KU-188-225

Between Naturalism and Religion

Philosophical Essays

University of Nottingham
Hallward Library

By Jürgen Habermas

Translated by Ciaran Cronin

polity

First published in German as *Zwischen Naturalismus und Religion* © Suhrkamp Verlag Frankfurt am Main, 2005

This English edition © Polity Press, 2008

Polity Press
65 Bridge Street
Cambridge CB2 1UR, UK

Polity Press
350 Main Street
Malden, MA 02148, USA

All rights reserved. Except for the quotation of short passages for the purpose of criticism and review, no part of this publication may be reproduced, stored in a retrieval system, or transmitted, in any form or by any means, electronic, mechanical, photocopying, recording or otherwise, without the prior permission of the publisher.

ISBN-13: 978-07456-3824-9
ISBN-13: 978-07456-3825-6 (pb)

A catalogue record for this book is available from the British Library.

1005444932

Typeset in 11 on 13 pt Berling
by SNP Best-set Typesetter Ltd, Hong Kong
Printed and bound in India by Replika Press Pvt Ltd

For further information on Polity, visit our website:
www.polity.co.uk

The publication of this work was supported by a grant from the Goëthe-Institut

Contents

Introduction

Two countervailing trends mark the intellectual tenor of the age –
the spread of naturalistic worldviews and the growing political
influence of religious orthodoxies. On the one hand, advances in
biogenetics, brain research, and robotics driven by therapeutic and
eugenic motives are being successfully presented in a positive light.
This program is designed to facilitate the spread of ways of understanding ourselves in terms of the objectifying categories of natural
science into everyday contexts of communication and action.
Habituation to forms of self-objectification that reduce all meaning
and experience to what can be observed would also dispose individuals to corresponding forms of self-instrumentalization.[1] For
philosophy, this trend is associated with the challenge of scientistic
naturalism. The fact that all operations of the human mind depend
on underlying organic processes is not in dispute. Instead, the
controversial issue is what form the naturalization of the mind
should take. For an appropriate naturalistic conception of cultural
evolution must do justice to both the intersubjective constitution
of the mind and the normative character of its rule-guided
operations.

On the other hand, the spread of naturalistic worldviews is
encountering an unexpected revitalization of religious communities and traditions and their politicization across the world. For

[1] See Jürgen Habermas, *The Future of Human Nature*, trans. Hella Beister and
William Rehg (Cambridge: Polity, 2003).

philosophy, the revival of religious energies, to which Europe alone seems to be immune, is associated with a fundamental critique of the postmetaphysical and nonreligious self-understanding of Western modernity. The fact that, for want of alternatives, the scope for political action is henceforth restricted to the universe of scientific-technical and economic infrastructures that developed in the West is not in dispute. The source of controversy is rather the correct interpretation of the secularizing impacts of a process of cultural and social rationalization increasingly denounced by the champions of religious orthodoxies as a historical development peculiar to the West.

These conflicting intellectual trends are rooted in opposed traditions. "Hard" forms of naturalism can be understood as an implication of the Enlightenment's uncritical faith in science, whereas the political reawakening of religious consciousness breaks with the liberal assumptions of the Enlightenment. However, these intellectual and spiritual outlooks do not merely clash at the level of academic controversies. They also develop into powerful political forces both within the civil society of the leading Western nation and at the international level in the encounter between the major world religions and the dominant global cultures.

From the perspective of a political theory concerned with the normative foundations and the functional preconditions of the democratic constitutional state, this clash also reveals a tacit complicity. The two countervailing trends conspire, as though in a division of labor, to jeopardize the cohesion of the polity through ideological polarization when neither side exhibits a willingness to engage in self-reflection. A political culture that polarizes itself irreconcilably along the fault-line of secular versus religious conflicts, whether over issues of human embryo research, abortion, or the treatment of comatose patients, challenges civic common sense even in the world's oldest democracy. The ethos of liberal citizenship demands that both sides should determine the limits of faith and knowledge in a reflexive manner.

As the example of the United States shows, the modern constitutional state was also invented with the aim of promoting peaceful religious pluralism. Only the ideologically neutral exercise of secular governmental authority within the framework of the constitutional state can ensure that different communities of belief can coexist on a basis of equal rights and mutual tolerance, while nevertheless remaining unreconciled at the level of their substantive worldviews or doctrines. The secularization of the political power of the state and the positive and negative freedom to exercise one's religion are two sides of the same coin. They protected religious communities not only against the destructive effects of violent interconfessional conflicts but also against the hostility toward religion of a secularized society. The constitutional state can defend its religious and nonreligious citizens from each other, however, only when their civic interactions are not based on a mere *modus vivendi*; their coexistence within a democratic system must also be founded on conviction. The democratic state is sustained by a legally unenforceable form of solidarity among citizens who respect each other as free and equal members of their political community.

This kind of civic solidarity paid for in small change must prove its worth also – indeed especially – across religious and ideological divides within the political public arena. Mutual recognition implies, among other things, that religious and secular citizens are willing to listen and to learn from each other in public debates. The political virtue of treating each other civilly is an expression of distinctive cognitive attitudes. The latter cannot be prescribed – they can only be learned. This circumstance has an implication of particular interest in the present context. Insofar as the liberal state demands that its citizens cooperate with one another in spite of their ideological differences, it must *presuppose* that the cognitive attitudes that this requires from both the religious and the secular sides are the result of historical learning processes. These kinds of learning processes involve more than merely contingent changes in mentalities that "occur" independently of rationally reconstructible insights. But neither can they be produced and steered through the media of law and politics. The liberal state depends in the long run on mentalities that it cannot produce from its own resources.

This becomes obvious when one reflects on the expectations concerning tolerance that religious citizens must satisfy in the liberal state. Fundamentalist convictions cannot be reconciled with the mentality that a sufficient proportion of citizens must share if a democratic polity is not to disintegrate. From the perspective of the history of religion, the cognitive attitudes that religious citizens must adopt in their civic dealings with members of other confessions and nonbelievers can be understood as the result of a collective learning process. In the Christian West, theology evidently played the role of pacemaker in this hermeneutic self-reflection of transmitted doctrines. Whether the dogmatic response to the cognitive challenges of modern science, religious pluralism, constitutional law, and secular social morality has been "successful" – whether one can even speak of "learning processes" in this connection – can be judged, of course, only from the internal perspective of the traditions that in this way reconcile themselves with modern conditions of social life.

In short, opinion- and will-formation within the democratic public arena can function only if a sufficiently large number of citizens fulfill specific expectations concerning civil conduct even across deep religious and ideological divides. However, this can be demanded of religiously minded citizens only on the assumption that they actually satisfy the requisite cognitive presuppositions. They must have learned to relate their religious convictions in reflexively coherent ways to the fact of religious and ideological pluralism. Moreover, they must have found a way to reconcile the epistemological privilege of the socially institutionalized sciences and the primacy of the secular state and universalistic social morality with their faith. Philosophy, which, in contrast to theology, is not linked with any particular confession, cannot influence this process. Here philosophy restricts itself to the role of an external observer who is not entitled to pass judgment on what can and cannot count as a justification within a particular religious teaching.

Philosophy first comes into play on the secular side. For non-religious citizens can also satisfy the expectations concerning civic solidarity only on the condition that they adopt a particular cognitive attitude toward their religious fellow-citizens and toward the latters' utterances. When the two sides meet in the democratic confusion of voices of a pluralistic public arena and debate political questions, specific epistemic obligations follow from the demand that they must show one another suitable respect. Participants who express themselves in a religious language also have a claim to be taken seriously by their secular fellow-citizens. Thus the latter should not be allowed to reject out of hand the possibility that contributions formulated in religious language could have a rational content.

Granted, a shared understanding of the democratic constitution requires that all laws, all judicial decisions, and all decrees and directives must be formulated in a public language that is equally accessible to all citizens and that they must, in addition, be open to justification in secular terms. However, in the context of the informal conflict of opinions within the political public arena, citizens and civic organizations operate below the threshold at which the institutional sanctioning power of the state can be invoked. At this level, it is not permissible to channel opinion- and will-formation by censoring speech or cutting it off from possible sources of meaning.[2] To this extent, the respect that secularized citizens owe their religious fellow-citizens also has an epistemic dimension.

On the other hand, secular citizens can be expected to demonstrate openness toward the possible rational content of religious contributions – and, all the more so, a willingness to engage in the cooperative endeavor of translating these contents from religious idioms into a generally intelligible language – only under a cognitive presupposition that is essentially contested. For in their eyes the conflict between secular convictions and those founded on religious doctrines can assume the prima facie character of a reasonable disagreement only if it can also be made plausible from a secular perspective that religious traditions are not merely irrational or meaningless. Only on this presupposition can nonreligious citizens assume that the major world religions *could* involve rational intuitions and instructive moments of unfulfilled but legitimate demands.

However, this is an open question that cannot be prejudged by constitutional norms. It is by no means a foregone conclusion which side will prove to be correct. The secularism of the scientific worldview insists that the archaic ways of thinking of religious doctrines have been completely overtaken and made redundant by the advances in knowledge of established research. By contrast,

---

[2] Habermas, "Faith and Knowledge," in *The Future of Human Nature*, pp. 101–15.

fallibilistic but nondefeatist postmetaphysical thought differentiates itself from both sides by reflecting on its own limits – and on
its inherent tendency to overstep these limits. It is as wary of
naturalistic syntheses founded on science as it is of revealed
truths.

The ideological polarization into religious and secular camps
that threatens to undermine civic cohesion is a topic for political
theory. However, once the focus switches to the cognitive presuppositions that must be fulfilled if civic solidarity is to function
effectively, analysis must shift to a different level. In a similar way
to the process by which religious consciousness becomes reflexive
in the modern era, the reflexive overcoming of secularistic consciousness also has an epistemological aspect. The mere allusion
to these two complementary learning processes betrays a detached
description from the perspective of a postmetaphysical observer.
From the perspective of participants, among whom the observer
must count him- or herself, however, this controversy remains
open. The contentious issues are clear. The discussion concerns,
on the one hand, the correct way to naturalize an essentially
intersubjective and norm-governed mode of thought. Corresponding to this, on the other hand, is the debate over how we should
understand the cognitive advance marked by the emergence of
the major world religions around the middle of the first millennium before the Christian era (which Jaspers called the "Axial
Age").

In this dispute, I defend Hegel's thesis that the major world
religions belong to the history of reason itself. Postmetaphysical
thinking misunderstands itself if it fails to include the religious
traditions alongside metaphysics in its own genealogy. On these
premises, it would be irrational to reject those "strong" traditions
as "archaic" residua instead of elucidating their internal connection
with modern forms of thought. Even today, religious traditions
perform the function of articulating an awareness of what is
lacking or absent. They keep alive a sensitivity to failure and suffering. They rescue from oblivion the dimensions of our social and
personal relations in which advances in cultural and social rationalization have caused utter devastation. Who is to say that they
do not contain encoded semantic potentialities that could provide
inspiration if only their message were translated into rational discourse and their profane truth contents were set free?

*

The present volume collects essays located within the ambit of these questions. They were written in recent years for diverse occasions and do not constitute a systematic whole. However, a thread running through all of them is the objective of confronting the opposed, yet complementary, challenges of naturalism and religion with the stubborn postmetaphysical insistence on the normative meaning of a detranscendentalized reason.

The commentaries and essays in the first part revisit the inter-subjectivist program in the theory of mind that I have long advocated. If we take our cue from a form of pragmatism that links Kant with Darwin,[3] it is indeed possible to deflate the Platonic ideas using the concept of idealizing presuppositions without pushing anti-Platonism to such an extreme that the rule-governed operations of the mind are summarily reduced to nomological regularities. The essays comprising the second part develop the central problem sketched in an anticipatory way above from the perspective of a normative theory of the constitutional state. The texts in the third section address the epistemological problematic in an attempt to clarify the position of postmetaphysical thinking between naturalism and religion. The three remaining contributions return to topics in political theory. There I am interested mainly in the correspondences between the process of coming to terms with religious and ideological pluralism within the state, on the one hand, and the prospects of a political constitution for a pacified world society, on the other.[4]

[3] See the introduction to Habermas, *Truth and Justification*, trans. Barbara Fultner (Cambridge, Mass.: MIT Press, 2003), pp. 1–50.
[4] In the final essay I return to questions concerning the constitutionalization of international law previously discussed in the corresponding essay in Habermas, *The Divided West*, trans. Ciaran Cronin (Cambridge: Polity, 2006), pp. 115–93.

Part I

The Intersubjective Constitution of Norm-governed Thought

1

Public Space and Political Public Sphere – The Biographical Roots of Two Motifs in my Thought

Permit me first to confess to my discomfiture at the request that I should relate in plain terms something instructive about my life and personal experiences. President Inamori's request to prize-winners is "Please, talk about yourself" – "Tell us how you overcame hardships, what your guideline was when standing at the crossroads of your life." I am thereby addressed as an author, teacher, and intellectual who is accustomed to communicating with readers, students, and listeners. So, you might well ask, why should someone who leads a comparatively public life be at all disconcerted when expected to talk about himself? But that would be to overlook the fact that in general the life of a philosopher is rather poor in external events. And philosophers themselves feel more comfortable in the theoretical domain. So please allow me to begin by explaining my inhibitions when it comes to talking about private matters by offering you a theoretical remark on the relationship between the private and the public.

It helps to distinguish here between two types of public and publicity. In today's media society, the public sphere serves those who have gained celebrity as a stage on which to present themselves. Visibility is the real purpose of public appearances. The price that stars pay for this kind of presence in the mass media is the conflation of their private and public lives. The intention behind participation in political, literary, or scholarly debates or any other contribution to public discourse, by contrast, is quite different. Here reaching agreement on a particular topic or clarifying reasonable dissent takes priority over the self-presentation of the author. This public is not a space of viewers or listeners but an arena in which speakers and interlocutors exchange questions and answers. Rather than everyone else's gaze being focused on the celebrity, an exchange of opinions and reasons takes place. In discourses that focus on issues of common concern, participants turn their backs on their private lives. They have no need to talk about themselves. The line between public and private spheres does not become blurred but instead the two domains complement each other.

This kind of objectivity may explain why when philosophers deliver historical lectures on Aristotle or Thomas Aquinas or Kant they generally limit themselves to stating only the bare biographical facts of when these thinkers were born, lived, and died. Even stormy episodes in the lives of these philosophers – one need only think of Plato's visits to Syracuse – take a back seat to their ideas and arguments. The lives of philosophers are not the stuff of legends. What they leave behind is at best a new and often enigmatic set of thoughts formulated in a unique language with which later generations continue to struggle. Indeed, in our field we treat those thinkers as "classics" whose works have remained contemporary for us. The ideas of such a classical thinker are like the molten core beneath a volcano that has deposited biographical rings of hardened lava. The great thinkers of the past whose works have stood the test of time impress this image upon us. By contrast, we, the many living philosophers – who are in any case more professors of philosophy – are merely the contemporaries of our contemporaries. And the less original our ideas are, the more they remain bound to the context from which they emerged. At times, indeed, they are no more than an expression of the biography from which they spring.

On my seventieth birthday, my students honored me with a *Festschrift* that bore the title *Die Öffentlichkeit der Vernunft und die Vernunft der Öffentlichkeit* – "The public sphere of reason and the reason of the public sphere." The title is not a bad choice, because the public sphere as a space of reasoned communicative exchanges is the issue that has concerned me all my life. The conceptual triad of "public space," "discourse," and "reason," in fact, has dominated my work as a scholar and my political life. Any such obsession has biographical roots. I suspect that four experiences may have had some bearing on this theoretical interest. Following my birth and during early infancy I was exposed to the traumatic experience of a series of surgeries (1) – as it happens, experiences of illness or physical handicap can be found in the biographies of many philosophers; second, from the time when I was just starting school, I recall experiencing difficulties in communicating and humiliations connected with my handicap (2); third, during my adolescence I was deeply influenced by my generation's experience of the break in world history marked by the year 1945 (3); and, finally, in the course of my adult life I have been disturbed by the political experience of the painfully slow liberalization of German postwar society and culture and its repeated setbacks (4). Allow me to elaborate in turn on these conjectures concerning links between theory and biography.

(1) I shall begin with my early childhood, with an operation that I underwent directly after I was born. I do not believe that this surgery, as one might suppose, enduringly shook my faith in the world around me. However, that intervention may well have awakened the feelings of dependence and vulnerability and the sense of the relevance of our interactions *with others*. At any rate, the social nature of human beings later became the starting point for my philosophical reflections. There are many species of animals that live socially. Indeed, the primates, our closest relatives, live in hordes and families, though they lack the complex kinship systems first invented by *Homo sapiens*. It is not forms of social existence as such that set human beings apart from other species. To grasp what is special about the social nature of humans we need to translate Aristotle's famous characterization of man as a *zoon politikón*, quite literally: man is a political animal, that is, an animal that exists *in a public space*. To be more precise, human beings are animals that, by virtue of being embedded from the outset in public networks of social relationships, first develop the competences that make them into persons. If we compare the biological features of newborn mammals, we observe that no other species enters the world as immature and as helpless as we do. Nor is any other animal dependent for so long a period of rearing on the protection of the family and a public culture

intersubjectively shared with conspecifics. We humans learn *from one another*. And this is only possible in the public space of a culturally stimulating milieu.

Needless to say, I can no longer remember that first operation on my cleft palate. But when I had to undergo a repeat of the operation at the age of five – in other words, at a time that I remember clearly – it undoubtedly sharpened my awareness of the deep dependence of one person on others. At any rate, this heightened sensitivity to the social nature of human beings led me to those philosophical approaches that emphasize the intersubjective constitution of the human mind – to the hermeneutic tradition that originated with Wilhelm von Humboldt, to the American pragmatism of Charles Sanders Peirce and George Herbert Mead, to Ernst Cassirer's theory of symbolic forms, and to Ludwig Wittgenstein's philosophy of language.

The intuitive sense of the deeply rooted reciprocal dependence of one person on another finds expression in an image of "the human being's place in the world." Such paradigms define our everyday self-understanding, though sometimes they also define the conceptual parameters for entire scientific disciplines. I have in mind the image of a subjectivity that one must imagine as a glove turned inside out in order to reveal the structure of its fabric woven from the strands of intersubjectivity. Inside each individual person, we find a reflection of the external social world. For the individual mind is imbued with structure and content by locking into the "objective" mind of the intersubjective interactions of *intrinsically* socialized subjects. The individual does not encounter his social environment in the same way that the bare organism encounters its natural environment, namely, as something interior that demarcates itself from the outer world through an osmotic barrier. The abstract juxtaposition of subject and object, of inside and outside, is misleading here, because the organism of the newborn infant first develops into a person when it enters into social interaction. The infant becomes a person by entering the public space of a social world that receives him with open arms. And this public domain of the jointly inhabited interior of our lifeworld is at once inside and outside.

In the process of growing up, the child is able to form the *inner* centre of a consciously experienced life only by *externalizing* herself through communicatively constituted interpersonal relations. Even in expressions of its most personal feelings and its most intimate excitations, an ostensibly *private* consciousness thrives on the impulses it receives from the cultural network of *public*, symbolically expressed, and intersubjectively shared categories, thoughts, and meanings. Surprisingly, though, in the cognitive sciences today we are witnessing a renaissance of the misleading Cartesian image of the monadic, recursively self-enclosed consciousness that stands in an opaque relation to the organic substrate of its brain and its genome.

It never made sense to me to regard self-consciousness as an original phenomenon. Do we not first become aware of ourselves in the gaze of another person? In your gaze, as that of the second person who speaks to me as a first person, I become aware of myself not only as a conscious subject but also as a unique *individual*. The subjectifying gaze of others possesses an individuating power.

(2) So much for the paradigm within which my research moves. The approach to the philosophy of language and the kind of moral theory that I developed within this framework may have been inspired by two experiences I had as a schoolboy: first, that other people did not understand me very well (a) and, second, that they responded with annoyance or rejection (b).

(a) I remember the difficulties I encountered when I tried to make myself understood in class or during break while speaking with my nasal articulation and distorted pronunciation of which I was completely unaware. I had left the haven of family life and its familiar surroundings and had to find my feet in an "anonymous" domain. Failures of communication direct our attention to an otherwise unobtrusive intermediary world of symbols that cannot be grasped like physical objects. Only when communication fails do we become aware of the medium of linguistic communication as a shared stratum without which individual existence would also be impossible. We invariably find ourselves within the element of language. Only someone who speaks can remain silent. Only because we are inherently connected with one another can we feel lonely or isolated.

Philosophers have never been especially interested in the power of language to forge a community. Ever since Plato and Aristotle, Western philosophers have preferred to analyze language as a medium of *representation* rather than of communication. They studied the logical form of statements we use to refer to objects and to represent states of affairs. But language is primarily there for the purposes of communication, after all, a process in which each person can take a "yes" or a "no" position on the validity claims of others, and thereby *reach agreement* about something in the world. We make use of language for communicative more than for purely cognitive purposes. Language is not the mirror of the world, but makes the world accessible to us. In so doing, it shapes our view of the world in a particular way. Something like a worldview is inscribed in language. Fortunately, this prior knowledge that we acquire with a specific language is not fixed once and for all. Otherwise, we could never learn anything really new in our dealings with the world and when talking with others about it. And what holds for theoretical languages also holds in everyday life, namely, that we can revise the meaning of predicates or concepts in the light of the experiences that they facilitate.

Incidentally, my speech impediment may also explain why I have always been convinced of the superiority of the written over the spoken word. The written form disguises the taint of the spoken word. I have tended to judge my students less by their contributions to discussions during seminars, no matter how intelligent they were, than by their written work. And as you see, to this day, I still shy away from speaking without a script in public, to the detriment of my listeners. This retreat into the precision afforded by the written word may also have led me to a theoretically important distinction. In *communicative action*, we proceed naïvely, as it were, whereas in *discourse* we exchange reasons in order to assess validity claims that have become problematic. Rational discourse borrows this reflexivity from the written word, that is to say, from the published article or the scholarly treatise, because discourse is designed to include everyone concerned and to create a third platform on which all pertinent contributions are heard. It is supposed to ensure that the unforced force of the better argument prevails.

(b) This view of things helped me to process another biographical experience in theoretical terms, namely, the insults in the form of the more or less harmless acts of discrimination that many children suffer in the schoolyard or street if they are different from the others. Today, globalization, mass tourism, worldwide migration, in fact the growing pluralism of worldviews and cultural life forms, have familiarized us all with such experiences of exclusion and marginalization of outsiders and minorities. Each of us can now imagine what it means to be a foreigner in a foreign country, to be regarded as different by others. Such situations awaken our moral susceptibilities. For morality is a device woven with the threads of communication to shield the particular vulnerability of individuals socialized through communication.

The deeper the process of individuation shapes the inner life of a person, the deeper she becomes entangled toward the outside, as it were, in an ever denser and more fragile network of relationships of reciprocal recognition. In the process, she exposes herself to the risk that reciprocity will be *denied*. The morality of equal respect for everyone is designed to absorb such risks. For it is designed to abolish discrimination and to facilitate the inclusion of the marginalized in the network of reciprocal recognition. Social norms capable of founding such a universal solidarity even among strangers depend on general approval. We must engage in discourse if we are to develop such norms. For moral discourses allow all those concerned an equal say. They enjoin each participant to adopt the perspectives of the others when deliberating on what is in the equal interest of all. In this way, the parties to the discourse learn to incorporate each other's interpretations of themselves and of the world into their own.

(3) Thus far, I have spoken about personal motifs deriving from my childhood. They may have opened my eyes to the intersubjective constitution of the human mind and the social core of our subjectivity, as well as to the fragility of communicative forms of life and the fact that socialized individuals are in need of special protection. Yet it was the caesura of 1945 that first led to the eye-opening experience for my generation without which I would hardly have ended up in philosophy and social theory. Overnight, as it were, the society in which we had led what had seemed to be a halfway normal everyday life and the regime governing it were exposed as pathological and criminal. Through this experience, the confrontation with the legacy of the Nazi past became a fundamental theme of my adult political life. My interest in political progress, spurred by this concern with the past, became focused on conditions of life that escape the false alternative

between *Gemeinschaft* and *Gesellschaft*, "community" and "society."
What I have in mind are, as Brecht puts it, "friendly" forms of
social interaction that neither surrender the gains in differentiation of modern societies nor deny the dependence of upright
individuals on one another – and their reciprocal reliance upon
one another.

World War II came to an end a few months before my sixteenth
birthday. There followed four years of alert adolescence until the
foundation of the Federal Republic of Germany and the beginning
of my university studies in the summer of 1949. I had, in the
German phrase, *"die Gnade der späten Geburt,"* the "good fortune
to be born late." I was old enough to have witnessed the fundamental changes marked by the end of the Third Reich at a morally
impressionable age, yet young enough not to have been incrimi-
nated by its criminal practices. My generation had not been old
enough to serve in the army. We did not have to answer for choosing the wrong side and for political errors and their dire consequences. After the revelations concerning Auschwitz, nothing
could be taken at face value. What we had experienced as a more
or less normal childhood and adolescence now transpired to be
everyday life in the shadow of a rupture in civilization. Without
having done anything to deserve it, my cohort had the opportunity to learn without reservation from the Nuremberg war crimes
trials, which we followed on the radio. We made Karl Jaspers's
distinction between collective guilt and collective liability our
own and took very seriously the responsibility for the consequences of a regime that had been supported by the mass of the
population.

Today, many take a critical view of this stance of a generation
influenced by the liberation of 1945, and it is by no means something for which we can claim special credit. There is something
typical of the time, almost compulsory, in the responses encountered among persons of my age, whether on the right, the centre,
or the left of the political spectrum. The moral and political
insights that we gained free of charge, as it were, were linked at
the time with a global shift in mentality marked by the cultural
opening to the West. During the Third Reich, we who had not
known the Weimar Republic had grown up in a mind-numbing
enclave of "fatherland" kitsch, monumentalism, and a death cult
steeped in ressentiment. After 1945, the doors were opened to

Expressionist art, to Kafka, Thomas Mann, and Hermann Hesse, to world literature written in English, to the contemporary philosophy of Sartre and the French left-wing Catholics, to Freud and Marx, as well as to the pragmatism of a John Dewey, whose former students decisively influenced the re-education effort in Germany. Contemporary cinema also conveyed exciting messages. The liberating, revolutionary spirit of Modernism found compelling visual expression in Mondrian's constructivism, in the cool geometric lines of Bauhaus architecture, and in uncompromising industrial design.

The cultural opening to the West went hand in hand with an analogous political opening. For me, "democracy," not liberalism of the Anglo-American variety, was the magic word. The political constructions of social contract theory, in the more popular version I was acquainted with at the time, combined with the pioneering spirit and the emancipatory promise of Modernism. All the more reason why we students felt ourselves isolated in the unchanged authoritarian setting of a postwar society unreceptive to the emergence of the new. The continuity of social elites and cultural prejudices through which Konrad Adenauer marshaled consent for his policies was stifling. There had been no break with the past, no new beginning in terms of personnel, no change in mentality – neither a moral renewal nor a revolution of political mindset. I shared my deep political disenchantment with my wife, whom I first met during my student days. As late as the 1950s, we encountered the at once elitist and apolitical self-image of the German universities. We also encountered the baleful fusion of nationalism and anti-Semitism that had intellectually disarmed our academic teachers in 1933 or even driven them into the arms of the Nazis.

In such a climate, my left-leaning political convictions found little contact with what I was learning in philosophy courses. Politics and philosophy, these two intellectual universes, remained for a long time separate domains. They first collided one weekend in the summer semester in 1953, when my friend Karl-Otto Apel handed me a copy of Heidegger's *An Introduction to Metaphysics* fresh from the presses. Until then, Heidegger had been my most influential teacher, if only from a distance. The fame he had acquired since the 1920s was still untarnished. I had read *Being and Time* through Kierkegaard's eyes. Heidegger's fundamental ontology contained an ethics which, so I thought, appealed to the individual's conscience, to the individual's existential sincerity. And now this selfsame Heidegger had published his lectures from 1935 without any revisions or commentary. The vocabulary of the lectures reflected the idolatry of a nationalist spirit, the defiance of the World War I trenches, the collectivism of solemn yea saying. The "existence of the Volk" had unexpectedly taken the place of the "existence" of the individual person. The only way to come to terms with my incredulous outrage was to put it in writing.

"Thinking with Heidegger against Heidegger" was the title of the newspaper article that I wrote at the time, which still betrayed the devoted Heidegger disciple. My choice of quotations still reveals what upset me about Heidegger's text at the time. It was above all four things. First, there was the fatal linking of a heroic call to "creative violence" with a cult of sacrifice – the "most profound and broadest Yes to decline." Second, I was incensed by the Platonist prejudices of the German mandarin who devalued "intelligence" in favor of "spirit," "analysis" in favor of "authentic thought," and wanted to reserve the esoteric truth for "the few." I was also irritated by the anti-Christian and anti-Western sentiments directed against the egalitarian universalism of the Enlightenment. But what was really offensive was the Nazi philosopher's denial of moral and political responsibility for the consequences of the mass criminality about which almost no one talked any longer eight years after the end of the war. In the ensuing controversy, Heidegger's interpretation, in which he stylized fascism as a "destiny of Being" that relieved individuals of personal culpability, was lost from view. He simply shrugged off his disastrous political error as a mere reflex of a higher destiny that had "led him astray."

(4) This episode from my early days as a student marked the beginning of a critical inquiry into the oppressive political heritage that persisted even in German philosophy. In the years that followed, I gained a clearer understanding of the mindset shared by men such as Martin Heidegger, Carl Schmitt, Ernst Jünger, and Arnold Gehlen. In all of them contempt for the masses and the average was allied, on the one hand, with the celebration of the noble individual, the elect, and the extraordinary and, on the

other, with rejection of "idle talk," the public sphere, and the "inauthentic." They elevated silence above conversation, and command and obedience above equality and self-determination. In this way, young conservative thought defined itself in sharp opposition to the basic democratic impulse that had driven us forward since 1945. This "Weimar syndrome" became a negative point of reference for me when, after graduation, I worked through theoretically my disappointment with the sluggish process of democratization in postwar Germany that was constantly beset by setbacks. Into the 1980s, the fear of a political relapse continued to spur my scholarly work, which I had begun in the late 1950s with my study *The Structural Transformation of the Public Sphere*.

At that time, I was working as Theodor W. Adorno's research assistant in the Frankfurt Institute for Social Research. Critical social theory offered me a perspective from which I could embed the emergence of American, French, and English democracy, and the repeated failure of attempts to establish democracy in Germany, in the larger context of social modernization. In the late 1950s, the political culture in Germany had by no means acquired definite shape. It was as yet not at all certain that the principles of a democratic order that had been imposed "from without" would become firmly lodged in the hearts and minds of German citizens. Evidently, such a change in political mentality could not occur in isolation or be simply imposed by administrative fiat. Only a vibrant and, where possible, discursive type of public opinion-formation could propel such a process.

As a consequence, I focused my theoretical attention on the political public sphere. What had always interested me about the general phenomenon of a "public space" that already arises with simple interactions was the mysterious power of intersubjectivity to unite disparate elements without eliminating the differences between them. The forms of social integration can be read off from the structures of public spaces. The constitution of public spaces reveals most clearly the anomic traits of social disintegration or the ruptures caused by repressive social relations. Does the specific type of integration in a particular society correspond to its degree of complexity? Or do public spaces betray the pathological traits of anomie or repression? In modern societies, one particular social space – namely, the political public sphere of a

democratic community – acquires an especially important symptomatic role in the integration of society. For complex societies
can be normatively held together solely by civic solidarity, that is,
the abstract, legally mediated form of solidarity among citizens.
The process of public opinion- and will-formation alone can foster
and reproduce a fragile form of collective identity among citizens
who can no longer become personally acquainted. For this reason
the health of a democracy can be gauged from the pulse of its
political public arena.

Professors are, of course, not only scholars who are concerned
with public-political issues from the viewpoint of an academic
observer. They are also *participating* citizens. And on occasion
they also take active part in the political life of their country as
intellectuals. In the 1950s, I participated in the "Easter Marches,"
pacifist protests against nuclear weapons. In the late 1960s, I had
to take a public stance on the student protest movement. In the
1980s and 1990s, I took part in public debates on coming to terms
with the Nazi past, on civil disobedience, on the form German
unification should take, on the first Gulf War, on political asylum
laws, and so forth. Over the last ten years, I have taken positions
on problems of European unification and on bioethical issues. And
since the invasion of Iraq, which violated international law, I have
been concerned with the postnational constellation and the future
of the Kantian project of establishing a cosmopolitan order. I
mention these activities only because I wish, in conclusion, to
report briefly on what I think I have learned from my own mistakes and those of others about the role of the public intellectual
in our times.

Intellectuals should make public use of the professional knowledge that they possess – for example, as philosophers or writers,
social scientists or physicists – on their own initiative, without
being commissioned by anyone to do so. They need not be neutral
and eschew partisanship, but they should be aware of their own
fallibility. They should limit themselves to relevant issues, contribute sound information and good arguments; in other words,
they should endeavor to improve the deplorable discursive level
of public debates. Intellectuals must walk a difficult tightrope in
other respects as well. For they doubly betray their own authority
if they do not carefully separate their professional from their
public roles. And they should not use the influence they acquire

through their words as a means to gain power, thus confusing "influence" with "political power," i.e. with authority tied to positions in a party organization or a government. Intellectuals cease to be intellectuals once they assume public office.

It is hardly surprising that we generally fail to live up to these standards; but that in no way devalues the standards themselves. For if there is one thing that intellectuals – a species that has so often attacked its own kind and pronounced its demise – cannot allow themselves, then it is to become cynical.

2

Communicative Action and the Detranscendentalized "Use of Reason"

In his preface to *Ideals and Illusions*, Thomas McCarthy characterizes the two directions that critics of Kantian conceptions of reason have taken since Hegel: "On one side are those who, in the wakes of Nietzsche and Heidegger, attack Kantian conceptions of reason and the rational subject at their very roots; on the other side are those who, in the wakes of Hegel and Marx, recast them in sociohistorical molds."[1] Even in their desublimated pragmatic forms, the Kantian "ideas" retain their original dual role. They are used to guide critique and, at the same time, are exposed as the fertile ground of a transcendental illusion: ideals and illusions. McCarthy opposes not only an iconoclastic deconstructionism that throws out the baby with the bathwater, but also an overly normative reading of Kant that leaves the illusion of pure reason intact. Even after the pragmatic turn, he keeps both functions of reason in view: the norm-setting function that makes critique possible and the obfuscating function that calls for self-criticism: "If we take a pragmatic turn, we can appreciate both aspects of the social-practical ideas of reason: their irreplaceable function in cooperative interaction and their potential for misuse."[2]

Elsewhere, McCarthy speaks of the "social-practical *analogues* of Kant's ideas of reason."[3] He is referring primarily to three

---

[1] Thomas McCarthy, *Ideals and Illusions* (Cambridge, Mass.: MIT Press, 1991), p. 2.
[2] Ibid., p. 4.
[3] David Couzens Hoy and Thomas McCarthy, *Critical Theory* (Oxford: Blackwell, 1994), p. 38.

formal-pragmatic presuppositions of communicative action, namely, the common supposition of an objective world, the rationality that acting subjects mutually ascribe to one another, and the unconditional validity they claim for their statements in speech acts. These presuppositions are interrelated and represent aspects of a desublimated reason embodied in everyday communicative practice: "the idealizations of rational accountability and real world objectivity both figure in our idealized notion of truth, for objectivity is the other side of the intersubjective validity of certain types of truth claims."[4] Thus the transcendental tension between the ideal and the real, between the realm of the intelligible and the realm of appearances, enters into the social reality of situated interactions and institutions. It is this transformation of "pure" into "situated" reason that McCarthy masterfully brings to bear against the critiques that destroy reason through its abstract negation, such as Foucault's objectivating analysis or Derrida's use of paradox. Yet he does so without ignoring the insights gained by deconstructing those illusions of reason that seep into the capillaries of everyday discourses.

Both the historicist tradition from Dilthey to Heidegger and the pragmatist tradition from Peirce to Dewey (and, in a sense, Wittgenstein) understand the task of "situating reason" as one of detranscendentalizing the subject of knowledge. The finite subject is to be situated "in the world" without entirely losing its "world-constituting" spontaneity. In this respect, the controversy between McCarthy and the followers of Heidegger, Dewey, and Wittgenstein is a domestic dispute over which side accomplishes the detranscendentalization in the right way: whether the traces of a transcending reason vanish in the sands of historicism and contextualism or whether a reason embodied in historical contexts preserves the power of immanent transcendence.[5] If cooperating

---

[4] Ibid., p. 39.
[5] Here there is no need to revisit the family quarrel within the family quarrel. See McCarthy, "Practical Discourse: On the Relation of Morality to Politics," in *Ideals and Illusions*, pp. 181–99; "Legitimacy and Diversity: Dialectical Reflections on Analytical Distinctions," in Michael Rosenfeld and Andrew Arato (eds), *Habermas on Law and Democracy* (Berkeley: University of California Press, 1998), pp. 115–53; for my reply, see "Reply to Symposium Participants," ibid., pp. 391–404.

subjects intelligently cope with what they encounter in the world, do their learning processes empower them to make rationally motivated revisions in their pre-understanding of the world as a whole? Is reason simply at the mercy of the "world-disclosive" happening of language, or is it also a "world-transforming" power?[6]

In the debate with the deconstructionists, at least the question itself is not under dispute. However, for the heirs of Hume – and thus for a large segment of analytic philosophy – the dialectic between world-disclosing language and inner-worldly learning processes does not even have a clear meaning. Unless one sub-scribes to Kant's idea of a "world-constituting" reason and the conception of an understanding that "constitutes" the objects of possible experience, there can be no grounds for detrans-cendentalizing the "consciousness" of knowing and acting sub-jects, let alone for a controversy over the problems that arise from such a corrective. McCarthy defends a pragmatic explica-tion of the "situatedness of reason" against deconstructionist objections. I shall try to address the incomprehension of analytic philosophy for the very *issue* of the detranscendentalized use of reason.

However, I do not wish to plead directly for a formal-pragmatic theory of meaning and repeat the well-known arguments.[7] The difficulty in understanding lies not in the details but in the whole approach. Truth semantics also establishes an internal connection between the meaning of statements and their conditions of valid-ity and thereby points toward conceptions of linguistic, and even communicatively embodied, rationality (Davidson, Dummett, Brandom). However, the markers laid down by Hume and Kant for or against a nominalist account of the operations of the human mind continue to divert structurally similar ideas into different channels and in different directions.

Unless I am mistaken, the transformation of Kant's "ideas" of pure reason into "idealizing" presuppositions of communicative

---

[6] Habermas, *Truth and Justification*, trans. Barbara Fultner (Cambridge, Mass.: MIT Press, 2003).
[7] Habermas, *On the Pragmatics of Communication*, ed. and trans. Maeve Cook (Cambridge, Mass.: MIT Press, 1998).

action poses difficulties especially for understanding the *factual* role of performatively presupposed *counterfactual* assumptions. For they are actually effective in structuring processes of mutual understanding and in organizing contexts of interaction:

> This [move] has the effect of relocating the Kantian opposition between the real and the ideal *within* the domain of social practice. Cooperative interaction is seen to be structured around ideas of reason which are neither fully constitutive in the Platonic sense nor merely regulative in the Kantian sense. As *idealizing suppositions* we cannot avoid making while engaged in processes of mutual understanding, they are *actually effective* in ways that point beyond the limits of actual situations. As a result, social-practical ideas of reason are both "immanent" and "transcendent" to practices constitutive of forms of life.[8]

Formal pragmatics holds that the rational structure of action oriented toward reaching understanding is reflected in the presuppositions that actors *must* make if they are to engage in this practice at all. The necessity of this "must" has a Wittgensteinian rather than a Kantian character. That is, it does not have the transcendental meaning of universal, necessary, and noumenal [*intelligiblen*] conditions of possible experience, but has the grammatical meaning of an "unavoidability" stemming from the conceptual connections of a system of learned – but for us inescapable – rule-governed behavior. After the pragmatic deflation of the Kantian approach, "transcendental analysis" means the search for presumptively universal, but only *de facto* inescapable, conditions that must be met if certain fundamental practices or achievements are to be possible. All practices for which we cannot imagine functional equivalents in our sociocultural forms of life are "fundamental" in this sense. One natural language can be replaced by another. But we cannot conceive of a functionally equivalent replacement for propositionally differentiated language as such (as a "species endowment"). I would like to clarify this basic idea in a genealogical way by tracing it back to Kant.

---

[8] Hoy and McCarthy, *Critical Theory*, p. 38.

For present purposes, I am concerned not with the systematic task of explicating the concept of "communicative reason,"[9] but with the genealogical examination of the context in which this conception originated. I shall focus on the idealizing performative presuppositions of communicative action: the shared presupposition of a world of independently existing objects, the reciprocal presupposition of rationality or "accountability," the unconditionality of context-transcending validity claims such as truth and moral rightness, and the demanding presuppositions of argumentation that force participants to decenter their interpretive perspectives. I speak of "presuppositions" here because these are conditions that must be fulfilled so that that which is conditioned can take on one of two values: without a referential system, acts of referring can neither succeed nor fail; unless participants in communication presuppose that their interlocutors are rational, they can neither understand nor misunderstand one another; if propositions that are "true" in one context could lose that property in another, then the corresponding truth claim could not be called into question in any given context; finally, unless there are communicative situations that can bring out the unforced force of the better argument, neither pro nor con arguments can have any weight. The respects in which these presuppositions have an "ideal" content will occupy us shortly.

Certainly, there is a family resemblance between these presuppositions and Kantian concepts. Presumably, there is a genealogical connection between the following:

1   the "cosmological idea" of the unity of the world (or the totality of conditions in the sensory world) and the pragmatic presupposition of a common objective world;
2   the "idea of freedom" as a postulate of practical reason and the pragmatic presupposition of the rationality of accountable agents;
3   the totalizing movement of reason that, as a "faculty of ideas," transcends all that is conditioned toward an unconditioned and the unconditionality of the validity claims raised in communicative action; and

[9] See Habermas, "Some Further Clarifications of the Concept of Communicative Rationality," in *Pragmatics of Communication*, ch. 7.

4   finally, reason as the "faculty of principles," which takes on
the role of the highest court of appeal for all rights and claims,
and rational discourse as the inescapable forum of possible
justification.

In what follows, I lay out these four genealogical connections
in turn. To be sure, the ideas of pure reason cannot be translated
seamlessly from the idiom of transcendental philosophy into that
of formal pragmatics. Establishing "analogies" is not the end of the
matter. In the course of their transformation, Kant's oppositions
(constitutive vs. regulative, transcendental vs. empirical, immanent vs. transcendent, etc.) become blurred because detranscendentalization represents a profound intervention into the
architecture of his basic assumptions. In light of these genealogical
connections, we also discover the crossroads at which analytic
philosophy of language diverts the legacy of the Kantian ideas of
reason. Nevertheless, as I will show in the second part, it arrives
at a similar normative description of linguistic practice as a formal
pragmatics that is more deeply indebted to Kant. Beginning with
Frege's critique of psychologism (5), I trace the course of the
analytic discussion, taking my lead from Davidson's principle of
charity (6), Dummett's critical reception of Wittgenstein (7), and
Brandom's conception of communication as a discursive exchange
of reasons (8).

I

(1) In addition to the idea of the unity of the thinking subject
and the idea of God as the unitary origin of the conditions of all
objects of thought, Kant includes the cosmological *idea of a unitary
world* among the ideas of theoretical reason. When he speaks of
a "hypothetical" use of reason, Kant has in mind the heuristic
function of this idea for the progress of empirical research. The
totalizing anticipation of the entirety of the objects of possible
experience does not make cognition possible but rather guides it.
Whereas empirical cognition is "the touchstone of truth," the
cosmological idea plays the role of a methodological principle of
completeness; it points to the goal of a systematic unity of all

knowledge.[10] In contrast to the constitutive categories of the understanding and the forms of intuition, the "unity of the world" is a regulative idea.

Metaphysical thinking falls prey to the dialectical illusion of a hypostatized world order because it uses this regulative idea constitutively. The reifying use of theoretical reason confuses the constructive projection of a *focus imaginarius* for ongoing research with the constitution of an object that is accessible to experience. This "apodictic" – hence excessive – use of reason corresponds to the "transcendent" use of the categories of the understanding beyond the realm of possible experience. Transgressing this boundary results in an inadmissible assimilation of the concept of the "world" – as the totality of all objects that can be experienced – to the concept of an object writ large that represents the world as such. The differentiation between the world and the inner-worldly that Kant defends must be preserved even if the transcendental subject loses its position outside time and space and mutates into a multitude of subjects capable of speech and action.

Detranscendentalization leads, on the one hand, to the embedding of socialized subjects into the context of a lifeworld and, on the other hand, to the entwinement of cognition with speech and action. The concept of the "world" is altered along with the theoretical architectonic. I will first (a) explain what I mean by the "formal-pragmatic presupposition of the world" before drawing attention to some of its important implications, namely, (b) the replacement of transcendental idealism by internal realism, (c) the regulative function of the concept of truth, and (d) the embeddedness of references to the world [*Weltbezüge*] in contexts of the lifeworld.

(a) As subjects capable of speech and action, language-users must be able to "refer" "to something" in the objective world from within the horizon of their shared lifeworld if they are to reach an understanding "about something" in communicating with one another or if they are to succeed "with something" in their practical dealings. Whether in communicating about states of affairs or

---

[10] See Immanuel Kant, *Critique of Pure Reason*, ed. and trans. Paul Guyer and Allen W. Wood (Cambridge: Cambridge University Press, 1998), pp. 197–8, 216–17.

in practical dealings with people and things, subjects can refer to something only if they start – each on her own, yet in agreement with everyone else – with a pragmatic presupposition. They presuppose "the world" as the totality of independently existing objects that can be judged or dealt with. All objects about which it is possible to state facts can be "judged." But only spatio-temporally identifiable objects can be "dealt with" in the sense of being purposefully manipulated.

To say that the world is "objective" means that it is "given" to us as "the same for everyone." It is linguistic practice – especially the use of singular terms – that compels us to make the pragmatic presupposition that such a world is shared by all. The referential system built into natural languages ensures that any given speaker can formally anticipate possible objects of reference. Through this formal presupposition of the world, communication about something in the world is intertwined with practical interventions in the world. Speakers and actors reach an understanding about and intervene in one and the same objective world. To achieve secure semantic references, it is important that speakers, as agents, are in contact with the objects of everyday life and that they can put themselves in contact with them repeatedly.[11]

Like Kant's cosmological idea of reason, the conception of a presupposed world rests on the transcendental difference between the world and the inner-worldly, which reappears in Heidegger as the ontological difference between "Being" and "beings." On this supposition, the objective world that we posit is not of the same kind as what can occur in it as object (i.e. a state of affairs, thing, or event). Otherwise this conception no longer fits within the framework of the Kantian oppositions. Once the *a priori* categories of the understanding and forms of intuition have been detranscendentalized, and thus disarmed, the classic distinction between reason and understanding is blurred. Obviously, the pragmatic presupposition of the world is not a regulative idea, but is "constitutive" for referring to anything about which facts can be established. At the same time, the concept of the world remains

[11] On Putnam's theory of reference, which is relevant here, see Axel Mueller, *Referenz und Fallibilismus: Zu Hilary Putnams pragmatischem Kognitivismus* (Berlin: de Gruyter, 2001).

formal in such a way that the system of possible references does not fix in advance any specific properties of objects in general. All attempts to reconstruct a material *a priori* of meaning [*Sinn-Apriori*] for possible objects of reference – that is, to predetermine the descriptions under which it is possible to refer to objects – have failed.[12]

(b) From this perspective, the distinction between appearance and "thing-in-itself" also loses its meaning. Experiences and judgments are now linked back to a practice that copes with reality. They remain in contact with a surprising reality through problem-solving activities that are evaluated by their success. This reality either resists our grasp, or it "plays along." Viewed ontologically, transcendental idealism, which conceives the totality of objects of possible experience as a world "for us," as a world of appearances, is replaced by an internal realism. Accordingly, everything is "real" that can be represented in true statements, although facts are interpreted in a language that is always "ours." The world itself does not impose "its" language on us; it does not itself speak; and it "responds" only in a figurative sense.[13] In asserting a state of affairs, we say it "obtains." However, this "veridical being" of facts must not be construed as a kind of picturing of reality and thereby assimilated to the "existence" of objects, as representational models of knowledge propose.

The ascertaining of facts cannot completely shed the operative meaning of the learning processes, solutions to problems, and justification from which they *result*. Thus it makes sense to distinguish, following C. S. Peirce, between a "reality" that can be represented in true statements and the "world" of objects these statements are about – between "what is the case" and the mode of "existence" of the things we "encounter" and have to "cope with" in our contingent practical dealings and which we experience as recalcitrant. The "accommodation" or "resistance" of the objects being talked about is already processed in true statements. Accordingly, the "existence" of recalcitrant

---

[12] For a discussion of Peter Strawson's investigations on this topic, see Marcel Niquet, *Transzendentale Argumente* (Frankfurt am Main: Suhrkamp, 1991), chs. 4 and 5.

[13] On Putnam's "internal realism," see Habermas, "Norms and Values: On Hilary Putnam's Kantian Pragmatism," in *Truth and Justification*, pp. 213–36.

objects (or the facticity of constraining circumstances) is also indirectly expressed in the "being the case" or obtaining [*Bestehen*] of states of affairs. The "world" that we presuppose as the totality of objects, not of facts, must not be confused with the "reality" that consists of whatever can be represented in true statements.

(c) Both concepts, "world" and "reality," express totalities, but only the concept of reality can, in virtue of its internal connection with the concept of truth, be placed alongside the regulative ideas of reason. The Peircean concept of reality (as the totality of statable facts) is a regulative idea in Kant's sense because it commits the practice of fact-stating to an orientation toward truth that in turn has a regulative function. For Kant, "truth" is not an idea, nor is it connected with the ideas of reason, since the transcendental conditions of objective experience are also supposed to explain the truth of judgments of experience: "For Kant, the question . . . of the conditions of possibility of constituting objects, i.e., of constituting the meaning of objectivity, was the same as the question . . . of the conditions of possibility of the intersubjective validity of true knowledge."[14] Contrary to this, Karl-Otto Apel defends the distinction between the pragmatically interpreted *a priori* of experience [*Erfahrungsapriori*], which determines the meaning of the objects of possible experience, and the conditions of the argumentative justification of statements about such objects.

Peirce wanted to explain "truth" itself epistemically, in terms of progress toward truth. He defined the meaning of truth by anticipating a consensus that all participants in a self-correcting process of inquiry under ideal epistemic conditions would have to attain.[15] The unlimited ideal "community of investigators" constitutes the forum for the "highest court" of reason. There are

---

[14] Karl-Otto Apel, "Sinnkonstitution und Geltungsrechtfertigung," in *Martin Heidegger: Innen- und Außenansichten*, ed. Forum für Philosophie (Frankfurt am Main: Suhrkamp, 1989), p. 134.

[15] C. S. Peirce, *Collected Papers*, vols. 5 and 6 (Cambridge, Mass.: Harvard University Press, 1934), p. 268: "The opinion which is fated to be ultimately agreed to by all who investigate, is what we mean by the truth, and the object represented in this opinion is the real" (5.407). See also Karl-Otto Apel, *Charles S. Peirce: From Pragmatism to Pragmaticism*, trans. John Michael Krois (Amherst: University of Massachusetts Press, 1981).

good reasons against epistemologizing the concept of truth in this way, which assimilates "truth" to "ideal warranted assertability."[16] Nonetheless, the *orientation* toward truth – as a property that a proposition "cannot lose" – acquires an indispensable regulative function for fallible processes of justification precisely if such processes can lead at best to decisions about the rational acceptability of propositions and not about their truth.[17]

Even after objective knowledge is detranscendentalized and tied to discursive justification as the "touchstone of truth," the point of Kant's injunction against the apodictic use of reason and the transcendent use of the understanding remains valid. Only the boundary separating the transcendental from the transcendent use of our cognitive faculty is no longer defined by sensibility and understanding, but by the forum of rational discourse in which the power of good reasons to convince must unfold.

(d) In a certain sense, the distinction between truth and rational acceptability replaces the difference between "things in themselves" and appearances. Kant was not able to bridge this transcendental–empirical divide even by means of the regulative idea of the unity of the world. The reason is that the heuristic procedure of completing all conditioned cognitions does not lead the understanding *beyond* the realm of appearances. Even after the knowing subject is detranscendentalized, a gap remains between what is true and what is warranted or rationally acceptable to us. Although this gap cannot be definitively closed within discourse, it can be closed pragmatically through a rationally motivated transition from discourse to action. Because discourses *remain* rooted in the lifeworld, there is an internal connection between the two roles assumed by the idea of an orientation toward truth – as practical certainties in action [*Handlungsgewissheiten*] and as hypothetical validity claims in discourse.[18]

---

[16] See the critique of the discursive conception of truth in Albrecht Wellmer, "Ethics and Dialogue: Elements of Moral Judgment in Kant and Discourse Ethics," in *The Persistence of Modernity*, trans. David Midgley (Cambridge, Mass.: MIT Press, 1991), pp. 145ff.; Cristina Lafont, *The Linguistic Turn in Hermeneutic Philosophy* (Cambridge, Mass.: MIT Press, 1999), pp. 283ff.

[17] Habermas, "Richard Rorty's Pragmatic Turn," in *Pragmatics of Communication*, ch. 8.

[18] Habermas, *Truth and Justification*, pp. 36ff., 263ff.; "Rorty's Pragmatic Turn," pp. 373ff.

The regulative function of the orientation toward truth, supported by the supposition of an objective world, directs processes of justification toward a goal that mobilizes the highest court of reason. That is, in the course of detranscendentalization, the theoretical ideas of reason step out of the static "intelligible world" and unleash their dynamics *within* the lifeworld. Kant says that we have only an "idea," but not "knowledge," of the intelligible realm. After the cosmological idea has been transformed into the presupposition of a shared objective world, however, the orientation to unconditional validity claims makes the resources of Kant's intelligible world available for the acquisition of empirical knowledge. Giving up the background assumptions of Kant's transcendental philosophy turns ideas of reason into idealizations that orient subjects capable of speech and action. The rigid "ideal" that was elevated to an other-worldly realm is set aflow in this-worldly operations; it is transposed from a transcendent state into a process of "immanent transcendence." For in the discursive conflict over the correct interpretation of what we encounter in the world, lifeworld contexts that are drifting apart must be transcended "from within."

Language-users can direct themselves *toward* something innerworldly only *from within* the horizon of their lifeworld. There are no strictly context-independent references to something in the world. Heidegger and Wittgenstein each in his own way showed that Kant's transcendental consciousness of objects rests on false abstractions.[19] The lifeworld contexts and the linguistic practices in which socialized subjects "always already" find themselves disclose the world from the perspective of meaning constituting traditions and habits. Members of a local linguistic community experience everything that they encounter in the world in the light of a habitual "grammatical" pre-understanding, not as neutral objects. The linguistic mediation of our relations to the world explains why the objectivity of the world that we presuppose in acting and speaking refers back to a communicative

---

[19] On the "hermeneutics of an always already linguistically interpreted being-in-the-world," see Karl-Otto Apel, "Wittgenstein und Heidegger," in Brian McGuinness et al., *Der Löwe spricht . . . und wir können ihn nicht verstehen* (Frankfurt am Main: Suhrkamp, 1991), pp. 27–68.

intersubjectivity among interlocutors. A fact about some object must be stated and, if necessary, *justified* before others who can object to my assertion. The particular demand for interpretation arises because we cannot disregard the world-disclosive character of language, even when we use it descriptively.

These translation problems shed light on the thicket of life-world contexts, but they are not grounds for subscribing to the incommensurability thesis in any form.[20] Interlocutors can achieve mutual understanding across the divides separating lifeworlds because, in presupposing a shared objective world, they orient themselves toward the claim to truth, that is, to the unconditional validity they claim when they make a statement. I shall return to this orientation to truth below.

(2) The cosmological idea of the unity of the world branches, on the one hand, into the pragmatic presupposition of an objective world as the totality of objects and, on the other, into the orientation to a reality conceived as the totality of facts. We encounter a different kind of idealization in the interpersonal relationships among language-users who take one another "at their word" and hold one another "to account." In their cooperative interactions, each must ascribe rationality to the other, at least provisionally. In certain circumstances, it may turn out that such a presupposition was unwarranted. Contrary to expectations, it might happen that the other person cannot account for her actions and utterances and that we cannot see how she could justify her behavior. In contexts of action oriented toward reaching understanding, this kind of frustration can occur only against the background supposition of rationality that anyone engaged in communicative action must assume. This supposition states that a subject who is acting intentionally is capable, in the right circumstances, of providing a more or less plausible reason for why she did or did not behave or express herself this way rather than some other way. Unintelligible, odd, bizarre, or enigmatic expressions prompt follow-up questions because they implicitly contradict an unavoidable presupposition of communication and therefore trigger puzzled or irritated reactions.

---

[20] Richard F. Bernstein, *Beyond Objectivism and Relativism* (Philadelphia: University of Pennsylvania Press, 1983).

Someone who cannot account for her actions and utterances to others is suspected of not having acted reasonably or "accountably." Even a criminal judge must first determine whether the accused could be held responsible for her alleged crime. Furthermore, the judge examines whether there are exculpatory grounds. In order to judge an offense fairly, we have to know whether the perpetrator was accountable and whether the offense should be attributed to the circumstances or to the agent herself. Exculpatory grounds confirm the supposition of rationality that we make about other agents not only in judicial proceedings, but also in everyday life. But the example of legal discourse is a good one for comparing the pragmatic presupposition of accountability with Kant's idea of freedom.

Until now, we have considered reason "in its theoretical use" as "the faculty of judging according to principles." Reason becomes "practical" insofar as it determines the will and action according to principles. Through the moral law expressed in the categorical imperative, the idea of freedom acquires its own "special kind of causality," namely, the rationally motivating force of good reasons.[21] Unlike the ideas of theoretical reason, which merely regulate the use of the understanding, freedom is constitutive for action because it is an "irrefutable demand of practical reason." Of course, we can always consider actions under the description of observable behavior as processes determined by natural laws. However, from a practical point of view, we have to relate actions to the reasons a rational subject might have had for doing them. The "practical point of view" signifies a shift in perspective to the kind of normative judgment in which we also engage when acting communicatively by presupposing rationality.

Of course the reasons that are relevant to "freedom" (in the Kantian sense) constitute only a fraction of the spectrum of the reasons for assessing the accountability of communicatively acting subjects. Kant characterizes freedom in general as an agent's capacity to subordinate her will to maxims, that is, to orient her actions by rules whose concept she has mastered. Thus

---

[21] The quoted phrase is to be found in Kant's *Groundwork of the Metaphysics of Morals*, ed. and trans. Mary Gregor (Cambridge: Cambridge University Press, 1998), p. 64 (Ak. 4: 460).

freedom of choice [*Willkürfreiheit*] enables one to adopt rules of prudence or skill depending on one's inclinations and subjectively selected ends, whereas "free will" [*freie Wille*] obeys universally valid laws it has imposed on itself from a moral point of view. Freedom of choice precedes free will, but the former remains subordinate to the latter when it comes to the moral evaluation of ends. Kant thus confines himself to technical-practical and moral-practical reasons. Communicative action draws on a broader spectrum of reasons: epistemic reasons for the truth of statements, ethical orientations for the authenticity of life choices, indicators for the sincerity of confessions, and, depending on the issue, aesthetic experiences, narrative explanations, cultural standards of value, legal claims, conventions, and so forth. Accountability is not measured simply by the standards of morality and purposive rationality – indeed, it involves more than just practical reason. Accountability consists, rather, in an agent's *general* ability to orient her action by validity claims.[22]

According to Kant, freedom is the only one among the practical ideas of reason whose possible realization we can *conceive* [*einsehen*] *a priori*. Hence this idea acquires legislative force for every rational being. It receives concrete expression in the ideal of a "kingdom of ends" in which all rational beings join together under common laws so that they never treat one another merely as means but as ends in themselves. Every member of this kingdom "gives universal laws in it but is also himself subject to these laws."[23] We have an *a priori* understanding of this model of self-legislation, which signifies two things: on the one hand, it has the categorical meaning of an obligation (namely of realizing the kingdom of ends by one's own actions and omissions); on the other hand, it has the transcendental meaning of a certainty (that this kingdom *can* be advanced by our moral actions and omissions). We can know *a priori* that it *is possible* to actualize this practical idea.

Considered under the first aspect, comparing the idea of freedom with the supposition of rationality in communicative action is not very fruitful. Rationality is not an obligation. Even with regard to moral or legal behavior, the supposition of

---

[22] Habermas, *Between Facts and Norms*, trans. William Rehg (Cambridge, Mass.: MIT Press, 1996), p. 5.
[23] Kant, *Groundwork*, p. 41 (Ak. 4: 433).

rationality does not mean that the other feels obligated to obey norms; knowledge of what it means to act autonomously is merely imputed to her. The second aspect is more promising: the idea of freedom provides the certainty that autonomous action (and the realization of the kingdom of ends) is *possible* – and not merely counterfactually demanded of us. According to Kant, rational beings think of themselves as agents who act on the basis of good reasons. With regard to moral action, they have an *a priori* knowledge of the possibility of actualizing the idea of freedom. In communicative action we also tacitly begin by assuming that all participants *are* accountable agents. It is simply part of the self-understanding of subjects acting communicatively that they take rationally motivated positions on claims to validity; agents mutually presuppose that they *do indeed* act on the basis of rationally warrantable reasons.

Of course we do not need social-scientific or psychological studies of behavior to show us that this performative practical "knowledge" is problematic. In everyday practice we are at once participant and observer and we discover that many assertions are not motivated by good reasons. From this empirical point of view, the accountability of communicative actors is no less a counterfactual presupposition than Kant's idea of freedom. Yet oddly enough, for the acting subjects *themselves* this empirical knowledge loses its contradictory character as they perform their actions. The contrast between the objective knowledge of an observer and the performatively engaged knowledge of an actor is of no significance *in actu*. First-year sociology students learn that all norms are valid counterfactually, even if they are obeyed on average because, for the sociologist-observer, statistically probable cases of deviant behavior go hand in hand with any prevailing norm.[24] Knowing this, however, will generally not prevent addressees from accepting as binding any norm that the community recognizes.

Someone who is acting morally does not credit herself with "more or less" autonomy; and participants in communicative

[24] This insight can be found in Emile Durkheim, *The Rules of Sociological Method*, 8th edn, ed. G. E. G. Catlin, trans. S. A. Soloray and J. H. Mueller (New York: Free Press, 1966).

action do not sometimes attribute "a little more" and sometimes "a little less" rationality to one another. From the perspective of the participants, these concepts are coded in a binary manner. As soon as we act out of "respect for the law" or "with an orientation to reaching mutual understanding," we cannot at the same time act from the objectivating perspective of an observer. While carrying out our actions, we bracket empirical self-descriptions in favor of the agents' rational self-understanding. Nevertheless, the supposition of rationality is a *defeasible* assumption and not *a priori* knowledge. It "functions" as a frequently corroborated pragmatic presupposition that is constitutive of communicative action. But it can be falsified in any given instance. This difference in the status of practical knowledge cannot be explained solely in terms of the detranscendentalization of the acting subject who has been dislodged from the kingdom of intelligible beings into the linguistically articulated lifeworld of socialized subjects. This paradigm shift alters the whole orientation of the analysis.

Within his mentalistic conceptual framework, Kant construes an agent's rational self-understanding as a person's knowledge of herself, and he opposes this first-person knowledge to an observer's third-person knowledge in an abstract way. The transcendental gap between these two forms of knowledge is such that the self-understanding of subjects as members of the intelligible realm cannot be corrected in principle by empirical knowledge. As speakers and addressees, however, communicatively acting subjects encounter one another literally at eye level by taking on first- and *second*-person roles. By reaching an understanding about something in the objective world and adopting the same relation to the world, they enter into an interpersonal relationship. In this performative attitude *toward* one another, they share communicative experiences *with* one another against the background of an intersubjectively shared – that is, sufficiently overlapping – lifeworld. Each can understand what the other one says or means. They learn from the information and objections that their interlocutor conveys and draw their own conclusions from irony, silence, paradoxical expressions, allusions, and so on. Cases in which opaque behavior becomes unintelligible or communication breaks down represent a reflexive mode of communicative experience. At this level, the presupposition of rationality cannot be refuted as such, but it can be indirectly disproven.

This kind of defeasibility does not seem to apply to idealizations in the domain of cognition, even if they also take the form of pragmatic presuppositions. The supposition of a shared objective world projects a system of possible references to the world and hence makes interventions in the world and interpretations of something in the world possible in the first place. The supposition of a shared objective world is "transcendentally" necessary in the sense that it cannot be corrected by experiences that would not be possible without it. The content of our descriptions is of course subject to revision, but the formal projection [*Entwurf*] of the totality of identifiable objects in general is not – at least not as long as our form of life is shaped by natural languages that have the familiar kind of propositional structure. At best, we may find out *a posteriori* that the projection was insufficiently formal. But "unavoidable" presuppositions are apparently "constitutive" for *practices* in a different sense than they are for *object domains*.

For rule-governed behavior, constitutive rules always offer the agent the alternative between following or violating them. Beyond that, there is the possibility in principle of being able to do something and not being able to do it. Someone who has not mastered the rules of a game and is not even capable of making mistakes is not a player. This becomes clear *in* the course of the practice. Thus only during communicative action does it become clear who is frustrating the pragmatic presupposition of accountability and is not even "playing the game." Whereas the supposition of a shared objective world cannot be checked against the kinds of experiences that it makes possible, the necessary supposition of rationality in communicative action holds only *pro tempore*. It is open to being contradicted by experiences that participants have in the course of this very practice.

(3) Until now, we have examined the detranscendentalized use of reason in terms of the supposition of a shared objective world and the mutual supposition of rationality that agents must make when they engage in communicative action. We have touched on another sense of "idealization" in passing in connection with the regulative function of the orientation to truth that complements reference to the world. The practice of action oriented to mutual understanding forces its participants to make certain totalizing

anticipations, abstractions, and transgressions of boundaries. Certainly the genealogical connection with Kant's "ideas" suggests the term "idealization" in these cases. But what do the various kinds of idealizations really have in common when we consider them in practice?

The relation to the world of a propositionally differentiated, representational language compels language-users to project a shared system of independently existing objects of reference about which they can form beliefs and which they can intentionally influence. The formal-pragmatic supposition of the world creates placeholders for objects to which speaking and acting subjects can refer. However, grammar cannot "impose" any laws on nature. A "transcendental projection" in the weak sense depends on nature "meeting us halfway." Thus in the "vertical" dimension of relating to the world, idealization consists in the anticipation of the totality of possible references. In the horizontal dimension of intersubjective relationships, the mutual supposition of rationality points to what subjects expect of one another *in principle*. If it is to be possible to reach understanding, and thereby coordinate action, at all, then agents must be able to take a warranted stance on criticizable validity claims and to orient themselves by such claims in their own actions.

Here idealization consists in a provisional abstraction from deviations, individual differences, and limiting contexts. Disturbances and, in extreme cases, breakdowns in communication occur only when these deviations exceed the limits of tolerance. In contrast to the Kantian projection of totalities, here a Platonic sense of idealization makes itself felt. As long as they maintain a performative attitude, actors are immune to acknowledging empirically observable imperfections until these reach a threshold at which the discrepancy between the ideal and its incomplete realization in a given instance becomes too gross. The decisive issue in this dimension is not the totalizing anticipation but rather the neutralization *in actu* of negligible deviations from the ideal from which even objectively deviant action takes its orientation.

Finally, the orientation toward truth in the critical testing of unconditional claims to validity first mobilizes yet another kind of idealization that seems excessive because it combines the Kantian and the Platonic senses of "idealization" to form an

apparent hybrid. Because our contact with the world is linguistically mediated, the world eludes both the direct grasp of the
senses and an immediate constitution through the forms of intuition and the concepts of the understanding. The presupposed
objectivity of the world is so deeply intertwined with the intersubjectivity of reaching an understanding about something in the
world that we cannot transcend this connection and escape the
linguistically disclosed horizon of our intersubjectively shared lifeworld. However, this does not rule out communication across the
divides between particular lifeworlds. We can reflexively transcend our respective hermeneutic starting points and reach intersubjectively shared views on disputed issues. Gadamer describes
this as a "fusion of horizons."[25]

The supposition of a common world of independently existing
objects about which we can state facts is complemented by the
idea of truth as a property that assertoric sentences cannot "lose."
However, if fallible sentences cannot immediately confront the
world, but can only be justified or refuted by means of further
propositions, and if no basis of self-warranting, self-evident propositions exists, then claims to truth can only be tested discursively.
Thus the two-place relation of the validity [*Gültigkeit*] of propositions is extended into the three-place relation of a validity
[*Geltung*] that valid propositions have "for us." Their truth must
be knowable for an audience. But then claims to *unconditional*
truth acquire, under the prevailing epistemic *conditions* of their
possible justification, an explosive power *within* the existing
communicative relationships. The epistemic reflection of unconditionality is the ideal elevation of the critical audience into a
"final" court of appeal. Peirce uses the image of the socially
and historically unlimited ideal community of inquirers who continued to engage in a joint process of inquiry – until they reach
the ideal limit of a "final opinion."

[25] Hans-Georg Gadamer, *Truth and Method*, 2nd edn, trans. Joel Weinsheimer
and Donald G. Marshall (New York: Continuum, 1993). Because Gadamer
has in mind the appropriation of classical works, however, he is misled into
aestheticizing the problem of truth; see Habermas, "Wie ist nach dem Historis-
mus noch Metaphysik möglich?" in *"Sein, das verstanden werden kann, ist
Sprache": Hommage an Hans-Georg Gadamer* (Frankfurt am Main: Suhrkamp,
2001), pp. 89–99.

This image is misleading in two respects. To begin with, it suggests that truth can be conceived as idealized warranted assertibility; and this in turn is assessed in terms of a consensus arrived at under ideal conditions. But a proposition is agreed to by all rational subjects because it is true; it is not true because it could be the content of a consensus reached under ideal conditions. Furthermore, Peirce's image does not direct our attention to the *process* of justification in the course of which true propositions must meet all objections, but to the *end state* of an agreement that is not subject to revision. This is contrary to a fallibilist self-understanding expressed in the "cautionary use" of the truth-predicate. Since our minds are finite, we have no way of foreseeing changes in epistemic conditions; hence we cannot rule out that a proposition, no matter how ideally justified, will turn out to be false.[26] Notwithstanding these objections to an epistemic conception of truth, the idea of a maximally inclusive process of argumentation that can be continued at any time plays an important part in explaining "rational acceptability," if not "truth," even after we have abandoned foundationalist justifications. As fallible, situated beings, we have no way of *ascertaining truth* other than through discourses that are both rational and open-ended.

No matter how misleading the image of an ideally extended communication community (Apel) that reaches a warranted mutual agreement [*Einverständnis*] under ideal epistemic conditions (Putnam), before an ideal audience (Perelman), or in an ideal speech situation (Habermas) may be, we cannot dispense with some such idealizations. For the rift opened up in everyday practice by a truth claim that has become problematic must be healed in a discourse that cannot be terminated "once and for all" either by "decisive" evidence or by "conclusive" arguments. Though truth claims cannot be definitively redeemed in discourses, it is through arguments alone that we let ourselves be *convinced* of the truth of problematic propositions. What is convincing is what we can accept as rational. Rational acceptability depends on a procedure that does not shield "our" arguments from anyone or anything. The process of argumentation as such must remain open

---

[26] See Wellmer's critique in "Ethics and Dialogue," pp. 160ff.

to any relevant objections and any improvements in our epistemic conditions. This kind of maximally inclusive and continuous argumentative practice falls under the idea of continually going beyond the limitations of current forms of communication as regards their social scope, their historical location, and levels of expertise in the relevant subject matter. The discursive process thereby increases the responsive potential by which rationally accepted claims to validity prove their worth.

With their intuitive understanding of the meaning of argumentation in general, proponents and opponents force one another into decentering their interpretive perspectives. Thus Kant's idealizing anticipation of the whole is carried over from the *objective* to the *social* world. This "totalization" is connected with a "neutralization" in the performative attitude of participants in argumentation. The latter prescind from the obvious gap between the ideal model of an "endless conversation" that is completely inclusive both socially and thematically, on the one hand, and the finite, spatio-temporally limited discourses that we actually engage in, on the other hand. Because the participants seek the truth, the concept of an absolutely valid truth is reflected at the level of the discursive ascertainment of truth in performative idealizations that make this argumentative practice so demanding.

Before I can enter into the details of these pragmatic presuppositions of rational discourse, I must briefly sketch the spectrum of validity claims that extends beyond "truth." According to the Kantian concept of practical reason, we claim unconditional validity not only for true assertoric propositions but also for correct moral – and with some reservations, legal – propositions.

(4) Until now, whenever I have spoken about communicatively acting subjects reaching an understanding about something in "the" world, I had in mind the reference to a common objective world. The claims to truth raised for assertoric sentences served as the paradigm for claims to validity in general. In regulative speech acts, such as recommendations, requests, and commands, agents refer to actions that (they believe) their interlocutors are obliged to perform. As members of a social group, they share certain practices and value orientations, they jointly recognize certain norms, have become accustomed to certain

conventions, and so forth. In the regulative use of language, speakers rely on an intersubjectively recognized or customary constellation of habits, institutions, or rules that regulate interpersonal relations within the group so that its members know what kind of behavior they may legitimately expect from one another. (With commissive speech acts, a speaker produces a legitimate relationship by entering into an obligation; in so doing, participants assume that communicatively acting subjects can bind their will to maxims and take responsibility for what they promise to do.)

In such normative language games, agents also refer to something in the objective world via the propositional contents of their utterances, but they do so only incidentally. They mention the circumstances and conditions of success of the actions they demand, request, recommend, accuse someone of, excuse, promise, and so on. But they refer directly to actions and norms as "something in the social world." However, they do not conceive of norm-governed actions as social facts that form a segment of the objective world, as it were. To be sure, from the objectivating point of view of the sociologist-observer there "really" are normative expectations, practices, habits, institutions, and regulations of all sorts "in the world" in addition to physical things and mental states. However, agents who are immediately involved have a different attitude toward the network of their normatively regulated interactions, namely, the performative attitude of actors who can "violate" norms only because they accept them as binding. Adopting the perspective of a second person whose "good will" is subject to normative expectations, they use a reference system that complements that of the objective world. This reference system detaches the relevant segment for their norm-governed action from the encompassing context of their *life*world for the purpose of thematization. Thus members comprehend their "social world" as the totality of possible legitimately regulated interpersonal relationships. Like the "objective world," this system of reference is also a necessary supposition that is grammatically coupled to regulative (as opposed to constative) language use.

The expressive use of first-person sentences completes this architectonic of "worlds." Based on a speaker's epistemic authority concerning sincere expressions of her own "experiences," we delimit an "inner world" from the objective and social worlds. The discussion of first-person perceptual and experiential reports, which arose in connection with Wittgenstein's private language argument and Wilfrid Sellars's critique of mentalism, shows that the totality of experiences to which a subject has privileged access cannot simply be understood as one more system of reference analogous to the objective and social worlds. "My" experiences are subjectively certain; unlike objective data or normative expectations, they do not have to be identified, nor can they be. Rather, the subjective "world" is determined negatively as the totality of what neither occurs in the objective world nor is taken to be valid or intersubjectively recognized in the social world. The subjective world complements these two publicly accessible worlds in that it includes all experiences that a speaker can turn into the content of first-person sentences when she wants to reveal something about herself to an audience in the expressive mode of self-presentation.

The claim to rightness of normative statements relies on the presumed validity of an underlying norm. Unlike the truth of descriptive statements, the sphere of validity of a rightness claim varies according to the legitimizing background, that is, according to the boundaries of a social world in general. Only *moral* imperatives (and legal norms such as human rights that can only be justified morally) claim absolute validity, that is, universal recognition, as assertions do. This explains Kant's demand that valid moral laws must be "universalizable." Moral norms must be able to command the rationally motivated recognition of *all* subjects capable of speech and action, beyond the historical and cultural confines of any particular social world. Thus the idea of a thoroughly morally ordered community implies the counterfactual extension of the social world in which we find ourselves to a completely inclusive world of well-ordered interpersonal relationships: all human beings become brothers and sisters.

Of course, to hypostatize such a universal community of persons capable of moral judgment and action in the sense of a spatio-temporally unlimited community would again be mistaken. The image of the self-determined "kingdom of ends" suggests the existence of a republic of rational beings, although it is a construct that, as Kant notes, "does not exist but . . . can become real by means of our conduct."[27] It ought to and can be brought about in accordance with the practical idea of freedom. The kingdom of ends "exists" in a certain sense, yet it is more a task [*aufgegeben*] than something given [*gegeben*]. This ambiguity was not the least of Kant's motives for dividing human practices into the intelligible realm and the realm of appearances. As soon as we no longer subscribe to this transcendental bipartition, we have to bring out the *constructive meaning* of morality in some other way.

We can represent moral learning processes as an intelligent expansion and reciprocal interpenetration of social worlds that in particular cases of conflict do not yet sufficiently overlap. The disputing parties learn to *include* one another in a world they construct together so as to be able to judge and hence resolve controversial actions in the light of compatible standards of evaluation. G. H. Mead described this as the expansion of a reversible exchange of interpretive perspectives. At first rooted in their own particular lifeworlds, the participants' perspectives become increasingly "decentered" (as Piaget puts it) as the process of intermeshing of one another's perspectives approaches the ideal limit of complete inclusiveness. Interestingly, this is precisely what the practice of argumentation aims at by its very structure. From the moral point of view, only those norms that are equally good for everybody deserve recognition. Hence rational discourse presents itself as the appropriate procedure for resolving conflicts because it ensures the inclusion of all those affected and the equal consideration of all the interests concerned.

"Impartiality" in the sense of justice converges with "impartiality" in the sense of the discursive ascertainment of cognitive claims to validity.[28] This convergence makes sense if we compare the orientation of moral learning processes with the conditions for participating in argumentation as such. Conflicts are triggered by contradictions among social adversaries with opposed value orientations. Moral learning processes resolve such conflicts through each participant's reciprocal inclusion of the other(s). As it turns out, however, argumentation as a form of communication is

---

[27] Kant, *Groundwork*, p. 44n. (Ak. 4: 436).
[28] William Rehg, *Insight and Solidarity* (Berkeley: University of California Press, 1994).

already tailored to such an interpenetration of perspectives and enriching expansion of world horizons. Lest the discussion of disputed validity claims forfeit its cognitive purpose, participants in argumentation must subscribe to an egalitarian universalism that is structurally mandated and that initially has only a formal-pragmatic meaning, rather than a moral one.

The cooperative nature of the competition for better arguments is explained by the goal or function constitutive for the language game of argumentation: participants want to convince one another. In continuing everyday communicative action at the reflexive level of thematized claims to validity, they are still guided by the goal of mutual understanding inasmuch as a proponent can win the game only if she *convinces* her opponents that her validity claim is warranted. The rational acceptability of the corresponding statement is based on the convincing force of the better arguments. Which argument does convince is not decided by private insight but by the stances that, bundled together in a rationally motivated agreement, are adopted by everyone who participates in the public practice of exchanging reasons.

Now, standards for whether something counts as a good or a bad argument may themselves become controversial. Anything can be caught up in the tumult of opposing reasons. Hence the rational acceptability of validity claims is *ultimately* based only on reasons that withstand objections under certain demanding conditions of communication. If the process of argumentation is to live up to its meaning, communication in the form of rational discourse must allow, if possible, all relevant information and explanations to be brought up and weighed so that the stance participants take can be inherently motivated solely by the revisionary power of free-floating reasons. However, if this is the intuitive meaning that we associate with argumentation in general, then we also know that a practice may not seriously count as argumentation unless it meets certain pragmatic presuppositions.[29]

---

[29] On the following, see Habermas, "A Genealogical Analysis of the Cognitive Content of Morality," in *The Inclusion of the Other*, ed. and trans. Ciaran Cronin and Pablo De Greiff (Cambridge, Mass.: MIT Press, 1998), pp. 3–46, here 43f.

The four most important presuppositions are: (a) publicity and inclusiveness: no one who could make a relevant contribution concerning a controversial validity claim must be excluded; (b) equal rights to engage in communication: everyone must have the same opportunity to speak to the matter at hand; (c) exclusion of deception and illusion: participants must mean what they say; and (d) absence of coercion: communication must be free from restrictions that prevent the better argument from being raised and determining the outcome of the discussion. Presuppositions (a), (b), and (d) subject one's behavior in argumentation to the rules of an egalitarian universalism. *With regard to moral-practical issues,* it follows from these rules that the interests and value orientations of every affected person are given equal consideration. And since the participants in practical discourses are simultaneously the ones who are affected, presupposition (c) – which *in theoretical-empirical disputes* requires only a sincere and unconstrained weighing of the arguments – takes on the additional significance that one must remain critically alert to self-deception and hermeneutically open and responsive to how others understand themselves and the world.

These argumentative presuppositions obviously contain such strong idealizations that they invite the suspicion that they represent tendentious description of argumentation. How is it even possible for participants in argumentation to make such obviously counterfactual assumptions in their performances? After all, people engaged in discourse are aware, among other things, that the circle of participants is highly selective, that one side enjoys greater communicative latitude than the other, that one person or another remains prejudiced concerning this topic or that, that many people on occasion behave strategically, or that "yes" and "no" positions are often determined by motives other than a better understanding of the issue. To be sure, an observer analyzing a discourse could more accurately spot such deviations from an "ideal speech situation" than could the engaged participants, who presume they have approximated the ideal. But even when taking a performative attitude, participants do not allow themselves to be wholeheartedly consumed by their engagement to the point of not being aware – at least intuitively – of much that they could know thematically by taking an observer's objectivating attitude.

At the same time, these unavoidable presuppositions of argumentative practice, no matter how counterfactual they may be, are by no means mere constructs. Rather they are *actually efficacious* in the behavior of the participants themselves. Someone who seriously takes part in an argument proceeds *de facto* from such presuppositions. This is evident from the inferences participants will draw, if necessary, from perceived inconsistencies. The process of argumentation is self-correcting in the sense that an unsatisfactory discussion, for example, spontaneously generates reasons for an "overdue" liberalization of the rules of procedure and discussion, for changing an insufficiently representative circle of participants, for expanding the agenda or improving the information base. One *can tell* when new arguments must be taken into account or when marginalized voices have to be taken seriously. On the other hand, perceived inconsistencies are not *always* the motive for these or similar repairs. This is explained by the fact that participants in argumentation are *immediately* convinced by the substance of the reasons rather than by the communicative design of the exchange of reasons. The procedural properties of the process of argumentation warrant the rational expectation that the relevant information and reasons get "put on the table" and can influence the outcome. As long as participants in argumentation proceed from the assumption that this is the case, from their perspective there is no reason to be worried about inadequate procedural properties of the process of communication.

The formal properties of argumentation bear on the difference between rational assertibility and truth. Because no evidence is decisive and no arguments are compelling "in the final instance," because no assertion, however well justified, is infallible, it is only the quality of the discursive truth-seeking procedure that warrants the reasonable expectation that the best attainable information and reasons are indeed available and do "count" in the end. Perceived inconsistencies that provoke doubts about the genuineness of an argumentative exchange do not arise until clearly *relevant participants* are excluded, *relevant contributions* are suppressed, and yes/no stances are manipulated or conditioned by other kinds of influences. The idealizing anticipation associated with argumentative presuppositions displays its operative efficacy in its critical function: an absolute claim to validity has to be justifiable in ever wider forums before an ever more competent and larger audience and against ever new objections. This dynamic of the progressive decentering of one's interpretive perspective inherent in argumentation specifically propels practical discourses, which are concerned not with ascertaining truth claims but with the insightful construction and application of moral (and legal) norms.[30]

The validity of such norms "consists" in the universal recognition that they merit. Because moral claims to validity lack the ontological connotations that are characteristic of claims to truth, reference to the objective world is replaced by an orientation toward an expansion of the social world, that is, toward the progressive inclusion of strangers and their claims. The validity of a moral statement has the epistemic significance that it would be accepted under ideal conditions of justification. However, if the meaning of "moral rightness," unlike that of "truth," is *exhausted* by rational acceptability, then our moral convictions must ultimately rely on the critical potential of self-transcendence and decentering that is built into the practice of argumentation – and the self-understanding of its participants – with the "disruptiveness" of idealizing anticipations.

II

(5) Kant operated within a paradigm that does not accord language any constitutive role for theory and practice. Mentalism develops a more constructive or more passive image of the mind that processes its perceptually mediated contacts with the world into representations of, and purposive effects on, objects, without being essentially influenced in these operations by language and its structures. As long as language does not trouble the mind with its idols, its merely handed-down images and ideals, the mind sees through the medium of language as through polished glass. In the retrospective genealogical analysis of the mentalistic origins of a detranscendentalized use of reason, therefore, language cannot as

---

[30] On the following, see Habermas, "Rightness versus Truth: On the Sense of Normative Validity in Moral Judgments and Norms," in Habermas, *Truth and Justification*, pp. 237–76.

yet function as the structure-forming medium of the mind that first transposes transcendental consciousness back into the historical and social contexts of the lifeworld.

Reason, for Kant, finds its true home in the domain of practice, because it is constitutive only for moral action alone. This is what inspires the search for traces of detranscendentalized reason in communicative *action*. The expression "communicative action" refers to those social interactions in which the use of language oriented to reaching understanding takes on a coordinating role.[31] The idealizing presuppositions migrate via linguistic communication into action oriented to reaching understanding. Hence, the theory of language, and in particular semantics, which explicates the meaning of linguistic expressions in terms of the conditions of linguistic understanding, represents the place in which a formal pragmatics in the Kantian tradition could meet up with investigations from the analytic side. In fact, with Frege the analytic research tradition takes as its point of departure the elementary case of an idealizing presupposition that only became discernible following the linguistic turn. For if the mind's structures are shaped by the grammar of language, we must ask how propositions and predicate expressions in their diverse contexts of use can acquire the universality and identity of meaning that judgments and concepts in the mental sphere have by their very nature.

Frege, who still belongs to the Kantian tradition and whom Dummett correctly places alongside Husserl, proposes to differentiate between the semantic concept of "thought" and the psychological concept of "representation." If it is to be possible to communicate thoughts, they must overstep the boundaries of an individual consciousness *unaltered*, whereas representations belong to a particular subject who is individuated in space and time. Propositions preserve the same thought content even when they are uttered or understood as propositions by different subjects in different contexts. This leads Frege to ascribe an ideal status – i.e. one removed from space and time – to thoughts and conceptual contents. He explicates the characteristic difference in status

---

[31] Habermas, "Actions, Speech Acts, Linguistically Mediated Interactions, and the Lifeworld," in *On the Pragmatics of Communication*, pp. 215–56.

between thoughts and representations in terms of the grammatical forms in which they are expressed. In contrast to Husserl, Frege explores the structure of judgment or thought in terms of the structure of the assertoric sentence composed of words as the smallest grammatical unit that can be true or false. The structure of propositions and the intermeshing of reference and predication show how thought contents differ from the objects of representational thinking.[32]

The fact that thought overshoots the boundaries of a spatio-temporally individuated consciousness, and the independence of the ideal thought content from the stream of experience of the thinking subject, are preconditions for the ability of linguistic expressions to preserve *the same* meaning for different people in different situations. Already at the elementary level of the sign substrate, speakers and hearers must be able to recognize the same sign type in the multiplicity of the corresponding sign tokens. This corresponds to the assumption of invariant meanings at the semantic level. At any rate, the members of a language community must assume in practice that the grammatical expressions they utter.have a *general* meaning that is *identical* for all participants across their various contexts of use. Only on this supposition can utterances sometimes prove to be unintelligible. Of course, the *in actu* unavoidable assumption that the expressions of a shared language are used with identical meanings precludes neither the linguistic division of labor nor historical changes in meaning. Changes in our knowledge of the world provoke changes in linguistic knowledge, and advances in knowledge are reflected in changes in the meaning of basic theoretical concepts.[33]

The ideal generality of the meaning of grammatical expressions also involves an idealizing presupposition that often proves to be incorrect from the perspective of an observer; indeed, when viewed under the microscope of the ethnomethodologist, it always proves to be incorrect. But as a counterfactual supposition it is unavoidable when language is used with the goal of reaching

[32] Ernst Tugendhat, *Einführung in die sprachanalytische Philosophie* (Frankfurt am Main: Suhrkamp, 1976), pp. 35ff.
[33] Hilary Putnam, "The Meaning of Meaning," in Putnam, *Mind, Language and Reality* (Cambridge: Cambridge University Press, 1975), pp. 215–71.

understanding. However, Frege was misled by his justified critique of psychologism into a platonism concerning meaning, which, as it happens, Husserl also shared under different premises. The late Frege believed that the mentalistic two-worlds architectonic, which juxtaposes a subjective world of representations to an objective world of things, had to be supplemented by a third, ideal world of propositions. With this unfortunate move, he maneuvered himself into a difficult position. If propositional meanings are hypostasized into an ideal in-itself [*Ansichsein*] it remains mysterious how these ethereal entities of a "third realm"[34] can enter into relations with the physical things of the objective world, on the one hand, and with representing subjects, on the other. The relation of the mental "presentation" [*Darstellung*] of entities in thought becomes independent of a subjective mind. And as for the latter, it remains unclear how it manages to "grasp" and "judge" propositions.

That the "thoughts banished from consciousness" (Dummett) lead an equivocal, indeed incomprehensible, existence is one of the problems that Frege bequeathed to his successors. The other is the reverse side of the groundbreaking idea of introducing "truth" as the basic semantic concept for explicating the meaning of linguistic expressions. To understand a proposition one must know the conditions under which it is true, that is, one must know, as Wittgenstein later puts it, "what is the case if it is true." This poses the task of explicating the meaning of truth, i.e. the "fulfillment" of truth conditions. Frege's proposal that the truth value of a proposition should be identified with its object of reference is clearly unsatisfactory. For his own analysis of the structure of statements makes clear that truth cannot be assimilated to reference. Thus the tradition of truth semantics was burdened from the outset with two stubborn problems.

The propositional contents elevated out of the stream of experience as meanings had to be incorporated into the medium of linguistic expressions in such a way that the ghostly twilight world

[34] Gottlob Frege, "The Thought: A Logical Enquiry," *Mind* 55 (1956): 289–311. There Frege concludes: "So the result seems to be: thoughts are neither things of the outer world nor ideas. A third realm must be recognized" (p. 302).

of free-floating propositions dissolved. But explicating the meaning of propositions in terms of truth semantics could accomplish this only if the explanatory basic concept of "truth" did not remain obscure. Both questions: How should we treat propositions? and: How should we understand the truth predicate? can be understood as the unresolved problems bequeathed by a repressed mentalistic concept of reason. From a linguistic point of view, two responses suggest themselves. Either the concept of reason itself is liquidated along with the mentalistic paradigm, or it is freed from its mentalistic framework and is transposed into the concept of communicative reason. Donald Davidson adopts the first strategy. Starting from empiricist premises, he wants to defuse the distinctive normativity of language, which is reflected in the relation of speaking and acting subjects to the world as well as in their relations to one another (6); Michael Dummett and Robert Brandom pursue the opposite course and seek to reconstruct the normativity of the practice of linguistic communication in a series of steps (7 and 8). The following sketch represents an attempt to trace the route along which the internal normative logic of the reason embodied in language also makes itself felt within the analytic philosophy of language.

(6) Davidson objectifies the phenomenon in need of explanation, i.e. what it means to understand a linguistic expression. In a methodological decision with far-reaching consequences, he changes the role of the analyst of language by detaching him from the role of the reader or hearer who tries to understand the texts or utterances of an author or speaker. Instead he accords the interpreter the role of an empirical theorist who makes behavioral observations of a foreign culture and, in contrast to Wittgenstein's ethnologist, looks for causal explanations of the unintelligible linguistic behavior of the natives. In this way the communicative behavior of speaking and acting subjects is shifted entirely onto the side of the object, as it were. The forceful assimilation of intelligible symbolic utterances to the category of observable natural phenomena is the counterpart of the assimilation of the understanding of meaning to explanations that call for an empirical theory. Davidson employs Tarski's truth convention as an *undefined* basic concept for generating meaning-equivalences in developing such a theory.

With this move, Davidson can defuse the problem of how to deal with the idea of truth and the ideal content of truth claims raised in communication. As for the other problem associated with the use of grammatical expressions with identical meanings – namely, how to avoid a platonic doubling of sentence meanings in propositions – he proposes to eliminate the concept of meaning altogether.

Davidson regards the fact that he does not have to make use of "meanings as entities" as one of the advantages of his approach: "no objects are introduced to correspond to predicates or sentences."[35] However, the problem does not disappear without trace. It reappears at the methodological level in the question of how the interpreter can correctly correlate the evidence collected in the field, i.e. the linguistic behavior and the indicators of the attitudes of foreign speakers, with the theoretically generated T-sentences. In order to be able to read a logical structure into the observed stream of data, the interpreter must first be able to divide these behavioral sequences into sentence-like units that can be correlated with the biconditionals of the Tarski theory. Even if this division is successful, however, the observed covariance of isolated utterances with the typical circumstances in which they occur is not sufficient to establish a clear correlation.

Generally speaking, a competent speaker utters a perceptual statement on the basis of the known *lexical meaning* of the expressions used only in connection with what he *thinks* he perceives in the given situation, and thus what he *believes* to be true. Because word meaning and belief can vary independently of each other, the observational data – hence, in addition to the behavior of the foreign speaker, the circumstances in which it occurs – can provide the interpreter with information concerning the meaning of the utterance to be interpreted only when the foreign speaker takes what he says to be true. An observer needs to know whether the foreign speaker believes what he says in order to find out what the speaker's utterance means. In order to neutralize the unwelcome interdependence of belief and meaning, therefore, the interpreter must assume as a constant that the observed speaker takes

---

[35] Donald Davidson, *Inquiries into Truth and Interpretation* (New York: Oxford University Press, 1984), p. xv.

what he says to be true. Only the *assumption that what is said is taken to be true* makes the observed covariance of utterance and situation of utterance into sufficient evidence for the theoretically informed choice of the correct interpretation. For this reason, Davidson introduces as a *defeasible assumption* the principle that the speakers observed in the field generally *behave rationally*. This means that they generally believe what they say and do not become entangled in contradictions in the course of their utterances. On this presupposition, the interpreter can assume that in most situations the observed speaker perceives and believes the same things as he does, so that both sides share a large number of convictions. This does not preclude discrepancies in individual cases, but the principle enjoins the interpreter to "maximize agreement."

Here it must be emphasized that the methodological principle of charity forces an interpreter to ascribe "rationality" to a foreign speaker as a behavioral disposition *from the observer perspective*. This ascription should not be confused with the supposition of rationality made by participants in a *performative* attitude. In the former case, the concept of rationality is used descriptively, in the latter, normatively. In both cases, it is a matter of a fallible presupposition: "The methodological advice to interpret in a way that optimizes agreement should not be conceived as resting on a charitable assumption about human intelligence . . . If we cannot find a way to interpret the utterances and other behavior of a creature as revealing a set of beliefs largely consistent and true by our standards, we have no reason to count that creature as rational, as having beliefs, or as saying anything."[36]

This formulation (which recurs in Davidson's argument against the distinction between conceptual scheme and content) already implies that the methodological principle has a quasi-transcendental status.[37] The ascription of rationality is an unavoidable presupposition not just for radical interpretation but also for everyday

[36] Davidson, "Radical Interpretation," in Davidson, *Inquiries into Truth and Interpretation*, pp. 125–40, here p. 137.
[37] Barbara Fultner, "Radical Interpretation of Communicative Action: Holism in Davidson and Habermas" (PhD Dissertation, Northwestern University, 1995), pp. 178ff.

communication between members of the same linguistic community.[38] Without the mutual ascription of rationality, we
would not find a sufficient common basis of communication
that leads beyond our respective theories of interpretation (or idio-
lects).[39] Then "taking-to-be-true" is reconnected with the general
"preference" for true sentences ("preferring one sentence true to
another") within the context of the integrated theory of speech and
action.[40]

Practical rationality is measured by the usual standards of logical
consistency, general principles of success-oriented action, and
responsiveness to empirical evidence. In his reply to an intervention by Richard Rorty, Davidson recently reformulated the
principle of charity as follows:

> Charity is a matter of finding enough rationality in those we
> would understand to make sense of what they say and do, for
> unless we succeed in this, we cannot identify the contents of their
> words and thoughts. Seeing rationality in others is a matter of
> recognizing our own norms of rationality in their speech and
> behavior. These norms include the norms of logical consistency,
> of action in reasonable accord with essential or basic interests of
> the agent, and the acceptance of views that are sensible in the light
> of evidence.[41]

Interestingly, the normativity of human behavior that informs
the supposition of rationality also serves Davidson as a criterion
of demarcation of the language of physics from mental language:
"There are several reasons for the irreducibility of the mental to

---

[38] Andrew Cutrofello, "On the Transcendental Pretensions of the Principle of
Charity," in Lewis E. Hahn (ed.), *The Philosophy of Donald Davidson* (LaSalle,
Ill.: Open Court, 1999), p. 333: "The principle of charity is supposed to be a
universally binding condition for the very possibility of interpreting anyone at
all." In his reply, Davidson accepts the expression "transcendental" in the weak
sense of factual unavoidability; at least he speaks of "the inevitability of the
appeal to that principle" (ibid., p. 342).
[39] Davidson, "A Nice Derangement of Epitaphs," in Davidson, *Truth, Language,
and History* (Oxford: Oxford University Press, 2005), pp. 89–107.
[40] Davidson, *Essays on Actions and Events* (Oxford: Oxford University Press,
1980).
[41] See Hahn, *The Philosophy of Donald Davidson*, p. 600.

the physical. One reason . . . is the normative element in interpretation introduced by the necessity (!) of appealing to charity in matching the sentences of others to our own."[42] Davidson wants to maintain at least a thin line of demarcation between mind and nature against the monistic viewpoint of scientistic naturalism. Richard Rorty can muster powerful arguments against this heroic endeavor for, in doing so, he merely radicalizes the strategy of defusing the rational potential implicit in linguistic communication pursued by Davidson himself.[43] It is by no means clear how Davidson can uphold a dualism of the body–mind perspectives once he has shifted rational behavior completely to the object side and has traced the understanding of linguistic expressions back to the *theoretical* explanations of an interpreter who adopts an *objectivating* standpoint. For the understanding of language and the standards of rationality that Davidson at first presupposes on the side of the radical interpreter did not materialize out of thin air. They require further explanation.

Radical interpretation cannot explain within the chosen empiricist framework how the interpreter himself could have learned to speak, or how language could have arisen in the first place. If subjects capable of speech and action are "mental beings" because they can adopt intentional attitudes toward logically articulated propositional contents, and if the intentional construction of their speech acts and their actions is what requires the interpreter to make the supposition of rationality and to employ mentalistic concepts, then the question of how something like intentionality could itself have arisen remains open. Davidson famously responds to this question with the model of a "triangular" learning situation in which two organisms react simultaneously to "the world" and to each other. Davidson wants to show in terms of the model of a logical genesis of the acquisition of elementary linguistic expressions how from "our" perspective, but on naturalistic premises, two conspecific, highly developed, intelligent, though still

---

[42] Davidson, "Could There be a Theory of Rationality?," *International Journal of Philosophical Studies* 3 (1995), pp. 1–16, here p. 4. Also Davidson, *Problems of Rationality* (Oxford: Oxford University Press, 2004), pp. 117–34.
[43] Richard Rorty, "Davidson's Mental-Physical Distinction," in Hahn, *The Philosophy of Donald Davidson*, pp. 575–94.

prelinguistic, organisms that are adapted to their natural environment could learn to achieve the distance from their sensible surroundings that we call "intentional" by means of symbols employed with identical meanings.

The supposition of an objective world of things toward which we can *relate* is constitutive for the intentional constitution of mind. This world-relation is a precondition for our being able to make statements concerning objects and to adopt different attitudes toward the contents of statements. Under this description, intentional consciousness is coeval with propositionally differentiated language. We are now supposed to conceive of the genesis of this consciousness as if it emerged from a kind of interaction with the world for which the relation to a *presumptively objective* world is not yet constitutive. The world is connected with language only in causal ways. This naturalistic premise coheres with "externalism," which holds that language is "anchored in the world" through an elementary perceptual vocabulary and owes its semantic content to an intelligent processing of causally generated sensory stimuli: "in the simplest and most basic cases, words and sentences derive their meanings from the objects and circumstances in whose presence they were learned. A sentence which one has been conditioned by the learning process to be caused to hold true by the presence of fires will (usually) be true when there is a fire present."[44]

This explanation traces the *meaning* of an expression and the *truth* of a statement back to the *causal* conditions under which they were learned. However, the procedure described as "conditioning" in the causal language game clashes in a counterintuitive way with our self-understanding as rational beings. Hence Davidson wants to explain how the *intentional distance toward and from* the world could be brought about by the world itself in accordance with the stimulus-response model. Two interacting creatures achieve the specific distance from the initially immediately conditioning stimulus to which they react in similar ways based on their conspecific dispositions not

[44] Davidson, "The Myth of the Subjective," in Davidson, *Subjective, Intersubjective, Objective: Philosophical Essays* (Oxford: Oxford University Press, 2001), p. 44.

only because they perceive the stimulus itself but also because they simultaneously perceive through mutual observation that the other responds to the same stimulus in the same way: "Enough features are in place to give a meaning to the idea that the stimulus has an objective location in a common space; it's a matter of two private perspectives converging to mark a position in intersubjective space. So far, however, nothing in this picture shows that . . . our subjects . . . *have* the concept of the objective."[45]

Of course, it remains unclear how one individual can know that the other is reacting to *the same* object as himself. Each must discover whether the other means the same object. They have to communicate about this. However, they can enter into a corresponding communication with each other only if they use the reaction pattern (or a part of it) at the same time as a symbolic expression and address it as a communication to the other. They must communicate with one another *about what exactly* triggered the reaction for the other: "For two people to know of each other that they are so related, that their thoughts are so related, requires that they be in communication. Each of them must speak to the other and be understood by the other."[46] A stimulus that triggers a similar reaction in both of the parties involves changes into an object "for them," hence into something in a shared objective world, once they go beyond mutual observation of similarities in their reactions and communicate "about it," i.e. the triggering stimulus thereby transformed into an object. They do this by means of their behavioral reactions, which they now *address to one another as symbols*. The pattern of the two similar behavioral reactions acquires at the same time an identical meaning for both sides only through such a communicative use.

The intuition that Davidson expresses with the image of triangulation is clear: references to and intentional attitudes toward something in the objective world are only possible from a speaker

[45] Davidson, "The Conditions of Thought," in *Le Cahier du Collège International de Philosophie* (Paris: Editions Osiris, 1989), p. 169.
[46] Ibid., p. 171.

perspective that is coordinated with the perspective of at least one other speaker via communicatively generated intersubjective relations. Objectivity is a product of intentional distance from the world. The speakers can achieve this distance only by learning to communicate with one another about *the same* things. However, it is difficult to understand how Davidson could explain this interconnection between objectivity and a coeval intersubjectivity in terms of his fictional learning situation. The problems are generated not by the externalism of the basic epistemological assumption but by the methodological solipsism of the solitary observer.

How is it possible for these two organisms, which find themselves in the same environment and observe each other reacting in similar ways to *a single* stimulus from this environment, to reach an understanding that they have *the same* stimulus in mind – unless, that is, they already possess a corresponding concept? But they can acquire the latter only with the aid of a criterion that they employ in the same way – in other words, by means of a symbol that has the same meaning for both of them. Only then could they also reach an agreement concerning objective similarities. To be sure, if someone, let us say a teacher, could already assume the role of a radical interpreter toward a child, he would discover whether he and the child "mean the same thing" – and could correct the child if necessary. However, in this case triangulation would explain at best how children growing up within an already existing language community can learn the elementary components of the perceptual vocabulary. As yet it does not tell us anything about the possibility of an *original* emergence of intentionality from the mutual behavioral observations of organisms that react to specific features of the environment in similar, though not yet intentional, ways.

The mutual ascription of *the same* reaction pattern can result from the reciprocal perception of objectively *similar* reactions only when those involved employ *the same* criterion. For different subjects can register objective similarities only in specific respects that remain intersubjectively constant. In Wittgenstein's terms, they must be able to follow a rule. It is not enough that they exhibit similar reactions from the perspective of an uninvolved observer; the participants themselves must *notice* a similarity in the reactions in respect of the same stimulus or object.[47] This presupposes what is to be explained: "All awareness of sorts, resemblances, facts etc. . . . is a linguistic affair."[48] To be sure, Davidson emphasizes the social core of the normativity of a mind characterized, among other things, by intentionality, the relation to a *shared* objective world. But he does not understand this sociality from the perspective of a participant who "finds himself" within a form of life shared with others, and hence is not only objectively equipped with similar behavioral dispositions but also has at least an intuitive awareness of this agreement.

Belonging or "membership" involves an antecedent, socially shared understanding of what makes one's mode of life into a common one. The choice of an objectivistic approach that assimilates the understanding of meaning to theoretically informed explanation amounts to a decision in favor of methodological solipsism. The latter requires us to trace the communicative agreement back to the constructive result of the coordination and overlapping of acts of interpretation that each undertakes for him- or herself from the position of an observer without being able to draw upon a store of existing, objectively adjusted, yet at the same time subjectively available, commonalities. Otherwise it would have seemed natural to introduce triangulation, following G. H. Mead for example, as a mechanism that explains how two conspecifics interacting with each other arrive at an awareness of the meaning of their species-typical reaction patterns through mutual

---

[47] After writing this I came across the same objection in John Fennell, "Davidson on Meaning Normativity: Public or Social," *European Journal of Philosophy* 8 (2000), pp. 139–54: "The regularity in the environment, the identification of the common stimuli as *the* ones we are both responding to involves a normative similarity judgment . . . In order to make the required judgment of normative similarity the interpreter must exceed what is available to an external observer . . . Hence triangulation faces the problem of the identification of the common stimuli, . . . and triangulation, if it is understood in purely causal terms as the correlation of stimulus-response groupings, leaves this problem unanswered" (p. 149).

[48] Wilfrid Sellars, *Empiricism and the Philosophy of Mind* (1956) (Cambridge, Mass.: Harvard University Press, 1997), p. 63.

perspective-taking, and how this meaning thereby becomes symbolically available to both of them.[49]

(7) Philosophical hermeneutics is opposed to objectivistic
approaches. It holds that the process of interpretation is guided
by a pre-understanding that is not tested through observations of
the behavior of others like an empirical hypothesis, but is made
explicit and corrected through question and answer on the model
of a dialogue with the second person. Partners in conversation
move within the horizon of an already shared background understanding, even when they must first develop a shared language.
This procedure is circular inasmuch as everything an interpreter
learns is the fallible product of the explication of a pre-
understanding, however vague. In this process, the interpreter, as
Gadamer emphasizes in agreement with Davidson, proceeds from
the pragmatic supposition that the text to be interpreted can only
have a clear meaning as the expression of a rational author. Only
against the background of such a "fore-conception of completeness" [*Vorgriff auf Volkommenheit*] can texts turn out to be incomprehensible or utterances opaque: "But this, too, is obviously a
formal condition of all understanding. It states that only what
really constitutes a unity of meaning is intelligible."[50]
  The hermeneutic presupposition of rationality exhibits a striking affinity with Davidson's principle of charity. Indeed, the affinity goes even further. Just as the "radical interpreter" must direct
his attention to the conditions under which a foreign speaker
makes a presumptively true utterance, so too must Gadamer's
interpreter direct his attention simultaneously to the text *and* to
the subject matter treated in it. One must first "understand the
content of what is said" before one can "isolate and understand
another's meaning as such."[51] This is the hermeneutic version of
the principle of formal semantics according to which the meaning
of a proposition is determined by its truth conditions. In another

---

[49] Habermas, *The Theory of Communicative Action*, Vol. 2, trans. Thomas
McCarthy (Cambridge, Mass.: Beacon Press, 1987), pp. 3–43.
[50] Hans-Georg Gadamer, *Truth and Method*, 2nd rev. edn, trans. Joel
Weinsheimer and Donald G. Marshall (New York: Continuum, 1993), p. 294.
[51] Ibid.

respect, however, there is a major difference between the two principles. Davidson's interpreter, adopting the observer perspective, ascribes to the stranger the disposition to take as his frame of reference the norms of rationality from which the interpreter also takes his orientation. By contrast, Gadamer's interpreter, taking the participant perspective, assumes that the utterances of his conversation partner are rational according to *shared* standards of rationality. The performative supposition of rationality, in contrast to the objectifying ascription of rationality, assumes a shared understanding of rationality and not just an objective agreement between their respective understandings.

However, the global model of a conversation sustained by life-world traditions takes on board quite a number of unclarified presuppositions. In order to make it accessible to more precise analysis, formal pragmatics reduces this hermeneutic scenario *in toto* to the bare skeleton of an elementary exchange of speech acts oriented to reaching understanding. The rational potential that operates at the macro-level of communicative action is subjected to microscopic re-examination by Wittgenstein at the level of rule-governed behavior. With this move, Wittgenstein inspired the non-empiricist branch of the Fregean tradition leading to Dummett and Brandom. In contrast to the Carnap–Quine–Davidson tradition, these authors take as their point of departure joint normatively regulated practices that establish an intersubjectively shared context of meaning. They take their methodological orientation from the perspective of fellow-players who make explicit the ability of competent speakers.

What a formal pragmatic analysis that proceeds "from above" represents as a network of idealizing presuppositions, the analytic approach, proceeding in the opposite direction to detranscendentalization, discovers "from below," as it were. For from this side it also transpires that the assumption of identical word meanings *points* to the more complex assumptions of a shared objective world, of the rationality of subjects capable of speech and action, and of the unconditional character of truth claims. The lowest stage of idealization cannot be *thought* independently of these further idealizations. Wittgenstein annuls Frege's meaning-platonism without abandoning the insight concerning the public communicability of general and identical meanings. Dummett preserves the independence of the representative function of language, and hence of the relation to the objective world, vis-à-vis the intersubjectively shared form of life and the background consensus of the language community. Finally, Brandom construes the rationality and accountability that the participants in discourse ascribe to each other in a detailed fashion in terms of a formal pragmatics. Of course, here I can recall these stages of an extraordinarily dense train of argument only in broad outlines with the goal of rendering the network of idealizing presuppositions visible also from this perspective.

The meaning of a symbolic expression overshoots the particular circumstances of its instantiations. Wittgenstein analyzes this platonic moment of the universality of meaning associated with every predicate or concept via the concept of "rule-governed" behavior. Whereas "regular" behavior merely conforms to a rule from the perspective of an observer, "rule-governed" behavior requires that the acting subject must orient himself to a rule of which he must have a concept. This is reminiscent of Kant's distinction between action "in conformity with the law" and acting "out of respect for the law." But Wittgenstein is not yet thinking of complex norms of action but of the generative rules of simple operations, of arithmetical, logical, or grammatical rules that he investigates on the model of game rules.

Using this approach, he analyzes the deepest level of the normativity that sets mental activities apart. Rules must be mastered practically because, as Aristotle was already aware, they could not regulate their own application without trapping the agent in an infinite regress. The implicit knowledge of how to follow a rule precedes the explicit knowledge of what rule one is following. One must first "master" a rule-governed practice before one can make this ability explicit and formulate the intuitively known rule as such. Wittgenstein concludes from the fact that knowledge of rules is founded on an ability that anyone who tries to clarify his practical knowledge in a sense finds himself to be already a participant in a practice.[52]

---

[52] Karl-Otto Apel already made this point in "Wittgenstein and the Problem of Hermeneutic Understanding," in Apel, *Toward a Transformation of Philosophy*, trans. Glyn Adey and David Frisby (London: Routledge & Kegan Paul, 1980), pp. 1–45.

The analysis of the peculiar normativity of this kind of elementary rule-governed behavior indicates, further, that these practices are exercised in common, and hence have an inherently social character. Rules are "normative" in the weak sense, still free from any connotations of *obligatory* norms of action, that they bind the free will of the subject by "steering" his intention in a particular direction:

- rules "bind" the will in the sense that acting subjects try to avoid possible rule violations; to follow a rule implies refraining from "transgressions";
- someone who follows a rule can make mistakes and exposes himself to criticism of possible errors; in contrast to the practical knowledge of how to follow a rule, judging whether some behavior is correct requires explicit rule knowledge;
- someone who is following a rule must be able to justify himself to a critic in principle; hence the virtual division of labor between the roles and the knowledge of the critic and of the actor belongs to the concept of following a rule itself;
- hence nobody can follow a rule in a solipsistic manner for himself alone; practical mastery of a rule implies the ability to participate *socially* in an established practice in which the subjects already find themselves once they offer each other reflexive assurances of their intuitive knowledge for the purpose of justification.

Wittgenstein explicates Frege's ideal universality of meaning in terms of the always already existing "agreement" among participants in a shared practice. This agreement expresses the intersubjective recognition of tacitly followed rules. Against such a background, members can "take" a specific behavior as an example of a rule or understand it as "satisfying" a rule. Because the correctness of a given behavior is in principle a matter of controversy, the implicitly accompanying "yes" or "no" of a possible critic belongs essentially to the meaning of the normative validity of a rule. At the same time, the "right" or "wrong" binary coding itself represents a self-corrective mechanism inherent in rule-governed behavior.

Of course, at first it remains unclear by what standard public criticism is *ultimately* measured. Criticism does not seem to be able to extend to the underlying intuitive rules themselves because these are constitutive for a given practice, for example, chess. Since Wittgenstein analyzes the grammar of language games on the model of parlor games, he regards (though this interpretation is not uncontroversial) the *de facto* agreement of a language community as the incontrovertible authority for judging what is right and wrong – as constituting the kind of bedrock certainty against which "one's spade is turned." One can at any rate understand the transition from truth semantics to the use theory of meaning made by the late Wittgenstein in this way. After all, Frege determined the meaning of a statement by means of truth conditions that stipulate how a sentence is correctly used. If we can now deduce the truth conditions from the local background consensus that has been established as a convention among the members of a language community, it is easier to dispense with the awkward concept of the truth or falsity of propositions and to describe the prevailing use of language directly: "The meaning of a statement or form of statement is therefore not to be explained by stating the condition for it to *be* true, but by describing its use."[53]

This argument loses plausibility, however, when one recalls Frege's *context principle*, which states that the meaning of individual words is determined by their potential contribution to constituting the meaning of true sentences. According to this principle, the meaning of individual predicates or concepts does not derive directly from the circumstances of use of individual words but from the context of the sentences in which they are used correctly, *assuming these sentences are true.* For the meaning of these sentences is determined as a whole by the circumstances under which they can be used in conformity with the truth. Whether someone uses the predicate "red" correctly, and thus has mastered the corresponding rule of predication, is determined by sample sentences that must be true if they are to express the results of successful tests, for example, a series of acts of pointing to red objects.

Similarly, practical mastery of mathematical or logical rules is measured by the correctness of corresponding propositions. As

---

[53] Michael Dummett, "Language and Communication," in Dummett, *The Seas of Language* (Oxford: Oxford University Press, 1993), p. 181.

long as we are dealing with operative rules with a cognitive function, their "validity" does not seem to be explicable on the basis
of existing conventions – as in the case of explicitly agreed-upon
game rules that are not based upon prior practical knowledge –
but on the contribution that the properly performed operations
make to forming true statements. In the sphere of simple cognitive operations, therefore, rule-governed behavior exhibits a normativity that already *points* to the truth and rational acceptability
of the statements of a natural language. The elementary "yes" or
"no" of a Wittgensteinian teacher who checks how a pupil proceeds in applying the rule first unfolds – first reveals its mode of
validity entirely – at the more complex level of the explicit yes-
and no-positions taken by participants in argumentation toward
truth claims with empirical content.

Dummett brings Frege's original insight to bear against the late
Wittgenstein in a similar way. His objection is based in essence
on the fact that the judgment of the truth of a statement is measured by the fact that the latter reproduces a state of affairs and
not by the fact that the speaker conforms to the way language is
used in his environment. The epistemic authority of warranted
assertability cannot be reduced to the social authority of the language community. Admittedly, it is clear following the linguistic
turn that the representation of states of affairs is contingent on
the medium of language, for every clear thought finds expression
only in the propositional form of a corresponding assertoric sentence. Thinking is linked to the representative function of language. But a correctly uttered assertoric sentence is not true
because the rules governing the use of the sentence reflect the
consensus or the worldview of a particular language community,
but because they guarantee the rational acceptability of the sentence when it is used correctly. The rules geared to the representative function of language make possible a reference to objects
and a relation to a state of affairs whose existence or pertaining
is not decided by local customs but by a world posited as objective. Speakers cannot communicate about something in the world
if the presumptively objective world does not at the same time
"communicate" with them.

Wittgenstein uses the expression "the grammar of language" in
the broad sense of a "grammar of forms of life" because every
natural language is "interwoven" through its communicative

function with the basic conceptual articulation of the worldview and of the social structure of a language community. Nevertheless, the language rules must not be assimilated to "customs" because every language enjoys a certain autonomy vis-à-vis the cultural background and the social practices of the language community. It owes this autonomy to the exchange between linguistic knowledge and factual knowledge [*Weltwissen*]. Although linguistic world-disclosure first makes possible the inner-worldly learning process on which factual knowledge draws, the latter preserves in turn a revisionary power vis-à-vis linguistic knowledge because the representative function of language is not reducible to its communicative uses: "A statement's satisfying the condition for it to *be* true is certainly not in itself a feature of its use . . . Statements do not in general acquire authority from the frequency with which they are made. We need, rather, to distinguish what is merely customarily said from what the principles governing our use of language and determinative of the meanings of our utterances *require* or *entitle* us to say."[54] This inherent logic of the representative function of language recalls the shared supposition of an objective world that participants in communication must make when they make assertions about something in the world.

(8) On the other hand, Dummett remains committed to Wittgenstein's insight, against Frege, that language is rooted in communicative action and that its structure can only be made transparent through the explication of the ability of practiced speakers. However, he stresses one particular practice from the complex contexts of use, namely, the language game of assertions, objections, and justifications in which semantically grounded "obligations" and "justifications" ("what the principles of language *require* and *entitle* us to say") are explicitly thematized. The epistemic orientation that Dummett lends truth semantics accounts for the privileged status of rational discourse. Since nobody has linguistically unmediated access to truth conditions, one can understand a sentence only if one is able to recognize that its truth conditions are fulfilled. We know the conditions that make a sentence true only by means of the reasons, or the correct kind

---

[54] Ibid., pp. 182f.

of reasons, that a speaker could adduce when he asserts that the sentence is true: "Identifying someone's taking a sentence to be true with his willingness to assert it, we distinguished two criteria of correctness: how the speakers establish or come to recognize sentences as true; and how so recognizing them affects their subsequent course of action."[55]

Of course, this internal discursive structure of linguistic communication only becomes manifest when there is reason to doubt the intelligibility or validity of a speech act. But the communicative exchange always takes place against the background of an implicitly accompanying discursive shadow theatre, as it were, because an utterance is only intelligible for someone who knows for what reasons (or what kind of reasons) it is acceptable. On this model, the speakers *tacitly* offer each other reasons for the acceptability of their utterances even in everyday communication. They ask each other for such reasons and they make judgments concerning the status of each other's utterances. One speaker decides whether he regards the argumentative obligation that the other has incurred as justified or not.

Robert Brandom adopts this approach as the starting point for a formal pragmatics that combines Wilfrid Sellars's inferential semantics with an impressive logical investigation into the practice of "giving and asking for reasons." He replaces the basic semantic question of the theory of meaning – namely, what it means to understand a proposition – with the pragmatic question of what an interpreter does when he correctly "takes and treats" an interpreter as someone who claims truth for the statement "p" with his speech act. The interpreter ascribes a commitment [*Verpflichtung*] to the speaker to justify "p" if called upon to do so; and he himself takes a position on this truth claim insofar as he ascribes or denies the speaker an entitlement [*Berechtigung*] to assert "p." I have discussed this theory at length elsewhere.[56] Here I am only interested in the unavoidable supposition of rationality made in such discourses. Admittedly, Brandom assumes that speaker and hearer

---

[55] Dummett, "Language and Truth," in Dummett, *The Seas of Language*, p. 143.

[56] Habermas, "From Kant to Hegel: On Robert Brandom's Pragmatic Philosophy of Language," in Habermas, *Truth and Justification*, pp. 131–74.

treat each other as rational beings for whom reasons "count." The speaker and the hearer allow themselves to be obligated or entitled by arguments to recognize validity claims that are in principle criticizable. However, Brandom overlooks the intersubjective interpretation of objective validity that views the practice of argumentation as linked to a strong idealizing anticipation.

Brandom localizes the normativity of language that is capable of "constraining" rational subjects in the unforced force of the better argument. This unfolds via a discursive practice in which the participants offer each other rational justifications of their utterances: "This force is a species of normative force, a rational 'ought'. Being rational is being bound or constrained by these norms, being subject to the authority of reasons. Saying 'we' in this sense is placing ourselves and each other in the space of reasons, by giving and asking for reasons for our attitudes and performances."[57] This kind of rational responsibility is constitutive for the self-understanding that distinguishes us as subjects capable of speech and action. Rational self-understanding is at the same time authoritative for the inclusive "we" perspective from which a person qualifies as "one of us."

Interestingly, Brandom begins his book squarely in the tradition of Peirce, Royce, and Mead with the intersubjectivistic version of a universalistic concept of reason. These pragmatists understood universalism in principle as the avoidance of exclusion. The "we" perspective from which rational beings differentiate themselves from other living creatures as "sapient rather than sentient" excludes particularism but not pluralism:

> The most cosmopolitan approach begins with a pluralist insight. When we ask, Who are we? or What sort of thing are we? the answers can vary without competing. Each one defines a different way of saying "we"; each kind of "we"-saying defines a different community. It points to the one great Community comprising members of all particular communities – the Community of those who say "we" with and to someone, whether the members of those different communities recognize each other or not.[58]

---

[57] Brandom, *Making it Explicit* (Cambridge, Mass.: Harvard University Press, 1994), p. 5.
[58] Ibid., p. 4.

This capital "c" could signify the ideal reference point for the rational acceptability of those unconditional, i.e. context-transcending, validity claims that must be justified before an "ever-wider" public. There is no pragmatic equivalent for this idea in Brandom – for example, in the form of those presuppositions of argumentation that sustain the dynamics of a progressive decentering of the pluralistic interpretive perspectives. One aspect of this largely impressive work that I would like to highlight for critical examination is instructive in this regard.

In common with the analytic tradition as a whole, Brandom neglects the cognitive relevance of the role of the second person. He accords no weight to the performative attitude of the speaker toward an addressee that is constitutive for every conversation, and he does not construe the pragmatic relation between question and answer as a genuinely dialogical exchange. This subjectivism becomes apparent, for example, in his treatment of the problem of how the methodological "priority of the social" can be discerned without leaving the last word in questions of epistemic validity to the consensus of a language community. To the collectivistic image of a language community that commands authority, Brandom opposes the individualistic image of isolated dyadic relationships. In each instance, two individuals ascribe "commitments" to each other and grant or deny each other "entitlements." Each side performs its judgment monologically, that is, in such a way that neither can "join with" the other in intersubjectively recognizing a validity claim. Although Brandom speaks of "I–you relations," he actually construes the latter as relations between a first person committed to the truth of a statement and a third person who ascribes a truth claim to the other, while reserving his own judgment. The act of ascription fundamental to the whole practice of discourse objectifies the second person into an observed third person.

It is no accident that Brandom prefers to equate the interpreter with a public that judges the utterance of an *observed* speaker, and not with an addressee from whom the speaker expects an answer. Because he does not even consider the possibility of a dialogical attitude toward a second person, Brandom is ultimately compelled to dissolve the internal relation between objectivity and intersubjectivity in favor of a "priority of the objective." The individual seems to be able to achieve epistemic independence from the collective authority of the respective language community through monological distance alone. This individualistic description fails to do justice to linguistic communication.

Everyday communications are sustained by the context of shared background assumptions, so that the need for communication arises primarily when the opinions and intentions of independently judging and deciding subjects must be brought into harmony. At any rate, the practical need to coordinate action plans first confers a sharper profile on the expectation of participants in communication that the addressees should take a stance on their own validity claims. The participants expect an affirmative or negative reaction that counts as an answer because only the intersubjective recognition of criticizable validity claims generates the kind of commonality on which interaction-relevant commitments on which both sides can rely can be based.

The practice of argumentation is merely the continuation of this communicative action, though at a reflexive level. Hence the participants in argumentation who persist in trying to reach understanding remain, on the one hand, bound into a shared practice; on the other hand, they must adopt a justified stand on the thematized validity claims, that is, they must be led by the gentle force of reasons to their own autonomous judgment. No collective authority restricts the individual's room for judgment or preempts his capacity to make judgments. These two aspects reflect the peculiar Janus-faced character of unconditional validity claims. As *claims*, they depend on intersubjective recognition; hence the public authority of a consensus arrived at under discursive conditions in which it is possible to say "no" cannot ultimately be replaced by the private insight of an individual who knows better. As claims to *unconditional* validity, however, they point beyond every factual agreement. What is accepted as rational here and now can turn out to be false under more favorable epistemic conditions, before a different public, or when confronted with future objections.

A discussion does justice to this Janus-faced character of unconditional validity claims only under the idealizing presupposition that all relevant reasons and information that are in any way accessible are taken into consideration. With this radical idealization, the finite mind accommodates the transcendental insight into the irreducible foundation of objectivity in linguistic intersubjectivity.

3

On the Architectonics of Discursive Differentiation: A Brief Response to a Major Controversy

I will not be able to offer my friend Karl-Otto Apel even a halfway adequate response to his three critical proposals for discussion.[1] This deficit is due not only to the sheer scope and complexity of his careful and wide-ranging reflections but above all to the nature of our differences. These differences bear on questions of theoretical architecture about which it is difficult to argue at the level of premises because theoretical orientations must be measured by the fruitfulness of their consequences. This is not something which the authors involved can decide for themselves. In comparing theories whose intentions are so closely related, those directly involved also frequently lack the hermeneutic stamina required to follow the arguments of the other with the requisite detachment. My impression is that the existing commonalities so impede criticism that we are too quick to interrupt each other and to rush to introduce our own arguments. The critical but sympathetic qualms may have become more acute in the decades between *Knowledge and Human Interests* (1968), the time of our greatest agreement, and *Between Facts and Norms* (1992). On the one hand, during this time the gap between Apel's strong transcendental claim and my detranscendentalizing approach became

---

[1] Karl-Otto Apel, *Auseinandersetzungen* (Frankfurt am Main: Suhrkamp, 1998), pp. 689–838.

wider. At the same time, I hope that I gained a better understanding of the various strategies of argumentation in seminars I taught together with Apel. Our continued cooperation has afforded me the insights that now form the background of our dialogue.

In the present context, I will restrict myself to a central objection that Apel raises against the specification of the discourse principle offered in *Between Facts and Norms* (1). To defuse the objection, I will first distinguish between the normative content of unavoidable presuppositions of argumentation and the aspects of validity under which this rational potential can be exploited (2). Thus the moral principle cannot be derived exclusively, as Apel claims, from the presuppositions of argumentation that are normative in a transcendental sense. Rather, it borrows its deontological binding force from the connection between the transcendental content of discourses and the meaning of the validity of moral practical norms that are introduced into discourses of justification (3). Modern law is subjective, coercive, and positive law that is contingent on the decisions of a political lawmaker and, in virtue of these formal characteristics, it differs from rational morality both in its function and in its need for justification (4). Finally, the requirement of a justification of a law interwoven with politics that is neutral with respect to worldviews explains why the principle of democracy acquires an independent status vis-à-vis the principle of morality (5). The differences between the architectures of our respective theories, which are also reflected in Apel's supplementation of discourse ethics by an ethics of responsibility that offers guidance in applying morality, are ultimately grounded in different metaphilosophical conceptions. I will be able to address this at the end of the essay only in a very cursory manner (6).

(1) In *Between Facts and Norms* I developed a proposal for grounding the system of basic rights that attempts to do justice to the intuition concerning the co-originality of private and public autonomy.[2] In the course of grounding constitutional democracy, the two principles of legitimation – namely, the "rule of law" and

---

[2] Jürgen Habermas, *Between Facts and Norms*, trans. William Rehg (Cambridge, Mass.: MIT Press, 1996), pp. 104ff.

"popular sovereignty" – presuppose each other. By contrast, the tradition of liberalism that goes back to Locke accords the freedoms of the moderns priority over the freedoms of the ancients. I want to avoid this counterintuitive subordination of the principle of democracy to the rule of law because it amounts to founding coercive and positive law on basic moral norms in accordance with natural law. It shields the founding principles of the democratic constitution from democratic will-formation. I do not need to recapitulate here the strategy of argumentation through which I justify the co-originality of the principle of democracy and human rights.[3] The motivation should be sufficient to clarify the starting point of my controversy with Apel.

The fact that moral and legal norms are simultaneously differentiated from religious and natural law forms of traditional ethical life [*Sittlichkeit*] under modern social conditions is not just a matter of historical interest. Rather, this parallelism in their respective geneses speaks for the fact that the two complementary sorts of highly abstract practical norms differ in their mode rather than in the level of justification. Modern coercive law must be generated in accordance with a legitimacy-guaranteeing procedure that meets the same postmetaphysical, and hence worldview-neutral, standards of justification as rational morality. But this democratic procedure cannot draw its legitimizing force from a morality that is accorded *priority over* law without destroying the performative meaning of the democratic self-determination of a concrete collectivity bounded in space and time.

However, the procedure of lawmaking must in turn be legally institutionalized if it is to guarantee the equal inclusion of all members of the political community in the democratic process of opinion- and will-formation. The principle of democracy is itself constituted in the language of law. It takes on positive contours in the equal political participation rights of all citizens. Of course, the citizens should *also* be capable of making moral judgments; but they do not make them within the extra-legal context of the lifeworld of natural persons but in their legally constituted role as citizens who are authorized to make use of their democratic

---

[3] Habermas, "Constitutional Democracy – A Paradoxical Union of Contradictory Principles?," *Political Theory* 29 (2001): 766–81.

rights. Otherwise, the addressees of law could not understand themselves *consistently* as its authors. They could adequately fulfill the role of citizens only if they were to slough off their identities as legal persons and draw upon their capacity for moral judgment as natural persons.

The thesis that the legitimacy of existing law is explained *exclusively* in terms of the procedure of democratic opinion- and will-formation also stands or falls with the independence of a "morally freestanding" principle of democracy. Thus I specified the principle of discourse, which was initially geared exclusively to the principle of moral universalization, "U," so abstractly that it expresses the postmetaphysical need of justification only in very general terms with respect to action norms as such. For the principle is supposed to leave room for a later specification of the demands of justification.

> This principle certainly has a normative content inasmuch as it explicates the meaning of impartiality in practical judgments. However, despite its normative content, it lies at the level of abstraction that is *still neutral* with respect to morality and law, for it refers to action norms in general:
> D: Just those action norms are valid to which all possibly affected persons could agree as participants in rational discourses.[4]

Only at the level of the moral principle and the principle of democracy[5] (as we shall see) is the content of "D" specified with respect to the conditions of validity that moral rules and legal

---

[4] Habermas, *Between Facts and Norms*, p. 107.

[5] To recall, the moral principle takes the form of a principle of universalization introduced as a rule of argumentation. According to this principle, valid moral practical norms must satisfy the condition that the foreseeable consequences and side-effects of their general observance for the interests of each individual must be acceptable by all those possibly affected in their role as participants in discourse. The principle of democracy, which takes the form of political participation and communication rights in the basic rights section of democratic constitutions, guarantees the self-determination of a voluntary association of free and equal legal subjects. It states that only those laws can claim legitimate validity that meet with the agreement of all citizens in a discursively constituted process of legislation that commands the agreement of all citizens and is itself legally operationalized.

norms, respectively, must satisfy if they are to merit universal recognition in their, albeit overlapping, but not identical spheres of validity.

Against this, Apel wonders whether the complete content of the moral principle is not already contained in "D": "I do not see how one could deny that the 'normative content' of the 'principle of impartiality of practical judgments' . . . has a moral character if, as Habermas subsequently posits, one is to derive a moral principle from the universal principle of discourse via its 'specification', a moral principle for which the viewpoint of 'the equal consideration of the interests' of all affected is supposed to be authoritative, though now 'alone.'"[6] No one disputes that moral reasons, in addition to empirical, pragmatic, ethical, and legal reasons, also play an important role, and often even the decisive role, in justifying norms that exhibit the formal characteristics of modern law. After all, laws must in general be so constituted that they can be obeyed "out of respect for the law."

However, if law must not violate morality, the principle of democracy that guides the creation of legitimate law may not be morally "neutral." It seems to owe its moral content to the same principle "D" that also underlies the moral principle. Thus, the controversy is sparked by the question of whether Apel can deduce on this basis the priority of the principle of morality over the principle of democracy that is authoritative for legitimizing law. Apel's hierarchical conception rests on a specific, and in my view problematic, understanding of the moral principle. To clarify my reservations about this foundationalism, I must first recall the shared starting point of departure of our reflections in discourse ethics.

(2) The discourse theory of truth, morality, and law can be understood as a response to the predicament generated by the fact that postmetaphysical thinking turns its back on strong ontological conceptions that deduce normativity entirely from the constitution of being [*des Seienden*] or of subjectivity. Instead, it derives a normative content from the practice of argumentation on which we always depend in situations of uncertainty, not only in the role

---

[6] Apel, *Auseinandersetzungen*, pp. 761f.

of philosophers or scientists, but already in everyday communicative practice when the disruption of routines leads us to reflect momentarily in an attempt to reassure ourselves of our well-founded expectations. Hence the starting point is the normative content of those "unavoidable" pragmatic presuppositions that participants in argumentation must implicitly accept once they participate in a cooperative search for the truth geared to redeeming controversial validity claims in the form of a competition for better arguments. After all, the performative meaning of the practice of argumentation consists in the fact that the "unforced force of the better argument" is supposed to have the final say (!) as regards the relevant questions and on the basis of all pertinent information. In the absence of conclusive arguments or compelling evidence, even the decision concerning what can count as a good or a bad argument in a given context can be controversial. Hence the rational acceptability of contested statements is *ultimately* based on the connection between "good reasons" and those idealizations of the epistemic situation that the participants must make when they engage in rational discourse as a form of communication. I call the four most important of these unavoidable pragmatic presuppositions:

(a) inclusivity: no one who could make a relevant contribution may be prevented from participating;

(b) equal distribution of communicative freedoms: everyone has an equal opportunity to make contributions;

(c) truthfulness: the participants must mean what they say; and

(d) absence of contingent external constraints or constraints inherent to the structure of communication: the yes/no positions of participants on criticizable validity claims should be motivated only by the power of cogent reasons to convince.

Here we encounter the premise on which Apel bases his objection. For he interprets the binding force of the normative content of these presuppositions of argumentation directly in a strong, deontologically binding sense and thinks that he can derive basic norms, such as the duty of equal treatment or the precept of truthfulness, directly from the reflexive confirmation of this content. He even wants to derive, and I will return to this point, a future-oriented principle of "co-responsibility" from what we must presuppose in argumentation. According to this principle, we can determine that all participants in discourse are liable "for conducting, indeed for initiating, practical discourses to resolve conflicts of interest."[7] I must confess that, from the beginning, I could not follow this *direct* extrapolation. For it is far from obvious that rules that are constitutive for the practice of argumentation as such, and hence are unavoidable *within* discourses, also remain binding for regulating action *outside* of this improbable practice.[8]

The (weak)[9] transcendental presuppositions of argumentation differ from moral obligations in that they cannot be systematically violated without destroying the game of argumentation as such. By contrast, we do not have to abandon the moral language game when we violate moral rules. Even if we understand the equal distribution of communicative freedoms and the truthfulness condition for participation in discourse in the sense of *rights* and *duties* of argumentation, their transcendental-pragmatic necessitation cannot be transferred directly from discourse to action and be translated into the deontological, hence action-regulating, force of moral rights and duties. The "inclusivity" condition does not provide any more support for the demand that practical norms should be universal, beyond requiring that there should be no restrictions on access to discourse. Even the presupposition of noncoercion refers only to the constitution of the process of argumentation itself, not to interpersonal relations outside of this practice.

---

[7] Ibid., p. 756; Apel, "Diskursethik als Ethik der Mitverantwortung vor den Sachzwängen der Politik, des Rechts und der Marktwirtschaft," in Karl-Otto Apel and Holger Burckhart (eds), *Prinzip Mitverantwortung: Grundlage für Ethik und Pädagogik* (Würzburg: Königshausen & Neumann, 2001), pp. 69–96.

[8] Habermas, "Discourse Ethics: Notes on a Program of Philosophical Justification," in Habermas, *Moral Consciousness and Communicative Action*, trans. Christian Lenhardt and Shierry Weber Nicholson (Cambridge, Mass.: MIT Press, 1990), pp. 43–115.

[9] Here I cannot address the discussion concerning the language-pragmatic meaning and the status of transcendental arguments.

The normative content of the game of argumentation represents a rational potential that can only be realized in the epistemic dimension of testing validity claims. Specifically, it can only be realized in such a way that the publicness, equal rights, truthfulness, and noncoercion presupposed in the practice of argumentation set standards for a self-correcting learning process. For the demanding form of communication represented by rational discourse compels participants to decenter their cognitive perspectives progressively as they mobilize all available and relevant reasons and information. To this extent, the normative substance contained in the presuppositions of argumentation has "practical relevance" only in the limited sense that it makes it possible to judge criticizable validity claims and thereby contributes to learning processes. However, one point is especially important in this context. This rational potential develops in different directions according to the type of validity claim thematized and the corresponding type of discourse.

The direction that the transfer of rationality takes is also determined by the connotations of the validity claim and by the relevant schemes of justification. We must first clarify the difference between the transcendental-pragmatic content of the communicative form of rational discourses and the specific meaning of the validity of the various justified action norms. This is necessary if we want to understand the independence of the principle of discourse that prescribes a certain level of justification – namely, one not dependent on metaphysical background assumptions – without for that reason already prejudicing the instrumental or utilitarian, ethical, moral, or legal meaning of the validity of possible normative statements. That the normative content of presuppositions of argumentation represents a general rational potential that enters into specific relations to the validity of the forms of statements introduced into discourse is already shown by the justification of straightforward descriptive statements.

(3) The meaning of *truth claims* that we associate with assertoric statements cannot be reduced to ideal acceptability. For we relate the asserted states of affairs to objects that we *assume* pragmatically to be components of an objective world, thus a world that is identical for all observers and exists independently of our

descriptions.[10] This ontological assumption accredits truth discourse with a point of reference beyond discourse and grounds the difference between truth and justified acceptability. Nevertheless, the participants in discourse who thematize a controversial truth claim are still ultimately constrained, even under the most favorable epistemic conditions, to accept the best possible justification of "p" instead of the truth of "p" – even when, as we say, they have "exhausted all reasons." Aware of our own fallibility, we willingly accept this *quid pro quo* because we have confidence in an epistemic situation that we know fosters a progressive decentering of our perspectives.

Much the same holds in discourses in which the *purposive or instrumental rationality of decisions,* thus the expediency of the choice of means or the utility of the choice between practical alternatives, is tested. Beyond the assumption of an objective world of possible, causally linked objects, here participants in discourse must master the language game of effectively realizing rationally chosen ends if they are to know what it means to justify rules of instrumental action or complex choice strategies. But here, too, the core empirical issue is the discursive redemption of truth claims.

A different validity claim comes into play with "strong" evaluative statements once the values in light of which the actors choose goals or adopt purposes themselves become problematic.[11] Discourses that serve to clarify such value orientations have relatively weak epistemic force. They make possible clinical advice that relates to the context of a consciously affirmed individual life history or collective form of life; they are geared to the *claims to authenticity of one's self-understanding* or the life plans of a first person singular or plural. We associate with the epistemic authority of the first person the supposition of a subjective world to which those involved have privileged access. A completely different perspective takes the lead once it becomes a matter of

---

[10] Habermas, *Truth and Justification,* trans. Barbara Fultner (Cambridge, Mass.: MIT Press, 2003), Introduction VII, pp. 35–41.

[11] Habermas, "On the Pragmatic, the Ethical, and the Moral Employments of Practical Reason," in Habermas, *Justification and Application: Remarks on Discourse Ethics,* trans. Ciaran Cronin (Cambridge, Mass.: MIT Press, 1993), pp. 1–18.

selecting from the standpoint of justice *generalized* values that enter into moral practical norms.

With the basic question of morality – i.e. which ways of acting are "equally good" for all members – we relate to a world of legitimately regulated interpersonal relations. *The claim to rightness of moral statements* has the meaning that the corresponding norms *merit* universal recognition among the circle of addressees. In contrast to truth claims, truth-analogous claims to rightness do not have any meaning over and above justification; their meaning is exhausted by ideally justified acceptability.[12] Rational acceptability is not only evidence for the validity of norms but constitutes the meaning of the validity of norms that are supposed to provide equally convincing, i.e. impartial, reasons for all of the parties involved in dispute in situations of conflict. This "impartiality," initially embodied in the figure of the judge, coincides with the epistemic "impartiality" of participants in discourse who are required to decenter their perspectives in the game of argumentation, only after it is expanded to include the post-traditional idea of justice. The happy convergence of "justice" in the sense of impartial conflict-resolution with "rightness" in the sense of the discursive justification of corresponding normative statements first occurs at the post-traditional level of justification.

However, the mutual adoption of epistemic interpretive perspectives, which participants in argumentation are always compelled to undertake if they want to test the rational acceptability of any statement, is *transformed* into the requirement of *existentially demanding* exchange of perspectives from the moral standpoint of according equal consideration to the interests of *all* possibly affected. Only regarding practical questions in which those concerned are personally involved do the communicative conditions of argumentation cease to have the meaning of merely ensuring that all relevant contributions are brought into play and lead to rationally motivated "yes" or "no" positions. The innocuous presupposition of an honest and impartial balancing of all arguments forces the participants in practical discourses to adopt a

---

[12] Habermas, "Rightness versus Truth: On the Sense of Normative Validity in Moral Judgments and Norms," in *Truth and Justification*, pp. 237–77.

self-critical stance toward their own interests and evaluations of situations and to take into account the interests of others from the perspective of the self-understandings and conceptions of the world of others.

Hence the moral principle of according the interests of all equal consideration cannot be justified by appealing to the normative content of presuppositions of argumentation alone. One can invoke this rational potential implicit in discourses in general with this goal only when one already knows what it means to have obligations and to justify actions in moral terms. Knowledge of how to participate in argumentation must be *joined* with knowledge drawn from the experience of a moral community. That we must be acquainted with the binding validity of moral precepts and the justification of norms becomes clear when we examine the genealogy of the challenge to which rational morality provides the answer.[13]

The beginnings of modernity are marked by the emergence of a pluralism of worldviews. In this situation, the members of moral communities face the dilemma that they must continue to engage in disputes about their actions and omissions in cases of conflict by appealing to moral reasons, despite the fact that the cultural and religious consensus in which these reasons were embedded has disintegrated. The only unifying context that the sons and daughters of "homeless" modernity still share is the practice of moral argumentation, now conducted with inadequate reasons. Thus the store of commonalities has shrunk to the formal features of these discourses. The only resource upon which the participants can draw is the normative content of the presuppositions of argumentation that they have already accepted once they engage in moral arguments.

However, the telos of this construction of a new background consensus on the slender basis of the formal features of this shared discursive practice also betrays the background knowledge stemming from past moral experiences. Without being able to draw upon prior acquaintance with the intact relations of

---

[13] Habermas, "A Genealogical Analysis of the Cognitive Content of Morality," in *The Inclusion of the Other*, ed. and trans. Ciaran Cronin and Pablo De Greiff (Cambridge, Mass.: MIT Press, 1998), pp. 3–46, here pp. 39ff.

recognition sustained by the "strong" traditions of the moral community to which they belonged under premodern conditions, the participants could not even form the intention to reconstruct a post-traditional morality from the sources of communicative reason alone. They already know what it means to have moral duties and to justify an action in light of binding norms. Only in connection with this *background knowledge* can the rationality potential inherent in argumentation as such be used to justify an autonomous morality liberated from the contexts of particular worldviews.[14]

Under conditions of discourse, the deontological meaning of the validity of norms that have in the meantime become problematic turns out to be the post-traditional idea of justice of the equal consideration of the interests of all. The need for justification extended to the norms themselves then highlights the need for a corresponding moral principle that, as a rule of argumentation, could facilitate a justified consensus concerning disputed norms and hence preserve the cognitive meaning of morality also under modern conditions. The purified, post-traditional idea of justice inspires the principle of universalization, "U," which is initially introduced in a hypothetical sense.[15] Assuming that it can claim a general, transcultural binding force, this principle could explain how moral questions can be rationally decided at all. The universal validity of "U" itself is then "derived" from the content of transcendentally constraining presuppositions of argumentation in light of the attendant knowledge of what it means to justify practical norms. With this move, I follow the nondeductive model of justification developed by Apel, which proceeds by uncovering the performative contradictions of a skeptic who disputes the possibility of justifying moral claims.

(4) The point of contention between Apel and me is not this justification move but its status in a nonfoundational game of justification. For if we – appealing to the distinction between transcendental and deontological meanings of normativity – do

---

[14] On the following justification sketch, see Habermas, *The Inclusion of the Other*, pp. 43–5.

[15] See n. 5.

not conceive of the rational potential inherent in discourses in general as binding in the deontological sense, then the impartial judgment required in an unspecific sense by "D" concerning the ability of norms to command consensus can indeed be understood so that it "remains neutral with respect to morality and law." Insofar as "D"[16] speaks of "norms of action" as such and "rational discourses" in general, it is situated at a higher level of abstraction than the moral principle and the principle of democracy. This formulation abstracts both from the type of actions in need of justification and from the specific aspect of validity under which they are justified in particular cases. To be sure, the discourse principle is tailored to practical questions; it impinges on questions of truth only insofar as facts are relevant for justifying actions. As regards the conditions of discourse under which a consensus is supposed to be reached, "D" demands a postconventional justification of norms of action in general, but without specifying a particular respect in which the consensus-generating force of reasons is supposed to be mobilized.

The rational potential implicit in discourses in general can be invoked to justify rules of instrumental and strategic action under the aspects of truth, effectiveness, and conceptual consistency, to justify ethical value orientations under the aspect of authenticity, and to justify moral judgments and norms under the aspect of justice. As we have seen, each of these types of norms and statements involves different connotations. Empirical statements suggest ontological connotations of the existence of states of affairs; success-oriented interventions evoke instrumental connotations of effectiveness and of utility maximization; ethical questions involve axiological connotations of the preferability of goods; and moral questions involve connotations of the recognition-worthiness of well-ordered interpersonal relations. These references to the constitution of the objective, subjective, or social world first determine the respects under which "D" takes on concrete meaning. For example, with reference to the world of legitimately ordered social relations, the moral principle can be understood as a special operationalization of "D" that enables

[16] See above, pp. 80–1.

us to make rational judgments concerning actions and norms under the aspect of justice.

Although legal norms may *also* be selected under the aspect of justice and must not *contradict* morality, the principle of democracy that empowers the citizens to create legitimate law is not subordinate to the moral principle, as Apel assumes. In order to show that the subsumption of law under morality and the natural-law subsumption of positive law under a hierarchy of legal norms [*Legeshierarchie*] does not go far enough, I must address the distinctive status that the law assumes among the kinds of norms already mentioned simply because it represents *an action system fused with political power*. This can be explained in terms of the formal characteristics of law that differentiate it from morality as (a) subjective, (b) binding, and (c) positive law.

(a) Modern law is constructed out of individual or "subjective" rights that guarantee individual persons carefully circumscribed spaces of freedom, i.e. domains in which they can make free choices and pursue autonomous life plans. Whereas from the moral standpoint we first determine our duties and only then deduce our rights from the obligations that others have toward us, modern law begins with the specification of "permissions" rather than of imperatives ("You ought to . . ."). Legal duties follow from the justified expectations that others direct toward us based on equal rights. This asymmetry is a function of the self-restriction of modern law, which permits everything that is not explicitly forbidden. Whereas the overwhelming force of morality embraces all areas of life and does not acknowledge any threshold between private conscience and public accountability, the law serves primarily to free private and autonomous domains of life from the arbitrary interference of public power. Law represents a selective, non-holistic way of regulating behavior and does not affect individuals in their concrete existence as persons individuated by their life histories, but only insofar as they as natural persons acquire the artificial and carefully circumscribed status of legal persons, i.e. of bearers of subjective rights.

(b) Modern law is connected with the threat of state sanctions. State power guarantees an average observance of the laws and, insofar as obedience to the law can be coerced, it fulfills a side-condition of the legitimacy of general legal principles. For one can be reasonably expected to obey a norm only when each addressee can count on its also being obeyed by all other address-ees. Even rational morality that is no longer embedded in reli-gious worldviews must be linked with socialization patterns and cultural traditions in order to ensure an average translation of moral judgments into moral action. But such an autonomous morality is inherently geared to the cognitive goal of fostering insights alone. It remains up to the subjects who have these insights to form good motives and convictions. By contrast, the institutional character of law liberates individuals from the burden of motivation. In contrast to morality, law is not just a cognitive system but also a practical system. Whereas morality appeals to insight and a good will, law restricts itself to requiring action in conformity with the law. This uncoupling of behavior in confor-mity with law from the motive of "respect for the law" also explains why legal norms can apply essentially only to "external behavior."

(c) Of course, politics not only equips the law with the means of sanction of the state but also itself makes use of the law, both as a medium for its administrative and organizational activities and as a source of legitimation. Positive law that is subject to the political will of the legislator is an appropriate means of organizing political rule. This positive character of law entails the separation between the role of authors who make law and that of addressees who are subject to the law. This voluntarism of lawmaking is also alien to a morality conceived in constructivist terms. Moreover, the law incorporates political goals and programs that cannot be justified solely from the moral standpoint. The matters in need of regulation require complex justifications involving reasons of an empirical, instrumental-pragmatic, strategic, and ethical charac-ter. Here the legal form remains intact only as long as each new regulation fits consistently into the existing legal system and does not violate principles of justice. The proviso that moral reasons must not be overridden is already satisfied by tying legislation to democratic constitutional principles.

(5) If we are to grasp finally the systematic autonomy of the principle of democracy criticized by Apel, we must analyze the need for justification generated by the specific interconnection

between law and politics. Law is constitutive for political power[17] and, at the same time, itself depends on the exercise of political power: legal programs are the product of a political will. This political will loses the character of an arbitrary use of political power not only when it is subjected to *constitutional* constraints. The process of lawmaking first acquires the ability to produce legitimacy by being applied to itself with the aim of instituting a *democratic procedure*. In this way, the decisions of the political lawmaker are made contingent on the outcome of an inclusive process of opinion-formation within the wide public sphere facilitated by the media and within the discursively structured deliberations of democratically elected bodies. The legal institutionalization of procedures of deliberative politics derives its legitimizing power from the guiding idea of a rational procedure of self-legislation that is independent of the premises of particular worldviews.

Here there is unquestionably an analogy to the Kantian concept of moral self-determination. Democratic self-legislation calls for a procedure of discursive will-formation that makes possible the self-binding of the democratic lawmaker to insights of practical reason, in such a way that the addressees of law can understand themselves at the same time as its authors in more than a merely voluntaristic sense. From this follows the principle of democracy, which states that only those laws can claim legitimate validity that can meet with the assent of all citizens in a discursive legislative process that is in turn legally organized. Here it is important not to misunderstand the *inherently political meaning* of the analogy to moral autonomy.

Given the collective character of the political will-formation of the citizens of a concrete polity, the analogy to the model of the moral self-determination of individual persons consists in the simulation of the *self-binding of free choice based on insight*. However, this structural similarity between political lawmaking and moral self-determination does not imply an assimilation of the one to the other. Certainly, the citizens who take their orientation from the common good must remain open to moral considerations. However, the deliberative decision-making prac-

---

[17] Habermas, *Between Facts and Norms*, pp. 133–51.

tice is part of a political system that is also, if not in the first instance, legitimized through the effectiveness of the imperatives of prudent self-preservation pursued in conformity with the constitution. This is why the democratic lawmaking procedure must exploit the rational potential of deliberations across the full spectrum of possible aspects of validity, and by no means merely under the moral aspect of the equal universalization of interests.

With the transition from morality to law, our perspective shifts from individual actors to the level of the institutional system. Norms that orient the individual in instrumental, purposive, ethical, and moral action are justified from the perspective of an acting subject, even if the latter is represented as a participant in discourses. As a participant in discourse, the actor seeks to answer the question of what he should do from the standpoint of success, advantage, the good, or the just. Practical reason is embodied in discourses that the participants enter into on an *ad hoc* basis in order to resolve practical issues. This cognitive reference is also preserved in the citizens' discourse. But legal norms are inherently institutional. Here practical reason does not only come into play in the practice of discourse itself or in the rules of argumentation that guide the latter. Rather, it is embodied at the systematic level in the principles that govern the constitution of the political system of action as such. This explains why the principle of democracy, as a component of a constitutional order, in contrast to the moral principle, does not intervene in discourses by prescribing a pattern of argumentation but instead lays down standards for *instituting* and *interconnecting* political discourses.

The discourses in which the citizens and their representatives engage are from the outset tied into a system of political action that obeys its own functional imperatives. Legitimate law must indeed ensure that interpersonal relations within a given collective are regulated in a just manner. However, at the same time it constitutes the language for programming a legally constituted system of action that ensures the stability and reproduction of the whole society; hence it is responsible for the collective life as a whole and not just for legitimate social relations. Therefore law *inherently* calls for different criteria of evaluation from morality, whose imperatives are oriented exclusively to justice, and even to the justified consent of all, and not primarily that of one's fellow-citizens. The imperatives of political, economic, and cultural self-preservation represent viewpoints that cannot be casually ignored, from which legally consistent regulations can be subjected to empirical, pragmatic, and ethical criticism without coming into conflict with the moral foundations of the constitution.

In this way, a self-correcting democratic constitutional order can put the reform-oriented realization of the system of rights on a permanent footing[18] and solve in a morally consistent way the very problem that leads Apel to introduce an ethics of responsibility that goes beyond morality as such.

(6) In virtue of the interconnection between modern law and political power, the principle of democracy that regulates law-making enjoys independence from the moral principle. Because Apel does not accord sufficient importance to this internal relation between law and power, he also fails to appreciate the role law plays in domesticating power. On the contrary, he is preoccupied with the moral taming of political power, and thereby plays into the hands of the political creation of moral relations. At any rate, a "problem of the historically sensitive application of morality"[19] cannot arise *within* moral discourses because a deontological ethics in the Kantian tradition excludes compromises for good reasons. Unconditionally valid moral precepts cannot make compromises, however well meaning, with political programs, no matter how lofty their goals may be. But does it even need to be supplemented by the ethics of responsibility to which Apel devotes the so-called Part B of his ethics?

The categorical meaning of moral imperatives remains intact even when confronted with the dismaying spectacle of intolerable injustice. At any rate, it need not have any truck with compromises by way of a "supplement" as long as we take into

---

[18] On the aporias of prudent advocacy of the creation of the conditions under which moral conduct can first be reasonably expected of all, see Habermas, "From Kant to Hegel and Back Again: The Move toward Detranscendentalization," in *Truth and Justification*, pp. 175–212.

[19] Apel, *Diskurs und Verantwortung* (Frankfurt am Main: Suhrkamp, 1988), pp. 103–53.

account a "moral division of labor" regarding positive duties that does justice to the principle (which is itself morally justified) that we are only obliged to do what is *de facto* within our power: *nemo ultra posse obligatur*. Even well-justified norms sacrifice none of their strict categorical meaning on account of the fact that they are only *prima facie* valid prior to application. Although in cases of conflict with other valid norms they do need to be carefully judged as regards their "appropriateness," their validity remains unaffected by the fact that they must "cede" to other norms in particular cases.[20] The claim to binding validity [*Sollgeltungsanspruch*] of moral imperatives would be relativized and tied to the conditions of success of strategic – or, as Apel puts it, "strategy-counterstrategic" – action if the (in a broad sense) "political" concern with the "approximate success of morality in general" (for example, in the form of an additional principle of the ethics of responsibility) were to be incorporated into morality itself.[21]

If the normative content of universal presuppositions of argumentation does not have any deontologically binding implications – and certainly does not contribute anything to the *direct* derivation of the precepts of equal treatment and reciprocity that are binding outside the practice of argumentation – it is even less clear to me what can be extracted from this normative substance for more ambitious demands. Apel wants to justify in a single move the "co-responsibility of all human beings for the consequences of collective activities, and hence also for institutions."[22] He wants to derive from the self-reflection on the norms that are always already presupposed in argumentation, without further mediation, the moral obligation to pursue policies that aim to

---

[20] Klaus Günther, *The Sense of Appropriateness: Application Discourses in Morality and Law*, trans. John Farrell (Albany, N.Y.: SUNY Press, 1993).
[21] Apel, "Diskursethik als Ethik der Mitverantwortung," pp. 77f.
[22] Ibid., p. 82. See also Dietrich Böhler, "Warum moralisch sein? Die Verbindlichkeit der dialogbezogenen Selbst- und Mitverantwortung," in Apel and Burckhardt (eds), *Prinzip Mitverantwortung*, p. 50: "Co-responsibility for what? First of all, for examining one's own validity claims, then for preserving, and if possible improving, the real conditions for open and cosmopolitan critical discourses (at any rate concerning human rights), and finally for the practical (political, economic, and ecological) consideration or application of their results."

create moral conditions of life for all human beings across the globe.

On the one hand, political power remains the sole medium through which deliberate and collectively binding effects can be exercised on the systemic conditions and institutional forms of our social existence. On the other hand, politics cannot be immediately moralized, whether on the Platonic model of the "good ruler," or via revolutionary action, or, as Apel seems to think, through a general moral strengthening of the virtues of political action. Against this, the institutional taming of political power through a democratically organized legislative process seems to be the only viable way to reform our conduct along moral lines. What is possible can be seen by studying the complex developments undergone by constitutional democracies and the social welfare guarantees that were achieved on this basis. The politics which has for the time being been tamed at least in part by national constitutions will have to change once again within the framework of a cosmopolitan legal system if it is to overcome its aggressive and self-destructive aspects and transform itself into a global civilizing regulatory power.[23]

Morality is much too imprecise and misleading to serve as a compass along this political route. What Apel offers in "Part B" as the compromise-form of morality that gauges its chances of success as a whole fails to recognize the dimension of a progressive democratic juridification of politics that would result in a civilizing of social conditions. In the course of the neoliberal self-dissolution of politics through economic globalization, however, this strategy runs the risk of losing sight of its goal. Politics, as a medium for conscious self-transformation, shrinks to the extent that it cedes its steering functions to markets. Under the banner of the "War on Terror," "the disappearance of politics" is, at any rate, counteracted only by the strengthening of the military, the secret services, and the police.

Apel imposes a triple burden on the discourse of the philosopher who, in conducting an argument, reflects on the content of the necessary presuppositions of argumentation. This discourse must (a) justify basic moral norms directly, i.e. without the detour

---

[23] See below, pp. 312ff.

of justifying a principle of universalization, (b) demonstrate an existential obligation "to be moral," and (c) supplement morality with a duty to realize morality in history based on an ethics of responsibility. Apel calls this discourse "primordial" in an allusion to Husserl's transcendental original founding [*Urstiftung*]. I suspect that our disagreement over the correct theoretical architecture can ultimately be traced back to a conflict over the role of philosophy itself. Apel offers a compelling reconstruction of the history of Western philosophy as a sequence of three paradigms, correlated, respectively, with ontology, epistemology, and linguistic philosophy. He is aware of the self-critical starting point of modern thought and at the same time of the fallibilistic limits of postmetaphysical thinking. Nevertheless, he inclines toward a foundationalist understanding of philosophy when he sets philosophical self-reflection apart in the manner of an original discourse burdened with excessive goals. Yet, in the end Apel puts his faith in the infallible certainties of a direct, pre-analytic recourse to the linguistic intuitions of a detached participant in argumentation who is skilled in reflection. For the transcendental-pragmatic argument, which he accords the role of an "ultimate justification," has in reality the status of a presumptively infallible, and at any rate discursively nontestable, reassurance. If it were an argument, it would be located in a linguistic context that offers as many opportunities for criticism as it has facets.

Of course, the concept of "strict reflection" introduced by Wolfgang Kuhlmann raises further issues that I cannot address here. I have confined my remarks to the differences that Apel has elaborated in his treatment of my philosophy of law. These are differences in our theoretical approaches. They can disguise neither the commonalities in our results nor the insights that I owe since my student days in Bonn to the unique instruction of a friend who remains for me a constant intellectual presence.

Part II

Religious Pluralism and Civic Solidarity

4

Prepolitical Foundations of the Constitutional State?

The topic proposed for our discussion[1] brings to mind a question that Ernst Wolfgang Böckenförde formulated succinctly in the mid-1960s, namely, whether the pacified, secular state is reliant on normative presuppositions that it cannot itself guarantee.[2] This question reflects doubt over whether the constitutional state can regenerate its normative infrastructure through its own resources and the supposition that it depends on autochthonous worldviews or religious – or at any rate collectively binding ethical – traditions. Although this would spell trouble for the modern state committed to neutrality toward competing worldviews due to the "fact of pluralism" (Rawls), this does not speak against the conjecture itself.

I would first like to specify the problem in two respects. From a cognitive point of view, the doubt expressed concerns whether political authority still even admits of a secular – i.e. a non-religious or postmetaphysical – justification once law has been completely positivized (1). Even if such a legitimation is granted, from a motivational point of view the doubt remains whether a pluralistic political community can stabilize itself

---

[1] I.e. the discussion conducted by the author with Joseph Cardinal Ratzinger on 19 January 2004 in Munich at the invitation of the Catholic Academy of Bavaria. – *Trans.*

[2] Ernst-Wolfgang Böckenförde, "Die Entstehung des Staates als Vorgang der Säkularisation" (1967), in *Recht, Staat, Freiheit* (Frankfurt am Main: Suhrkamp, 1991), pp. 92ff., here p. 112.

normatively – i.e. in a way that goes beyond a mere *modus vivendi* – on the supposition of an at best formal background consensus limited to procedures and principles (2). Even if this doubt can be dispelled, liberal political orders remain dependent upon solidarity among their citizens, a solidarity whose sources could dry up as a result of an "uncontrolled" secularization of society as a whole. This diagnosis cannot be dismissed out of hand; but it should not be understood in such a way that the learned defenders of religion derive an unearned benefit from it, as it were (3). I will propose, by contrast, that we construe social and cultural secularization as a twofold learning process that compels the traditions of the Enlightenment and religious teachings to reflect on each other's limits (4). Finally, regarding post-secular societies, there is the question of what cognitive attitudes and normative expectations the liberal state must demand of its religious and nonreligious citizens in their dealings with one another (5).

(1) I understand political liberalism (which I defend in the specific form of Kantian republicanism)[3] as a nonreligious, post-metaphysical justification of the normative foundations of constitutional democracy. This theory is situated in the tradition of rational natural law that eschews the strong cosmological or soteriological assumptions of classical and religious natural law. Of course, the history of Christian theology in the Middle Ages, and of late scholasticism in Spain in particular, belongs to the genealogy of human rights. However, the form of state power that remains neutral toward different worldviews ultimately derives its legitimation from the profane sources of seventeenth- and eighteenth-century philosophy. Only much later did theology and the Church come to terms with the intellectual challenges of the revolutionary constitutional state. If I understand it correctly, however, there is no obstacle in principle to an autonomous foundation of morality and law (i.e. one independent of revealed truths) from the Catholic side, which is congenial to the *lumen naturale* (i.e. the natural light of reason).

[3] Jürgen Habermas, *The Inclusion of the Other*, ed. and trans. Ciaran Cronin and Pablo De Greiff (Cambridge: Polity, 1998).

The post-Kantian justification of liberal constitutional principles in the twentieth century had less trouble with the remnants of objective natural law (and the material ethics of values) than with historicist and empiricist forms of criticism. In my view, weak assumptions concerning the normative meaning of the communicative constitution of sociocultural forms of life provide a sufficient basis for defending a nondefeatist concept of reason against contextualism and a nondecisionistic concept of legal validity against legal positivism. The principal task is to explain:

- why the democratic process counts as a procedure of legitimate lawmaking; and
- why democracy and human rights are interrelated in a coeval manner in the process of founding a constitution.

The explanation consists in proving:

- that the democratic process warrants the supposition that its outcomes are rationally acceptable to the extent that it fulfils the preconditions of an inclusive and discursive process of opinion- and will-formation; and
- that the legal institutionalization of such a democratic lawgiving procedure requires that both the liberal and the political basic rights be guaranteed simultaneously.[4]

The point of reference for this justification strategy is the constitution that the citizens jointly confirm upon themselves rather than the domestication of an existing state power, for the latter is supposed to be first created in the course of founding a democratic constitution. A "constituted" (rather than merely a constitutionally "tamed") state power is legally regulated to its very core, so that law permeates political power through and through. Whereas the positivist idea of the will of the state [*Staatswillen-positivismus*] that marked the German constitutional theory of the Wilhelmine period (from Laband and Jellinek to Carl Schmitt) left an opening for the idea of the ethical substance of "the State"

---

[4] Habermas, *Between Facts and Norms*, trans. William Rehg (Cambridge: Polity, 1996), ch. 3.

or "the Political" free from law, in the constitutional state there is no subject of power that draws its sustenance from pre-legal sources.[5] Preconstitutional princely sovereignty has not bequeathed any empty space that must be filled by a comparable substantive popular sovereignty in the form of the ethos of a more or less homogeneous people [*Volk*].

In light of this problematic heritage, Böckenförde's question has been taken to imply that a completely positive constitutional system requires religion or some other "sustaining power" to lend cognitive support to its legitimizing principles. The claim to validity of positive law, on this reading, is supposed to require grounding in the prepolitical ethical convictions of religious or national communities, because such a legal order cannot legitimate itself in a self-reflexive fashion through a democratic legal procedure alone. If, on the contrary, we understand the democratic procedure as a method by which legitimacy is generated from legality, rather than in a positivist way following Kelsen or Luhmann, then the issue of a deficit of validity that must be compensated for by "ethical life" never arises. In contrast to a right-Hegelian understanding of the constitutional state, the proceduralist conception of Kantian inspiration insists on an autonomous grounding of constitutional principles that claims to be rationally acceptable to all citizens.

(2) In what follows, I assume that the constitution of the liberal state can satisfy its need for legitimation in a modest way by drawing on the cognitive resources of a set of arguments that are independent of religious or metaphysical traditions. Even granting this premise, however, there remain doubts from the motivational side. For the basic normative preconditions of the constitutional state are more demanding with regard to the role of citizens who understand themselves as the authors of law than to the role of citizens as addressees of the law. Addressees of the law are only expected not to overstep legal boundaries in exercising their individual liberties (and claims). The motivations and attitudes expected of citizens in their role as democratic co-legislators are

---

[5] Hauke Brunkhorst, "Der lange Schatten des Staatswillenpositivismus," *Leviathan* 31 (2003): 362–81.

a different matter from the obedience toward coercive laws designed to protect individual liberties.

Citizens as co-legislators are supposed to make active use of their communication and participation rights, which means using them not only in their enlightened self-interest but also with a view to promoting the common good. This demands a more costly form of motivation that cannot be legally exacted. A *duty* to vote would be as alien to a constitutional democracy as legally *prescribed* solidarity. The willingness to take responsibility if need be for anonymous fellow-citizens who remain strangers to us and to make sacrifices in the common interest can only be *requested* of the citizens of a liberal polity. Hence, political virtues are essential for the survival of a democracy even though they are only "levied" in small change. They are a matter of socialization and habituation into the practices and attitudes of a liberal political culture. Citizenship is "embedded" in a civil society that is nourished by spontaneous and, if you will, "prepolitical" sources.

This does not imply that the liberal state is incapable of reproducing the motivations on which it depends from its own secular resources. Citizens' motives for participating in political opinion- and will-formation do indeed draw their sustenance from ethical lifeworlds and cultural forms of life. But democratic practices generate their own political dynamism. Only a rule of law without democracy, such as existed for long enough in Germany, would imply a negative answer to Böckenförde's question: "To what extent can peoples united into states live off guarantees of individual freedom alone without a unifying bond that precedes this freedom?"[6] After all, the democratic constitutional state does not only guarantee negative liberties for citizens concerned with their own well-being; by fostering communicative freedoms, it also *mobilizes* citizen participation in public debates over matters that concern them all. The "unifying bond" sought for is a democratic process in which the correct understanding of the constitution is ultimately under discussion.

Thus in the current debates over the reform of the welfare state, immigration policy, the war in Iraq, and the abolition of

---

[6] Böckenförde, "Die Entstehung des Staates als Vorgang der Säkularisation," p. 111.

obligatory military service, for example, we are not simply dealing with isolated policies but always also with disagreements over the interpretation of constitutional principles. In such cases, we are also implicitly dealing with our understanding of ourselves as citizens of the Federal Republic and as Europeans, in light of the diversity of our cultural forms of life and the pluralism of our worldviews and religious convictions. With historical hindsight, to be sure, a shared religious background, a common language, and, above all, the newly awakened national consciousness contributed to the emergence of a highly abstract form of civic solidarity. However, the republican ethos has in the meantime largely freed itself from these prepolitical anchors – the fact that we are not ready to die "for Nice"[7] is no longer an objection against a European constitution. Think of the ethical-political discourses concerning the Holocaust and mass crimes that fostered an awareness of the constitution as an achievement among the citizens of the Federal Republic. The example of a self-critical "politics of memory" (which is by no means exceptional any longer but has been adopted by other countries) shows how constitutional patriotic bonds form and renew themselves in the medium of politics *itself*.

Contrary to a widespread misunderstanding, "constitutional patriotism" means that the citizens make the principles of the constitution their own not merely in an abstract sense but also in the concrete historical context of their respective national histories. The cognitive approach does not go far enough if the moral contents of basic rights are to gain a foothold in convictions. Moral insights and worldwide agreement in reactions of moral outrage against gross violations of human rights alone would ensure only the paper-thin integration of the citizens into a politically constituted world society (should it one day come into existence). A solidarity among citizens, however abstract and legally mediated, develops only when the principles of justice become woven into the more finely spun web of cultural values.

---

[7] The reference is to the Treaty of Nice adopted by the European Council in December 2000 in which major reforms of the institutions of the EU were agreed upon in anticipation of the impending enlargement of the union. – *Trans.*

(3) In light of the foregoing reflections, the secular character of the constitutional state does not exhibit any internal weakness inherent in the political system as such that jeopardizes its ability to stabilize itself in a cognitive or motivational sense. This does not exclude external reasons. An uncontrolled modernization of society as a whole could certainly corrode democratic bonds and undermine the form of solidarity on which the democratic state depends even though it cannot enforce it. Then the very constellation that Böckenförde has in mind would transpire, namely, the transformation of the citizens of prosperous and peaceful liberal societies into isolated, self-interested monads who use their individual liberties exclusively against one another like weapons. Evidence of such a corrosion of civic solidarity can be found in the larger context of the politically uncontrolled dynamics of the global economy and global society.

Markets, which, unlike state administrations, cannot be democratized, are increasingly assuming regulatory functions in domains of life that used to be held together by norms – in other words, by political means or through prepolitical forms of communication. Not only are private spheres as a consequence becoming increasingly recalibrated to the mechanisms of instrumental action guided by individual preferences but the domain open to public legitimation pressures is also shrinking. Civic privatism is being reinforced by the discouraging loss of function of a mode of democratic opinion- and will-formation that in the meantime operates more or less satisfactorily only within national arenas, with the result that decision-making processes that have been displaced onto supranational levels are now beyond its reach. The fading hope in the political capacity of the international community is also promoting the trend toward the depoliticization of citizens. In the light of the conflicts and glaring social injustices of a highly fragmented global society, the disappointment is growing with every additional setback to the process of constitutionalization of international law initiated after 1945.[8]

Postmodern theories frame these crises in terms of a critique of reason. They do not see them as a function of the selective exploitation of the rational resources implicit in Western

---

[8] See below, p. 314.

modernity but as the logical result of a self-destructive program of intellectual and social rationalization. Although radical skepticism concerning reason is fundamentally alien to the Catholic tradition, Catholicism found it difficult to come to terms with the secular ideas of humanism, enlightenment, and political liberalism as late as the 1960s. Hence, the thesis that a religious orientation to a transcendent reality alone can show a contrite modernity the way out of its impasse is once again gaining adherents. In Tehran, a colleague asked me whether, viewed from the perspective of the comparative study of cultures and the sociology of religion, European secularization was not actually the special path [*Sonderweg*] in need of correction. This is reminiscent of the mood of the Weimar Republic associated with such figures as Carl Schmitt, Heidegger, and Leo Strauss.

I think it would be a mistake to radicalize the question of whether an ambivalent modernity will achieve stability on the basis of the secular resources of communicative reason alone into a critique of reason as such; instead, we should treat it less dramatically as an open empirical question. I do not thereby mean to treat the phenomenon of the continued existence of religion in an environment shaped by continuing secularization as a mere social fact. Philosophy must take this phenomenon seriously also from within as a *cognitive* challenge. Before pursuing this line of discussion, however, I would like to mention a natural branching of the dialogue in another direction. The move to radicalize the critique of reason has led philosophy to reflect on its own religious-metaphysical origins, and on occasion to be drawn into conversations with a theology that, for its part, has sought inspiration from philosophical attempts at a post-Hegelian self-reflection of reason.[9]

Excursus. The point of departure for the philosophical discourse on reason and revelation is the recurring idea of a reason reflecting on its deepest foundations and discovering its source in an Other whose ominous power it must acknowledge if it is not to lose its rational orientation in the dead end of a

---

[9] Peter Neuner and Gunther Wenz (eds), *Theologen des 20. Jahrhunderts* (Darmstadt: Wissenschaftliche Buchgesellschaft, 2002).

hybrid self-subjection [*hybrider Selbstbemächtigung*]. Here the self-empowered, or at any rate self-initiated, spiritual exercise of conversion – a conversion of reason by reason – serves as a model. It makes no difference whether reflection begins with the self-awareness of the knowing and acting subject, as in Schleiermacher, or with the historicality of each individual's existential self-confirmation, as in Kierkegaard, or with the provocative inner turmoil of ethical life, as in Hegel, Feuerbach, and Marx. A reason initially free of theological intent becoming aware of its limits transcends itself toward an Other, whether in the mystical union with an encompassing cosmic consciousness, in the despairing hope in the historical advent of redemptive tidings, or in the form of a future-oriented solidarity with the humiliated and the downtrodden that seeks to accelerate the advent of messianic salvation. These anonymous deities of post-Hegelian metaphysics – the inclusive consciousness, the archaic event, and the non-alienated society – are easy prey for theology. They invite interpretation as pseudonyms for the self-proclaiming personal God of the Trinity.

These attempts to renew philosophical theology following Hegel remain more congenial than the Nietzscheanism that merely borrows the Christian connotations of concepts like listening, hearing, devotion, grace, advent, and event to trace a propositionally hollowed-out thinking back to an undifferentiated pre-Christian and pre-Socratic archaic source. A philosophy aware of its fallibility and its precarious foothold within the differentiated framework of modern society, by contrast, insists on the generic, though by no means pejorative, distinction between secular discourse that claims to be universally accessible, and religious discourse that appeals to revealed truths. In contrast to Kant and Hegel, this grammatical distinction is not bound up with the philosophical claim to determine what is true or false in the contents of religious traditions over and above socially institutionalized secular knowledge [*Weltwissen*]. The respect that goes hand in hand with this cognitive stance of refraining from judgment is founded on respect for persons and forms of life that clearly derive their integrity and authenticity from religious convictions. But it is not just a matter of respect. Philosophy also has good reasons to be open to learning from religious traditions.

(4) Postmetaphysical thinking is ethically modest in the sense that it is resistant to any generally binding concept of the good and exemplary life. Holy scriptures and religious traditions, by contrast, have articulated intuitions concerning transgression and salvation and the redemption of lives experienced as hopeless, keeping them hermeneutically vibrant by skillfully working out their implications over centuries. This is why religious communities, provided that they eschew dogmatism and respect freedom of conscience, can preserve intact something that has been lost elsewhere and cannot be recovered through the professional knowledge of experts alone. I have in mind sufficiently differentiated expressions of and sensitivity to squandered lives, social pathologies, failed existences, and deformed and distorted social relations. A willingness on the part of philosophy to learn from religion can be justified on the basis of the asymmetry of epistemic claims, not just for functional but – in the light of its successful "Hegelian" learning processes – also for substantive reasons.

The cross-fertilization of Christianity and Greek metaphysics gave rise not only to the discipline of dogmatic theology and a – not always propitious – Hellenization of the Christian faith. It also promoted an assimilation of genuine Christian elements by philosophy. This process of assimilation led to such normatively charged networks of concepts as responsibility, autonomy and justification, history and remembrance, rebirth, innovation and return, emancipation and fulfillment, renunciation, internalization and incarnation, individuality and community. Although philosophy transformed the original religious meanings of these terms, it did not deflate them and exhaust their meaning. The translation of the theological doctrine of creation in God's image into the idea of the equal and unconditional dignity of all human beings constitutes one such conserving translation. It makes the content of biblical concepts available to the general public of unbelievers and members of other faiths beyond the boundaries of a particular religious community. Walter Benjamin was among the thinkers who at times succeeded in making such translations.

In view of this experience of the secularizing recovery of religious meanings, we can lend an unproblematic meaning to Böckenförde's theorem. I mentioned the diagnosis according to which the balance between the three principal media of societal integration achieved over the course of modernity is being jeopardized because markets and administrative power are displacing social solidarity – i.e. the coordination of action through values, norms, and language use oriented to reaching understanding – from ever more domains of social life. Thus, it is also in the interest of the constitutional state to conserve all cultural sources that nurture citizens' solidarity and their normative awareness. This conservative turn finds expression in talk of the "postsecular society."[10]

By this is meant not only the fact that religion must maintain its position in an increasingly secular environment and that society must anticipate that religious communities will continue to exist. In addition, the expression "postsecular" does not merely grant religious communities public recognition for their functional contribution to the reproduction of desirable motives and attitudes. The public consciousness of a postsecular society reflects, rather, a normative insight that has implications for political interactions between religious and nonreligious citizens. In the postsecular society, the conviction is gaining ground that the "modernization of public consciousness" affects and reflexively transforms religious and secular mentalities, though not simultaneously. Both sides can then take each other's contributions to controversial public debates seriously for cognitive reasons as well, assuming that they share an understanding of the secularization of society as a *complementary* learning process.

(5) On the one hand, religious consciousness is forced to undergo adaptation. Every religion is originally a "*world*view" or "comprehensive doctrine" also in the sense that it claims the authority to structure a form of life *as a whole*. Religion had to renounce this claim to a monopoly on interpretation and to shape life as a whole with the secularization of scientific knowledge, the neutralization of state power, and the universalization of religious freedom. As social subsystems become functionally differentiated, the life of the religious community also detaches itself from its social

---

[10] Klaus Eder, "Europäische Säkularisierung – ein Sonderweg in die postsäkulare Gesellschaft?" *Berliner Journal für Soziologie* 3 (2002): 331–43.

environment. The role of a member of a religious community becomes differentiated from that of a citizen. And since the liberal state depends on a political integration of citizens that goes beyond a mere *modus vivendi*, this differentiation of memberships must not be confined to a cognitively undemanding conformity of the religious ethos to the *imposed* laws of secular society. Rather, the universalistic legal order and egalitarian social morality must be connected with the ethos of the community from within in such a way that the one follows consistently *from the other*. John Rawls chose the image of a module to describe this kind of "embedding": the module of secular justice should fit into each orthodox context of justification even though it was constructed with the help of reasons that are neutral toward different worldviews.[11]

This normative expectation with which the liberal state confronts religious communities accords with their interests to the extent that they thereby gain the opportunity to exercise influence of their own on society as a whole through the political public arena. Admittedly, the burdens of tolerance are not shared equally by believers and unbelievers, as is shown by more or less liberal abortion regimes; but secular consciousness does not enjoy negative freedom of religion for free either. It is expected to adopt a self-reflexive critical stance toward the limits of enlightenment. The conception of tolerance of pluralistic liberal societies not only requires believers to recognize that they must *reasonably* reckon with the persistence of disagreement in their dealings with non-believers and members of other faiths. The same recognition is also required of unbelievers in their dealings with believers in a liberal political culture.

For religiously tone-deaf citizens, this implies the by no means trivial requirement to determine the relation between faith and knowledge *self-critically* from the perspective of secular knowledge [*Weltwissen*]. For the expectation that the disagreement between faith and knowledge will persist deserves the title "reasonable" only if religious convictions are also accorded an epistemic status as not simply "irrational" from the perspective of secular knowledge. Hence, naturalistic worldviews based upon speculative

---

[11] John Rawls, *Political Liberalism* (New York: Columbia University Press, 1993), pp. 58ff.

elaborations of scientific findings that have implications for citizens' ethical self-understanding by no means enjoy *prima facie* priority over competing worldviews or religious outlooks in the political public sphere.[12]

The neutrality of state power vis-à-vis different worldviews, which guarantees equal individual liberties for all citizens, is incompatible with the political generalization of a secularized worldview. Secular citizens, in their role as citizens, may neither deny that religious worldviews are in principle capable of truth nor question the right of their devout fellow-citizens to couch their contributions to public discussions in religious language. A liberal political culture can even expect its secular citizens to take part in the efforts to translate relevant contributions from religious language into a publicly intelligible language.[13]

---

[12] See, for example, Wolf Singer, "Keiner kann anders sein, als er ist: Verschaltungen legen uns fest: Wir sollten aufhören, von Freiheit zu reden," *Frankfurter Allgemeine Zeitung*, January 8, 2004, p. 33.

[13] See Jürgen Habermas, "Faith and Knowledge," in *The Future of Human Nature*, trans. Hella Beister and William Rehg (Cambridge: Polity, 2003).

5

Religion in the Public Sphere: Cognitive Presuppositions for the "Public Use of Reason" by Religious and Secular Citizens[1]

(1) Religious traditions and communities of faith have gained a new, hitherto unexpected political importance since the epoch-making historical juncture of 1989–90.[2] What initially spring to mind are, of course, the variants of religious fundamentalism that we encounter not only in the Middle East, but also in Africa, Southeast Asia, and the Indian subcontinent. They are often associated with national and ethnic conflicts and also provide the seedbed for the decentralized terrorism that operates globally and is directed against the perceived insults and injuries inflicted by a superior Western civilization. But these are not the only symptoms.

---

[1] I am indebted for their insightful comments to Rainer Forst and Thomas M. Schmidt, both of whom have already published several instructive works on this topic. I am also grateful to Melissa Yates for helpful references and stimulating discussions.
[2] See Peter L. Berger (ed.), *The Desecularization of the World* (Washington, DC: Ethics and Public Policy Center, 1999).

In Iran, for example, the protest against a corrupt regime set in place and supported by the West has given rise to a veritable theocracy that serves as a model for other movements. In several Muslim countries, and in Israel as well, religious family law has either replaced or represents an alternative to secular civil law. And in countries like Afghanistan and Iraq, the validity of a more or less liberal constitution is conditional upon its compatibility with Sharia. Likewise, religious conflicts are forcing their way onto the international stage. The hopes associated with the political agenda of *multiple modernities* are fueled by the cultural self-confidence of those world religions that to this day indelibly mark the physiognomy of the major civilizations. And on the Western side of the fence, how international relations are perceived has changed in the light of fears of a "clash of civilizations" – "the axis of evil" is merely one prominent example of this. Even Western intellectuals who to date have remained self-critical in this respect are beginning to go on the offensive in responding to the Occidentalist image that others have formed of the West.[3]

Fundamentalism in other corners of the earth can be construed, among other things, as a long-term result of violent colonization and failed decolonization. Capitalist modernization that forcibly penetrates these societies from the outside under unfavorable conditions triggers social uncertainty and cultural upheavals. On this reading, religious movements must come to terms with the upheavals in social structure and cultural time-lags that individuals may experience as deracination under conditions of an accelerated or failing modernization. What is more surprising is the political revitalization of religion within the United States, where the dynamism of modernization has enjoyed the greatest success. Certainly, in Europe since the days of the French Revolution we have been aware of the power of a religious form of traditionalism that regarded itself as counter-revolutionary. However, this evocation of religion as the power of tradition implicitly revealed the nagging doubt that the vitality of what is merely passed down as tradition may have been broken. By contrast, the political

---

[3] See Ian Buruma and Avishai Margalit, *Occidentalism: The West in the Eyes of its Enemies* (New York: Penguin, 2004).

awakening of an undiminished religious consciousness in the United States seems to be unaffected by such doubts.

During the period since the end of World War II all European countries, with the exception of Ireland and Poland, have been gripped by a wave of secularization that goes hand in hand with modernization. For the United States, by contrast, all survey data indicate that the comparatively large proportion of devout and religiously active citizens has remained constant over the past six decades.[4] More importantly, the current religious right in the United States is not traditionalist. It induces a sense of paralysis among its secular opponents precisely because it inspires spontaneous revivalist energies.

The movements for religious renewal at the heart of the civil society of the leading Western power are exacerbating at the *cultural* level the *political* division of the West prompted by the Iraq War.[5] Among the divisive issues are the abolition of the death penalty, more or less liberal regulations on abortion, setting homosexual partnerships on a par with heterosexual marriages, an unconditional rejection of torture, and in general the prioritization of rights over collective goods such as national security. The European states now seem to be continuing alone along the path which, since the two constitutional revolutions of the late eighteenth century, they had pursued side by side with the United States. In the meantime, the significance of religions used for political ends has increased throughout the world. Against this background, the split within the West is perceived as though Europe were isolating itself from the rest of the world. Viewed in terms of world history, Max Weber's "Occidental Rationalism" now appears to be the actual deviation.

From this revisionist perspective, religious traditions appear to be sweeping away with undiminished strength the thresholds hitherto upheld between "traditional" and "modern" societies, or at least to be leveling them. The West's own image of modernity seems to be undergoing a gestalt switch as if in a psychological

---

[4] See Pippa Norris and Ronald Inglehart, *Sacred and Secular: Religion and Politics Worldwide* (Cambridge: Cambridge University Press, 2004), ch. 4.
[5] See Habermas, *The Divided West*, ed. and trans. Ciaran Cronin (Cambridge: Polity, 2006).

experiment: what was assumed to be the normal model for the future of all other cultures is suddenly becoming the exception. Even if this suggestive image of a gestalt switch will not stand up to closer sociological scrutiny and the explanations of secularization offered by modernization theory can be brought into line with the countervailing evidence,[6] there can be no doubt concerning the evidence itself and above all concerning the symptomatic aggravation of the political mood.

Two days after the last US presidential elections, an essay appeared by a historian entitled "The Day the Enlightenment Went Out," which posed the alarmist question:

> Can a people that believes more fervently in the Virgin Birth than in evolution still be called an Enlightened nation? America, the first real democracy in history, was a product of Enlightenment values . . . Though the founders differed on many things, they shared these values of what was then modernity . . . Respect for evidence seems not to pertain any more, when a poll taken just before the election showed that 75% of Mr. Bush's supporters believe Iraq either worked closely with Al Qaeda or was directly involved in the attacks of 9/11.[7]

However one evaluates the facts, the analyses of the election confirm that the cultural division of the West runs right through the American nation itself: conflicting value orientations – God, gays, and guns – have evidently eclipsed more concrete conflicts of interests. Be that as it may, President Bush owes his victory to

---

[6] Norris and Inglehart (*Sacred and Secular*, ch. 10) defend the classical hypothesis that secularization prevails to the extent that a sense of "existential security" takes root together with improved economic and social conditions of life. Along with the demographic assumption that fertility rates decrease in developed societies, this hypothesis offers a preliminary explanation of why until now secularization has on the whole taken root only in the "West." The United States constitutes an exception, first, because the effects of its form of capitalism are less cushioned by a welfare state, so that its population is exposed to a higher average level of existential insecurity, and, second, because of its comparatively high rates of immigration from countries whose societies are still deeply shaped by tradition and whose fertility rates are correspondingly high.

[7] Gary Wills, "The Day the Enlightenment Went Out," *New York Times*, November 4, 2004.

a coalition of primarily religiously motivated voters.[8] This shift in the balance of political power points to a shift in mentality in civil society that also provides the backdrop for the academic debates on the political role of religion in the state and the public sphere.

Once again, the battle is over the substance of the first sentence of the First Amendment: "Congress shall make no law respecting an establishment of religion, or prohibiting the free exercise thereof." The United States was the political pacemaker on the path to establishing a freedom of religion that rests on mutual respect for the religious freedom of others.[9] The marvelous Article 16 of the Bill of Rights of Virginia of 1776 is the first document that features a constitutional guarantee of freedom of religion that democratic citizens accord *one another* across the divides between the different religious communities. Unlike in France, the introduction of the freedom of religion in the United States did not mark a victory of laicism over a state authority that had at most tolerated religious minorities according to its own standards which it *imposed* on the population. Here, the secularization of state power did not have the primarily negative meaning of protecting citizens from being compelled to adopt a faith against their conscience. It was designed instead to guarantee the settlers who had turned their backs on Old Europe the positive liberty to exercise their respective religions without hindrance. For this reason, in the current American debate over the political role of religion, all sides can affirm their loyalty to

[8] Laurie Goodstein and William Yardley, "President Bush Benefits from Efforts to Build a Coalition of Religious Voters," *New York Times*, November 5, 2004. Bush was elected by 60 per cent of the Spanish-speaking voters, 67 per cent of the white Protestants, and 78 per cent of the evangelical or born-again Christians. Even among the Catholics who otherwise vote Democrat, Bush was able to invert the traditional majorities to his advantage. The fact that the Catholic bishops sided with Bush is astonishing, notwithstanding the agreement on the abortion issue, if we bear in mind that the administration, in contrast to the Church, defends the death penalty and has put the lives of tens of thousands of US soldiers and Iraqi civilians at risk for a war of aggression that contravened international law and was based on flimsy reasons.
[9] On this "respect concept" of tolerance, see the wide-ranging historical and systematically convincing study by Rainer Forst, *Toleranz im Konflikt* (Frankfurt am Main: Suhrkamp, 2003).

the constitution. To what extent this claim is valid remains to be seen.

In what follows, I shall address the debate inspired by John Rawls's political theory, in particular his conception of the "public use of reason." How does the constitutional separation of state and church influence the role that religious traditions, communities, and organizations are permitted to play in civil society and the political public sphere, that is, in the political opinion- and will-formation of the citizens? Where, in the opinion of the revisionists, should the dividing line be drawn? Are the opponents who are currently on the warpath against the classical liberal conception of this division merely championing the pro-religious view that the secular state should remain neutral toward a *narrowly secularist* understanding of a pluralist society? Or are they changing the liberal agenda more or less imperceptibly from the ground up – and thus already arguing within the horizon of a *different* self-understanding of modernity?

First I would like to highlight the liberal premises of the constitutional state and the implications of John Rawls's conception of the public use of reason for the ethics of citizenship [*Ethos der Staatsbürger*] (2). Then I will turn to the most important objections to this rather restrictive idea of the political role of religion (3). Through a critical discussion of revisionist proposals that impinge upon the foundations of the liberal self-understanding, I will develop a conception that mediates between the two sides (4). Secular and devout citizens can fulfill the normative expectations of the liberal role of citizens, however, only if they likewise satisfy certain cognitive conditions and ascribe to each other the corresponding epistemic attitudes. I will offer a preliminary explanation of what this means by discussing the transformation of religious consciousness in response to the challenges of modernity (5). By contrast, the secular awareness that one is living in a postsecular society finds expression at the philosophical level in a postmetaphysical mode of thought (6). In both respects, however, the liberal state faces the problem that devout and secular citizens can acquire these attitudes only through complementary "learning processes," whose status as learning processes remains controversial, and over which the state cannot in any event exercise influence by the legal and political means at its disposal (7).

(2) The self-understanding of the constitutional state developed within the context of a philosophical tradition that relies on "natural" reason, in other words, that relies exclusively on public arguments that claim to be *equally accessible* to *all* persons. The assumption of a common human reason provides the epistemic basis for justifying a secular state that no longer depends on religious legitimation. And this in turn makes the separation between church and state possible at the institutional level. The overcoming of the early modern wars of religion and confessional disputes provided the historical backdrop against which the liberal conception emerged. The constitutional state responded by secularizing government and democratizing political power. This genealogy also forms the background to John Rawls's *Theory of Justice*.[10]

The constitutional freedom of conscience and religion is the appropriate political response to the challenges of religious pluralism. For it makes it possible to defuse at the level of the social interactions among citizens the potential for conflict between the existentially relevant convictions of believers, members of other faiths, and nonbelievers, which remains undiminished at the cognitive level. Yet the secular character of the state is a necessary, though not sufficient, condition for guaranteeing equal religious freedom for everybody. It is not enough to rely on the condescending indulgence of a secularized authority that comes to tolerate minorities who previously suffered discrimination. The parties *themselves* must come to an agreement on the precarious demarcations between the positive liberty to practice a religion of one's own and the negative liberty to remain unencumbered by the religious practices of others. If the principle of tolerance is to be above the suspicion of defining the *limits* of tolerance in an oppressive manner, then compelling reasons must be found for the definition of what can still be tolerated and what cannot, reasons equally acceptable to all sides.[11] Fair arrangements can be found only if the parties involved also learn

---

[10] Rawls, *A Theory of Justice* (Cambridge, Mass.: Harvard University Press, 1971), §§33f.

[11] On the concept of tolerance as reciprocal respect, see Forst, *Toleranz im Konflikt*.

to adopt the perspectives of the others. The deliberative mode of democratic will-formation is the most appropriate for this purpose.

In the secular state, government must in any case be put on a nonreligious footing. The democratic constitution must fill the gap in legitimation opened up by a secularization that deprives the state of religious legitimation. The practice of constitution-making generates those basic rights that free and equal citizens must accord one another if they wish to regulate their coexistence reasonably and autonomously by means of positive law.[12] The democratic procedure owes its legitimizing power to two components: first, the equal political participation of all citizens, which ensures that the addressees of the laws can also understand themselves to be the authors of these laws; and, second, the epistemic dimension of a deliberation that grounds the presumption of rationally acceptable outcomes.[13]

These two legitimacy components explain the legally noncoercible political virtues that the liberal state must expect from its citizens. The conditions for the successful participation in the shared practice of democratic self-determination define the role of the citizen. In spite of their ongoing dissent over questions concerning worldviews and religious doctrines, citizens should respect one another as free and equal members of their political community. And, based on this civic solidarity, they should seek a rationally motivated agreement when it comes to contentious political issues – they owe one another good reasons. Rawls speaks in this context of the "duty of civility" and "the public use of reason": "The ideal of citizenship imposes a moral, not a legal, duty – the duty of civility – to be able to explain to one another on those fundamental questions how the principles and policies they advocate and vote for can be supported by the values of public reason. This duty also involves a willingness to listen to

---

[12] See Habermas, *Between Facts and Norms*, trans. William Rehg (Cambridge: Polity, 1996), ch. 3.
[13] See Rawls, "The Idea of Public Reason Revisited," *University of Chicago Law Review* 64 (1997): 765–807, here p. 769: "Ideally citizens are to think of themselves as if they were legislators and ask themselves what statutes, supported by what reasons satisfying the principle of reciprocity, they would think it most reasonable to enact."

others and a fair-mindedness in deciding when accommodations to their views should reasonably be made."[14]

Only with the emergence of a self-governing association of free and equal citizens founded on legal norms does the point of reference arise for the use of public reason which requires citizens to justify their political statements and attitudes before one another in the light of a (reasonable interpretation)[15] of valid constitutional principles. Rawls refers here to "values of public reason," elsewhere to the "premises we accept and think others could reasonably accept."[16] In a secular state, only those political decisions can count as legitimate that can be impartially justified in the light of generally accessible reasons, in other words, that can be justified equally toward religious and nonreligious citizens and citizens of different confessions. The exercise of power that cannot be justified in an impartial manner is illegitimate because it reflects the fact that one party is forcing its will on another. Citizens of a democratic polity are obliged to provide each other with reasons, because only in this way can political power shed its repressive character. This explains the controversial "proviso" to which the public use of nonpublic reasons is supposed to be subject.

The principle of separation of church and state obliges politicians and officials within political institutions to formulate and justify laws, court rulings, decrees, and measures exclusively in a language that is equally accessible to all citizens.[17] By contrast, the proviso to which citizens, political parties and their candidates, social organizations, churches, and other religious associations are subject in the public arena is not quite so strict. Rawls writes: "The first is that reasonable comprehensive doctrines, religious or non-religious, may be introduced in public political discussion at

---

[14] Rawls, *Political Liberalism* (New York: Columbia University Press, 1993), p. 217.

[15] Rawls speaks of a "family of liberal conceptions of justice" to which the use of public reason can refer when interpreting constitutional principles; see Rawls, "The Idea of Public Reason Revisited," pp. 773f.

[16] Ibid., p. 786.

[17] For a specification of the demand for reasons in a "generally accessible" language, see Forst, *Contexts of Justice*, trans. John M. M. Farrell (Berkeley: University of California Press, 2002), pp. 126–33.

any time, *provided that in due course proper political reasons – and not reasons given solely by comprehensive doctrines – are presented that are sufficient to support whatever the comprehensive doctrines are said to support.*"[18] This means that the political reasons appealed to in each case may not be put forward simply as a pretext, but must "count" irrespective of the religious context in which they are embedded.[19]

On the liberal conception, the state guarantees citizens freedom of religion only on the condition that religious communities, each from the viewpoint of their respective doctrinal traditions, accept not only the neutrality of public institutions, and hence the separation of church and state, but also the restrictive definition of the public use of reason. Rawls insists on these requirements even in the face of an objection that he himself raises: "How is it possible . . . for those of faith . . . to endorse a constitutional regime even when their comprehensive doctrines may not prosper under it, and indeed may decline?"[20]

Rawls's conception of the public use of reason has met with sharp criticism. Objections are leveled in the first instance, not against his liberal premises per se, but against an overly narrow, secularist definition of the political role of religion within the context of a liberal political order. However, the dissent ultimately also seems to affect the real substance of the liberal state. What interests me here is how the line of demarcation to claims that are illegitimate on a liberal constitution is drawn. However, arguments for a more generous interpretation of the political role of religion which are incompatible with the secular character of the state should not be confused with well-founded

---

[18] Rawls, "The Idea of Public Reason Revisited," pp. 783f. (my italics). This represents a revision of the more narrowly formulated principle in Rawls, *Political Liberalism*, pp. 224f. Rawls confines the proviso to key issues affecting "constitutional essentials"; I consider this reservation unrealistic in the case of modern legal systems in which basic rights directly affect concrete legislation and adjudication, so that virtually any controversial legal issue can be heightened into an issue of principle.

[19] Rawls, "The Idea of Public Reason Revisited," p. 777: "They are not puppets manipulated from behind the scenes by comprehensive doctrines."

[20] Ibid., p. 781. I shall return to this objection later.

objections to a secularist understanding of democracy and the rule of law.

The separation of church and state demands that the institutions of the state should operate with strict impartiality vis-à-vis religious communities; parliaments, courts, and the administration must not violate the requirement of neutrality by favoring one side at the expense of another. However, this principle should not be reduced to the laicist demand that the state should refrain from adopting any political stance that would support or (in accordance with the guarantee of freedom of religion) constrain religion per se, even if this affects all religious communities equally. That would amount to an overly narrow interpretation of the separation of church and state.[21] At the same time, the rejection of secularism must not open the door for revisions that would undermine the principle itself. The toleration of religious justifications within the legislative process is a case in point, as we shall see. That said, Rawls's liberal position has drawn his critics' attention less to the impartiality of state institutions than to the normative implications of citizenship.

(3) Rawls's critics cite historical examples of the beneficial political influence that churches and religious movements have actually had on the realization or defense of democracy and human rights. Martin Luther King and the US Civil Rights Movement illustrate the successful struggle for a broader inclusion of minorities and marginal groups in the political process. In this context, the deep religious roots of the motivations of most social and socialist movements in both the Anglo-American and the European countries are highly impressive.[22] There are obvious historical counterexamples of the authoritarian or repressive role of churches and fundamentalist movements; however, in well-established constitutional states, churches and religious communities generally perform important functions for stabilizing and advancing a liberal

---

[21] See the debate between Robert Audi and Nicholas Wolterstorff in Audi and Wolterstorff, *Religion in the Public Square* (Lanham, Md.: Rowman & Littlefield, 1997), pp. 3f., 76f., and 167f.

[22] See Norman Birnbaum, *After Progress* (New York: Oxford University Press, 2001).

political culture. This is especially true of the form of civil religion so well developed in American society.[23]

Paul Weithman draws on these sociological findings to support a normative analysis of the ethics of democratic citizenship. He describes churches and religious communities as actors in civil society who fulfill indispensable functional imperatives for the reproduction of American democracy. They provide arguments for public debates on crucial morally loaded issues and fulfill tasks of political socialization by informing their members and encouraging them to participate in the political process. The churches' civic engagement would, however, wane, so the argument goes, if they constantly had to distinguish between religious and political values according to the yardstick laid down by Rawls's "proviso" – in other words, if they were obliged to find an equivalent in a universally accessible language for every religious statement they pronounce. Therefore, if only for functional reasons, the liberal state must refrain from obliging churches and religious communities to comply with such standards of self-censorship. And all the more so must it eschew imposing a similar limitation on its citizens.[24]

However, this is not the central objection to Rawls's theory. Irrespective of how the interests are balanced in the relationship

---

[23] See the influential study by Bellah, Madsen, Sullivan, Swidler, and Tipton, *Habits of the Heart* (New York: Harper & Row, 1985). On Bellah's relevant publications in this field, see the festschrift by Richard Madson et al. (eds), *Meaning and Modernity: Religion, Polity and Self* (Berkeley: University of California Press, 2001).

[24] On this empirical argument, see Paul J. Weithman, *Religion and the Obligations of Citizenship* (Cambridge: Cambridge University Press, 2002), p. 91: "I argued that churches contribute to democracy in the United States by fostering realized democratic citizenship. They encourage their members to accept democratic values as the basis for important political decisions and to accept democratic institutions as legitimate. The means by which they make their contributions, including their own interventions in civic argument and public political debate, affect the political arguments their members may be inclined to use, the basis on which they vote, and the specification of their citizenship with which they identify. They may encourage their members to think of themselves as bound by antecedently given moral norms with which political outcomes must be consistent. The realization of citizenship by those who are legally entitled to take part in political decision-making is an enormous achievement for a liberal democracy, one in which the institutions of civil society play a crucial role."

between the state and religious organizations, a state cannot encumber its citizens, to whom it guarantees freedom of religion, with duties that are incompatible with pursuing a devout life – it cannot expect something impossible of them. This objection merits closer scrutiny.

Robert Audi expresses the duty of civility postulated by Rawls as a special "principle of secular justifications": "One has a prima facie obligation not to advocate or support any law or public policy . . . unless one has, and is willing to offer, adequate secular reasons for this advocacy or support."[25] Audi supplements this principle with a requirement that goes even further, namely, the demand that the secular reasons must be strong enough to direct the citizen's own behavior, for example when voting in elections, quite independently of the concomitant religious motivations.[26] Now, the link between the actual motivation for a citizen's actions and those reasons he cites in public may be relevant for a moral judgment of the citizen, but it has no import for assessing his contribution to maintaining a liberal political culture. For in the final analysis, only the manifest reasons have institutional implications for the formation of majorities and decision-making within the relevant political bodies.

As regards the political consequences, all and only those issues, statements, facts, and reasons "count" that find their way into the impersonal circuits of public communication and contribute to the cognitive motivation of *some* decision (backed and implemented by state power). This holds both for direct influence on the decisions of voters and for indirect influence on the decisions taken by party leaders, members of parliament, or officeholders (such as judges, ministers, or civil servants). Hence I will ignore Audi's additional requirement for motivation as well as his distinction between publicly expressed reasons and those that motivate behavior in the polling booth.[27] What is essential for the standard version of political liberalism is simply the demand for "secular justifications": since only secular reasons count in

---

[25] Audi and Wolterstorff, *Religion in the Public Square*, p. 25.
[26] Ibid., p. 29.
[27] This distinction also prompts Paul Weithman to adapt his modified proviso accordingly; see Weithman, *Religion and the Obligations of Citizenship*, p. 3.

the liberal state, citizens who adhere to a religious faith are obliged to establish a kind of "balance" between their religious and their secular convictions – in Audi's words, a theo-ethical equilibrium.[28]

This demand is countered by the objection that many religious citizens would not be able to undertake such an artificial division within their own minds without jeopardizing the pious conduct of their lives. This objection must be distinguished from the empirical observation that many citizens who take a stance on political issues from a religious viewpoint do not have enough knowledge or imagination to find correspondingly secular justifications that are independent of their authentic beliefs. This fact is serious enough given that any "ought" implies a "can." Yet the central objection has normative implications, as it relates to the integral role that religion plays – i.e. its "seat" – in the life of a person of faith. A devout person conducts her daily existence *on the basis of* her faith. Genuine faith is not merely a doctrine, something believed, but is also a source of energy that the person of faith taps into performatively to nurture her whole life.[29]

However, this totalizing trait of a form of faith that permeates the very pores of daily life resists, so the objection goes, any nimble switchover of religiously rooted political convictions onto a *different* cognitive basis:

> It belongs to the religious convictions of a good many religious people in our society that *they ought to base* their decisions concerning fundamental issues of justice *on* their religious convictions.

---

[28] Audi has since introduced a counterpart to the principle of secular justification: "In liberal democracies, religious citizens have a prima facie obligation not to advocate or support any law or public policy that restricts human conduct, unless they have, and are willing to offer, adequate religiously acceptable reasons for this advocacy or support" (Audi, "Moral Foundations of Liberal Democracy, Secular Reasons, and Liberal Neutrality toward the Good," *Notre Dame Journal of Law, Ethics and Public Policy* 19 (2005): 197–218, here p. 217). This principle of religious justification is evidently meant to impose an obligation of critical self-scrutiny on citizens who are initially guided by religious reasons.

[29] On the Augustinian distinction of *fides quae creditur* [i.e. faith in the sense of what is believed] and *fides qua creditur* [i.e. faith in the sense of the act of believing], see Rudolf Bultmann, *Theologische Enzyklopädie* (Tübingen: Mohr, 1984), pp. 185ff.

They do not view it as an option whether or not to do it. It is their conviction that they ought to strive for wholeness, integrity, integration in their lives: that they ought to allow the Word of God, the teachings of the Torah, the command and example of Jesus, or whatever, to shape their existence as a whole, including, then, their social and political existence. Their religion is not, for them, about *something other* than their social and political existence.[30]

Their religiously grounded conception of justice tells them what is politically right and wrong, so that they are unable to discern "any 'pull' from any secular reasons."[31]

If we accept this, to my mind compelling, objection, then the liberal state, which expressly protects such forms of existence as a basic right, cannot at the same time expect *all* citizens in addition to justify their political positions independently of their religious convictions or worldviews. This strict demand can only be made of politicians operating within state institutions who have a duty to remain neutral among competing worldviews, in other words, of all those who hold a public office or are candidates for such.[32]

The neutrality of the state toward competing worldviews is the institutional precondition for the equal guarantee of freedom of religion for all. The consensus on constitutional principles in which all citizens must share pertains also to the principle of the separation of church and state. However, in light of the aforementioned key objection, to extend this principle from the

---

[30] Wolterstorff, in Audi and Wolterstorff, *Religion in the Public Square*, p. 105.
[31] Weithman, *Religion and the Obligations of Citizenship*, p. 157.
[32] This raises the interesting question of the extent to which during an election campaign candidates may confess or even indicate that they are religious persons. The principle of separation of church and state certainly extends to the platform, the manifesto, or the "line" that political parties and their candidates promise to realize. Electoral decisions that are driven by personality issues instead of programmatic ones are in any case problematic from a normative perspective. And it becomes even more problematic when the voters take their cue from candidates' religious self-presentations. See on this point the ideas elaborated by Weithman (ibid., pp. 117–20): "It would be good to have principles saying what role religion can play when candidates are assessed for what we might call their 'expressive value' – their fittingness to express the values of their constituencies . . . What is most important to remember about these cases, however, is that elections should not be decided nor votes cast entirely or primarily on the basis of various candidates' expressive value."

institutional level to statements put forward by organizations and citizens in the political public sphere would constitute an over-generalization of secularism. We cannot infer from the secular character of the state a direct personal obligation on all citizens to supplement their publicly expressed religious convictions by equivalents in a generally accessible language. And certainly the normative expectation that all religious citizens when casting their vote should *ultimately* let themselves be guided by secular considerations is to ignore the realities of a devout life, an existence *guided* by faith. This assertion has, however, been disputed by pointing to the actual situation of religious citizens in the secular milieus of a modern society.[33]

After all, the conflict between one's own religious convictions and secularly justified policies or proposed laws can only arise because even the religious citizen is already supposed to have accepted the constitution of the secular state for good reasons. He no longer lives as a member of a religiously homogeneous population within a religiously legitimated state. Hence certainties of faith are interconnected with fallible convictions of a secular nature; they have long since lost their purported immunity to the impositions of modern reflexivity – in the manner of "unmoved" but not "unmovable movers."[34] Religious certainties are in fact exposed to increasing reflective pressure in the differentiated architecture of modern societies. Religiously rooted existential convictions, by dint of their if necessary rationally justified reference to the dogmatic authority of an inviolable core of infallible revealed truths, evade that kind of *unreserved* discursive examination to which other ethical orientations and worldviews, i.e. secular "conceptions of the good," are exposed.[35]

---

[33] Thomas M. Schmidt, "Glaubensüberzeugungen und säkulare Gründe," *Zeitschrift für evangelische Ethik* 4 (2001): 248–61.

[34] Schmidt bases his objection on Gerald F. Gaus, *Justificatory Liberalism* (New York: Oxford University Press, 1996).

[35] As it happens, this special status prohibits a normative-political assimilation of religious convictions to ethical convictions, as practiced by Forst (*Contexts of Justice*, pp. 93–100) when he accords the principled priority of procedural over substantive criteria of justification precedence over the distinction between religious and secular reasons. Only conflicting religious beliefs teach us *a fortiori* that a justified consensus cannot be reached. In his more recent book, Forst (*Toleranz im Konflikt*, pp. 644ff.) acknowledges the special status of this category of beliefs.

This discursive extraterritoriality of a core of existential certainties *can* lend religious convictions (on certain readings) an integral character. At any rate, the liberal state, which protects all religious forms of life equally, must release religious citizens from the burden of having to make a strict separation between secular and religious reasons in the political public arena when they experience this as an attack on their personal identity.

(4) The liberal state must not transform the necessary *institutional* separation between religion and politics into an unreasonable *mental and psychological* burden for its religious citizens. It must, however, expect them to recognize the principle that the exercise of political authority must be neutral toward competing worldviews. Every citizen must know and accept that only secular reasons count beyond the institutional threshold separating the informal public sphere from parliaments, courts, ministries, and administrations. This only calls for the epistemic ability to consider one's own religious convictions reflexively from the outside and to connect them with secular views. Religious citizens can certainly acknowledge this "institutional translation proviso" without having to split their identity into public and private parts the moment they participate in public discourses. They should therefore also be allowed to express and justify their convictions in a religious language even when they cannot find secular "translations" for them.

This need not at all estrange "monolingual" citizens from the political process, because they also take political positions even when they adduce religious reasons.[36] Even if the religious language is the only one they speak in public, and if religiously justified opinions are the only ones they can or wish to contribute to political controversies, they nevertheless understand themselves as members of a *civitas terrena*, which empowers them to be the authors of laws to which they are subject as addressees. They may express themselves in a religious idiom only on the condition that they recognize the institutional translation proviso. Thus the citizens, confident that their fellow-citizens will cooperate in producing a translation, can understand themselves as partici-

[36] Here I am responding to a written objection of Rainer Forst.

pants in the legislative process, although only secular reasons count therein.

The admissibility of nontranslated religious utterances in the political arena can be justified not only on the normative grounds that it is not reasonable to *expect* Rawls's proviso to apply to those among the faithful who cannot abstain from the political use of "private" reasons without compromising their religious way of life. There are also functional reasons for not overhastily reducing the polyphonic complexity of public voices. For the liberal state has an interest in the free expression of religious voices in the public arena and in the political participation of religious organizations. It must not discourage religious persons and communities from also expressing themselves *as such* in the political arena, for it cannot be sure that secular society would not otherwise cut itself off from key resources for the creation of meaning and identity. Secular citizens or those of other religious persuasions can also learn something from religious contributions under certain circumstances, for example, when they recognize buried intuitions of their own in the normative truth contents of a religious utterance.

Religious traditions have a special power to articulate moral intuitions, especially with regard to vulnerable forms of communal life. In corresponding political debates, this potential makes religious speech into a serious vehicle for possible truth contents, which can then be translated from the vocabulary of a particular religious community into a generally accessible language. However, the institutional thresholds between the "wild" political public sphere and the formal proceedings within political bodies also function as a filter that allows only secular contributions from the Babel of voices in the informal flows of public communication to pass through. In parliament, for example, the rules of procedure must empower the house leader to strike religious positions or justifications from the official transcript. The truth contents of religious contributions can enter into the institutionalized practice of deliberation and decision-making only when the necessary translation already occurs in the pre-parliamentarian domain, i.e. in the political public sphere itself.

To be sure, this requirement of translation must be conceived as a cooperative task in which the nonreligious citizens must likewise participate if their religious fellow-citizens, who are ready and willing to participate, are not to be burdened in an asymmetrical way.[37] Whereas citizens of faith may make public contributions in their own religious language only subject to the translation proviso, by way of compensation secular citizens must open their minds to the possible truth content of those presentations and enter into dialogues from which religious reasons might well emerge in the transformed guise of generally accessible arguments.[38] Citizens of a democratic polity owe one another good reasons for their political positions. Even if the religious contributions are not subjected to self-censorship, they depend on cooperative acts of translation. For without a successful translation the substantive content of religious voices has no prospect of being taken up into the agendas and negotiations within political bodies and of gaining a hearing in the broader political process. By contrast, Nicholas Wolterstorff and Paul Weithman wish to jettison even this proviso. However, they thereby infringe against the principle that the state should remain neutral toward competing worldviews, contrary to their claim to remain in line with liberal premises.

In Weithman's opinion, citizens have the moral right to justify public political statements in the context of a comprehensive worldview or a religious doctrine. In this case, however, they are supposed to meet two conditions: first, they must be convinced

---

[37] In this sense, Forst (*Contexts of Justice*, p. 98) likewise speaks of "translation" when he requires that "a person (must) be able to make a (progressive) *translation* [his emphasis] of their arguments into reasons that are acceptable on the basis of the values and principles of public reason." However, he does not regard the process of translation as a cooperative search for the truth in which secular citizens should engage even if the other side limits itself to religious utterances. Forst, like Rawls and Audi, formulates the requirement as a civic duty incumbent upon the religious person him- or herself. Besides, the purely procedural definition of the act of translation aimed at "unrestricted reciprocal justification" does not do justice to the semantic problem of transposing the contents of religious speech into a postreligious and postmetaphysical mode of representation. As a result, the difference between ethical and religious discourse is lost from view. See, for example, Edmund Arens, *Kommunikative Handlungen* (Düsseldorf: Patmos, 1982), who interprets biblical parables as innovative speech acts.

[38] Habermas, "Faith and Knowledge," in Habermas, *The Future of Human Nature*, trans. Hella Beister and William Rehg (Cambridge: Polity, 2003), pp. 101–15.

that their government is justified in carrying out the laws or policies they support with religious arguments; and, second, they must be willing to explain why they believe this. This toned-down version of the proviso[39] amounts to the demand to undertake a universalization test from the first-person perspective. In this way, Weithman wants to ensure that citizens make their judgment from the standpoint of a conception of justice, even one grounded in terms of a religion or another substantive worldview. Citizens are supposed to consider in each case from the perspective of their own doctrine what would be equally good for everyone. However, the Golden Rule is not the Categorical Imperative. It does not oblige all those affected to *mutually* adopt each other's perspectives.[40] On this egocentric procedure, each person's worldview constitutes the insurmountable horizon of her deliberations on justice: "The person who argues in public for a measure must be prepared to say what she thinks would justify the government in enacting it, *but the justification she is prepared to offer may depend on claims, including religious claims, which proponents of the standard approach would deem inaccessible.*"[41]

Since no institutional filters are envisaged between the state and the public arena, this version does not exclude the possibility that policies and legal programs will be implemented solely on the basis of the specific religious or confessional beliefs of a ruling majority. This is the conclusion explicitly drawn by Nicholas Wolterstorff, who does not favor any constraint whatsoever on the political use of religious reasons – even the political legislator should be permitted to make use of religious arguments.[42]

---

[39] Weithman, *Religion and the Obligations of Citizenship*, p. 3: "Citizens of a liberal democracy may offer arguments in public political debate which depend on reasons drawn from their comprehensive moral views, including their religious views, without making them good by appeal to other arguments – provided they believe that their government would be justified in adopting the measures they favor and are prepared to indicate what they think would justify the adoption of the measures."

[40] Habermas, "On the Pragmatic, the Ethical, and the Moral Employments of Practical Reason," in *Justification and Application*, trans. Ciaran Cronin (Cambridge, Mass.: MIT Press, 1993), pp. 12–14.

[41] Weithman, *Religion and the Obligations of Citizenship*, p. 121 (my emphasis).

[42] Audi and Wolterstorff, *Religion in the Public Square*, pp. 117f.

However, by opening parliaments to conflicts over religious certainties, governmental authority can become the agent of a religious majority that imposes its will in violation of the democratic procedure.

Of course, it is not the majority vote itself, assuming that it has been correctly carried out, that is illegitimate, but the violation of the other essential components of the procedure, namely, the discursive character of the preceding deliberations. What is illegitimate is the violation of the principle of the neutrality of the exercise of political power which holds that all coercively enforceable political decisions must be *formulated* and be *justifiable* in a language that is equally intelligible to all citizens. Majority rule mutates into repression if the majority deploys religious arguments in the process of political opinion- and will-formation and refuses to offer publicly accessible justifications that the outvoted minority, be it secular or of a different faith, can follow and evaluate in the light of shared standards. The democratic procedure owes its power to generate legitimacy to its deliberative character in addition to the fact that it includes all participants; for the justified presumption of rational outcomes rests on this in the long run.

Wolterstorff pre-empts this objection by rejecting the whole idea of legitimation based on a reasonable background consensus on constitutional essentials. In the liberal view, political power sheds its inherently violent character by virtue of its binding legal connection to the exercise of power in accordance with principles capable of meeting with universal agreement.[43] Wolterstorff raises empirical objections to this conception. He ridicules the idealizing assumptions inscribed in the practices of the constitutional state as the "Quaker meeting ideal" (though the Quaker principle of unanimity is not typical of the democratic process). He maintains that the conflict between conceptions of justice grounded in competing religions or worldviews can never be resolved by the common assumption of a background consensus, however formal.

---

[43] Rawls, *Political Liberalism*, p. 137: "Our exercise of political power is fully proper only when it is exercised in accordance with a constitution the essentials of which all citizens as free and equal may reasonably be expected to endorse in the light of principles and ideals acceptable to their common human reason."

Although he wants to retain the majority principle from the liberal constitutional consensus, Wolterstorff can conceive of coexistence in an ideologically divided society based on majority decisions only as a reluctant adaptation to a kind of *modus vivendi*: "I do not agree, I *acquiesce* – unless I find the decision truly appalling."[44]

It remains unclear on this premise why the political community should not be in constant danger of disintegrating into religious conflicts. To be sure, the standard empiricist reading of liberal democracy has always construed majority decisions as the temporary subjection of a minority to the *de facto* power of the numerically superior party.[45] But according to this theory the acceptance of the voting procedure is explained by the willingness to compromise of parties who at any rate agree in their preference for the largest possible share of basic goods, such as money, security, or leisure time. The parties can reach compromises because they all aspire to the *same* categories of divisible goods. Yet precisely this condition is no longer met as soon as the conflicts are no longer triggered by agreed-upon basic goods, but by competing "goods of salvation." Conflicts over existential values between communities of faith cannot be resolved by compromise. They can only be alleviated by being depoliticized against the background of a jointly assumed consensus on constitutional principles.

(5) The competition between worldviews and religious doctrines that claim to explain human beings' position in the world as a whole cannot be resolved at the cognitive level. As soon as these cognitive dissonances penetrate the foundations of the normative regulation of the social interactions of citizens, the political community fragments into irreconcilable religious and ideological segments based on a precarious *modus vivendi*. In the absence of the uniting bond of a legally unenforceable civic solidarity, citizens do not regard themselves as free and equal participants in the shared practices of democratic opinion- and will-formation in

---

[44] Audi and Wolterstorff, *Religion in the Public Square*, p. 160.
[45] In the tradition of Hayek and Popper, see, for example, Werner Becker, *Die Freiheit, die wir meinen* (Munich: Piper, 1986).

which they *owe* one another *reasons* for their political stances. This reciprocity of expectations among citizens is what sets a liberal polity integrated by a constitution apart from a community segmented along the divisions between competing worldviews. Such a community frees religious and secular citizens in their dealings with one another from the reciprocal obligation to justify themselves in political controversies *toward one another*. Since here the dissonant background beliefs and subcultural bonds out-trump the supposed constitutional consensus and the expected civic solidarity, citizens need not adapt to or become involved with *one another* as second persons in deep conflicts.

Foregoing reciprocity and mutual indifference seems to be justi-fied by the fact that the liberal state contradicts itself if it demands that all citizens conform to a political ethos that imposes unequal cognitive burdens on them. The translation proviso for religious reasons and the institutional precedence of secular over religious reasons demand that religious citizens make an effort to learn and adapt that secular citizens are spared. This would, at any rate, concur with the empirical observation that a certain resentment has long persisted also within the churches toward the secular state. The duty to make public use of one's reason can be fulfilled only under certain cognitive preconditions. However, such epis-temic attitudes are an expression of an already existing mentality and cannot be made the content of normative expectations and political appeals to virtue, as motives can. Every "ought" presupposes a "can." The normative expectations associated with democratic citizenship remain ineffectual unless a corresponding change in mentality has taken place; otherwise they only serve to kindle resentment on the part of those who feel harried and misunderstood.

By contrast, Western culture has witnessed a transformation of religious consciousness since the Reformation and the Enlighten-ment. Sociologists describe this "modernization" of religious con-sciousness as a response of religious traditions to the challenges posed by the fact of religious pluralism, the emergence of modern science, and the spread of positive law and secular morality. In these three respects, traditional communities of faith must process cognitive dissonances that either do not arise for secular citizens, or arise only insofar as they adhere to doctrines anchored in simi-larly dogmatic ways:

- Religious citizens must develop an epistemic stance toward other religions and worldviews that they encounter within a universe of discourse hitherto occupied only by their own religion. They succeed in this to the extent that they relate their religious beliefs in a self-reflexive manner to the claims of competing doctrines of salvation so that they do not jeopardize their own exclusive claim to truth.
- Furthermore, religious citizens must develop an epistemic stance toward the internal logic of secular knowledge and toward the institutionalized monopoly on knowledge of modern scientific experts. They can succeed in this only to the extent that they conceive the relationship between dogmatic beliefs and secular knowledge from their religious viewpoint in such a way that the autonomous progress of secular knowledge cannot conflict with articles of faith.
- Finally, religious citizens must develop an epistemic stance toward the priority that secular reasons also enjoy in the political arena. This can succeed only to the extent that they embed the egalitarian individualism of modern natural law and universalistic morality in a convincing way in the context of their comprehensive doctrines.

This arduous work of hermeneutic self-reflection must be undertaken from within the perspective of religious traditions. In our culture, it has been accomplished in essence by theology and, on the Catholic side, also by an apologetic philosophy of religion that seeks to explicate the reasonableness of faith.[46]

---

[46] I am indebted to correspondence with Thomas M. Schmidt for the characterization of a non-agnostic philosophy of religion devoted to the self-enlightenment of religion that, unlike theology, does not speak "in the name of" a particular revealed religion, yet does not merely speak as "its observer" either. See also Matthias Lutz-Bachmann, "Religion-Philosophie-Religionsphilosophie," in Matthias Jung et al. (eds), *Religionsphilosophie* (Würzburg: Echter, 2000), pp. 19–26. Friedrich Schleiermacher played an exemplary role on the Protestant side. He made a careful distinction between the role of the theologian and that of the apologetic philosopher of religion (who draws on Kant's transcendental idealism rather than on the Thomist tradition) and united both in his own person. See the introduction to his explication of the Christian doctrine in Schleiermacher, *The Christian Faith*, trans. H. P. Mackintosh and J. S. Stewart (Edinburgh: T. & T. Clark, 1999), §§1–10.

Yet in the final instance it is the faith and practice of the religious community that decide whether a dogmatic processing of the cognitive challenges of modernity has been "successful" or not; only then can believers accept it as a "learning process." The new epistemic attitudes can be described as "acquired by learning" only if they result from a reconstruction of articles of faith that is convincing for people of faith, in the light of modern conditions of life to which there are no longer any alternatives. If those attitudes were merely the contingent result of conditioning or forced adaptation, then the question of how those cognitive preconditions for the reasonableness of a liberal civic ethos are met would have to be answered à la Foucault – namely, as a result of the kind of "discursive power" that imposes itself in the apparent transparency of enlightened knowledge. Of course, this answer would contradict the normative self-understanding of the constitutional state.

Within this liberal framework, what interests me is the open question of whether the revised concept of citizenship that I have proposed still imposes an *asymmetrical* burden on religious traditions and religious communities. Historically speaking, religious citizens had to learn to adopt epistemic attitudes toward their secular environment that come easily to enlightened secular citizens, since the latter are spared similar cognitive dissonances from the outset. However, the latter are not spared a cognitive burden either, for something more than a secularist attitude is called for by cooperation with religious fellow-citizens. This cognitive adaptation should not be confused with the political virtue of mere tolerance. What is at stake is not a respectful sensibility for the possible existential significance of religion for some other person, something also expected of secular citizens, but a self-reflexive overcoming of a rigid and exclusive secularist self-understanding of modernity.

As long as secular citizens are convinced that religious traditions and religious communities are, as it were, archaic relics of premodern societies persisting into the present, they can understand freedom of religion only as the cultural equivalent of the conservation of species threatened with extinction. Religion no longer has any intrinsic justification in their eyes. Even the principle of the separation of church and state can have for them only the laicist meaning of benign indifference. In the secularist reading, it can be anticipated that religious views will ultimately dissolve in the acid of scientific criticism and that religious communities will not be able to withstand the pressures of advancing cultural and social modernization. Clearly, citizens who adopt such an epistemic stance toward religion can no longer be expected to take religious contributions to contentious political issues seriously or to participate in a cooperative search for truth to determine whether they may contain elements that can be expressed in a secular language and be justified by rational arguments.

On the normative premises of the constitutional state and of a democratic civic ethos, the admission of religious assertions into the political arena only makes sense if *all* citizens can be reasonably expected not to exclude the possibility that these contributions may have cognitive substance – while at the same time respecting the priority of secular reasons and the institutional translation proviso. This is what the religious citizens assume in any case. Yet such an attitude presupposes a mentality on the part of secular citizens that is far from a matter of course in the secularized societies of the West. On the contrary, the recognition by secular citizens that they live in a postsecular society that is also *epistemically attuned* to the continued existence of religious communities is a consequence of a change in mentality that is no less cognitively exacting than the adaptation of religious consciousness to the challenges of an environment that is becoming progressively more secular. In line with the standards of an enlightenment endowed with a critical awareness of its own limits, the secular citizens understand their non-agreement with religious conceptions as a *disagreement* that it is *reasonable* to expect.

Without this cognitive presupposition, citizens cannot be reasonably expected to make a public use of their reason, at least not in the sense that secular citizens are willing to enter into a political discussion of the content of religious contributions with the intention of translating potentially morally convincing intuitions and reasons into a generally accessible language. This presupposes an epistemic mindset that is the result of a self-critical assessment of the limits of secular reason.[47] However, this cognitive precondition implies that it is reasonable to expect the version of an ethics of citizenship I have proposed of all citizens equally only if both religious and secular citizens have already undergone *complementary* learning processes.

(6) The critical overcoming of the to my mind narrow secularist mindset is itself, of course, essentially contested – at least as much as the theological responses to the cognitive challenges of modernity that have become influential since the Reformation (not merely among Protestants). Whereas we regard the "modernization of religious consciousness" as a matter for theology and can already describe it with historical hindsight, the naturalistic background of secularism is the focus of a continuing, open-ended philosophical debate. The secular awareness that we live in a postsecular society finds philosophical expression in postmetaphysical thinking. This mode of thought is not exhausted by emphasizing the finiteness of reason or by the combination of fallibilism with anti-skeptical conceptions of truth that has marked the self-understanding of modern empirical science since Kant and Peirce. The secular counterpart to reflexive religious consciousness is an agnostic, but nonreductionist form of postmetaphysical thinking. It refrains, on the one hand, from passing judgment on religious truths, while insisting (in a nonpolemical fashion) on making a strict demarcation between faith and knowledge. On the other hand, it rejects a scientistically truncated conception of reason and the exclusion of religious doctrines from the genealogy of reason.

Postmetaphysical thinking refrains from making ontological pronouncements on the constitution of being as such; however, this does not imply a reduction of our knowledge to the sum total of statements that represent the current "state of science." Scientism often misleads us into blurring the boundary between natural scientific knowledge which is relevant for understanding

---

[47] In his masterful study of the history of the notion of tolerance, Rainer Forst credits Pierre Bayle with being the "greatest thinker on tolerance" because Bayle provides such an exemplary reflexive self-limitation of reason in relation to religion. On Bayle, see Forst, *Toleranz im Konflikt*, §18, and, for the systematic argument, §§29 and 33.

ourselves and our place in nature as a whole, on the one hand, and a synthetic naturalistic worldview constructed on this basis, on the other.[48] This form of radical naturalism devalues all types of statements that cannot be traced back to empirical observations, statements of laws, or causal explanations, hence moral, legal, and evaluative statements no less than religious ones. As the revived discussion of freedom and determinism shows, advances in biogenetics, brain research, and robotics provide stimuli for a kind of naturalization of the human mind that places our practical self-understanding as responsibly acting persons in question[49] and preempts calls for a revision of criminal law.[50] However, the permeation of everyday life by a naturalistic self-objectification of speaking and acting subjects is incompatible with any conception of political integration that imputes a *normative* background consensus to citizens.

One route by which a multidimensional reason that is not exclusively fixated on its reference to the objective world can achieve a self-critical awareness of its boundaries is through a reconstruction of its own genesis that enables it to catch up with itself, as it were, and to overcome fixations. In the process, post-metaphysical thinking does not restrict itself to the heritage of Western metaphysics but also reconfirms its internal relationship to those world religions whose origins, like those of ancient philosophy, date back to the middle of the first millennium before Christ, i.e. to what Jaspers called the "Axial Age."[51] For the

---

[48] Wolterstorff alerts us in a general way to this in practice all-too-frequently blurred distinction between secular statements and reasons that should count, and secular worldviews that should count just as little as religious doctrines. See Audi and Wolterstorff, *Religion in the Public Square*, p. 105: "Much if not most of the time we will be able to spot religious reasons from a mile away . . . Typically, however, comprehensive secular perspectives will go undetected."

[49] Christian Geyer (ed.), *Hirnforschung und Willensfreiheit* (Frankfurt am Main: Suhrkamp, 2004); Michael Pauen, *Illusion Freiheit?* (Frankfurt am Main: Fischer, 2004).

[50] Hubert Rottleuthner, "Zur Soziologie und Neurobiologie richterlichen Handelns," in Reinhard Damm et al. (eds), *Festschrift für Thomas Raiser* (Berlin: de Gruyter, 2005), pp. 579–98.

[51] See the research program pursued since the 1970s by Samuel N. Eisenstadt, most recently in Johan P. Arnason et al. (eds), *Axial Civilizations and World History* (Leiden and Boston: Brill, 2005).

religions that have their roots in this period made the cognitive leap from mythical narratives to a logos that differentiates between essence and appearance in a very similar way to Greek philosophy. Since the Council of Nicaea, philosophy also took on board and assimilated many motifs and concepts, especially those associated with salvation, from monotheistic traditions in the course of a Hellenization of Christianity.[52]

The complex web of inheritance cannot be disentangled solely along the lines of a history of being, as Heidegger claimed.[53] Greek concepts such as "autonomy" and "individuality," or Roman concepts such as "emancipation" and "solidarity," have long since been invested with meanings of Judeo-Christian origin.[54] Philosophy has repeatedly learned through its encounters with religious traditions – and also, of course, with Muslim traditions – that it receives innovative impulses when it succeeds in freeing cognitive contents from their dogmatic encapsulation in the crucible of rational discourse. Kant and Hegel are the most influential examples of this. The encounters of many twentieth-century philosophers with a religious writer such as Kierkegaard, who thinks in postmetaphysical, but not post-Christian, terms, are also exemplary in this regard.

Religious traditions appear to have remained present in an even more vital sense than metaphysics, even if they at times present themselves as the opaque other of reason. It would be unreasonable to reject out of hand the idea that the major world religions – as the only surviving element of the now alien cultures of the Ancient Empires – can claim a place within the differentiated architecture of modernity because their cognitive substance has not yet been exhausted. At any rate, we cannot exclude that they involve semantic potentials capable of exercising an inspirational force on society *as a whole* as soon as they divulge their profane truth contents.

---

[52] M. Lutz-Bachmann, "Hellenisierung des Christentum?" in Carsten Colpe et al., *Spätantike und Christentum* (Berlin: Akademie, 1992), pp. 77–98.
[53] See the sketches of a history of Being in Heidegger, *Contributions to Philosophy: From Enowning* (Bloomington: Indiana University Press, 1999).
[54] See the interesting discussions in Hauke Brunkhorst, *Solidarität* (Frankfurt am Main: Suhrkamp, 2002), pp. 40–78.

In short, postmetaphysical thinking is prepared to learn from religion while at the same time remaining agnostic. It insists on the difference between the certainties of faith and publicly criticizable validity claims; but it eschews the rationalist presumption that it can itself decide which aspects of religious doctrines are rational and which irrational. The contents that reason appropriates through translation must not be lost for faith. However, providing an apology for faith employing philosophical means is not a task for philosophy proper. At best, philosophy *circumscribes* the opaque core of religious experience when it reflects on the specific character of religious language and on the intrinsic meaning of faith. This core remains as profoundly alien to discursive thought as the hermetic core of aesthetic experience, which likewise can be at best circumscribed, but not penetrated, by philosophical reflection.

I have discussed this ambivalent attitude of postmetaphysical thinking to religion because it also expresses the cognitive presupposition for the willingness to cooperate of secular citizens. This ambivalent attitude to religion corresponds exactly to the epistemic attitude that secular citizens must adopt if they are to be prepared to learn something from the contributions of their religious counterparts to public debates which are potentially translatable into a generally accessible language. The philosophical recapitulation of the genealogy of reason clearly plays a similar role for a self-reflection of secularism as the reconstructive work of theology plays for the self-reflection of religious faith in the modern world. The effort of philosophical reconstruction required shows that the role of democratic citizenship assumes a mentality on the part of secular citizens that is no less demanding than the corresponding mentality of their religious counterparts. This is why the cognitive burdens imposed on both sides by the acquisition of the appropriate epistemic attitudes are not at all asymmetrical.

(7) The fact that the "public use of reason" (in the proposed interpretation) depends on cognitive preconditions that are far from trivial has interesting but ambivalent implications. It reminds us, first, that constitutional democracy, which relies on a deliberative form of politics, is an epistemically demanding,

"truth sensitive" form of government.[55] A "post-truth democracy," which the *New York Times* declared to be in the ascendant during the last US presidential election, would no longer be a democracy. Moreover, the requirement of complex mentalities highlights an improbable functional imperative whose fulfillment the liberal state can scarcely influence through the legal and administrative means at its disposal. The polarization of a community into fundamentalist and secular camps demonstrates, for example, that political integration is jeopardized if too many citizens fail to live up to the standards of the public use of reason. However, mentalities are prepolitical in origin. They change incrementally and in unpredictable ways in response to social changes. A long-term process of this kind can at best be accelerated in the medium of public discourses conducted by the citizens themselves. Yet is this a cognitively steered process at all, one that may be described as a learning process?

A third implication is the most disquieting of all. We have assumed thus far that the citizens of a constitutional state can acquire the functionally requisite mentalities via "complementary learning processes." The examples cited show that this assumption is not unproblematic. From what perspective may we claim that the fragmentation caused by a collision of fundamentalist and secularist convictions is the result of "learning deficits"? Let us recall the change in perspective that we made when we moved from a normative explanation of a democratic civic ethos to an epistemological investigation of the cognitive preconditions under which such an ethos can be reasonably expected of citizens. A change in epistemic attitudes must occur if religious consciousness is to become reflexive and if the secularist mindset is to overcome its limitations. But these changes in mentality count as complementary "learning processes" only from the perspective of a specific normative self-understanding of modernity.

This view can certainly be defended within the framework of an evolutionary social theory. But even setting aside the controversial status of such theories within their own academic disciplines, from the viewpoint of normative political theory citizens

---

[55] See Julian Nida-Rümelin's Munich inaugural lecture, "Demokratie und Wahrheit" (MS, 2004).

can by no means be enjoined to describe themselves, for example, in terms of a theory of religious evolution and possibly to rate themselves as cognitively "backward." Only those concerned and their religious organizations can decide whether a "modernized" faith is still the "true" faith. And whether or not, on the other side, a scientist form of secularism will ultimately win out over the more comprehensive concept of reason underlying postmetaphysical thinking is, for the time being, an open question even among philosophers themselves. However, if political theory must leave open the question of whether the functionally requisite mentalities can be acquired through learning processes at all, then it must also accept that its normatively justified concept of "the public use of reason" remains "essentially contested" among citizens themselves. For the liberal state may only impose duties on its citizens that the latter can perceive as *reasonable* expectations, which presupposes in turn that they can acquire the necessary epistemic attitudes through insight, i.e. through "learning."

We must not be misled into drawing the wrong conclusions from this self-limitation of political theory. As philosophers and as citizens, we may well be convinced that a strong reading of the liberal and republican foundations of the constitutional state should *and can* be successfully defended both *intra muros* and in the political arena. However, this discourse concerning the correct understanding, and the correctness *tout court*, of a liberal constitution and a democratic civic ethos extends into a terrain where normative arguments do not go far enough. The controversy also extends to the epistemological question of the relationship between faith and knowledge, which itself impinges upon key elements of the background understanding of modernity. Interestingly enough, both the philosophical and the theological efforts to define the relationship between faith and knowledge in a self-reflexive manner throw up far-reaching questions concerning the genealogy of modernity.

Let us return to Rawls's question: "How is it possible for those of faith, as well as the nonreligious, to endorse a secular regime even when their comprehensive doctrines may not prosper under it, and indeed may decline?"[56] This question cannot ultimately be

---

[56] See note 20.

answered in terms of the normative explanations of political theory. Let us take the example of "radical orthodoxy," which takes up the intentions and basic ideas of the political theology of a Carl Schmitt and develops them further with the tools of deconstruction.[57] Theologians of this ilk dispute the validity of the modern age[58] with the aim of ontologically re-embedding a nominalistically uprooted modern world in the "reality of God." Controversies with such opponents must be conducted within the proper disciplinary terrain. This means that theological claims can only be met with theological counterarguments, historical and epistemological claims with historical and epistemological counterarguments.[59]

The same holds true for the opposite side. Rawls's question is addressed equally to the religious and the secular side. A debate on basic philosophical issues becomes especially urgent when a naturalistic worldview oversteps the boundaries of its scientific competence. The public demand that religious communities should at long last renounce traditional statements concerning the existence of God and a life after death cannot be deduced from recent neurological insights into the dependence of all mental operations on brain processes – at least not until we have achieved philosophical clarity concerning the pragmatic meaning of such biblical statements and their historical context of transmission.[60] The problem of how scientific claims relate to religious convictions impinges, in turn, upon the genealogy of modernity's understanding of itself. Is the practice of modern science fully understandable in its own terms? Does it provide the performative yardstick of all truth and falsehood? Or should it rather be

---

[57] John Milbank, *Theology and Social Theory: Beyond Secular Reason* (Oxford: Blackwell, 1991); Milbank et al. (eds), *Radical Orthodoxy: A New Theology* (London and New York: Routledge, 1999).

[58] For the contrary position, see the early work of Hans Blumenberg, *The Legitimacy of the Modern Age* (Cambridge, Mass.: MIT Press, 1983).

[59] Schmidt, "Postsäkulare Theologie des Rechts: Eine Kritik der radikalen Orthodoxie," in Martin Frühauf and Werner Löser (eds), *Biblische Aufklärung: Die Entdeckung der Tradition* (Frankfurt am Main: Alber, 2005), pp. 91–108.

[60] See the final comment by W. Detel in his wonderfully informed article "Forschungen über Hirn und Geist," *Deutsche Zeitschrift für Philosophie* 52 (2004): 891–920.

understood as the outcome of a history of reason of which the world religions are an integral part?

Rawls developed his "Theory of Justice" into a "Political Liberalism" because of his growing recognition of the relevance of the "fact of pluralism." He deserves the immense credit of having addressed the political role of religion at an early date. Yet these very phenomena can trigger an awareness of the limits of normative arguments in a supposedly "free-standing" political theory. For whether the liberal response to religious pluralism can be accepted by the citizens themselves as the single right answer depends not least on whether secular and religious citizens, from their respective points of view, are prepared to accept an interpretation of the relationship between faith and knowledge that first makes it possible for them to treat one another in a self-reflexive manner in the political arena.

Part III
Naturalism and Religion

6

Freedom and Determinism[1]

Free will is currently the subject of a lively debate in Germany that has even found its way into the national daily press.[2] It is almost as if one had been transported back into the nineteenth century. For the results of brain research, now with the support of imaging technology, are lending renewed currency to a venerable philosophical debate. Neurologists and cognitive scientists are arguing with philosophers and others in the humanities over the determinist view that a causally self-contained world leaves no room for freedom of choice between alternative actions. The current controversy stems from the results of a research tradition that goes back to the experiments conducted by Benjamin Libet in the 1970s.[3]

The findings seem to support reductionist research strategies that try to explain mental events *exclusively* in terms of observable physiological determinants.[4] These approaches assume that the

---

[1] This text formed the basis of a lecture delivered on receiving the Kyoto prize in 2004, the fourth time it was conferred – following Karl Popper, Willard van Orman Quine, and Paul Ricoeur – on a philosopher.
[2] Once again I would like to thank Lutz Wingert, who is more at home in this discussion than I am, for detailed advice that has advanced my thinking on these matters, and Tilman Habermas for helpful suggestions for improvements.
[3] Christian Geyer (ed.), *Hirnforschung und Willensfreiheit: Zur Deutung der neuesten Experimente* (Frankfurt am Main: Suhrkamp, 2004).
[4] Gerhard Roth, "Worüber dürfen Hirnforscher reden – und in welcher Weise?" *Deutsche Zeitschrift für Philosophie* 52 (2004): 223–34, here p. 231.

awareness of freedom that agents attribute to themselves rests on self-deception. The experience of making one's own decisions represents, as it were, a superfluous wheel that does no work. Hence freedom of the will understood as "mental causation" is an illusion that conceals an exclusively causal chain of neural states linked according to natural laws.[5]

However, this determinism is incompatible with the ordinary self-understanding of acting subjects. In everyday life, we cannot avoid provisionally attributing *responsible authorship* for our actions to one another. The prospect of our actions being explained scientifically by means of natural laws cannot seriously challenge our intuitively anchored understanding of ourselves as accountable agents that is confirmed by practice. The objectivating language of neurobiology attributes the grammatical role formerly played by the "I" to the "brain" but in so doing it fails to connect up with the language of folk psychology. The provocation involved in asserting that it is "the brain" and not my "self" that thinks and acts is assuredly merely a grammatical matter; but this is how the lifeworld successfully shields itself against cognitive dissonances.

Of course, this would not be the first time that a scientific theory clashed with common sense. It would unavoidably affect folk psychology at the latest when the technical applications of theoretical knowledge permeated everyday practice, for example with the adoption of therapeutic techniques. Future techniques through which the results of neurobiological research intervened in the lifeworld could acquire the ability to transform consciousness which this knowledge itself lacks. But is determinism a scientifically founded thesis, or is it merely a component of a naturalistic worldview based on a speculative interpretation of scientific knowledge? I would like to continue the debate over freedom and determinism as a dispute concerning the *right way* to naturalize the mind.

On the one hand, we want to do justice to the intuitive self-evidence of a sense of freedom that performatively accompanies every intentional action; on the other hand, we want to satisfy the

---

[5] Whether or not natural laws are interpreted probabilistically is immaterial for determinism, since free choice [*Willkür*] cannot be reduced to chance [*Zufall*].

need for a coherent picture of the universe that includes humans as part of nature. Kant was able to reconcile "causality through freedom" with natural causality only by adopting a dualism of the intelligible and phenomenal realms. Nowadays we would like to dispense with such metaphysical background assumptions. But then we have to reconcile what we learned from Kant about the transcendental conditions of knowledge with what Darwin has taught us about natural evolution.

I will begin by showing in a critical section of the chapter that the reductionist research programs can avoid the problems posed by the dualism of explanatory perspectives and language games only by embracing epiphenomenalism. In the second, constructive, part of the chapter I will recall the anthropological roots of this perspectival dualism, which is itself compatible with a monistic view of natural evolution. The more complex picture of the interaction between a brain that determines the mind and a mind that programs the brain is the product of philosophical reflection and is not itself a piece of natural scientific knowledge. I advocate a nonscientistic or "soft" naturalism. On this conception, just those states of affairs are "real" that can be represented in true statements. But reality is not exhausted by the totality of scientific statements that count as true according to current empirical scientific standards.

I For and Against Reductionism

Beginning with a critique of the design and import of Libet's experiments, I would first like to introduce a phenomenologically adequate concept of freedom of action (1). Analytic theory of action points to a nondeterministic concept of conditioned freedom and a conception of responsible agency. In contrast to causal explanations, both call for rational explanation of action (2 and 3). Reductionism tries to evade the epistemic cleavage between complementary explanatory perspectives and forms of knowledge. The difficulties generated by this research strategy inspire the question to be explored in the second part of the chapter, namely, whether the dualism of epistemic perspectives that at once structures and limits our access to the world could have been a result of the natural development of cultural forms of life itself (4).

(1) Benjamin Libet instructed his experimental subjects to make a particular spontaneous arm movement and to report the point at which the decision was made, during which time he observed their neurological processes. As expected, the decision precedes the bodily movement. The crucial issue, however, is the time interval between the occurrence of unconscious processes observed in the primary and associative regions of the cerebral cortex, on the one hand, and the conscious act experienced by the experimental subject as her own decision, on the other.[6] In the brain, an action-specific "readiness potential" appears to form *before* the person herself "decides" to act. This finding regarding the temporal sequence of neural processes and subjective experiences seems to prove that brain processes determine conscious actions without any causal role being played by the act of will that the agent ascribes to herself. Moreover, psychological experiments confirm the experience that under certain conditions agents perform actions to which they only subsequently ascribe intentions of their own.

However, the Libet experiments can hardly bear the entire burden of proof ascribed to them in defending the thesis of determinism. The overt experimental design was geared to arbitrary bodily movements that allowed the actors just a fraction of a second between the intention and the execution of the action. Hence we must ask whether the test results can be generalized beyond these classes of actions. Even an interpretation that is careful in this respect is open to the further objection that the meaning of the observed sequences remains unclear. The design seems to leave open the possibility that the experimental subjects, who were informed about the course of the experiment, had already concentrated on the plan of action before making the decision to perform a specific action. But then the observed

---

[6] For the experimental setup and later control experiments, see Gerhard Roth, *Fühlen, Denken, Handeln* (Frankfurt am Main: Suhrkamp, 2003), pp. 518–28; Benjamin Libet, *Mind Time: The Temporal Factor in Consciousness* (Cambridge, Mass.: Harvard University Press, 2004).

neurological buildup of the readiness potential would merely reflect the planning stage. Finally, an even more serious problem is the objection in principle against artificially producing abstract decision situations. As with any experimental design, we must ask what is being measured – quite apart from the prior philosophical question as to what *ought* to be measured in the first place.

Normally, conscious actions are the result of a complex chain of intentions and deliberations that weigh up ends and alternative means in light of opportunities, resources, and obstacles. An experimental design that condenses the planning, decision, and execution of a bodily movement into a brief moment and abstracts from justified alternatives can only register artifacts that lack what implicitly makes an action into a free action in the first place, namely, the internal connection to reasons. To treat Buridan's ass as the epitome of the freedom to act in one way rather than another is a misunderstanding. The "bare" decision to extend one's left or right arm is by no means a manifestation of freedom of action as long as a relation to reasons is lacking, for example, to reasons such as those that can motivate a cyclist to make a right or a left turn. Only such deliberations open up the realm of freedom, "for it is part of the very meaning of deliberation that we can act one way or another."[7]

Once reasons for or against an action come into play, we must assume that the conclusion that we first wish to arrive at as a result of weighing reasons is not fixed from the outset.[8] Were the question as to how to decide not open to begin with, we would not need to engage in deliberation at all. A will is formed, however imperceptibly, *in the course of* deliberations. And because a decision *comes about* as the result of deliberations, however fleeting and unclear they may be, we experience ourselves as free only

---

[7] Ernst Tugendhat, "Der Begriff der Willensfreiheit," in his *Philosophische Aufsätze* (Frankfurt am Main: Suhrkamp, 1992), pp. 334–51, here, p. 340.

[8] The empiricist counterargument according to which deliberations are exhausted by their function in testing the "emotional tolerability" of the consequences of actions presupposes what it is supposed to demonstrate. See Roth, *Fühlen, Denken, Handeln*, pp. 526f.: "Regardless of the outcome of rational reflection, it is subject to the final decision (!) of the limbic system because it must be *emotionally acceptable* . . . Contrary to folk psychology, it is not logical arguments *as such* that impel us to act rationally."

in the actions that we perform to some degree consciously. Of course, there are different types of actions, for example, compulsive, habitual, chance, neurotic-compulsive actions, etc. But all consciously performed actions can be examined retrospectively as to their imputability. Other persons can always require a responsible agent to account for his intentional actions: "what an agent does do intentionally is what he is free to do *and* has adequate reasons for doing."[9] Only a reflective will is free.

Benjamin Libet also later reflected on the role of conscious deliberation and interpreted his experimental results in a way that casts doubt upon how they are generally understood.[10] He now ascribes the free will a controlling function in the phase between intention and execution in the case of unconsciously initiated actions insofar as the latter would foreseeably conflict with other – for example, normative – expectations. On this interpretation, the free will would be able to play at least the negative role of a veto against the conscious realization of an unconscious, but unjustified, practical disposition.

(2) Peter Bieri has proposed a phenomenologically convincing resolution of the confusions attending the concept of an "unconditioned" and "originary" will.[11] If an act of "free decision" implies that the actor "binds" her will "through reasons," then the openness of the decision does not preclude its being *rationally* conditioned. The actor is free when she wills what she on deliberation takes to be correct. We experience as unfreedom only externally imposed constraints that force us to act otherwise than we, on reflection, want to act. The result is a conception of conditioned freedom that does equal justice to both aspects of a conditioned freedom.

On the one hand, the actor will not reach a conclusive practical judgment concerning how to act without weighing alternative

[9] Donald Davidson, "Freedom to Act," in Davidson, *Essays on Actions and Events* (Oxford: Clarendon Press, 1980), pp. 63–81, here p. 74.
[10] Libet, "Do We Have Free Will?" in Benjamin Libet, Anthony Freeman, and Keith Sutherland (eds), *The Volitional Brain: Toward a Neuroscience of Free Will* (Thorverton: Imprint Academic, 2000), pp. 47–58.
[11] Peter Bieri, *Das Handwerk der Freiheit: Über die Entdeckung des eigenen Willens* (Munich: Hanser, 2001).

courses of action. Granted, these alternatives present themselves within a field of possibilities that is limited by her capabilities, character, and circumstances. But in view of the alternatives to be weighed, the actor must believe that she is capable of acting in one way rather than another. This is because, for the reflective actor, her capabilities, her character, and the circumstances transform themselves into as many reasons for what she, within a given context, is "herself" capable of doing. In this sense, she is not *unconditionally* free to act one way or another. In the course of her reflections, the actor reaches a rationally motivated position that is not arbitrary because it is not unwarranted. Insights do not arise arbitrarily but are the result of a rule-governed process. Had the agent who reached a decision judged differently, she would have willed something else.

On the other hand, the motivating role of reasons cannot be understood on the model of an observable event being caused by a prior state of affairs. The judging process *empowers* the agent as the author of a decision. The agent would feel disempowered, i.e. robbed of initiative, by a causally explicable natural process. That is why it is not simply a grammatical error to say that, if the actor had judged differently, she would have "had to" will differently. The forceless force of the better argument that motivates us to take a "yes" or "no" position must be distinguished from the causal constraint of an imposed restriction that compels us to perform actions that we do not want to perform: "If we experience a failure of agency, then it is because we fail to influence our willing and doing as thinking and judging subjects. Freedom in this sense is not only *compatible* with conditionality . . . ; it *requires* conditionality and would be unthinkable without it."[12]

We can explain what it means to be rationally motivated by reasons only from the perspective of a participant in the public process of "giving and asking for reasons" (Robert Brandom). That is why an observer has to describe the discursive events in mentalistic language, that is, in a language that includes predicates such as "believes," "convinces," "approves," and "rejects." In an empiricist language, she would have to eliminate – for grammatical reasons – any reference to the propositional attitudes of

[12] Ibid., p. 166.

subjects who take things to be true or false. From this perspective, a discursive event is transformed into a natural event that takes place "behind the backs" of subjects.

Peter Bieri attempts to reconcile the concept of conditioned freedom with determinism concerning the course of nature: "Reflection on the alternatives is on the whole an occurrence that will ultimately bind me and my history to a specific will."[13] But his further statement "I know that and it doesn't bother me" suggests that something is wrong here. The conditioned character of my decision does not bother me as long as I can understand this "occurrence" retrospectively as an unfolding process of reflection (however implicit) in which I *take part* as a participant in discourse or as a subject reflecting *in foro interno*. For in that case I make the decision based on *my own* understanding. However, it would certainly bother me if my decision were determined by a neural event in which I was no longer involved as a person who takes a position; for then it would no longer be *my* decision. Only the *unnoticed* switch from the participant to the observer perspective can create the impression that the motivating of action by intelligible reasons forms a bridge to the determination of action by observable causes.

The correct concept of conditioned freedom does not lend support to the overhasty ontological monism that declares that reasons and causes are two aspects of a single phenomenon. On this conception, reasons represent the subjective side – the "experiential form" – of neurologically observable processes. "Complex chains of neurophysiological events" are supposedly mirrored in the logical-semantic links between propositional contents and attitudes: "Reasons would accordingly be the 'inner,' lived aspect, causes the 'external' neurophysiological aspect of an inclusive third that evidently unfolds in a deterministic manner but remains fundamentally inaccessible to us."[14] This naturalistic interpretation mistakenly appeals to Donald Davidson's "causal theory of action," which holds that desires, attitudes, intentions, convictions, and value orientations count as the causes of action when they are the reasons *from which* an agent performs this action.

---

[13] Ibid., pp. 287f.
[14] Roth, "Worüber dürfen Hirnforscher reden," p. 232.

Although Davidson himself rejects reductionism,[15] the conceptualization of reasons as causes has suggested an interpretation of freedom of action that promises to bridge the gap between mental and physical reality. But the theory cannot fulfill this promise. Admittedly, the exaggeratedly idealistic concept of an unconditioned spontaneous freedom that is supposed to have the power to give rise to new causal series can be refuted from the perspective of this theory of action. However, embedding freedom of action in a context of motivating reasons cannot obscure the difference between explanations of actions in terms of rational motives and explanations in terms of causes. The concept of conditioned freedom provides just as little support for the thesis that we can relate these explanations of action to each other like two sides of the same – *at present unknown* – coin.[16]

(3) In contrast to standard causal explanations, a rational explanation of an action does not specify *sufficient* conditions for the actual occurrence of an action-event. For the motivating power of reasons for action presupposes that under certain conditions they are "decisive" for the acting subject, that is, they are sufficient to "bind" the agent's will. Motivation by reasons requires not merely a rational, position-taking agent for whom reasons count, but one who *lets* herself be *determined* by her judgment. This reference to a subject who can also act against her better judgment

---

[15] See Davidson's reply to Richard Rorty in Lewis Edwin Hahn (ed.), *The Philosophy of Donald Davidson* (Chicago: Open Court, 1999), p. 599: "What I have chiefly emphasized is the irreducibility of our mental concepts. They are irreducible in two senses. First, they cannot be defined in the vocabularies of the natural sciences, nor are there empirical laws linking them with physical phenomena in such a way as to make them disposable. Second, they are not an optional part of our conceptual resources. They are just as important and indispensable as our common-sense means of talking and thinking about phenomena in non-psychological ways."

[16] Thomas Nagel develops this variant of ontological monism linked to aspect dualism in his program of providing an empirical scientific verification of an as yet merely postulated "third." This future theory is then supposed to provide the basis to which the two complementary physical and mental descriptions can be reduced along familiar lines. See "The Psychophysical Nexus," in Thomas Nagel, *Concealment and Exposure* (New York: Oxford University Press, 2002), pp. 194–235.

already shows why the statement that S performed action A for reason R is not equivalent to the statement that R caused the action A.[17] Unlike standard causal explanations, rational explanations of action do not permit the inference that any given person would reach the same decision given the same antecedent conditions. Specifying the rational motives for action is not sufficient to transform the explanation into a prediction. Responsible agency is not merely a matter of being motivated by reasons but of taking the initiative for specific reasons and attributing the initiative to oneself. That is what makes the agent the "author" of her actions.

The idea that it is "up to her" to act one way rather than another requires two things: she must be convinced that she is doing the right thing, but she must also do it *herself*. The spontaneity we experience in acting is not an anonymous source but rather a subject that attributes to herself the capability to act. Indeed, an agent can regard herself as the author of her actions because she has identified with her own body [*Körper*] and exists as a lived body [*Leib*] that enables and empowers her to perform actions. The agent can allow herself to be "determined" by an organic substrate that she experiences as her lived body without diminishing her freedom because she experiences her subjective nature as a source of capabilities. From the perspective of this bodily experience, the vegetative processes steered by the limbic system – like all of the other brain processes that neurological observers regard as "unconscious" – are transformed for the agent from causal determinants into *enabling* conditions. In this sense, freedom of action is not just "rationally conditioned" but is also "naturally conditioned" freedom. Since the body, as a lived body, "is" in each case one's own body, it determines what one can do: "Being determined is a constitutive support of self-determination."[18]

Something similar holds for the character that each of us develops in the course of his or her life. The author is in each case the

---

[17] On this argument, see John Searle, *Freiheit und Neurobiologie* (Frankfurt: Suhrkamp, 2004), pp. 28–36. [*Freedom and Neurobiology: Reflections on Free Will, Language, and Political Power* (New York: Columbia University Press, 2007).]

[18] Martin Seel, *Sich bestimmen lassen* (Frankfurt: Suhrkamp, 2002), p. 288.

unique person we have become or the irreplaceable individual that we understand ourselves to be. This is why our desires and preferences can count as good reasons. However, these first order reasons can be overridden by ethical reasons that concern our individual lives, and ethical reason can in turn be trumped by moral reasons. The latter result from obligations that we owe each other as persons.[19] Kant speaks of autonomy or of a free will only when the will lets itself be bound by reasons of this sort, that is, by insights grounded not just in the person and the enlightened interest of the individual, but in the common and equal interest of all persons. The privileging of moral action and of the categorical ought has lent support to an inflationary notion of a spontaneous, intelligible freedom that is "absolute" in the sense of being cut off from all empirical contexts.

The phenomenology of responsible agency, by contrast, has led us to a conception of conditioned freedom rooted in the organism and the biography of the individual. This conception is compatible neither with Descartes's doctrine of two substances nor with Kant's two-worlds theory. The methodological dualism of participant and observer explanatory perspectives must not be ontologized into a dualism of mind and nature.[20] Rational explanations of action also assume that actors are embedded in contexts and entangled in biographical involvements when they make decisions. Actors are not situated outside of the world when they let their will be determined by what is within their power and what they regard as right. They are dependent on enabling organic conditions, on their biography, character, and capabilities, on their social and cultural surroundings, and not least on the actual circumstances of the situation of action. But the actor makes all of these factors her own, as it were, so that they no longer operate on the formation of her will like external causes and disrupt her

---

[19] Thomas Scanlon, *What We Owe to Each Other* (Cambridge, Mass.: Harvard University Press, 1998).

[20] This is the alternative that Singer employs as a foil for his deterministic conception: "One possibility is that ontologically different worlds actually exist, one material and one immaterial, that human beings participate in both, and that we cannot imagine how the one relates to the other." Wolf Singer, "Selbsterfahrung und neurobiologische Fremdbeschreibung," *Deutsche Zeitschrift für Philosophie* 52 (2004): 235–56, here p. 239.

sense of freedom. The author identifies herself with her own organism, with the biography and culture that shape her behavior, and with her motives and capabilities. Moreover, the judging subject incorporates perceived circumstances into her deliberation insofar as these are relevant as constraints or opportunities.

Thus far our discussion has developed a strong, though not idealistic, conception of freedom of action that is first supposed to cast the relevant phenomenon in the proper light. This conception is linked with a concept of the rational explanation of actions that draws attention to an inescapable dualism between different explanatory perspectives and language games. Granted, this is an epistemic dualism only in a methodological, not an ontological sense. However, it is not yet clear how it can be squared with a monistic conception of the universe that would satisfy our need for a coherent picture of the world. The proponents of reductionistic approaches cast doubt upon the equal status of the two perspectives, with good reason. For reductionism has repeatedly demonstrated its superiority over common sense by appealing to counterintuitive knowledge. A subjectively experienced phenomenon such as heat has been traced back to the movement of molecules, and nobody objects to the physicalistic concepts in terms of which we analyze color differences and the pitches of sounds. Even with regard to the supposed interaction between the mind and the brain, research strategies that rely solely on hard causal explanations and relegate soft rational explanations to the realm of illusory folk psychology could prove to be on the right track.

(4) There is also a good biological argument for this. Along the path to empirical scientific realism, we have already overcome the selectivity of the perceptual domains to which our contingent organic equipment restricts us. Evolutionary epistemology emphasizes the functional relevance for the survival of the species of logical thinking and the constructive, theory-building processing of perceptions:

> Although our sense organs are wonderfully adapted to enable us to establish the conditions relevant for behavior from very little data, they do not accord much importance to completeness and objectivity. They do not provide faithful representations; instead,

they reconstruct, and in the process draw upon the foreknowledge stored in the brain . . . Brains use this foreknowledge to interpret sense impulses and incorporate them into larger contexts . . . These knowledge-based reconstructions can compensate in part for the imperfections of the sense organs. For knowledge can be used to fill gaps and logical inference can help to uncover inconsistencies . . . In addition, technical sensors can open up sources of information that are not accessible to our natural senses.[21]

This argument invokes the biological adaptive value of the collective learning of organized research.

But how does this privileging of the scientific enterprise, whose adherents are specially trained in the cooperative search for truth and in the weighing of reasons, cohere with the supposed illusory character of reasons and justifications? When we draw on the premises of the theory of evolution to explain the reproductive value of natural scientific research, we attribute to the latter an important causal role for the survival of the species. This conflicts with the neurobiological perspective which classifies this practice as an epiphenomenon just like any other justificatory practice. This epiphenomenalist conception is a necessary implication of the reductionistic research program. Reasons are not observable physical conditions that vary in accordance with natural laws; hence, they cannot be identified with standard causes. Because reasons resist rigorous causal explanation, they can at best play the role of mere accompanying commentaries on the unconscious, neurologically explicable behavior that rationalize it after the fact. We act, so to speak, "from" causes, even when we justify our action toward others "with the aid of" reasons.

Reductionism pays a high price for this. If reasons and the logical processing of reasons do not play any causal role from a neurobiological point of view, it becomes mysterious from the perspective of the theory of evolution why nature allows itself the luxury of a "space of reasons" (Wilfrid Sellars) at all. Reasons do not swim about like globules of fat on the soup of consciousness. On the contrary, judging and acting are always associated with good reasons for the subjects concerned. If the process of "giving and asking for reasons" had to be dismissed as an epiphenomenon,

[21] Ibid., p. 236.

there would not be much left of the biological functions of the self-understanding of subjects capable of speech and action. Why do we have to demand justifications from each other? What purpose is served by having a whole superstructure of agencies of socialization that drill into children causally superfluous habits of this sort?[22]

John Searle has stated the obvious objection to this kind of epiphenomenalism concerning conscious life: "The processes of conscious rationality are such an important part of our lives, and above all such a biologically expensive part of our lives, that it would be unlike anything we know in evolution if a phenotype of this magnitude played no functional role at all in the life and survival of the organism."[23] Gerhard Roth presumably has this objection in mind when he declares that the self-understanding of agents and, in particular, the freedom of action that the "virtual ego" ascribes to itself are an illusion, while at the same time warning against understanding ego-consciousness[24] and freedom of will[25] as mere epiphenomena.

This warning does not fit very well with Roth's own premises. An independent causal role for conscious life coheres with the reductionistic research program only on the assumption that one "conceives of mind and consciousness . . . as physical states" that "stand in reciprocal relations" with other physical states.[26] However, semantic entities such as reasons or propositional

---

[22] The explanations offered by Roth (*Fühlen, Denken, Handeln*, pp. 528ff.) are strangely tautological. The question, after all, is why the illusion of the freedom of will arises if it plays no causal role.

[23] Searle, "Free Will as a Problem in Neurobiology," *Philosophy* 76 (2001): 509. The biological reasons that Singer ("Selbsterfahrung und neurobiologische Fremd-beschreibung," pp. 253f.) cites for differentiating a conscious level of decision-making would be conclusive only on the assumption that the sense of freedom, as the expression of rational action, is not an illusion.

[24] Roth, *Fühlen, Denken, Handeln*, p. 397: "The decisive point is that we should not regard this virtual agent as an epiphenomenon. The brain could not perform those complex functions that it performs without the possibility of virtual perception and virtual action."

[25] Ibid., p. 512f.: "We can assume that the will is not a mere epiphenomenon, i.e. a subjective state, without which everything in the brain and in its relations would proceed exactly as it does with it."

[26] Ibid., p. 253.

contents are not generally instantiated as observable states. Hence, Roth himself categorizes reasons and the logical processing of reasons as epiphenomena. Therefore, the causal role of ego-consciousness and freedom of the will cannot amount to much.

In tracing all mental processes back to the causal interaction between the brain and its environment in a deterministic manner and in denying the capacity of the "space of reasons" – or, if you will, the level of culture and society – to intervene, reductionism seems no less dogmatic than idealism, which sees the originary power of the mind also at work in all natural processes. But bottom-up monism is only more scientific than top-down monism in its procedure, not in its conclusions.

In light of these alternatives, a form of perspectival dualism that withdraws our sense of freedom from the currently established standards of natural science – though not, to be sure, from the broader perspective of natural evolution – starts to look more attractive. In this spirit, Richard Rorty explains the grammatical split in our explanatory vocabularies into those that direct our attention to observable causes and those that direct it to understandable reasons as the result of the functional adaptation of our species to different surroundings, namely, the natural and the social environments. The fact that the one language game cannot be reduced to the other need not bother us any more than the fact that one tool cannot be replaced by another.[27] Of course, this comparison would only satisfy our longing for a coherent image of the universe if we were ready to follow Rorty in understanding the truth claim of theories from the functionalist perspective of their adaptive success.[28] However, the truth of theories is not reducible to the success of the instruments we are able to construct with their aid; and hence the desire for a monistic interpretation of reality remains unfulfilled. Nevertheless, if we want to find a place in the world for epistemic dualism, then the pragmatist theory of knowledge, with its project of detranscendentalizing the Kantian presuppositions of knowledge, at least points in the right direction.

---

[27] Rorty, "The Brain as Hardware, Culture or Software," *Inquiry* 47 (2004): 219–35.

[28] Eve-Marie Engels, *Erkenntnis als Anpassung? Eine Studie zur Evolutionären Erkenntnistheorie* (Frankfurt am Main: Suhrkamp, 1989).

From the anthropocentric perspective of a form of life composed of individuals who have been socialized into problem-solving linguistic and cooperative communities, the two vocabularies and explanatory perspectives that we *impose* on the world remain "inescapable" for us. This accounts for the stability of our sense of freedom in the face of the determinism of the natural sciences. On the other hand, we can conceive of the organically rooted mind as an entity in the world only as long as we avoid ascribing a kind of *a priori* validity to these two complementary forms of knowledge. Epistemic dualism must not be conjured up out of transcendental thin air. It must have *emerged* in the course of an evolutionary learning process and have already proven itself in the cognitive efforts of *Homo sapiens* to come to terms with the challenges of a risky environment.[29] On this assumption, the continuity of a natural history that we can conceive at least *on an analogy with* Darwinian evolution, though we cannot form a theoretically satisfying concept of it, can ensure the unity of a universe to which human beings belong as natural creatures. This enables us to bridge the epistemic gap between nature as objectified by the natural sciences and a culture that we always already intuitively understand because it is intersubjectively shared.

II On the Interaction between Nature and Mind

I would first like to return to the "inescapability" of the language games specialized in causal versus rational explanations because it is not at all clear from the perspective of the theory of knowledge whether we can dispense with one of these two perspectives (5). I will then draw upon some well-known anthropological results to retrieve methodologically grounded dualism in the form of a "soft" naturalism. These results are intended to show how such an epistemic dualism could have developed through the

---

[29] Regarding this "Kantian pragmatism," see also my introduction to Habermas, *Truth and Justification*, trans. Barbara Fultner (Cambridge, Mass.: MIT Press, 2003).

socialization of the cognition of interdependent members of the same species (6). From a neurobiological perspective, of course, even a methodological dualism encounters the problem – crucial for the question of determinism – of how the "interaction" between individual brains and cultural programs should be understood (7).

(5) To say that it is not possible to "retreat" behind the dualism of epistemic perspectives means, in the first place, that the corresponding language games and patterns of explanation cannot be reduced to one another. Thoughts that can be expressed in mentalistic terms cannot be translated without loss of meaning into an empirical vocabulary geared to things and events. This is the Achilles heel of those research traditions that must perform precisely this kind of translation if they want to realize their goal of naturalizing the mind in accordance with established scientific standards.[30] This holds equally for forms of materialism committed to reducing intentional states or propositional contents and attitudes to physical states and events and for forms of functionalism committed to the view that electrical circuits in computers or natural physiological states in the cerebral cortex can "realize" the causal role ascribed to mental processes or semantic contents. These attempts to naturalize the mind fail at the basic conceptual level because they cannot perform the required translation. The translations these theories attempt either themselves tacitly draw upon the meaning of the mentalistic expressions they are supposed to replace or they miss essential aspects of the initial phenomena and thereby arrive at untenable redefinitions.

That is not particularly surprising because incompatible ontologies are built into the grammar of these two language games. We have known since Frege and Husserl that neither propositional contents nor intentional objects can be individuated in the spatiotemporal frame of reference of causally efficient events and states.

---

[30] See Vincent Descombes, *The Mind's Provisions: A Critique of Cognitivism* (Princeton, N.J.: Princeton University Press, 2001), and Wolf-Jürgen Cramm, "Repräsentation oder Verständigung? Eine Kritik naturalistischer Philosophien der Bedeutung und des Geistes" (PhD Dissertation, Frankfurt University, 2003).

This can also be explained in terms of how the concept of causation intermeshes with the functional circuit of instrumental action.
When we interpret the succession of two observable states of the
world, A and B, as a causal relation (in the strict sense that state
A is a sufficient condition for the occurrence of state B), we
implicitly assume that we could give rise to state B ourselves by
intervening instrumentally in the world to produce state A.[31] This
interventionist background of the concept of causation makes
clear why mental states and semantic contents, which cannot be
manipulated instrumentally like things and events, elude this sort
of causal explanation.

The fact that the language games tailored to the mental and
the physical cannot be reduced to one another raises the interesting question as to whether we must regard the world from both
perspectives simultaneously if we are to be able to learn something about it. Clearly, the observer perspective, to which the
empiricist perspective *limits* us, must be combined with that of
participants in communicative and social practices in order to give
socialized subjects like us cognitive access to the world. We
combine the roles of observers and participants in communication
in one person.

With the system of personal pronouns, we learn the observer
role of the "third" person only in tandem with the "first"- and
"second"-person roles of speaker and hearer. It is no accident that
the two interdependent basic functions of language, description
of state of affairs and communication, are equally original.[32] This
view of the philosophy of language on speakers and addressees
who, by exchanging the first- and second-person roles, communicate with one another about something in the objective world
against the background of an intersubjectively shared lifeworld
can be inverted from the perspective of the theory of knowledge:
objective reality is constituted for an observer only together with

[31] G. H. von Wright, *Explanation and Understanding* (London: Routledge &
Kegan Paul, 1971), part 2; on this, see Albrecht Wellmer, "Georg Henryk von
Wright über 'Erklären' und 'Verstehen,'" *Philosophische Rundschau* 26 (1979):
1–27, here pp. 4ff.
[32] Michael Dummett, "Language and Communication," in Dummett, *The Seas
of Language* (Oxford: Oxford University Press, 1993), pp. 166–87.

the intersubjectivity of possible communication concerning his cognition of events in the world. The intersubjective testing of subjective evidence first makes possible the progressive objectivation of nature. This is why processes of reaching mutual understanding cannot be located entirely on the "object side," and hence cannot be exhaustively described as causally determined events in the world and thereby be drawn into the domain of objectivating descriptions.[33]

It is not only social cognition and the development of moral consciousness,[34] but also the cognitive processing of the experiences that we make in our encounters with the natural environment, that are rooted in the complementary relation between participant and observer perspectives. Truth claims must simultaneously withstand both the test of experience and the objections that others can raise against the authenticity of one's experiences, or of one's interpretations thereof. In this respect, the scientific enterprise is no different from everyday life.[35]

Concept and intuition, construction and discovery, interpretation and experience are moments that cannot be isolated from one another in the research process either. Experimental observations are prestructured in far-reaching ways by the choice of a theoretical design. They can serve as an independent check only insofar as they count as arguments and can be defended against opponents. At this level of reflection, the perspective of an observer who, in having experiences, adopts an objectivating stance toward something in the world is *a fortiori* interwoven with the perspective of participants in discourse who, in presenting

[33] On this, see the classic – i.e. still instructive – 1960 article by Wilfrid Sellars, "Philosophy and the Scientific Image of Man," in *Science, Perception, and Reality* (Atascadero, CA: Ridgeview, 1991), pp. 1–40.
[34] Robert L. Selman, *The Growth of Interpersonal Understanding: Developmental and Clinical Analyses* (New York: Academic Press, 1980); Jürgen Habermas, *Moral Consciousness and Communicative Action*, trans. Christian Lenhardt and Shierry Weber Nicholsen (Cambridge, Mass.: MIT Press, 1990), pp. 116–94.
[35] On this issue, see Lutz Wingert, "Die eigenen Sinne und die fremde Stimme," in Matthias Vogel and Lutz Wingert (eds), *Wissen zwischen Entdeckung und Konstruktion* (Frankfurt am Main: Suhrkamp, 2003), pp. 218–49; Wingert, "Epistemisch nützliche Konfrontationen mit der Welt," in Lutz Wingert and Klaus Günther (eds), *Die Öffentlichkeit der Vernunft und die Vernunft der Öffentlichkeit* (Frankfurt am Main: Suhrkamp, 2001), pp. 77–105.

arguments, adopt a performative stance toward their critics: "Experience and argument constitute two dependent components of the basis or foundation of our claims to know something about the world."[36]

From the claim that the increase in theoretical knowledge remains dependent upon the complementarity of the observer and participant perspectives, Wingert infers that the conditions of mutual understanding that are only accessible from the performative perspective of participants in lifeworld practices cannot be cognitively retrieved with the means of the natural sciences, i.e. they cannot be *exhaustively* objectified. For this reason a deterministic view of the world can also claim only a regional validity. However, this argument by no means necessarily implies a transcendental independence of the "for us" of a scientifically objectified "in-itself." On the contrary, the bifocal access to the world of observers and participants on which even the objectifying knowledge of nature depends could also be the result of an evolutionary learning process.[37]

(6) From a pragmatist perspective that seeks to reconcile Kant with Darwin, the inescapability thesis supports the view that the interdependence of complementary epistemic perspectives deeply rooted in human nature emerged in tandem with the sociocultural form of life itself. The vulnerability of biologically immature neonates and the correspondingly extended nurturing period make humans dependent from the moment of birth on social interactions that penetrate deeper into the organization and character of our cognitive capacities than in the case of any other species. From early in life, human beings' social existence affects the communicative socialization of learning and cognitive development. Michael Tomasello highlights the social-cognitive capacity (already emphasized by G. H. Mead) to perceive and understand members of the same species as intentionally acting beings[38] as the evolutionary

[36] Wingert, "Die eigenen Sinne und die fremde Stimme," p. 240.

[37] Habermas, "Introduction" to *Truth and Justification*, pp. 1–50, especially pp. 26–30.

[38] G. H. Mead, *Mind, Self, and Society* (Chicago: University of Chicago Press, 1934); on this, see Jürgen Habermas, *Theory of Communicative Action*, vol. 2, trans. Thomas McCarthy (Cambridge, Mass.: MIT Press, 1987), pp. 1–42.

achievement that separates *Homo sapiens* from its closest relatives and makes it capable of cultural development.[39]

Primates can act intentionally and differentiate between social objects and inanimate objects, but other primates remain for them literally "social objects," since they neither take the perspective of others nor recognize others as alter egos. They do not understand others as intentional actors in a way that allows them to forge commonalities that are "intersubjective" in the strict sense, whereas prelinguistic nine-month-old children already learn to direct their attention *together* with their caregiver to the *same* object. Insofar as they take the perspective of an other, the latter is transformed into a counterpart who adopts the communicative role of the second person toward them. A shared perspective, which already emerges at this early stage from the incipient relationship of a first to a second person, is constitutive for the objectivating, distancing "take" on the world and on oneself: "what infants' new-found social-cognitive skills do is to open up the possibility that they may now learn about the world from the point of view of others, and one of the things they may learn about in this way is themselves."[40] Based on social understanding, children's cognitive coping with the physical environment comes to depend on their cognitive interaction with one another. The interweaving of the perspective of an observer on what is going on in the world with the perspective of a participant in interaction *socializes* the cognition of the developing child with her fellow humans. This interweaving of perspectives becomes fixed in the grammatically regulated exchange of the communicative roles of speaker, addressee, and observer as the child learns to master the system of personal pronouns in the course of acquiring language.

Whereas chimpanzees do not point to things or teach things to conspecifics, human beings learn both through cooperation and through instruction. In their dealings with existing cultural artifacts, they also discover for themselves the functions embodied in them. The kinds of traditions, rituals, and tool use that are also

---

[39] On the following, see Michael Tomasello, *The Cultural Origins of Human Cognition* (Cambridge, Mass.: Harvard University Press, 1999).
[40] Ibid., p. 90.

encountered among chimpanzees do not reveal an intersubjectively shared cultural background knowledge. Without intersubjective understanding, there can be no objective knowledge. Without the reorganizing "connection" of the subjective mind [*subjektiver Geist*] and its natural substrate, the brain, to an objective mind [*objektiver Geist*] – that is, to symbolically stored collective knowledge – there can be no propositional attitudes to a world that is distanced in a way that allows for objectivation. Nor can there be any of the technical achievements in coping with an objectivated world of that sort. Only *socialized brains*, linked up with a cultural milieu, become bearers of those highly accelerated, cumulative learning processes that have become uncoupled from the genetic mechanism of natural evolution.

Of course, neurobiology also acknowledges the role of culture and the socialization of cognition. Thus, Wolf Singer, for example, distinguishes the innate knowledge stored in the genes and embodied in the human brain's genetically encoded basic neural connections [*Grundverschaltung*] from knowledge acquired by individuals and cultural knowledge. Society and culture clearly exercise a structuring influence on the brain into adolescence and continue to exercise an efficiency-enhancing influence throughout adulthood:

> Until the onset of puberty, education and experience influence the structural development of the neural networks within the genetically defined limits. Later, when the brain has matured, such fundamental changes in its architecture are no longer possible. All learning is then restricted to changes in the efficiency of existing connections. Hence, the knowledge acquired since the beginning of cultural evolution concerning the conditions in the world, knowledge of social realities, is reflected in the culturally specific forms assumed by individual brains. In this connection, early influences program occurrences in the brain almost as enduringly as genetic factors, since the two processes affect the specification of the networking patterns equally.[41]

These statements seem to suggest something like a "programming" of the brain by cultural traditions and social practices, and

---

[41] Singer, "Selbsterfahrung und neurobiologische Fremdbeschreibung," p. 249.

hence also interaction between mind and nature. However, the undisputed fact that all conscious and unconscious experiences alike are "realized" by decentralized occurrences in the brain seems to be enough for Wolf Singer to exclude the possibility that grammatically regulated and culturally sustained processes of conscious judgment and action influence the neural occurrences: "If it is admitted that conscious argumentation rests on neural processes, then it must be subject to neural determinism in the same way as conscious decision-making."[42] However, the *neural realization* of thoughts need not preclude a *programming* of the brain by thought.[43]

(7) Freedom of action belongs to the dimension of objective mind. Conscious participation in the symbolically structured "space of reasons" jointly inhabited by linguistically socialized minds is reflected in the accompanying performative sense of freedom. The rational motivation of convictions and actions takes place in this dimension and follows logical, linguistic, and pragmatic rules that are not reducible to natural laws. Why should there not also be a "mental causation," in the sense of the programming of the brain by objective mind, running counter to the determination of the individual mind by the brain? Singer presents three main counterarguments: (a) We have no idea how we should conceive of a mental causation of observable processes in the brain that is inaccessible to observation. (b) The neural occurrences that enter consciousness through attention are dependent variables of the broad stream of processes that remain unconscious. (c) Neurobiology can discover no correlate of the "self" of an agent who ascribes conscious decisions to himself among the decentralized operations in the brain.

(a) The inescapability of the complementary interlinked epistemic perspectives does indeed give rise to the "problem of causation": it seems that our cognitive apparatus is ill-adapted to understanding how the deterministic causal connections between stimulation states in the brain can interact with a cultural

---

[42] Ibid., p. 215.
[43] See also H. P. Krüger, "Das Hirn im Kontext exzentrischer Positionierung," *Deutsche Zeitschrift für Philosophie* 52 (2004): 257–93.

programming that we experience as motivation through reasons. To put this in Kantian terminology, it is incomprehensible how natural causation and causation through freedom can interact. However, this mystery causes difficulties for both sides. On the one hand, the "mental causation" of neurologically explicable bodily movements by rational intentions remains mysterious. For if we identify this kind of programming with natural causation something essential gets lost, namely, the reference to conditions of validity without which propositional contents and propositional attitudes remain unintelligible.[44] But the converse view pays an equally steep price. Determinism must declare the self-understanding of rational judging subjects to be a self-deception.

The costs of epiphenomenalism are not reduced by caricaturing the opposed position: "If this immaterial mental entity that takes possession of us and endows us with freedom and dignity exists, how is it supposed to interact with the material processes in our brain?"[45] In fact, something like the mind only "exists" in virtue of its embodiment in acoustically or visually perceptible sign tokens, that is, in observable actions and communicative utterances, in symbolic objects or artifacts. Alongside propositionally differentiated language, the heart of cultural forms of life, there are many other symbolic forms, media, and rule systems whose semantic content is intersubjectively shared and reproduced. We can understand these systems of symbols as emergent properties that evolved in the course of the evolutionary advance to the "socialization of cognition."

Two aspects are important for grasping the ontological status of "objective" mind, or mind as symbolically embodied in signs, practices, and objects. On the one hand, objective mind evolved out of the interaction between the brains of intelligent animals who had already developed the capacity for reciprocal perspective-taking; and it reproduces itself at a new level of interaction via the communicative and social practices of these "brains" and their organisms. On the other hand, "objective mind" claims relative

---

[44] Lutz Wingert, "Die Schere im Kopf: Grenzen der Naturalisierung," in Geyer (ed.), *Hirnforschung und Willensfreiheit*, pp. 155–8.
[45] Singer, "Selbsterfahrung und neurobiologische Fremdbeschreibung," pp. 239f.

independence vis-à-vis these individuals, since the universe of intersubjectively shared meanings, organized according to its own grammar, has taken on symbolic form. These meaning systems can, in turn, influence the brains of participants through the grammatically regulated use of symbols. The "subjective mind" of those individuated participants in shared practices develops only in the course of the socialization of their cognitive capacities. This is what we mean by the self-understanding of a subject who can step into the public space of a shared culture. As actors, they develop the awareness of being able to act one way or another because they are confronted in the public space of reasons with validity claims that challenge them to take positions.

Talking of the mind "programming" the brain evokes metaphors from computer language. The computer analogy puts us on the wrong track insofar as it suggests the Cartesian model of isolated conscious monads, each of which develops its own "inner representation of the external world." What is missing here is the socialization of cognition that is peculiar to the human mind. However, the mistaken metaphor is not "programming." Clearly, at the evolutionary level of human nature and culture, a symbolically materialized layer of intersubjectively shared, grammatically structured meanings emerges from the intensified interaction among conspecifics. Although the physiology of the brain does not permit any distinction between "software" and "hardware," the objective mind, in contrast to the subjective mind, can acquire the power to structure the individual brain. Singer himself speaks of an early "imprinting" of the brain associated with language acquisition. In the course of ontogeny, the individual brain apparently acquires the dispositions required to "access" the programs of society and culture.

Wolf Singer's skepticism is based, among other things, on the fact that neurological observation cannot establish any differences in the reactions in the brain activated by sense impulses depending on whether the signals come from the natural or the cultural environment. The stimulation patterns in the brain provide no indication as to whether they were produced via the direct perception of a "flowering meadow" or by a corresponding symbolically coded perception thereof – for example, by viewing an impressionist painting of this flowering meadow or by a memory of the flowering meadow evoked by reading a novel. Should there prove to be systematic differences, these should not be explained in terms of the symbolic coding of the sensory input, i.e. as a consequence of the interpretation that the flowering meadow acquires through the style of a Renoir or through the surplus of meaning endowed by a fictional narrative: "Hence, cultural understandings and social interactions influence brain functions like any other factors that affect neural connections and the stimulation patterns based upon them. It is completely irrelevant for the functions unfolding in the neural networks whether . . . the activity of the neurons is produced by normal sensory inputs or by social signals."[46]

Nobody doubts the thoroughgoing causal determination of the states observed by neurologists; however, the fact that cultural programs must be realized through operations of the brain does not of itself imply that we must level the distinction between understanding the meaning of perceived symbolic signs and processing noncoded "normal sensory inputs." The *tacitly presupposed* causal model already precludes the possibility that a programmed "mind" could influence processes in the brain. After all, the brain does not encounter the physical environment directly in the symbolically articulated propositional content of signs. Rather, the confrontation with the physical environment is mediated by the symbolically stored collective knowledge that has been assembled out of the shared cognitive achievements of past generations. The physical features of the received signals disclose to the brain, now mutated into a subjective mind, the grammatically organized meanings that demarcate the public space of an intersubjectively shared lifeworld from a surrounding environment that is henceforth objectified. And the formation of judgment and action constitutive for our performative awareness of freedom occurs in this "space of reasons."

(b) The phenomenon of freedom of will arises only in the dimension of *conscious* life. Thus a further objection refers to the irrelevance of the distinction between conscious and unconscious processes from a neurological point of view: "It is only true that the variables on which the process of deliberation is founded are of a more abstract nature, and can presumably be interlinked in

---

[46] Ibid., p. 249.

accordance with more complex rules, in the case of conscious deliberation than in the case of decisions originating primarily in unconscious motives."[47] In general, only those experiences find their way into consciousness that attract attention and can be stored in short-term memory, articulated in language, and retrieved from declarative memory. And these experiences constitute at best fleeting islands in the sea of unconscious processes that unfold in accordance with older and more fundamental evolutionary patterns.

The evolutionary priority of unconscious over conscious processes suggests that the latter are no less subject to deterministic natural laws than the former. "The variables involved in conscious decisions are for the most part things learned late, specifically, articulate cultural knowledge, ethical precepts, laws, discursive rules, and consensual behavioral norms. Therefore, strategies of deliberation, evaluations, and implicit cognitive contents that find their way into the brain as a result of genetic programming, early childhood training or unconscious learning processes, and thus evade consciousness, are not available as variables for conscious decisions."[48]

However, evolutionary stratification would only provide an argument for preferring a completely deterministic view if we could exclude *from the beginning* that the brain also realizes *cultural guidelines* via conscious processes. To be sure, even cultural programs do not affect behavior without supportive brain processes. The dependence of conscious life on an organic substrate is reflected in consciousness itself as the sense of embodiment. While we are acting, we are aware in a trivial sense of our dependence on a body with which we identify as our lived body. But because we *are* this lived body, we experience the self-regulating organism as a collection of enabling conditions. The ability to act goes hand in hand with the awareness of embodiment. The lived body, character, and biography are not felt as causal determinants as long as they define – as our own lived body, character, and biography – the "self" that makes actions into our actions.

---

[47] Ibid., p. 248.
[48] Ibid., p. 252.

(c) The third objection relates to this socially constituted "self" in the sense of the self-understanding of agents who assume that they are capable of acting in one way or another. Yet neurobiology seeks in vain for a controlling instance in the brain that coordinates everything and with which the subjectively experienced "I" can be correlated. This neurological observation leads Singer to infer that ego-consciousness is an illusion and that the sense of freedom must be treated as an epiphenomenon. Singer insists that

> our intuition errs dramatically on this point. Circuit diagrams of the networks in the cerebral cortex do not provide even the slightest indication for the existence of a single point of convergence. There is no command centre . . . in which the "I" could constitute itself. Highly developed vertebrates are, rather, densely networked, distributive systems in which a huge number of operations unfold simultaneously. These parallel processes organize themselves without any need of a single convergent centre and combine to produce coherent perceptions and coordinated behavior.

This gives rise to the so-called connection problem, the question of "how so many effective processes unfolding simultaneously in different areas of the cerebral cortex coordinate themselves in a way that makes coherent interpretations of the diverse sensory stimuli possible, resulting in clear determinations in favor of specific behaviors and in coordinated motor reactions."[49]

This observation can count as an argument against freedom of will, however, only on the assumption that the self-relation of the responsible agent presupposes a command centre for which there is a neural correlate. This idea belongs to the heritage of a philosophy of consciousness that sees the experiencing subject as centered in self-consciousness and as standing over against the world as the totality of perceivable objects. The fact that the neurological critique thinks that it must contend with the image of a hierarchical ego-authority is explained by the tacit affinity between cognitive science and this philosophy of consciousness. Taking as their starting point the two-place relation between "I" and "world" or "brain" and "environment," both positions end up

---

[49] Ibid., p. 243.

with the paradigm of the mind as a subjective consciousness that discloses itself from the first-person perspective of an experiencing subject. This concept of the "mental" shared by both positions is the result of neglecting the perspective of the second person toward which a first person relates as a participant in a joint practice.

As Wittgenstein, among others, shows through an analysis of the use of personal pronouns, behind the reifying utterance of the first-person pronoun there is no instance to which we could refer as to an entity in the world.[50] The expression "I" plays a number of different grammatical roles over and above the referential function. In the expressive use of language, first-person sentences perform the function of revealing subjective states to a public that attributes the discovered states to the speaker. The performance of illocutionary acts (verbalized by means of "I" and a performative expression) fulfills the unthematized ancillary function of claiming for the speaker, as a source of responsible actions, a place in the network of social relations.[51] In the present context, it is important that the expression "I" fulfills each of these functions only as a component of the system of personal pronouns, without assuming a privileged status within this system.

The system of personal pronouns founds a decentered network of systematically interchangeable relations between first, second, and third persons. Since the social relations that the alter ego enters into with the speaker first make the ego's relations to self possible, the "I" can indeed be understood as a social construction[52] – but it is not therefore an illusion. In the consciousness of the "I" is reflected, as it were, the individual brain's link to cultural

---

[50] See Ernst Tugendhat's excellent analysis that draws upon Wittgenstein's private language argument, in *Self-consciousness and Self-determination*, trans. Paul Stern (Cambridge, Mass.: MIT Press, 1986), Lectures 4–6.

[51] Habermas, "Individuation through Socialization: On George Herbert Mead's Theory of Subjectivity," in *Postmetaphysical Thinking*, trans. William Mark Hohengarten (Cambridge, Mass.: MIT Press, 1992), pp. 149–204. For the corresponding discussion between Tugendhat, Dieter Henrich, and myself, see Barbara Mauersberg, *Der lange Abschied von der Bewusstseinsphilosophie* (Frankfurt am Main: Peter Lang, 2000).

[52] On this, see the introduction to Rainer Döbert, Jürgen Habermas, and Gertrud Nunner-Winkler (eds), *Entwicklung des Ichs* (Cologne: Kiepenheuer & Witsch, 1977), pp. 9–31.

programs. These programs are reproduced only through social communication, branching out over the communicative roles of speaker, addressee, and observer. The reciprocally interchangeable roles of the first, second, and third person also facilitate the individuating embedding of the single organism in the public "space of reasons," where socialized individuals take stances on validity claims and can act deliberately, and thus freely, as the responsible authors of their own actions.

7

"I Myself am Part of Nature" – Adorno on the Intrication of Reason in Nature: Reflections on the Relation between Freedom and Unavailability

The Adorno anniversary has been copiously commemorated with books, biographies, photo albums, and conferences, not to mention countless events involving the media, enthusiasts, and voyeurs. Not that Adorno would not have been pleased by this. But this lively interest of a wider and more clamorous public stands in stark contrast to the hesitancy of the specialists who are again turning to the work of the great philosopher and sociologist to mark the occasion – and are finding it tough going. Adorno's philosophy and social theory is even farther removed from our current discussions than at the time of the previous Adorno conference here twenty years ago.[1] Today's event is an attempt to examine the relevance of his theory for contemporary concerns. What value does the philosopher and sociologist Adorno have in the context of present-day controversies? In addressing this question, I will discuss the issue of freedom that Adorno addressed in his lectures on moral philosophy[2] and in

---

[1] Ludwig von Friedeburg and Jürgen Habermas (eds), *Adorno-Konferenz* (Frankfurt am Main: Suhrkamp, 1983).
[2] Theodor W. Adorno, *Problems of Moral Philosophy*, trans. Rodney Livingstone (Cambridge: Polity, 2001) (cited in the text as "PM" followed by page numbers).

Negative Dialectics[3] primarily in conversation with Kant's moral philosophy.

The accelerating advances in the life sciences and in research on artificial intelligence have lent renewed relevance to naturalistic approaches in the philosophy of mind. As a result, the hallowed controversy over freedom and determinism is finding a surprising response within the natural sciences themselves. This is true in Germany at any rate, where, in contrast to the United States, a secular mentality has put down firm social roots, whereas the basic assumptions of scientistic naturalism are by no means deeply rooted in the philosophical tradition. Here we are still struggling to reconcile Kant with Darwin and to understand the apparent paradox that Adorno described in the following terms: "That reason is different from nature and yet a moment of the latter is its prehistory become its immanent determination" (ND, 285).

This formulation reflects the intuition that even subjects who are guided by reason, and hence act freely, by no means stand above the course of nature. They cannot sever themselves from their natural origins by transposing themselves into an intelligible original position [*Ursprungsort*]. Of course, this abandonment of the Kantian dualism between the realm of transcendental freedom and that of causally linked natural phenomena encounters the old problem in a new form: How can a freedom of will that is bound to nature be intelligently situated within a causally closed world? "Conversely, however, if empirical subjects really can act freely, then, because they are themselves part of nature, the Kantian unity of nature, founded on the categories, will be destroyed. Nature will then have a gap, and this gap will violate the unity of our knowledge of nature to which . . . the natural sciences aspire" (PM, 101).

---

[3] Adorno, *Negative Dialektik*, Gesammelte Schriften vol. 6 (Frankfurt am Main: Suhrkamp, 1973) (cited in the text as "ND" followed by page numbers). [In the absence of a reliable English translation, in translating quotations from *Negative Dialektik* I have drawn freely on a fine interim translation made available online by Dennis Redmond, at http://www.efn.org/~dredmond/ndtrans. html – *Trans.*]

Here Adorno expressly reaffirms Kant's characterization of the natural sciences in order to reiterate the aporia generated by the fact that the concept of free will is incompatible with the concept of natural causality as "the connection of a state with a preceding state . . . according to a rule."[4] His argument seeks to resolve the antinomy of freedom and determinism through a momentous semantic shift in the concept of nature. He subordinates the scientific concept of nature, i.e. the object domain of the causally explanatory natural sciences, to the Romantic concept of a nonreified *natura naturans* in Schelling's sense, a natural history that, from "our" retrospective standpoint, can be interpreted as the prehistory of mind. However, within the sphere of mind itself, a second, as it were, *inverted* nature in the guise of quasi-natural social relations is supposed to have emerged through an assimilation to an objectified nature that has been made available [*verfügbar*]. The stigma of this inverted nature is the causal power of unconscious motives in which two things seem to be fused: causality in conformity with natural laws and the form of causality through reasons that is compatible with the self-understanding of an author of responsible actions. Thus psychoanalytic explanations of moral development form a bridge between freedom and determinism.

This conception of a derailed natural history cannot really resolve the antinomy; nevertheless it will in the end offer us an interesting clue. First I will address the phenomenology of the everyday, intuitive consciousness of freedom that Adorno develops in passing. This contains a detranscendentalized concept of *naturally conditioned freedom*, though one which does not yet concern the antinomy of freedom and determinism (I). Adorno's intuition concerning the remembrance of nature within the subject [*Eingedenken der Natur im Subjekt*] is aimed at freedom in the more exacting sense of an emancipation from natural determination. But this critique of a reason that has *succumbed to nature* cannot solve the riddle of a reason that is *intricated in nature* set forth in Kant's third antinomy either (II). Nevertheless, the two

---

[4] Immanuel Kant, *Critique of Pure Reason*, ed. and trans. Paul Guyer and Allen W. Wood (Cambridge: Cambridge University Press, 1998), p. 532.

speculative moments of *naturally conditioned* freedom – namely, the unavailability [*Unverfügbarkeit*]⁵ of the opinions of the non-identical other and the unavailability of subjective nature – lead us to the heart of the current disputes with naturalistic approaches (III).

I On the Phenomenology of the Consciousness of Freedom

The first move is crucial for an undistorted phenomenology of acting subjects' consciousness of freedom. We must not become fixated on the subject of self-observation and on the subjectivity of experience. The consciousness of freedom is implicit practical consciousness. The phenomenological gaze must focus on the *performance* of the action and trace the intuitive background knowledge that it contains. The anticipation of something that occurs in an unthematized way while doing something else which is intentionally thematized has a performative character. Adorno stresses this when he invokes the "temporal actualization" of the self-experience of the actor against the supposedly intelligible character of freedom. "It is unfathomable, how freedom, the principal attribute of the temporal act . . . is supposed to be predicable by something radically non-temporal" (ND, 251).

The illocutionary meaning of speech acts is present to us in this way when we "make" statements without explicitly thematizing them as assertions, objections, questions, or advice. However, this procedural knowledge [*Moduswissen*] remains superficial. One need only switch from the participant perspective to that of a third person to make the illocutionary meaning of a speech act into the content of a further anaphoric description. In this way

---

⁵ The terms "*unverfügbar*" and "*Unverfügbarkeit*" are used here in Adorno's sense to describe features of inner nature or "subjective mind," such as emotional impulses, motives, or thoughts, that are not subject to natural determination and hence resist technical control. Since there does not seem to be any English word that adequately captures the connotations of Adorno's use of these terms, I have favored the literal translations "unavailable" and "unavailability." By contrast, "*verfügbar*," "*Verfügbarkeit*" ("available," "availability") refer to features of external nature that are subject to causal determination and hence are open to technological manipulation. – *Trans.*

one can transform "knowledge of how to do something" into "knowledge of something." However, one cannot analyze every kind of practice on the model of Wittgenstein's language games as an instance of following implicitly known rules. The consciousness of freedom that silently accompanies all of our actions lies so deeply buried or so far in the background that it is not easy to bring it to light. What is important is that the performative character alerts us to the participant perspective from which alone the self-experience of the freely acting subject is accessible.

This is contradicted by the classical experimental setup that likens us to Buridan's ass in an attempt to isolate the moment of freedom of choice involved in being able to act one way or another. It invites us to adopt the perspective of a person *observing* himself, although the performative consciousness of freedom eludes the perspective of an observer. Thus this kind of experiment rubs Adorno the wrong way. He uses the example of lifting the book in front of him and letting it fall to demonstrate "free choice" only to alert his students to the public space of reasons from which the solipsistic concept of freedom of choice abstracts. For it is only within the social horizon of expectations created by a university lecture that such a performance loses its absurd character:

> So if I may come back once again to this idiotic example of dropping a book, this is in the first instance my own free decision. But it may at the same time be regarded as the product of a whole series of other events. For example, I find myself under the necessity of demonstrating to you this phenomenon of a so-called free act, and have nothing else to hand but this accursed book. So I drop it and this can in its turn be referred back to all sorts of other things. (PM, 51–2)

A person acting freely always moves within an intersubjective space where other people can challenge them to explain themselves: "Why did you lift the book and then let it fall again?" This impinges upon the *first substantive aspect* of what we are intuitively aware of when we act. An actor would not feel free if he could not *give an account of* the motive on which he acted if called upon to do so. Involuntary reactions or movements, blushing and turning pale or blindly acting on desires, for instance, do not fall under the category of action. Actions must display an intention if they are to be imputable to a subject. In everyday action, we feel "free" intuitively only if our actions can be interpreted as executing an intention, i.e. as an expression of will. Otherwise we are not accountable for our actions.[6] Reasons are what differentiate the will from brute drives. This includes all kinds of reasons, provided that they lead to a considered decision. Because the will is always formed in the medium of reasons, the acting subject can be interrogated concerning "his reasons." And Adorno's statement that "reason in the shape of the will takes possession of the instinctual drive" (PM, 128) makes sense because reason is the faculty of reasons. In weighing reasons, reason shapes the will out of its "material," i.e. vague moods and stirrings (ND, 327).

However, this rather brusque formulation, which already relocates Kant within a Freudian perspective, reveals that this first aspect of the consciousness of freedom – namely, the rational character of the will as the foundation of accountability toward others – does not exhaust the meaning of freedom. As an impersonal faculty, reason could shape the wills of an arbitrary number of subjects in an anonymous way without allowing each individual room for *his own* action. But someone who acts in an awareness of freedom understands himself as the author of his actions. On closer inspection, two different moments are linked in this sense of *authorship*, namely, that I take the *initiative* and that it is *I alone* who take the initiative.

Having a sense of oneself as free means, in the first place, being able to initiate something new. Concerning this ability to initiate something, Adorno adheres to a conventional reading of Kant's third antinomy: subjects who act freely intervene in law-governed natural processes and "found," as he puts it, new causal series. An agent who takes an initiative assumes that, in doing so, he initiates something that would not happen of its own accord. For in a performative attitude the question of what the "objective connections" of our actions "may be with the causality of nature" (PM, 40) cannot even arise.

---

[6] Ernst Tugendhat, "Der Begriff der Willensfreiheit," in Tugendhat, *Philosophische Aufsätze* (Frankfurt am Main: Suhrkamp, 1992), pp. 334–52.

If one is to experience an initiative as *one's own*, the further moment of self-attribution must be added. I must be able to relate to "myself" reflexively as the ultimately decisive author of the positing or initiation of a new series of causal determinations. It must remain "up to me" whether I take an initiative and do one thing rather than another. Under the aspects of the will shaped by reasons and of the initiation of something new discussed thus far, the phenomenology of the consciousness of freedom registers the performative presuppositions of *responsible authorship*. But who is the "self" of the self-ascription of the actions of which I experience myself as the author? Adorno answers this question in his critical examination of Kant's concept of intelligible freedom with the claim that my lived body [*Leib*] and my life history constitute the common point of reference for the actions imputed to me.

The spontaneity of my action that is part of my self-experience as an actor does not spring from an anonymous source but from a center that I *am*, hence one with which I know myself to be identical. Kant situates the source of the relation to self in the transcendental subjectivity of the free will, in the noumenal ego. But the *individual* ego can hardly be grounded in the free will if the latter is identical with the rational will. The free will lacks individuating power because it owes its structure to an impersonal reason. Adorno's detranscendentalizing countermove begins with a differentiation that drives a wedge between judgment and action. If not a merely "good," i.e. ineffectual, will is to follow from good reasons but the right action, "something must be added" to the mere consciousness: "praxis also requires something other, something that does not exhaust itself in consciousness, something corporeal [*Leibhaften*], rationally mediated but qualitatively different from reason" (ND, 228). The practical element that overshoots the theoretical element of good reasons in the performance of the action, in the actual execution of the intention, Adorno characterizes as "impulse," as "that which abruptly springs forth," as "the spontaneity that Kant likewise transplanted into pure consciousness" (ND, 229).

In this "supplement," which is both mental and somatic, and hence also overshoots the realm of consciousness to which it belongs, the organic substrate of the body, which constitutes my body only because I inhabit this body as my lived body, announces itself.[7] I experience "internal" or subjective nature in the modality of the lived bodily existence in which I live: "Kant turns the issue on its head. No matter how much more sublimated the supplement becomes with increasing consciousness, indeed regardless of whether this first gives rise to the concept of the will as something substantial and uniform – if the motor form of reaction were totally liquidated, if the hand no longer twitched, then there would be no will" (ND, 229). Not the rational will as such but the subjective nature into which it extends – its organic roots in the lived nature of my bodily existence – is the point of reference of selfhood and of the self-ascription of "my" actions.

The centering of my existence that I experience as a lived body is a necessary, though not sufficient, condition for my reflexive relation to myself as the author of my actions. The lived body is the organic substrate of the life of a physically *irreplaceable* person who first acquires the characteristics of a *unique* individual in the course of his life *history*. It is not only the bodily impulse – the "twitching hand" – that is supplemented in translating judgment into action but also one's life history as the framework for the anticipatory existential concern with one's own well-being. Rational reflection first arises in the form of the prudent pursuit of one's own goals. This first, immediate sublimation of "stirrings," of affects and impulses, springs from an already reflexively distanced and more far-reaching striving for happiness. Linked back to bodily existence, a farsighted ethical will projects the individual self-understanding within whose horizon the moral concern for the equal interests of others is then first supposed to be integrated.

The at first self-related ethical will that is open to moral considerations is the character-forming force that, together with the personal understanding of self, constitutes a self who can address itself as "I." Adorno sees in the "character" that first makes a

---

[7] Helmut Plessner treats the dualism of being a body [*Leibsein*] and having a body [*Körpersein*] as the key to analyzing the "eccentric position" of human beings; see Plessner, *Gesammelte Schriften*, Vol. IV (Frankfurt am Main: Suhrkamp, 1981). Michael Weingarten takes up this motif in connection with the discussion in bioethics; see Weingarten, *Leben (bioethisch)* (Bielefeld: Bibliothek dialektischer Grundbegriffe, 2003).

person into an individual "that middle ground between nature and the *mundus intelligibilis* that Benjamin contrasted to fate" (ND, 237). Practical reason and moral freedom, which are Kant's concerns, evolve only in the context of the life history of persons who are concerned with their own welfare. The phenomenology of the consciousness of freedom that clarifies those aspects of responsible agency that we are aware of in naïvely performing actions does not yet refer, as we now see, to the "free will" in the strict Kantian sense at all. The intuitive meaning of responsible agency is connected with all actions, not just with moral actions.

Adorno describes this general practical consciousness – not yet specified according to pragmatic, ethical, or moral reasons – without projecting this experience of freedom onto an intelligible ego situated beyond nature and history. His description points to the natural origin of a subject buoyed by moods and driven by impulses who first constitutes himself as a responsibly acting subject on the basis of his lived bodily mode of existence and through the individuating power of the ethical concern with his own life history. From a genetic standpoint, the relation between reason and nature is asymmetrical: the one first evolves, in good Darwinian fashion, out of the other: "Ephemerally escaping the latter [i.e. nature], reason is identical and non-identical with nature" (ND, 285). In short, following the detranscendentalization of the free will, the boundary between reason and nature can no longer be specified as one between the intelligible and the empirical realms; rather, this boundary runs "right through the empirical" (ND, 213). But what do we mean by "nature" and natural causality in this context?

By withdrawing the reason-guided will from the sphere of the intelligible and relocating it in the domain of lived bodily experience and the individuating life histories of acting persons, Adorno replaces the aporetic concept of *unconditional* freedom with that of a freedom issuing from nature. From the perspective of an actor who understands himself as the author of actions for which he is accountable, this concept of a *naturally conditioned* freedom inserted into life-historical contexts does not pose a riddle. For, in acting, we encounter nature head on as our environment, as a causally determined sphere of constraining conditions, enticing opportunities, and available means. We pass no

remarks to the natural causality that operates behind our backs
when we perform actions – it remains invisible from the participant perspective.

The stability of the consciousness of freedom can be reflexively threatened only through a form of knowledge that origi-
nates in the objectivating attitude of an observer of objective
nature or of nature as constituted in the empirical sciences. Only
after undertaking such a shift from the participant to the observer
perspective can our practical motives become entangled in a
counterintuitive way in the network of law-governed occurrences of the causally closed world. The problem of how freedom
and the causality of nature can be reconciled cannot arise for the
practical consciousness of the acting subject. An actor does not
feel himself, *as* actor, to be subjected to the nature that confronts him and in which he intervenes, any more than he can
feel himself to be dependent on his own subjective nature; for
in acting spontaneously he knows that he is identical with this
subjective nature, with the lived body that he is. Given this unity
with his lived body, the structure of conditions that constitute
his internal nature appears to him to be an ensemble of enabling
conditions of his own freedom. And to the extent that the
organic substrate of natural drives [*Triebnatur*] conditions his life
history, the actor cognizes himself as the author who distances
himself from his own impulses and transforms them into motivating reasons.

This also holds for the ethical reasons for acting in which character and life history acquire the power to shape the will. As in
the identification with one's own body and somatic moods and
stirrings, this is also a matter of active appropriation, an act of
more or less conscious identification that explains why the identity-forming influences of socialization and of the milieu in which
one grows up are not experienced as a fate that restricts one's
freedom. The young person can in principle take a retrospective
stance toward his own development and decide which of the
"determining" cultural forms of life, traditions, and role models
he wishes to make his own and which not. Letting oneself be
determined by them is part of, rather than an impediment to,
freedom. The acting subject can experience reasons that spring
from his "character" and its development as constraining only
when he "stands outside himself" and regards his own life history

like a natural occurrence that is of no personal concern and escapes all evaluation.[8]

Reasons and the exchange of reasons constitute the logical space in which the free will is formed. Reasons can certainly constrain us – to change our opinion, for example. But good reasons force us to grasp something in a cognitive sense; they cannot constrain our freedom of will, which is, after all, free only as a reflective will.[9] Reasons do not "compel" in the sense of restricting our freedom but are constitutive for the consciousness of freedom that serves as a foil for experiences of unfreedom. As Peter Bieri rightly states: "Not to be able to decide to do something other than what one takes to be right constitutes the reliable freedom of choice."[10] Reasons can motivate actions or cause them, but only insofar as the reflecting subject is convinced of their efficacy. Reasons acquire the power to motivate actions only insofar as, in the course of practical reflection, they tip the balance in favor of practical alternatives that are ripe for decision. To the extent that they thereby assume the role of motives, they acquire their causal efficacy not in accordance with laws of nature but in accordance with grammatical rules. The logical-semantic link between a statement and a preceding statement is not of the same kind as the nomological connection between one state of affairs and a preceding one.

II Freedom as Emancipation from Nature – Remembrance of Nature within the Subject

The phenomenology of the consciousness of freedom leads in this way to a consistent concept of naturally conditioned freedom.

[8] Letting oneself be determined is not an impediment to, but a precondition of, freedom. On this, see Martin Seel, *Sich bestimmen lassen* (Frankfurt am Main: Suhrkamp, 2002), p. 288: "Someone who was not determined in many respects could not determine anything himself . . . Being determined is a constitutive prop of self-determination."
[9] Herbert Schnädelbach, "Vermutungen über Willensfreiheit," in Schnädelbach, *Vernunft und Geschichte* (Frankfurt am Main: Suhrkamp, 1987), pp. 96–125.
[10] Bieri, *Das Handwerk der Freiheit* (Munich: Hanser, 2001), p. 83.

Contrary to the Kantian construction of freedom as an intelligible
faculty, we can infer from this that freedom and unfreedom
cannot be traced back to the contrast between being conditioned
and being unconditioned.[11] However, the unworldliness of intelligible freedom must not be negated for the wrong reasons either.
Adorno works with an image of reason that springs from nature
and remains entwined with it. Inner nature, experienced as the
totality of the enabling conditions of freedom, includes the somatic
impulses of a lived bodily existence as well as moods and strivings
– hence the "material" accessible to self-experience out of which
a particular will is initially forged in the embers of discursive
reflections. The free will is conditioned by the motivating power
of considerations that reflect as much upon one's own desires and
conceptions as on conditions, opportunities, means, and possible
consequences. These will-constituting thoughts spring from his
subjective nature also for the agent himself. However, *from his
standpoint*, they cannot be simultaneously projected into the scientifically reified nature.

The networks of conditions into which a subject, as the responsible author of his actions, knows that he is inserted in acting are
not simultaneously reflected in his consciousness as determining
connections in the sense of natural causality (as Kant understands
this). Whereas the phenomena of the hidden accompanying consciousness of freedom are accessible from the performative attitude of an agent, we can ascribe causality, in the sense of a
law-governed connection linking a series of events, to nature only
in the objectivating attitude of an observer. Hence, in order to
resolve the antinomy of freedom and determinism, an *intelligible
connection* must be established between the self-experience of the
intuitive act of reflective choice and the "objective" events that
occur simultaneously in the substrate of the body. The phenomenological analysis of freedom conditioned by nature does not
itself possess the means to construct such a bridge between the
language of philosophy, which is tied to the actor perspective, and
the language of neurology, which is tied to the observer perspec-

---

[11] Ibid., p. 243.

tive.[12] *How can the responsible assumption of authorship of one's actions be translated into an observable and causally explicable occurrence in such a way that we can still know when we are talking about the same phenomena?*

Anyone who wants to resolve the antinomy of freedom and determinism must confront this question. But it never arises in Adorno. Instead he displaces causality out of the "first" nature constituted by empirical science into the sphere of a "second nature" that is *socially* constituted through the repression of freedom. This strange conception of a quasi-natural [*naturwüchsig*] society enables him to investigate the relationship between causality and freedom *within* the experiential horizon of freely acting subjects. After all, only within this horizon of the everyday consciousness of freedom can causality be experienced as "constraint" at all – i.e. as a restriction of the scope for rationally weighing alternative possible courses of action.

Adorno takes the antinomy of freedom and determinism seriously from this internal perspective with the goal of resolving it in favor of preserving freedom: "The subject's decisions do not form a causal chain, but are discontinuous occurrences" (ND, 226). However, the phenomenology of freedom as conditioned by nature precludes any recourse to the intelligible realm: "This supplement, the factical, which realizes itself in consciousness, is

---

[12] Bieri (ibid., pp. 287f.) erroneously levels the linguistic difference between an analysis of conditions in terms of concepts of reasons and an analysis of conditions in terms of causal concepts when he describes the process of weighing alternative courses of action from the observer perspective as an "occurrence," but introduces this third-person knowledge into practical consciousness itself: "Reflection on the alternative courses of action is, taken as a whole, an occurrence that in the end commits me, as well as my history, to a specific will. I know this but I am not bothered by it; on the contrary, this is precisely what constitutes freedom of choice." In fact, however, the reflexive stability of the consciousness of freedom is jeopardized by objectifying knowledge; in this sense, Kant's antinomy is justified. The switch to a naturalistic description of practical reflections – of what appears to us as our own reflection – as neural processes in the cerebrum does indeed give rise to cognitive dissonance, because the consciousness of freedom, together with all of the associated assumptions, is so closely tied to the performative attitude of the present action that it collapses the moment it is exposed to objectifying examination.

again interpreted by the philosophical tradition merely as consciousness . . . as though intervention by pure mind [*Geist*] were
somehow conceivable" (ibid.). Adorno remains true to the intuition that Kant tried to grasp with his dualistic solution: "the
reflection of the subject alone would be capable, if not of breaking
through natural causality, then at least of altering its direction by
inserting other chains of motivations" (ibid.). But because the
idealist solution is inconsistent and naturalism no longer even
attempts to satisfy the evidentiary requirements of an explanation
that is *true to the phenomena*, he must seek a materialist solution
– "materialist" in the sense of a causal examination of the social
pathologies in which a structural repression of freedom is
expressed. He situates this materialistic social theory within the
framework of a conception of human history as a *derailed* natural
history.

The concept of internal or subjective nature, familiar from the
phenomenology of naturally conditioned freedom, plays a key role
in the three delicate conceptual operations that the development
of this concept calls for. The crucial contrast is between the
unavailability of subjective nature as experienced in our spontaneous lived body existence, on the one hand, and the subjugation
of objectified external nature, on the other. In the clash of these
two modalities – of an unavailable subjective nature and of an
objective nature that has been made available – lurks the residue
of the suppressed normativity of natural law that is overcome in
the philosophy of life (I will return to this below).

First, with the concept of naturalness [*Naturwüchsigkeit*],
Adorno introduces the social causality of a freedom that has been
denied and driven out of consciousness (1). He then radicalizes
ordinary freedom into the extra-ordinary emancipation from
natural conditions (2). Finally, he restricts the natural causality of
law-governed sequences of states of affairs to a nature that is
constituted for the purposes of technical manipulability [*Verfüg-
barmachung*], i.e. to the object domain of the causally explanatory
natural sciences. The expanding dimension of human beings'
natural fate eludes the grasp of the instrumental reason that
belongs in this domain. The causality of quasi-natural social relations feeds off repressed freedom in a parasitic manner and hence
can be overcome through reflection. In this way, freedom can
have the last word (3).

(1) The starting point for the concept of naturalness is the fate suffered by the internal nature of the acting subject as a result of a socially organized and intensifying subjugation of external nature. Reason initially splits itself off from primary needs only to satisfy the requirements of an unobjectionable self-preservation, without denying the origin of these needs in nature. The feelings and needs are sublimated through rational reflections, at the first level, into preferences of purposive action and, at the next level, into conceptions of happiness or ideals of a successful life. And insofar as reason promotes the formation of the prudent and ethical will in harmony with subjective nature, it is "psychic power diverted into the ends of self-preservation; once split off and contrasted to nature, it also becomes its other" (ND, 285). However, the reason sprung from nature becomes *hostile* toward nature once it devotes itself, in pursuit of self-preservation elevated into an end in itself, to the socially unleashed frenzy of subjugating external nature and in addition repudiates the nature in itself. "The more unscrupulously . . . reason in this dialectic makes itself into the absolute opposite of nature and forgets this nature in itself, the more it regresses, as self-preservation run wild, to nature" (ND, 285).

With this, a different, pejorative concept of nature comes into play, namely, the inadvertent quasi-naturalness of systemically rigidified social relations. In contrast to internal nature that inscribes an orientation to happiness in the reason that it generates, instrumental reason reduced to narrow self-preservation has become the driving force of a quasi-natural society. "Quasi-naturalness" here refers to a society assimilated to the law-like regularities of objectified nature, because it forces social interactions below the level of free action through an inversion of freedom. In the unrestrained competition and the opaque functional socialization of actors competing to assert themselves, those imperatives of self-preservation that are not inherently irrational turn against their proper goal, i.e. the happiness of the individual and society. For, in the egocentric competition between individuals who are systemically chained to one another, the very solidarity among strangers that inspires the socialist dream of the emancipated society that guarantees equal freedom for all is extinguished.[13]

---

[13] Hauke Brunkhorst, *Solidarität unter Fremden* (Frankfurt am Main: Suhrkamp, 1997).

The critique of the quasi-natural character of society reveals Adorno's sole concern in his phenomenology of the consciousness of freedom. It has the propaedeutic task of elucidating the intuitive background for experiences of unfreedom. Unfreedom can occur only within the horizon of freedom. We feel unfree when we experience restrictions on our leeway for acting as external or internal compulsion. We act under constraint when we do something against our will, either through external subjection and coercion or through psychological dependencies and drives.[14] We are unfree in a heightened, uncanny sense above all when we no longer experience internalized constraints as such at all. Adorno is interested in the mechanisms of social constraint that assume the false appearance of freedom by being transposed into neurotic, hence unconscious, compulsions through the internalization of normative principles. Quasi-natural societies function *as if* they were subject to natural laws. Systemic regulation occurs through the still intact medium of free action, but it takes place behind the backs of acting subjects and downgrades the subjective consciousness of freedom to an illusion.

(2) We need not address the totalizing assumption that the mechanisms of the market and of bureaucratic normalization lead to an unlimited expansion of the principle of exchange and to the *hermetic* functionalism of a completely regulated world.[15] Foucault developed this line of argument further. What interests me in Adorno's controversy with Kant is a different question, namely, whether in Adorno's view Kant's moral philosophy contradicts the quasi-naturalness of society or whether it is itself a reflex of the latter – merely a reflection of self-assertion gone wild. It sounds like this when Adorno describes the categorical imperative as nothing but "the principle for achieving the domination of nature, raised to a norm, elevated into an absolute" (PM, 104). The abstract principle of according equal consideration to the interests of all seems to center instinctual energies on an ego

[14] Bieri, *Das Handwerk der Freiheit*, ch. 4, pp. 84ff.
[15] Habermas, *Theory of Communicative Action*, trans. Thomas McCarthy (Boston: Beacon Press, 1984), Volume I, pp. 366–99; *The Philosophical Discourse of Modernity*, trans. Frederick G. Lawrence (Cambridge, Mass.: MIT Press, 1985), ch. 5.

that imposes the norms of society under the rigorous yoke of a superego alien to the ego and against the individual striving for happiness of the libidinal impulses.

On the other hand, Adorno does not attempt to hide from his students the social critic who also speaks in the person of the moral philosopher Kant. In the formalism and pathos of the unconditionality of the moral law, in particular, Adorno discovers the corrective to the "imageless image of the possible" that Kant opposed to the tendency toward reductive functionalization [*Fungibilisierung*] (PM, 151). The injunction to treat every person always also as an end and never merely as a means goes counter to the general tendency to reduce the intrinsic logic of action to the satisfaction of the functions of the market and bureaucracy. Adorno repeatedly frustrates his own critique of the reckless leveling power of abstract general laws – of the "identity that annexes everything non-identical" (ND, 248), as though he suspected that the intersubjectivistic freedom of egalitarian universalism no longer needs to defend itself against a difference-sensitive justification and a context-sensitive application of norms. The opposition between duty and inclination does not invariably mean the suppression of sympathy or even "the suppression of every natural impulse." After all, Adorno traces the difference between desire and will back to the intervention of reasons that take account of individual welfare in the context of the equal consideration of the interests of others. Only the reflected will is free.

The only bone of contention is the supranatural status of the intelligible to which Adorno opposes practical reason's intrication in nature. He is interested in freedom not so much in the trivial form of the consciousness of responsible authorship that accompanies all of our actions but as emancipation from the spell of a quasi-natural society: "Freedom becomes concrete in the changing forms of repression, in resistance against them. Freedom of will extended as far as human beings' desire to liberate themselves" (ND, 262). Adorno ascribes liberation to a second-order will, the will to become conscious of one's own unfreedom. This calls for a self-reflexive exertion of reason that undermines the false constellation of reason and nature.

Following the model of the Freudian analysis of motives that have been split off and excluded from consciousness, condition behavior by evading a reflective will, and find expression in pathological symptoms, the "remembrance of nature within the subject" is also supposed to trigger liberation from the natural compulsion of society.[16] Once again it is the needs and interests that have been excluded from public discourse that must be raised to consciousness if they are to lose their blind determining force. It is not the making available of external nature through science and technology as such that severs the communication between internal nature and rational will-formation. It is the self-assertion of a quasi-natural society organized in accordance with the principle of "blind adherence to purposes of nature" gone wild that first brings a freedom-restricting causality into play. It triggers the vicious circle of the inexorably expanding mastery of external nature and the corresponding suppression of inner nature.

(3) Given these premises, Adorno thinks he has found a solution to the antinomy of freedom and determinism. For, on the one hand, an increase in freedom results when neurotic restrictions on the scope for action are overcome through reflection and the interrupted communication between reason and the elements of inner nature that have been split off is re-established. On the other hand, this liberating act of recollection does not material-ize out of thin air. Motivated by the suffering resulting from constraints on freedom, this self-reflection must be seconded by an understanding of the *law-governed* connection between trauma, resistance, and symptom-formation. However, it also becomes clear that the problem of freedom itself shifts with the semantic displacement of causality from "first" nature into "second" nature. The emancipation from the compulsions of a quasi-natural society does not impinge upon the *original* antin-omy between the agent's consciousness of freedom and the subsequent destabilizing knowledge of the world as a closed causal system.

---

[16] Max Horkheimer and Theodor W. Adorno, *Dialectic of Enlightenment*, trans. John Cumming (New York: Continuum, 1993), p. 40. (Cited in the text as "DE" followed by page number.) On this, see Gunzelin Schmid Noerr, *Das Eingeden-ken der Natur im Subjekt* (Darmstadt: Wissenschaftliche Buchgesellschaft, 1990).

Adorno could have responded to this objection with his version of a "natural history" that leaves a double imprint on the history of humankind. Under the influence of Simmel's philosophy of life – and also by this time of Benjamin – the young Adorno assimilated the idea of "second nature" in the version expressed by the young Lukács in *The Theory of the Novel* as follows: "This nature is not mute, corporeal and foreign to the senses like first nature: it is a petrified, estranged complex of meaning that is no longer able to awaken inwardness; it is a charnel-house of rotted interiorities. This second nature could only be brought back to life, if ever, by a metaphysical act of reawakening the spiritual element that created or maintained it in its earlier or ideal existence, but could never be experienced by another interiority."[17] Adorno interprets this diagnosis in such a way that the fate of a split with nature caused by culture avenges itself on modern society. Hence "the unacknowledged truth of all culture lies hidden" in the operation of reflection on this split (DE, 40).

The "dialectic of enlightenment" completes this thought. Here the "remembrance of nature in the subject" (DE, 40) is supposed to reveal the archaic origins – reconstructed as the prehistory of subjective nature – of the not-yet-split nature which can still be read off from the ciphers of its mutilation. The derailment of natural history is ascribed to an instrumental reason that lets the making available of an objective nature, in itself harmless, "run wild." It subjects a ruthlessly exploited nature to a social imperative to free productive forces from all constraints that has assumed an independent systemic character. The crucial point for our concerns is the transcendental-pragmatic assumption that *the same instrumental reason is also embodied in the sciences that first subsume surrounding nature under the concepts of causality and law-governedness in order to make them technologically manipulable.* With this move, the naturalistic image of a world determined

---

[17] Quoted from Robert Hullot-Kentor, *Things Beyond Resemblance: Collected Essays on Theodor W. Adorno* (New York: Columbia University Press, 2006), pp. 261–2. See Axel Honneth, "A Fragmented World: On the Implicit Relevance of Lukács' Early Work," in Honneth, *The Fragmented World of the Social: Essays in Social and Political Philosophy*, ed. Charles W. Wright (Albany: SUNY Press, 1995), pp. 50–60.

through and through in accordance with laws loses its power over the self-understanding of subjects. For once the remembrance of nature within the subject reveals the unbridgeable difference between this nature constituted "for us" and nature-in-itself, the claims of the biological sciences concerning the objectified nature of human beings can no longer provide the unquestioned yardstick against which the reflexive stability of acting subjects' consciousness of freedom must be measured.

III The Naturalistic Assault on Subjective Nature

A mode of thought that wants to remain in solidarity with metaphysics at the moment of its downfall need not balk at the metaphysical assumption of the primacy of a nonreified nature over nature as constituted by the empirical sciences. But we who belong to a younger generation are no longer altogether comfortable with this normatively charged conception of a derailed natural history – of a natural law animated by the history of philosophy. Once we renounce this speculative framing narrative, our knowledge of nature as constituted can no longer be relativized to the fate of a supposedly "other" nature. If we accept the nature of the natural sciences founded on realist epistemological assumptions as the standard against which our knowledge must ultimately be measured, however, in adopting this sobering perspective we squander the advantage promised by the idea of natural history for resolving the antinomy of freedom. For then knowledge of the world as a closed causal system to which human beings belong as products of natural evolution remains in conflict with the performatively ineradicable consciousness of freedom.

I would like to examine, in conclusion, whether, even on these sobering premises, we can still learn something from Adorno's diagnoses for resolving the Kantian antinomy. It seems natural to consider the debate in bioethics over the implications of the technical manipulation of the human genome in light of the dialectic of enlightenment, for this also concerns the limits of a *practical* making available of subjective nature (1). However, the problem of freedom and determinism concerns the limits of the *epistemic* making available of the experiencing and active subjectivity of a reason that is entangled in nature. The normative content of Adorno's idea of natural history is not exhausted by the idea of the non-availability of subjective nature but extends to the non-identical that escapes objectification in the encounter with the other. This consideration casts light on the current debate over attempts to naturalize the mind (2).

(1) The non-availability of the organic beginnings of conscious life already plays a role in the phenomenology of naturally conditioned freedom. The intuition that the rational orientation to longer-term goals should harmonize with the spontaneous sensations and impulses of an inner nature over which nobody may exercise control is unproblematic from a metaphysical point of view. The sensitivity to the moral limits to the availability of subjective nature can be justified without appealing to the normative logic of an orthogenesis that Adorno ascribes to the derailed natural history *as a whole*. Would we not feel restricted in our ethical freedom to shape our lives if the successful manipulation of the genetic code of the human organism were one day to become a socially accepted custom?[18] We do not know whether we will ever acquire the technologies that would permit the genetic manipulation of desirable characteristics, dispositions, or capabilities in our offspring. However, advances in biogenetic research and gene technology have opened up the prospect of eugenic practices while at the same time evoking fantasies of *shopping in the genetic supermarket* (Peter Singer) that lend the basic ideas developed in *Dialectic of Enlightenment* a surprising topicality. According to the latter, a self-empowering subject that transforms everything around it into an object can extend control over external nature only at the cost of repressing its own inner nature. The objectification of the natural environment propels self-objectification within the subject: "Man's domination over himself . . . is almost always the destruction of the subject . . . for the substance which is dominated, suppressed, and dissolved by virtue of self-preservation is none other than that very life . . . in fact, what is to be preserved" (DE, 54).

---

[18] Habermas, *The Future of Human Nature*, trans. Hella Beister and William Rehg (Cambridge: Polity, 2003).

To be sure, this dialectical relation between the domination of nature and the disintegration of the subject is supposed to be produced through the second nature represented by the *social organization* of a relentless increase in productive forces. But today we also already see this dialectic at work when we detach the relation of a genetically engineered person to his (we assume) well-meaning and considerate parents from its wider social context. On this scenario, the embryonic body of the future person represents the external nature that is made available; and the organism that develops out of this embryo, which the growing person experiences as his prenatally manipulated lived body, represents the disintegrating subjective nature.

A person can regard his actions as accountable only when he identifies with his body as his own lived body. Otherwise he would not have any basis for an original awareness of himself as the responsible author of his actions. The prenatal prehistory of his subjective nature must also be shielded from external interference. For even the most prudent, liberal, and empathetic parents cannot preclude that their child may one day fail to identify with the genetic dowry that they conferred upon him. In the event of such a rejection, the programmed individual would reproach his parents for failing to choose a different design that would have provided better initial conditions for his own life plan. From the perspective of the affected child, the parents would appear as unwelcome co-authors of a life history for which each individual must claim exclusive authorship if he is to be able to experience his actions as free. The parents had to decide *in accordance with their own preferences* concerning the allocation of the natural resources required to secure the creative space within which another person must later develop and pursue his own life plan. Their choice represents a potential restriction on the child's freedom because nobody can foresee what significance particular genetic characteristics will acquire for the programmed person himself under the unforeseeable circumstances of his future life history.

On the normative assumptions of a pluralistic society in which each citizen has the right to arrange his life in accordance with his own values, it is an inadmissible presumption to interfere in defining the parameters within which *another* person will one day exercise his freedom to shape his life, a matter that is otherwise left up to the natural lottery. To the extent that the difference between what has evolved [*das Gewordene*] and what has been made [*das Gemachte*] intrudes into the unborn organism itself, an alien will takes root within the domain of the individual's lived body and undermines the basis for his self-ascription of initiatives and an autonomous conduct of life. As such practices became customary, parents making themselves into co-authors of the life histories of their children in this instrumental way would be increasingly felt to be normal. An ever-denser intergenerational web of action would spread inexorably through the present network of interaction and damage the everyday consciousness of freedom that accompanies our actions, which is bound up with the practical unavailability of subjective nature.

This thought experiment shows how a non-naturalistic self-understanding of acting subjects could become established through the tacit imposition of new technologies and transformed practices. But this *unspoken* undermining of the consciousness of freedom does not really affect our question concerning the reflexive stability of this consciousness. Only the *epistemic*, not the practical, reification of human beings' experiencing and active subjectivity could produce a destabilizing knowledge of the natural determination of our supposedly free will. Mental phenomena such as thoughts, propositional attitudes, intentions, and experiences would become "epistemically available" in an empirical scientific sense once they could be translated into an observational language and be *exhaustively* described as mental processes. Such a language is geared to the nominalistic ontology of observable, and hence spatio-temporally identifiable, things and events and makes possible the interpretation of inner-worldly conditions in terms of the concepts of causal determination. If naturalistic research programs of this kind were successful, they would make it possible to replace the phenomena that are accessible from the participant perspective with objectifying self-descriptions. In this way, the functional equivalents that make possible a naturalistic resolution of Kant's third antinomy would also be found for the intuitive consciousness of freedom.

(2) Adorno was not satisfied with such reductionist strategies. However, he could have interpreted the semantic gaps that regularly appear in previous attempts to reconceptualize reasons as

causes as traces of the non-identical. Just as the objectifying violence of an all-subjugating reason runs up against the resistance
[*Eigensinn*] of a spontaneous internal nature at the level of the
subject's relation to self, so too in the horizontal dimension of
social relations it seems to run up against the individuality and
autonomous will of second persons – of persons who are different
and who can raise objections. The attempt to make the alter
ego available through objectification harms the other person
in two respects and thereby highlights two further aspects of
unavailability.

The integrity of others makes itself felt, on the one hand,
as the individuality of a *unique person* who eludes the grasp of
universal determinations. The Adorno of *Negative Dialectics*
resolutely works out this moment of the non-identical.[19] The
uniqueness of a person who is individuated by his life history
becomes visible only from a performative perspective, through
the recognition of the other person's difference that must be
forthcoming in interaction.[20] Only an intact intersubjectivity can
preserve the non-identical from assimilation to the identical. It
would protect one individual from annexation by another and
enable both "to remain distant and divergent in the nearness
accorded, beyond the heterogeneous and the own" (ND, 192).
On the other hand, the normative integrity of the other also finds
expression in the nonmanipulable positions of an interlocutor.
Every attempt to instrumentalize the other denies him the status
of an *irreplaceable person* who, with his "yes" or "no," takes a critical stance on the basis of his own judgment and accordingly acts

---

[19] In her Adorno lecture (*Giving an Account of Oneself: A Critique of Ethical
Power* [New York: Fordham University Press, 2005]), Judith Butler addresses
the ethical implications of the "non-identical." Her intersubjectivist approach
reveals aspects of the work that Adorno himself leaves obscure because of his
skepticism concerning communication. However, Butler dramatizes responsibility toward the second person from the crypto-theological perspective of Emman-
uel Lévinas who – in contrast to Adorno, who in this respect thinks in Kantian
terms – conceives of the interpersonal relation not in egalitarian terms but as a
triadic, asymmetrical relation. See Lévinas, *Discovering Existence with Husserl*
(Evanston, Ill.: Northwestern University Press, 1998).
[20] Habermas, "Individuation through Socialization: On George Herbert Mead's
Theory of Subjectivity," in *Postmetaphysical Thinking*, trans. William Mark
Hohengarten (Cambridge, Mass.: MIT Press, 1993), pp. 149–204.

on his own will.[21] The autonomous positions of the other cannot be choreographed.

The conceptual problems encountered by attempts to reduce reasons to causes are reminiscent of these peculiar resistances.[22] This is the first move in the epistemic game of naturalizing the consciousness of freedom. Because the free will is a will determined by good reasons, rational motivation through reasons must be traced back to causation in accordance with the nomological model. However, reasons are not valid in an absolute sense but are intrinsically communicable – they are always reasons *for somebody*. Reasons are communicated in the medium of a shared language, so that the "yes" or "no" of those involved is governed by "grammatical" rules. That the one party cannot control the positions of the other in the objectivating attitude of a third person is explained by the primacy of the shared language over the intentions of the individual speakers. *Meanings ain't something in the head* (Putnam). The primacy of a structure of interconnected perspectives compels participants in communication to relate to one another in the second person. In this way, each makes himself dependent on the unforeseeable positions of the other. People enter the public space of reasons by being socialized into a natural language and by gradually acquiring the status of a member of a linguistic community through practice. Only with the ability to participate in the practice of exchanging reasons do they acquire the status of *responsible* authors of actions that is definitive of persons as such, i.e. the ability to account for themselves toward others.

The counterpart of this social-ontological primacy of language is the methodological primacy enjoyed by the intersubjectively shared meanings embodied in joint practices in the sequence of explanation prior to internal states of the individuals involved. Until now, all attempts to replace the social-pragmatic image of a mind embodied in intersubjectively shared practices by the naturalistic image of neural processes in the brain or of operations

[21] Klaus Günther, "Grund, der sich selbst begründet, oder: Was es heißt eine Person zu sein," *Neue Rundschau* 114 (2003): 66-81.
[22] See Wolf-Jürgen Cramm, "Repräsentation oder Verständigung: Eine Kritik naturalistischer Philosophen der Bedeutung und des Geistes" (Doctoral Dissertation, Frankfurt 2003).

in computers have been thwarted by an inescapable dualism of language games.[23] This unbridgeable semantic chasm between the normatively charged vocabulary of everyday languages in which first and second persons communicate with one another about something and the nominalistic orientation of the languages of science specialized in descriptive statements is grounded in the profound difference between the observer and participant perspectives. These two perspectives are complementary in the sense that not everything that is accessible from the one perspective can be encompassed by the other. This complementarity can be underpinned, in turn, by an epistemological argument that undermines scientistic naturalism's basic faith in the primacy of the observer perspective.[24]

In one respect, the "hard" factual knowledge of the natural sciences enjoys a privilege over the "soft" understanding of symbolically constituted meanings and practices. The one kind of knowledge can appeal to "experience" in the sense of a systematic confrontation with "the world" based on observation, where this is understood as an "objectively" existing world of objects (i.e. of possible referents), in other words, a world that is identical for all observers and is independent of their descriptions. The other form of knowledge is based on the interpretation or explication of meanings and essences [*Bewandtnissen*] that can be tested through hypothetical questions and answers. The meaning of symbolic utterances is disclosed to interpreters only through their performatively acquired linguistic and practical competences, hence through a pre-understanding that they have acquired as participants in shared practices. Natural scientific knowledge enjoys the advantage of explanatory power and predictive ability over hermeneutic knowledge. The seal on the empirical content of this factual knowledge is its technical exploitability. This creates the impression that this is ultimately the only way to gain assurance concerning reality. The progressive "disenchantment of the world" (Max Weber) seems to confirm the suggestion that knowledge

---

[23] Geert Keil and Herbert Schnädelbach (eds), *Naturalismus: Philosophische Beiträge* (Frankfurt am Main: Suhrkamp, 2000), "Einleitung."

[24] On the following, see Lutz Wingert, "Die eigenen Sinne und die fremde Stimme," in Matthias Vogel and Lutz Wingert (eds), *Wissen zwischen Entdeckung und Konstruktion* (Frankfurt am Main: Suhrkamp, 2003), pp. 219–48.

based on observation enjoys a priority over understanding based on communication.

This conviction underlies the naturalistic assumption that soft hermeneutic knowledge tied to the participant perspective can be *replaced in toto* by "hard" factual knowledge. However, this program is already thwarted by the fact that investigation of the objective world itself rests on an argumentative dispute, which, although it appeals to events accessible from the observer perspective, is nourished by hermeneutic resources. For experiences are inherently conceptually structured and can take on the role of a controlling authority in the acquisition of knowledge only insofar as they count as arguments and can be defended vis-à-vis second persons. Concept and intuition, construction and discovery, interpretation and experience represent two moments that cannot be isolated from one another in the epistemic process. The perspectivē of the observer who takes an objectivating stance on something in the world in the course of experience cannot be separated from the perspective of the participant in a theoretical dispute who, in offering arguments, takes a performative attitude toward his critics: "Experience and argument represent two independent components of the basis or foundation of our claims to know something about the world."[25]

However, reductionist programs become implausible when the complementarity of the intertwined epistemic perspectives in the activity of research itself cannot be renounced in favor of subordinating the intersubjectivity of understanding to the objectivity of observation. The empirical authority of the veto of objective reality and the representation of something in the world remain internally related to the justificatory authority of the objections raised by participants in argumentation and to communication with them about something in the world. We can learn something from the confrontation with reality only to the extent that we are at the same time able to learn from the criticism of others. The ontologization of natural scientific knowledge into a naturalistic worldview reduced to "hard" facts is not science but bad metaphysics.

[25] Ibid., p. 218.

The inescapable linguistic dualism compels us to assume that the complementarity of anthropologically deep-seated epistemic perspectives arose concurrently with the sociocultural form of life itself. The coeval emergence of the observer and participant perspectives would provide an evolutionary explanation for why the meanings that become accessible in our encounters with second persons do not admit of *exhaustive* objectification through the instruments of natural science. This may force us to revise certain epistemological conceptions.[26] However, the "epistemic unavailability" of the experiencing and active subjectivity of human beings does not imply any immunization of an intelligible reality removed from the world. The perspective-dependent linguistic dualism is compatible with a "soft" naturalism if it is understood as an emergent feature of cultural forms of life.

This conception of a reason intricated in nature that respects neo-Darwinian discoveries poses just as little threat to the reflexive stability of our consciousness of freedom. Once we recognize that the consciousness of freedom that accompanies our performances is coeval with the linguistically structured form of life as such, we need not be troubled by the thought that this form of life itself evolved naturally.

[26] Habermas, *Truth and Justification*, trans. Barbara Fultner (Cambridge, Mass.: MIT Press, 2003), "Introduction."

8

The Boundary between
Faith and Knowledge:
On the Reception and
Contemporary Importance
of Kant's Philosophy
# of Religion[1]

Far from being a one-sided process, the Hellenization of Christianity also involved a theological assimilation and utilization of Greek philosophy. Throughout the Middle Ages in Europe, theology was the protectress of philosophy. Natural reason had its justification as the counterpart of revelation. The discourse on faith and knowledge emerged from its spiritual cloister only following the anthropocentric turn spurred by humanism in the early modern period. The burden of proof was inverted once factual knowledge became autonomous and no longer had to justify its existence as secular knowledge: religion was brought before the bar of reason. With this, the philosophy of religion was born.[2]

[1] I would like to thank Rudolf Langthaler for helpful textual references and comments. His objections and the critical results of a rereading of Kant during a seminar on the philosophy of religion held at Northwestern University compelled me to make corrections to the version originally presented in Vienna and subsequently published.
[2] Matthias Lutz-Bachmann, "Religion, Philosophie, Religionsphilosophie," in Matthias Jung, Michael Moxter, and Thomas M. Schmidt (eds), *Religionsphilosophie* (Würzburg: Echter, 2000), pp. 19–26; Lutz-Bachmann, "Religion nach der Religionskritik," *Theologie und Philosophie* 77 (2002): 374–88.

Kant's self-criticism of reason was aimed both at the stance adopted by theoretical reason toward the metaphysical tradition and at the stance of practical reason toward Christian doctrine. Philosophical thought proceeds from transcendental self-reflection both as postmetaphysical and as post-Christian – which does not mean unchristian – thought.

With his demarcation between the speculative and the transcendental uses of reason, Kant laid the groundwork for postmetaphysical thinking, even though he did not abandon the terminology of a "metaphysics" of nature or of morals. Moreover, by separating the intelligible world from the world of the senses, he continued to employ a metaphysical background supposition as a supporting pillar for the "architectonic" of his theoretical construction. It is transcendental reason itself that outlines the structure of the world as a whole with its unifying ideas; this is why it must prescind from hypostasizing assertions concerning the ontological or teleological constitution of nature and history. Being as a whole or the moral world as such are not possible objects of cognition. This epistemological restriction of theoretical reason to the employment of the understanding in relation to experience finds its counterpart in the philosophy of religion in the "restriction of reason with regard to our ideas of the supersensible to the conditions of its practical use."[3] Kant opposes the "presumptions of reason" in both directions.

To be sure, the critique of metaphysics retains its priority over the critique of religion for the self-understanding of philosophy. Through the former, Kant combats the speculative illusion of a reason that springs not only from *errors*, i.e. false statements, but from a more deep-seated illusion of reason concerning the operation and scope of its own cognitive faculty. By placing restrictions on the theoretical use of reason, Kant wants to open up the "secure path of science" to a philosophy that had previously merely groped around on the battlefield of metaphysics. The destruction of metaphysics is also supposed to liberate an autonomous morality based on pure practical reason; however, it refers directly to the theoretical business of philosophy itself. The demarcation of

---

[3] Immanuel Kant, *Critique of the Power of Judgment*, trans. Paul Geyer and Eric Matthews (Cambridge: Cambridge University Press, 2000), p. 323.

the practical use of reason from positive faith has a different thrust. The taming of religion through reason is not a matter of philosophical self-therapy; its aim is not the purification of its own thought but to protect the general public against two forms of dogmatism. On the one hand, Kant the enlightener wants to bring the authority of reason and of individual conscience to bear against a rigid ecclesiastical orthodoxy imposed by the Church that "regards the natural principles of morality as of secondary importance."[4] On the other hand, however, Kant the moralist also opposes the enlightened defeatism of unbelief. Against skepticism, he wants to rescue the contents of faith and the religious commitments that can be justified within the bounds of reason alone.[5] The *critique* of religion is bound up with the motive of a *saving* appropriation.

Nowadays religious fundamentalism, which also exists within Christianity, lends the critique of religion a regrettable topicality. Nevertheless, the focus of attention in the West has in the meantime shifted. Here, in the European part of the West, the aggressive conflict between anthropocentric and theocentric understandings of self and world is yesterday's battle. Hence the project of *incorporating* central contents of the Bible into a rational faith has become more interesting than combating priestcraft and obscurantism. Pure practical reason can no longer be so confident in its ability to counteract a modernization spinning out of control armed solely with the insights of a theory of justice. The latter lacks the creativity of linguistic world-disclosure that a normative consciousness afflicted with accelerating decline requires in order to regenerate itself.

Thus I am interested in Kant's philosophy of religion from the perspective of how one can assimilate the semantic legacy of religious traditions without effacing the boundary between the universes of faith and knowledge. In the preface to *The Conflict*

---

[4] Kant, *The Conflict of the Faculties*, trans. Mary J. Gregor and Robert Anchor, in Kant, *Religion and Rational Theology*, ed. Allen W. Wood and George di Giovanni (Cambridge: Cambridge University Press, 1996), pp. 233–327, here p. 281.
[5] Kant, "Preface" to the second edition of the *Critique of Pure Reason*, ed. and trans. Paul Geyer and Allen W. Wood (Cambridge: Cambridge University Press, 1998), pp. 106–24.

of the Faculties, Kant himself recalls – and not just out of self-protective motives – "the *theoretical* deficiency which our pure rational belief admits it has." Making good this defect he conceives as a matter of satisfying "a rational need" and argues that impulses from historically transmitted religious doctrines may be "more or less" hopeful in this regard. Hence, even from the perspective of rational faith, "revelation as contingent tenets of faith" is not regarded as "idle and superfluous."[6] Why and in what sense can religious traditions claim to be not "superfluous" even for an agnostic, and hence non-apologetic, philosophy of religion? The answer I want to derive from a critical reading will draw less on Kant's systematic assertions than on his motives and declared intentions.

I will first recall the boundaries that Kant draws in his philosophy of religion (1–5) and then turn to the historical reception and contemporary relevance of this attempt to appropriate religious contents on a rational basis (6–12).

(1) Kant's philosophy of religion, inspired by the spirit of the Enlightenment's critique of religion, initially reads like the proud declaration of independence of the secular morality of reason from the apron strings of theology. Even the "Preface" opens with a trumpet blast: "So far as morality is based on the conception of the human being as one who is free but who also, just because of that, binds himself through his reason to unconditional laws, it is in need neither of the idea of another being above him in order that he recognize his duty, nor, that he observe it, of an incentive other than the law itself."[7] Neither belief in God as the creator of the world nor belief in God as the redeemer who promises eternal life is required to know the moral law and to recognize that it is categorically binding.

The morality of equal respect for everybody holds independently of any religious context in which it may be embedded. Granted, elsewhere Kant concedes that "we cannot very well

---

[6] Kant, *Conflict of the Faculties*, p. 242.
[7] Kant, *Religion within the Boundaries of Mere Reason*, ed. and trans. Allen W. Wood and George di Giovanni (Cambridge: Cambridge University Press, 1998), p. 33.

make obligation (moral constraint)" – i.e. the categorical validity of moral obligations – "intuitive for ourselves without thereby thinking of *another's* will, namely God's (of which reason in giving universal laws is only the spokesman)." But this "making intuitive" only serves to strengthen "the moral incentive in our own lawgiving reason."[8] Whether we regard God or reason as the moral legislator has no bearing on the content of the moral law: "As far as its matter, i.e. object, is concerned, religion does not differ in any point from morality, for it is concerned with duties as such."[9] A theory of religion is possible as a philosophical discipline only in the guise of the *critical application* of moral theory to existing historical traditions. Hence the philosophy of religion is not part of the ethics developed from practical reason alone either.[10]

Kant describes positive religion from the perspective of the critique of religion as merely external and particular "ecclesiastical faiths" [*Kirchenglauben*]. The major world religions, which were founded by prophets, were handed down in doctrinal form, and are practiced as cults, found faiths each of which is tied to particular historical testimonies and facts and exercises its effects only within the confines of a particular religious community. Ecclesiastical faiths founded on revealed truths always arise in the plural, whereas the pure moral content of natural religion "is communicated to everyone": "There is only one (true) religion; but there can be several kinds of faith."[11] The religion based on pure practical reason does not need any organizational structures and statutes; it is not anchored "in dogmas and observances" but in the inwardness of "the heart's disposition to observe all human duties as divine commands."[12] The biblical teachings constitute

---

[8] Kant, *The Metaphysics of Morals*, ed. and trans. Mary Gregor (Cambridge: Cambridge University Press, 1996), "Doctrine of Virtue," pp. 229–30.

[9] Kant, *Conflict of the Faculties*, p. 262.

[10] Viewed in this light, the following assertion from the "Conclusion" of the "Doctrine of Virtue," which preempts mistaken interpretations, also acquires an unproblematic meaning: "We can indeed speak of a 'Religion *within the Bounds of Mere Reason*' which is not, however, derived *from* the reason alone but is also based on the teachings of history and revelation." Kant, *Metaphysics of Morals*, p. 230.

[11] Kant, *Religion*, p. 116.

[12] Ibid., p. 98.

the shell and must not be confused with the rational content of religion.[13]

The claim of the philosophical "scholar of reason" to challenge the exclusive right of the theological "scriptural scholar" to interpret the Bible with respect to what is essential to religion ("which consists in the morally practical (in what we *ought* to do)")[14] is based on these premises. Kant elevates reason to the standard for interpreting ecclesiastical faith and thus makes "the moral improvement of human beings . . . the true end of all religion of reason" into "the supreme principle of all scriptural exegesis."[15] In *The Conflict of the Faculties* his tone takes on a sharper edge. Here he is explicitly concerned with the claim of philosophy to make independent judgments concerning the truth contents of the Bible and to excise whatever cannot be recognized "by concepts of *our* reason, insofar as they are pure moral concepts."[16] The italicized reference to "our" reason can be understood as an ironical reference to the Protestant principle of individual exegesis by laypersons. The authentic interpreter is only "the God in ourselves" who is attested by the fact of reason, in other words, the moral law.[17]

Assuming this anthropocentric foundation, rational hermeneutics must reject many articles of faith, such as the resurrection of the body, for example, as historical embellishments. It must also strip central articles of faith, such as that God became man in the person of Jesus Christ, of their essential meaning and reinterpret divine mercy, for example, into an imperative of self-reliance: "Scriptural texts which seem to enjoin a merely passive surrender to an external power that produces holiness in us must, then, be interpreted differently. It has to be made clear from them that *we ourselves must work* at developing that moral disposition . . ."[18] The soteriological context of sin, repentance, and reconciliation, and thus the eschatological faith in the retroactive power of a redemptive God, take a back seat to the duty of earthly moral exertion. The referring back of all transcendent articles of faith to human

[13] Kant, *Conflict of the Faculties*, p. 270.
[14] Ibid., p. 242.
[15] Kant, *Religion*, pp. 119–20.
[16] Kant, *Conflict of the Faculties*, p. 272.
[17] Ibid., pp. 285–6.
[18] Ibid., p. 268.

beings' pure practical reason in a subjective manner exacts a price. Faced with the question of what assumption we should proceed from in acting morally, "whether from faith in what God has done for our sake, or from what we ought to do in order to become worthy of it (whatever this may be),"[19] Kant opts for the inherent worth of the moral form of life: "The human being must make or have made *himself* into whatever he is or should become in a moral sense, good or evil."[20] However, he does not acquire any claim to happiness through moral conduct but shows himself at most to be worthy of experiencing happiness. Morality is supposed to make the virtuous person worthy of happiness, not happy as such.

(2) Insofar as religious traditions can in this way be reduced solely to their moral content, one might get the impression that the only task of the philosophy of religion, like the critique of metaphysics, is to destroy transcendental illusions. But Kant does not reduce the philosophy of religion to the critique of religion. At the very point where Kant reminds theology that "the moral law of itself still does not *promise* any happiness,"[21] it becomes clear that the philosophy of religion has the additional constructive meaning of directing reason to religious sources from which philosophy itself can in turn gain impulses, and thus learn something. Although "there is not the least ground in the moral law" itself to discover "a necessary connection"[22] between the *worthiness* of a morally praiseworthy person to be happy and the actual amount of happiness that falls to his lot, the phenomenon of unjust suffering violates a deep sentiment. Our outrage at injustice in the world tells us in no uncertain terms "that it could not in the end make no difference if the person has conducted himself honestly or falsely, fairly or violently, even if to the end of his life he has found at least no visible reward for his virtues or punishment for his crimes. *It is as if they heard an inner voice that things must come out differently.*"[23] Of course, individual happiness, which we

---

[19] Kant, *Religion*, p. 124.
[20] Ibid., p. 65.
[21] Kant, *Critique of Practical Reason*, p. 107.
[22] Ibid., p. 104.
[23] Kant, *Critique of the Power of Judgment*, p. 323 (emphasis added).

would like to experience in proportion to virtuous behavior, is merely the subjective natural goal of worldly rational beings. Almost more insulting for a practical reason that strives for the universal than the absence of a guarantee of happiness for those who act rightly, however, is the additional thought that all moral actions in the world *taken together* are powerless to bring about an overall improvement in the disastrous condition of human existence. Clearly, it is this protest against the contingency of a social natural destiny that "flings them, who were capable of having believed themselves to be the final end of creation, back into the abyss of the purposeless chaos of matter from which they were drawn"[24] that finds a response in the "doctrine of Christianity."

The religious message responds to the peculiar insensitivity of unconditionally valid moral imperatives to the consequences of moral action in history and society with a promise: "But the moral law of itself still does not *promise* any happiness . . . The Christian doctrine of morals now supplements this lack . . . by representing the world in which rational beings devote themselves with their whole soul to the moral law as a *kingdom of God*, in which nature and morals come into a harmony . . . through a holy author who makes the derived highest good possible."[25] Although Kant translates the biblical notion of the "kingdom of God" into the metaphysical concept of the "highest good," his intention is not, as one might expect, the metaphysical-critical one of placing restrictions on the excesses of speculative reason. The concern of the philosophy of religion is not to *restrict* a theoretical reason plagued by unanswerable questions, but to *extend* the use of practical reason beyond the moral legislation of a strict ethics of duties to the presumptively rational postulates of God and immortality.

Already in the preface to his work on religion, Kant highlights the supplementary element that differentiates pure religious belief from the mere awareness of moral duties. As rational beings, we take an interest in promoting a final end, even though we can conceive of its fulfillment only as the result of a fortunate summation of the unforeseeable side-effects of unconditional moral

---

[24] Ibid., p. 318.
[25] Kant, *Critique of Practical Reason*, p. 107.

actions brought about by a higher power. Morally right action does not need an end. Any idea of an end would distract moral actors from the unconditionality of what is categorically enjoined in any given situation. Nevertheless, "it cannot possibly be a matter of indifference to reason how to answer the question, *What is then the result of this right conduct of ours?* nor to what we are to direct our doings or nondoings, even granted this is not fully in our control."[26] What first makes religious belief into *faith* is the rational *need* that goes beyond moral consciousness "to assume a power capable of procuring for them [i.e. the moral laws and actions in accordance with the law] the full effect possible in this world in conformity with the moral final end."[27]

Practical reason itself must show why precisely this need, and the associated interest, should be rational. For proof we do not have to await philosophy's encounter with the historical teachings of religion. It must be provided already by moral theory (with the aid of the critique of theological judgment, and hence the support of the heuristic reflections of natural philosophy).[28] The ancient concept of the "highest good," which becomes charged with eschatological meaning only when it is equated with the biblical concept of the "kingdom of God," serves here as a bridge. In fact, only by discreetly anticipating the world-disclosing power of religious semantics can Kant advance tentatively toward a doctrine of postulates that paradoxically enable practical reason to inspire confidence in a "promise of the moral law" after all.[29]

(3) Strictly speaking, the competence of practical reason extends only to the moral injunctions that it makes a duty for every individual person according to the moral law. The "kingdom of ends," too, in which all persons are thought of as being *united* as simultaneously lawmaking and law-abiding citizens, is an idea that adds nothing to the content of the moral law addressed to each individual. With this transcendental idea, Kant spells out a "republican" form of social coexistence that results from the general

---

[26] Kant, *Religion*, p. 34.

[27] Ibid., p. 113.

[28] Aside from a couple of references to specific passages, I cannot address these remarks in sections 82–91 of the *Critique of the Power of Judgment*.

[29] Kant, *Critique of the Power of Judgment*, p. 335n.

observance of the moral law (i.e. when "everyone does what he ought to do"). But only if this idea were no longer merely geared to individual moral action, but were translated into the ideal of a social-political condition to be realized cooperatively in the world of appearances, would the intelligible kingdom of ends be transformed into a kingdom of this world. In the philosophy of religion, Kant will actually undertake such a translation under the heading of an "ethical community." But in his moral theory he introduces as an interim stage the notion of the "highest good" that likewise depicts the "agreement between morality and happiness" as a condition in the world. However, this ideal is not represented as a goal to be pursued cooperatively but as the hoped-for collective effect of all particular ends pursued individually under the moral laws.

Such an ideal condition of universal happiness that follows only indirectly from the sum of all moral actions cannot actually be made into a duty on the premises of Kant's moral theory. When Kant asserts that "we *ought* to strive to promote the highest good,"[30] this, we must assume, weak ought runs up against the limits of human prudence, which quickly becomes engulfed in the turmoil of unintended side-effects in the shared pursuit of high-minded goals.[31] Practical reason in itself may not venture further than the phenomenal depiction of the noumenal reality of the kingdom of ends in feeble and, at any rate, morally non-binding *ideals* of the highest good. Kant also describes "ideals" as "Platonic" in a dismissive sense. The human understanding is not capable of foreseeing the complexity of the consequences of moral cooperation in a world governed by natural laws. Hence only someone who takes his orientation from *ideas* and restricts his choice of ends in accordance with moral norms acts from duty; he cannot be morally obligated to realize an extravagant goal of bringing about an ideal condition in the world which overshoots moral laws.

---

[30] Kant, *Critique of Practical Reason*, p. 104.

[31] On the realization of the highest good, see the excellent analysis of Rainer Wimmer, *Kants kritische Religionsphilosopie* (Berlin: de Gruyter, 1990), pp. 57–76 and 186–206. However, I do not see how one can understand (pp. 70f.) the "promotion" of the highest good as a morally obligatory idea, whereas the "realization" of this final end merely counts as an ideal. One can "promote" a goal only by trying to contribute to its realization.

Interestingly, Kant still pulls out all the conceptual stops in an attempt to elevate the *realization* of the highest good in the world to the status of a moral duty. The imperative that everybody should make the highest good attainable in the world – i.e. a general agreement of morality with happiness – into the final end of his action is contained in the moral laws themselves, and hence cannot be justified *from* the moral law like all other concrete duties ("In the question of the *principle* of morals the doctrine of the *highest good* . . . can be completely passed over and set aside").[32] Nevertheless Kant wants to convince us that "aiming at the highest good" is already contained in "respect for the moral law."[33] We should conceive of the highest good as "the whole object of pure practical reason" because "it commands us to contribute every-thing possible to its production."[34] One understands this supra-moral injunction only if one knows that it is an answer to the question: Why should one be moral at all?[35]

This question should not even arise for Kant, however, given the unconditionally binding character of a moral law based exclu-sively on the fact of the sense of duty. We can convince ourselves of the binding character of the moral law without any prospect of effectively promoting a highest good and without assuming the corresponding postulates. For, as Kant states with reference to Spinoza: "Suppose, then, that a person were to convince him-self . . . of the proposition that there is no God: he would still be worthless in his own eyes if on that account he were to hold the laws of duty to be merely imaginary, invalid, and nonobligatory."[36] For this reason, Kant's various attempted justifications are not really convincing. A deontological ethics that construes all moral action as action in conformity with morally justified norms cannot

---

[32] Kant, "On the Common Saying: That May be Correct in Theory, but it is of No Use in Practice," in Kant, *Practical Philosophy*, ed. and trans. Mary Gregor (Cambridge: Cambridge University Press, 1996), p. 283.

[33] Kant, *Critique of Practical Reason*, p. 110.

[34] Ibid., p. 100.

[35] As it happens, Karl-Otto Apel seems to take precisely this step with "Part B" of his ethics, which leads to a teleological fallacy on deontological assumptions: Apel, *Diskurs und Verantwortung* (Frankfurt am Main: Suhrkamp, 1988), pp. 103–53; for a critique, see chapter 2 of this volume.

[36] Kant, *Critique of the Power of Judgment*, p. 317.

make the self-binding of the autonomous will to moral insights in turn contingent on an end.

Against this Kant asserts: "For without some end there can be no *will*, although, if it is a question only of lawful necessitation of actions, one must abstract from any end . . ."[37] Should one then associate the decision to abide by moral laws in general rather than to act wrongly with an end? But if all ends are subject to moral judgment, how could a final end that justifies being moral as such "proceed" from the totality of all legitimate ends? Kant is content to refer to the unselfishness of the need to cooperate in realizing the final end, which is conceivable only under the condition of consistently moral action:

> With the human being too, accordingly, the incentive which is present in the idea of the highest good possible in the world by his cooperation is not his own happiness thereby intended but only this idea as end in itself, and hence [?] compliance with it as duty. For it contains no prospect of happiness absolutely, but only of a proportion between it and the worthiness of a subject, whatever that may be. But a determination of will which limits itself and its aim of belonging to such a whole to this condition is *not selfish*.[38]

Unselfishness, however, does not constitute the meaning of the duty but is the presupposition in particular cases for following a *specific* duty that conflicts with one's desires. Kant must ultimately acknowledge that this is a matter of "a special kind of determination of the will"[39] that cannot be situated at the same level as "duties" as he generally understands them.

(4) Why does Kant nevertheless insist that we have a duty to promote the highest good? One answer is suggested by the postulate of the existence of God. Even assuming that we should accept such an excessive duty, we must ask how adherence to moral laws, however thoroughgoing, could realize the highest good in a world governed by natural causality. Practical reason can make it morally obligatory to cooperate in realizing this goal

---

[37] Kant, "On the Common Saying," p. 282n.
[38] Ibid., p. 283n.
[39] Ibid., p. 282n.

only if it is not impossible from the beginning to realize the ideal. Hence its realization must be at least conceivable. Since this task manifestly exceeds human powers, therefore, in imposing it upon us, practical reason simultaneously enjoins us to assume the possibility of a supreme intelligence which harmonizes the unforeseeable effects of morality with the course of events governed by natural laws: "we *ought* to strive to promote the highest good (which must therefore be possible). Accordingly, the existence of a cause of all nature, distinct from nature, which contains the ground of this connection, namely of the exact correspondence of happiness with morality, is also *postulated*."[40]

Does this mean that we must assume, with reference to a conception of the highest good that does not automatically cohere with the foundations of moral theory, that Kant accepts a convoluted argument in order to be able at least to postulate the existence of God? Apart from being unseemly, it would be implausible to ascribe such a motive to him, given the integrity that radiates from every sentence of this philosophy. No, Kant supplements moral thought with the dimension of the prospect of a better world for the sake of morality itself, to reinforce its confidence in itself and to preserve it from defeatism. Adorno's dictum that the secret of Kant's philosophy is "the unthinkability of despair," as I understand it, is not a critique of the naïvety of the enlightener but an expression of agreement with Kant the dialectician who stares into the abyss of an enlightenment that is becoming subjectively rigidified. Kant wants to immunize the secular Spinoza, "who takes himself to be firmly convinced that there is no God and . . . also no future life,"[41] against despair over the pitiable effects of moral action that has its end only in itself.

To be sure, Kant wanted to overcome metaphysics in order to make room for faith. But he was interested in "faith" as form [*Modus*] rather than as content. He was looking for a rational equivalent for the attitude of faith, the cognitive posture of the believer: "Faith (simply so-called [*hence not just religious faith but also rational faith*]) is trust in the attainment of an aim the promotion of which is a duty but the possibility of the realization

---

[40] Kant, *Critique of Practical Reason*, p. 104.
[41] Kant, *Critique of the Power of Judgment*, p. 317.

of which it is not possible for us to have insight into."[42] He offers the following explanation in a footnote: "It is a matter of trusting the promise of the moral law: not a promise that is contained in the moral law, but one that I put into it, and indeed on a morally adequate basis."[43] Kant wants to preserve a moment of promise, but stripped of its sacred character. In order to insulate the moral disposition from discouraging appearances, it must be supplemented by the dimension of confidence in a finite success as the possible summation of all moral actions in the world. Kant's primary concern here is not to subsume all religious contents under concepts but to integrate the pragmatic meaning of the religious *mode* of faith as such into reason. He describes his attempt here as "a flattering imitation" of the Christian concept of *fides*. For rational belief retains the special character of a taking-to-be-true that preserves the reference of moral knowledge to convincing reasons and the interest of religious faith in the fulfillment of existential hopes.[44]

If we construe the supplementation of the moral law by the duty to cooperate in realizing the final end, which is problematic on Kant's own assumptions, in terms of the motif of the "unthinkability of despair," then Kant's primary interest in the Judeo-Christian heritage becomes clear. Rather than the promise of the afterlife represented by the existence of God (or even the immortality of the human soul), what interests him is the prospect of the promised kingdom of God *on earth*: "The doctrine of Christianity, even if it is not regarded as a religious doctrine, gives . . . a concept of the highest good (of the kingdom of God) which alone satisfies the strictest demand of practical reason."[45] The eschatological notion of a God who acts in history, an idea that goes beyond all Platonic ideals, makes it possible to transpose the idea of the "kingdom of ends" from the transcendental insubstantiality of the intelligible world into an inner-worldly utopia. Human beings thereby gain the assurance that, by acting morally, they can contribute to realizing the "ethical community" which

---

[42] Ibid., p. 336.

[43] Ibid., p. 335n.

[44] This concept does not fit into the schema of the three modes of taking-to-be-true that Kant introduced in the *Critique of Pure Reason* (pp. 688–9).

[45] Kant, *Critique of Practical Reason*, pp. 106–7.

represents Kant's philosophical explication of the metaphor of God's dominion over the earth.

Without the historical credit advanced by positive religion, with its store of suggestive and inspiring images, practical reason would lack the epistemic stimulus to generate the postulates with which it attempts to recuperate a *need* articulated in religious terms within the horizon of rational reflection. Practical reason finds in religious traditions something that promises to compensate for a lack expressed as a "need of reason" – provided that it succeeds in assimilating what it already finds in history in accordance with its own rational standards.

Kant does not concede this epistemic dependence as long as he accords positive religion and ecclesiastical faith an instrumental function. He thinks that human beings need striking models, the exemplary biographies of prophets and saints, promises and miracles, suggestive images and edifying narratives, merely as "stimuli" to overcome their "moral unbelief," and explains this in terms of the weakness of human nature. Revelation merely shortens the route to the dissemination of rational truths. It makes truths accessible in doctrinal form that human beings *"could and ought to have* arrived at . . . on their own through the mere use of their reason"[46] even without instruction by authorities. Thus "pure moral faith" will ultimately emerge from the conventional shell of ecclesiastical faith: "The integuments within which the embryo is first formed into a human being must be laid aside . . . The leading-string of holy tradition, with its appendages, its statutes and observances, which in its time did good service, becomes bit by bit dispensable, yea, finally . . . turns into a fetter."[47]

(5) However, it does not sit very well with this acetic understanding of ecclesiastical faith as a mere "vehicle" for disseminating

---

[46] Kant, *Religion*, p. 154. See also *Conflict of the Faculties* (p. 263): "The biblical theologian says: 'Search the Scriptures, where you think you find external life.' But since the moral improvement of the human being is the sole condition of eternal life, the only way we can find eternal life in any Scripture whatsoever is by putting if there. For the concepts and principles required for eternal life cannot really be learned from anyone else: the teacher's exposition is only the occasion for him to develop them out of his own reason."

[47] Kant, *Religion*, p. 127 (translation amended).

rational belief based on a critique of religion when Kant describes the "transition of ecclesiastical faith toward the exclusive dominion of pure religious faith" under the aspect of an "approach of/to the kingdom of God"[48] (which is in turn a symbol for the condition of the realized "best state of the world") in such a way that the ecclesiastical forms of organization already anticipate essential features of this future constitution. Kant's use of the formulation "approach" [*Annäherung*] here can be understood either (in the sense of a subjective genitive) as the approach *of* the kingdom of God or (in the sense of an objective genitive) as the approach *to* the kingdom of God. Precisely if we understand the creation of "kingdom of God on earth" – in spite of the nonsense involved in saying "that *human beings* should *found* the kingdom of God"[49] – as the result of the cooperative efforts of the human race itself, then the institutions of salvation, which initially appear in the plural, play an important organizational role along the difficult path to the "true church." The approach to the kingdom of God "is represented in the visible form of a *church*, the founding of which . . . devolves on human beings as a work which is entrusted to them and can be required of them."[50]

The institution of the church community that understands itself as "a people of God under ethical laws"[51] leads Kant in the philosophy of religion to develop a concept that offers a concrete embodiment in the shape of a form of life in place of the pale metaphysical heirloom of the "highest good." Kant develops the concept of the "ethical community" not in the context of practical philosophy but in the course of its application "to a history handed down to us."[52] Evidently it is not only a matter of "religion within the boundaries of mere reason" extracting everything out of religious traditions that can withstand the scrutiny of reason;[53] rather, in the process reason itself also seems to acquire impulses for

---

[48] Ibid., p. 122 (translation amended).
[49] Ibid., p. 152.
[50] Ibid., p. 151.
[51] Ibid., p. 109.
[52] Kant, *Metaphysics of Morals*, p. 230.
[53] The declared goal of the philosophy of religion is "to set forth as a coherent whole only those things in the Bible – the text of the religion believed to be revealed – that can *also* be recognized by *mere reason*." "Preface" to Kant, *Conflict of the Faculties*, p. 239n. (translation amended).

extending contents of reason defined in narrowly deontological ways. In reconstructing the rational content of the "doctrines of history and revelation," Kant is particularly drawn to the contribution made by the organized religious communities to "establishing a kingdom of God on earth." The "applied doctrine of religion" develops the rational concept of the "ethical community" for the symbol of the kingdom of God on earth and thereby compels practical reason to go beyond a purely moral legislation in the intelligible "kingdom of ends."

As we have seen, moral theory ascribes an intelligible status to the "kingdom of ends" that does not require any worldly supplementation. This idea is directed in each case to the individual addressees of the moral law. It does not need to be realized in the form of a moral community because this model of a "systematic union of various rational beings through common laws"[54] does not have the meaning of an obligation to engage in any form of cooperation, i.e. to participate in a *shared* practice. The "kingdom of ends" exhibits only *in abstracto* the condition of a rule of categorically valid moral laws – without taking into account the actual consequences of action in the complex world of appearances. The *public* character of this *mundus intelligibilis* remains "virtual." Its real counterpart in the world is the community of republican citizens organized under juridical laws. Morality, conceived in internal terms, can turn outward and leave visible traces in law-abiding conduct only through the medium of coercive law.

Kant abandons this strict dualism between the internal and the external, between morality and legality, when he translates the idea of a universal and invisible church, which is inscribed in all religious communities, into the concept of the "ethical community." With this, the "kingdom of ends" leaves the sphere of internality and assumes institutional form, on an analogy with an inclusive global religious community: "An association of human beings merely under the laws of virtue, ruled by this idea, can be called an *ethical* and, so far as these laws are public, an *ethical-civil* (in contrast to a *juridical-civil*) society, or an *ethical community*."[55]

---

[54] Kant, *Groundwork of the Metaphysics of Morals*, ed. and trans. Mary Gregor (Cambridge: Cambridge University Press, 1997), p. 41.
[55] Kant, *Religion*, p. 106.

Here the *epistemic dependence* of the philosophical conceptualization and theorization of the *source of inspiration of religious tradition* becomes abundantly clear.

Kant lends the "final end of rational worldly beings" a new,
intersubjective reading with the idea of the "ethical-civic condition" of a community organized solely in accordance with laws of
virtue that takes its place alongside the "legal-civic condition" of
a political community. In this way the duty to cooperate in realizing the final end also acquires a different meaning. Hitherto, the
"production" of the highest good had to be conceived rather as an
unintended "product" of the sum of the unforeseeably complex
consequences and side-effects of all moral actions. This is why the
peculiar "duty" to cooperate in realizing the final end could not
have any direct influence on the orientation of action either, but
at most on the motivation *for* acting. The moral laws in accordance
with which each person decides for himself what duty requires in
each situation alone have the power to orient action. Even if the
ideal convergence between virtue and happiness is understood not
only with reference to personal salvation but also to the "best state
of the world" for all, the higher-level duty to promote this condition remains empty; for it can only be fulfilled indirectly through
the individual fulfillment of simple duties.

Each individual stands in an "immediate" relation to the moral
law. This changes when the highest good, which every righteous
person hopes to promote through consistent moral action, is
replaced by the vision of a form of life that Kant subsumes under
the concept of the ethical community. For the local practices of
a community that anticipates such a form of life, in however distorted a form, and embodies it to a greater or lesser extent through
approximation, can now become a "point of unification" for cooperative attempts at a closer approximation: "For only in this way
can we hope for a victory of the good principle over the evil one.
In addition to prescribing laws to each individual human being,
morally legislative reason also unfolds the banner of virtue as a
rallying point for all those who love the good, that they may
congregate under it . . ."[56] From this perspective, the individual

---

[56] Ibid.

duty to promote the highest good mutates into the duty of members of different, existing communities to unite into an "ethical state," that is, an all-encompassing, ever more inclusive "kingdom of virtue."[57]

(6) Reason cannot recuperate the idea of a progressive realization of the kingdom of God on earth, over and above what the moral law requires, through the postulates of God and immortality. Rather, the intuition underlying this projection points to the support that the right must seek in the concrete good of forms of life that have been made better. The guiding images of successful forms of life that could meet morality halfway strike us, even without the certainty of divine assistance, as both an enabling and a constraining horizon of action. However, unlike Kant's ethical community, they do not arise in the singular and they are not forced into the rigid mold of what is morally required. They inspire and encourage us to make – and to continue to make – the kinds of tentative attempts at cooperation that are so often unsuccessful because their success depends on *fortuitous* circumstances.

The doctrine of the postulates rests on introducing a problematic duty that drives the ought so far beyond human capabilities that this asymmetry must be rectified by extending knowledge through faith. This also reflects the dilemma in which Kant is landed by his contradictory intention to treat religion both as a heritage and as an opponent. He regards religion, on the one hand, as the source of a morality that satisfies the standards of reason and, on the other, as an obscure refuge to be cleansed of obscurantism and zealotry by philosophy. His goal of assimilating religious contents in a reflexive manner conflicts with the aim of the critique of religion to decide questions of the truth and falsity of these contents in a *philosophical* manner. Reason cannot have its religious cake and eat it. Nevertheless, the constructive intention of Kant's philosophy of religion still merits our attention if we want to know what we can learn from the articulatory power of the major world religions for the practical use of reason under conditions of postmetaphysical thinking.

[57] Ibid.

The translation of the idea of the rule of God on earth into the concept of a republic under laws of virtue shows in an exemplary way that Kant associates the at once critical and self-critical differentiation between knowledge and faith with receptiveness to the possible cognitive relevance of the contents preserved in religious traditions. Kant's moral philosophy can be understood in general terms as an attempt to reconstruct the categorical ought of divine imperatives in discursive terms. The transcendental philosophy, taken as a whole, has the practical meaning of transposing the transcendent divine standpoint into a functionally equivalent *inner-worldly* perspective and to preserve it in the form of the moral standpoint.[58] The attempt to deflate the mode of faith in rational terms without destroying it altogether also draws support from this genealogy.

Kant's disillusioned idealism is itself an expression of a cognitive attitude that combines a genuine openness to the pessimistic objections of theoretical reason with the optimistic determination of an unbowed practical reason. This combination protects a "posture of reason" that is inherently vulnerable to skepticism against defeatist indifference and cynical self-destruction. To be sure, Kant had not yet crossed the threshold to a historical consciousness whose philosophical relevance was first recognized by Hegel. He still understood the reflexive assimilation of religious contents in terms of a progressive replacement of positive religion by a pure rational religion rather than as the genealogical reconstruction of a historical context of emergence of which reason itself is a part. In a certain sense, however, the doctrine of the postulates already reconciles the self-assurance of a reason critical of religion with the goal of redeeming religious contents through translation.

Our hermeneutic approach to Kant's philosophy of religion is shaped by its historical reception over the past two centuries. In this context, it is worth recalling the apologetic character of the most important work in the philosophy of religion in the neo-Kantian tradition. Hermann Cohen used Kant's idea of rational

---

[58] Habermas, "A Genealogical Analysis of the Cognitive Content of Morality," in *The Inclusion of the Other*, ed. and trans. Ciaran Cronin and Pablo De Greiff (Cambridge: Polity, 1998), pp. 3–46.

religion as the key to a detailed interpretation of the literary sources of the Jewish tradition.[59] He sought to counter the pervasive intellectual anti-Semitism of his time by underlining the humanistic content and universalistic meaning of the Old Testament and by demonstrating the equal validity of Judaism and Christianity with philosophical means.[60]

However, the three figures who exercised the greatest influence and on whom I will concentrate in what follows were not part of the Kantian mainstream. Hegel, Schleiermacher, and Kierkegaard responded in different, but equally significant, ways to the differentiation between knowledge and faith of Kant's critique of religion. Each was convinced that Kant, as a critic of religion and a child of the eighteenth century, remained prisoner to an abstract form of the Enlightenment and stripped religious traditions of their inherent substance. In this branch of the historical reception – and it is no accident that it is dominated by Protestantism – the main controversy concerns the accurate description of the "religious phenomena" and the correct demarcation of reason from religion. Here I will be able to trace the three metacritical lines leading, respectively, from Hegel, Schleiermacher, and Kierkegaard up to the present constellation only in their broadest outlines.

(7) Hegel criticizes Kant as the enlightener who measures religion against the yardstick of abstract concepts of the understanding and dismisses its essential content as something merely positive. Although a presumptuous subjective reason thereby achieves a pyrrhic victory over alleged obscurantism, this false

---

[59] Cohen, *Religion of Reason: Out of the Sources of Judaism*, trans. Simon Kaplan (New York and Oxford: Oxford University Press, 1995): "If I am dependent upon the literary sources of the prophets for the concept of religion, so too would these remain mute and blind if I did not – under their tutelage, to be sure, but not just guided by their authority – approach them with the concept which I made the basis of my learning from them." Quoted from Habermas, *Religion and Rationality*, ed. Eduardo Mendieta (Cambridge: Polity, 2002), p. 44.

[60] Micha Brumlik acknowledges Cohen's work as an expression of "Hebraic humanism" in *Vernunft und Offenbarung* (Berlin and Vienna: Philo, 2001), pp. 11–28.

transcendental self-limitation of reason actually creates a positivistically abridged concept of religion as its adversary.[61] This critique itself can still be understood as a radicalization of the Kantian approach in that it also seeks to overcome the opposition between faith and knowledge within the horizon of a rationally *extended* knowledge. Although the history of religions for Hegel includes the full spectrum of ritual practices and representational worlds, nevertheless he understands it in terms of a genealogy of an inclusive reason of which philosophy is the spokesman. He too upholds the claim of the philosophical enlightenment to justify the truth content of religion in rational terms.[62]

On the other hand, the conceptual transcendence [*Aufhebung*] of religion as a whole now takes the place of a selective assimilation of individual religious contents by a reason aware of its limits. Philosophy grasps what is rational in the representing thought of religion. However, the unequal marriage into which the philosophical embrace ultimately forces an overwhelmed religion has double-edged implications for the apparently superior partner. With the concept of the absolute mind that externalizes itself in nature and history and then recuperates itself reflexively in this other, philosophy incorporates the fundamental idea of Christianity and makes the incarnation of God into the principle of its own dialectical thought. However, it pays a twofold price for this. On the one hand, its rejection of the self-critically drawn boundaries of transcendental reason thrusts it back into the arms of metaphysics; on the other, the fatalism of a mind turned in upon itself – which must discharge itself into nature again once it has reached the summit of absolute knowledge – bars the way

---

[61] Hegel, *Faith and Knowledge*, trans. H. S. Harris (Albany, N.Y.: SUNY Press, 1977), p. 1: "Enlightened Reason won a glorious victory over what it believed, in its limited conception of religion, to be faith as opposed to Reason. Yet seen in a clear light the victory comes to no more than this: the positive element with which Reason busied itself to do battle, is no longer religion, and virtuous Reason is no longer Reason." See Thomas M. Schmidt, *Anerkennung und absolute Religion* (Stuttgart-Bad Cannstatt: Frommann-Holzboog, 1997).

[62] Hegel, *Lectures on the Philosophy of Religion*, trans. E. B. Speirs and J. Burdon Sanderson (London: Routledge & Kegan Paul, 1962), vol. III, p. 122: "The true Christian content of faith is to be justified by philosophy."

to the very eschatological dimension of a new beginning to which the believer's hope of salvation is directed.[63]

The double disappointment – over the regression to metaphysics and over the quietistic retreat of theory from practice – inspired the left Hegelians to radicalize the Kantian critique of religion in a different, materialistic direction. Feuerbach and Marx turn the idealistic genealogy of absolute mind on its head from the perspective of an intersubjective reason incarnated in the body and language and situated in history and society, and reaffirm the Kantian priority of practical over theoretical reason. Admittedly, they conceive of religion in deflationary terms as the reflection of disrupted social conditions and at the same time as the mechanism that conceals this alienated life from itself.[64] Their critique of religion anticipates Freud's psychoanalytic explanation which represents religious consciousness as satisfying unfulfilled needs through projection. But, as in Kant, this destruction of false positivity is supposed to liberate a truth content that is waiting to be practically realized. The idea of the kingdom of God on earth as an ethical community is again supposed to find a secular embodiment in the revolutionary form of the emancipated society.[65]

---

[63] Karl Löwith, "Hegels Aufhebung der christlichen Religion," in Löwith, *Zur Kritik der christlichen Überlieferung* (Stuttgart: Kohlhammer, 1966), pp. 54–96.

[64] Marx, *Contribution to the Critique of Hegel's Philosophy of Right*: "Introduction": "Man is *the human world*, the state, Society. This state, this society, produce religion which is an *inverted world consciousness*, because they are an *inverted world*. Religion is the general theory of this world, . . . its enthusiasm, its moral sanction, its solemn complement, its general basis of consolation and justification. It is the *fantastic realization* of the human being in as much as the *human being* possesses no true reality. The struggle against religion is, therefore, indirectly struggle against *that world* whose spiritual *aroma* is religion." *The Marx–Engels Reader*, ed. Robert C. Tucker (New York: W. W. Norton, 1978), pp. 53–4.

[65] Ludwig Feuerbach, *Principles of Philosophy of the Future*: "The single man *in isolation* possesses in himself the *essence* of man neither as a *moral* nor as a *thinking* being. *The essence* of man is contained only in the community, in the *unity of man with man* – a unity, however, that rests on the *reality* of the *distinction* between 'I' and 'You'." *The Fiery Brook: Selected Writings of Ludwig Feuerbach*, ed. Zawar Hanfi (Garden City, N.Y.: Anchor Books, 1972), §59. Feuerbach anticipated essential motifs of Martin Buber's philosophy of dialogue; see Michael Theunissen, *Der Andere* (1965) (Berlin: de Gruyter, 1977), pp. 243–373.

This atheistic assimilation of religious contents has been actively pursued in Western Marxism. The theological motifs are not difficult to discern, whether in Bloch's philosophy of hope grounded in the philosophy of nature, in Benjamin's despairing, but messianically inspired notion of rescue and recovery, or in Adorno's austere negativism. Many of these philosophical ideas have found a sympathetic reception within theology itself, for example in Johann Baptist Metz or Jürgen Moltmann.

From Hegel to Marx and Hegelian Marxism, philosophy attempts to assimilate the *collective* emancipatory moment of the Judeo-Christian promise of salvation by drawing on the idea of the "people of God" inherited from Kant. For Schleiermacher and Kierkegaard, by contrast, *individual* salvation, which poses the greater difficulties for a philosophy oriented to the universal, constitutes the core of faith. They are both simultaneously Christian and postmetaphysical thinkers. The one switches between the roles of philosopher of religion and theologian that Kant distinguished; the other, in the role of a religious author, takes up the challenge of a Socrates philosophizing in a Kantian vein.

(8) In contrast to Hegel, Schleiermacher respects the boundary markers laid down by Kant in his critique of metaphysics. Although he shares Hegel's reservations concerning a critique that sees only morality in religion, from an epistemological perspective Schleiermacher remains true to the self-relation of subjective reason. He shifts the boundary-line between faith and knowledge to the advantage of an authentic faith beyond mere reason by working out the intrinsic logic and the autonomy of religion using the basic concepts of the philosophy of consciousness. As a philosopher, Schleiermacher is not interested in the contents of religious faith (*fides quae creditur*), but in the question of what it means in a performative sense to have faith (*fides qua creditur*).[66]

---

[66] See above ch. 5, n. 29. This explains how Bultmann can find a route leading from Schleiermacher to Kierkegaard; see Friederike Nüssel's article on Bultmann in Peter Neuner and Gunther Wenz (eds), *Theologen des 20. Jahrhunderts* (Darmstadt: Wissenschaftliche Buchgesellschaft, 2002), pp. 70–89.

He distinguishes between a scientific theology that treats the contents of faith in a dogmatic manner and the piety that inspires and sustains the personal conduct of the believer.

Schleiermacher extends the Kantian architectonics of the faculties of reason without going beyond it when he assigns religious belief a transcendental place of its own alongside knowledge, moral insight, and aesthetic experience. The religiosity of the person of faith now takes its place alongside the familiar faculties of reason. In the feeling of piety the person of faith is immediately aware of his own spontaneity and his absolute dependence on an other. Schleiermacher shows how self-reassurance and the awareness of God are intertwined. His famous argument begins with the inner-worldly position of a subject who is characterized by responsiveness and autonomy and by an alternation between passive and active relations to the world.[67] Neither absolute freedom nor absolute dependence is *conceivable* for a finite subject turned toward the world. Just as absolute freedom is incompatible with the restrictions that the world places on situated agency, so, too, conversely, absolute dependence is incompatible with the intentional distance from the world without which states of affairs cannot be grasped objectively and treated accordingly. But once it turns away from the world, this subject is overcome by a feeling of utter dependence as it becomes aware of the spontaneity of its own conscious life. In the process of intuitive self-reassurance, it becomes conscious of its dependence on another being who first makes conscious life possible prior to our intentional distance from what we receive from the world and what we bring about in it.

This transcendental analysis of the feeling of piety equips religious experience with a general basis independent of both theoretical and practical reason on which Schleiermacher develops a far-reaching alternative to the Enlightenment. Religious experience rooted in "immediate self-consciousness" can claim coeval status with a reason that springs from the same root. In contradistinction to the concept of rational religion, Schleiermacher's transcendental philosophical introduction of religiosity has the

---

[67] Schleiermacher, *The Christian Faith*, trans. H. P. Mackintosh and J. S. Stewart (Edinburgh: T. & T. Clark, 1999), §§3–5.

advantage of being able to accommodate religious pluralism within society and the state without violating the claims of positive religious traditions or denying them altogether. For the pietistic valorization of religious inwardness supports the additional argument that the feeling of dependence characteristic of the human species as a whole *branches out* into *different* traditions once the feeling of piety acquires a specific articulation by being raised above the threshold of symbolic expression and assumes the practical form of an *ecclesiastically practiced* faith as believers unite to form communicative communities.

The philosophical insight that all religions have the same rational origin enables the churches – and the dogmatic interpretation of the respective ecclesiastical faiths – to find a legitimate place within the differentiated structure of modern societies. On this premise, they can practice mutual tolerance, recognize the secular order of the liberal state, and respect the authority of the sciences specialized in factual knowledge without damaging their respective claims to truth vis-à-vis members of other confessions and nonbelievers. For the philosophical justification of religious experience in general frees theology from unnecessary burdens of proof. Metaphysical proofs of God's existence and similar speculations become superfluous. Theology can quietly take its place within the university as one practical discipline among others by employing the best scientific methods to elucidate its central dogmas. However, the Culture Protestantism of the late nineteenth and early twentieth centuries makes clear the price that Schleiermacher has to pay for this elegant reconciliation of religion and modernity, faith, and knowledge. The integration of the Church into society and the privatization of faith rob the religious relation to transcendence of its disruptive power within the world.

The life and work of Adolf von Harnack invited the suspicion of a blunting of religious seriousness. The accommodation of religion to the spirit of modernity in the course of modernization robs the solidaristic practice of the religious community of the power of a reforming – and especially the energy of a revolutionary – practice *in the world*. On this view, the presence of God withdraws into the depths of the individual soul: "The kingdom of God comes . . . to the individual, by entering into his soul and laying hold of it."[68] Like Schleiermacher, Max Weber and Ernst Troeltsch construe religion as a form of consciousness that preserves its independence and structure-forming power even in modern societies. For them, however, the meaning of religious tradition is revealed only by concrete empirical evidence. They are able to conjure a binding normative content of religion out of the current of historicism only by reflecting on the Christian roots of the liberal, enlightened, individualistic con- temporary culture which they see as the reflection of their own self-understanding.[69]

(9) Kierkegaard's work stands in contrast to Schleiermacher's comforting analysis of the pious existence reconciled with moder- nity. He shares with his contemporary Marx the sense of crisis of a *restless* modernity. Unlike the latter, however, he does not attempt to break out of speculative thought and the corruption of bourgeois society through an inversion of the relation between theory and practice but through an existential response to the Lutheran question concerning the merciful God that plagued him. Through the radicalized awareness of sinfulness, the autonomy of reason is overshadowed by the absolutely heterogeneous power of the unknowable, self-proclaiming God whose existence is attested exclusively by history. This neo-orthodox countermove to the anthropocentric self-understanding of modernity represents an important historical stage in the reception of Kant's philosophy of religion. For it reaffirms the demarcation between reason and religion, this time from the side of revealed faith. In this way, Kierkegaard turns Kant's transcendental self-restriction of reason against its own anthropocentrism. It is not reason that sets restric- tions on religion, but religious experience that shows reason its

[68] Von Harnack, *What is Christianity*, trans. Thomas Bailey Saunders (New York: Williams & Norgate, 1902), p. 61; see also Gunther Wenz, "A. von Harnack – Herzensfrömmigkeit und Wissenschaftsmanagement," in Neuner and Wenz (eds), *Theologen des 20. Jahrhunderts*, pp. 33–52.
[69] F. W. Graf and Ernst Troeltsch, "Theologie als Kulturwissenschaft des Histo- rismus," in Neuner and Wenz (eds), *Theologen des 20. Jahrhunderts*, pp. 53–69; on Max Weber, see Wolfgang Schluchter, "Die Zukunft der Religion," in Schuchter, *Religion und Lebensführung*, Vol. 2 (Frankfurt am Main: Suhrkamp, 1988), pp. 506–34.

place. Of course, Kierkegaard knows that reason can only be defeated with its own weapons. He must convince "Socrates," the figure who plays the role of his Kantian adversary, that the post-conventional morality of conscience can become the point of crystallization of a conscious life conduct only when it is embedded in a religious self-understanding.[70]

Thus Kierkegaard uses pathological forms of life to describe the symptomatic stages of a salutary "sickness unto death" – the figures of an at first repressed *despair* that makes the transition to consciousness and finally forces an inversion of consciousness centered on the ego. These various shapes of despair represent so many manifestations of the *transgression* of the basic existential relation that could make an authentic being-oneself possible. Kierkegaard depicts the disturbing states of a person who is aware that his vocation is that he must be a self, but who takes refuge in alternatives: "in despair not to will to be oneself. Or even lower: in despair not to will to be a self. Or lowest of all: in despair to will to be someone else."[71] Someone who finally recognizes that the source of despair does not lie in his circumstances but in his own attempts to flee will make the defiant, but equally unsuccessful, attempt "to will to be oneself."

The despairing failure of this ultimate heroic feat – namely, a willing to be oneself that is entirely fixated on oneself – should lead the finite mind to transcend itself and hence also to recognize its dependence on an absolute other in which individual freedom is founded. This reversal marks a turning point, namely, the overcoming of the secularized self-understanding of modern reason: "in relating itself to itself and in willing to be itself, the self rests transparently in the power that established it."[72] This consciousness alone makes it possible to be oneself authentically.[73] A reason

[70] Habermas, "Are There Postmetaphysical Answers to the Question: What is the Good Life?" in Habermas, *The Future of Human Nature*, trans. Hella Beister and William Rehg (Cambridge: Polity, 2003), pp. 1–15.
[71] Søren Kierkegaard, *The Sickness unto Death*, ed. and trans. Howard V. Hong and Edna H. Hong (Princeton, N.J.: Princeton University Press, 1980), pp. 52–3.
[72] Ibid., p. 14.
[73] Michael Theunissen, *Das Selbst auf dem Grund des Verzweiflung* (Meisenheim-Frankfurt am Main: Beltz Athenäum, 1991).

reflecting on its deepest foundations discovers its origin in an other; and it must acknowledge the latter's ominous power if it is not to lose its orientation in the dead end of hybrid self-subjection.

In Schleiermacher this conversion of reason by reason begins with the self-consciousness of the knowing and acting subject, in Kierkegaard it begins with the historicality of existential self-confirmation. In both cases, a reason becoming aware of its limits transcends itself toward an other, be it in the reassuring feeling of dependence on an all-encompassing cosmic being or in the despairing hope in a historical event of redemption. The key difference is that Kierkegaard construes the conversion of reason as its abdication before the authority of the self-proclaiming Christian God, whereas Schleiermacher upholds the anthropocentric perspective and provides a philosophical justification of the basic religious experience from which positive religious traditions first spring.

For Karl Barth, such a philosophical conception of religiosity and religion is plain "unbelief" – and the Christian revelation "transcendence of religion."[74] Barth and Bultmann side with Kierkegaard in a dogged attempt to do justice to the inner normative logic of revealed faith and the Christian life in faith against the tide of historical thought, the secularizing pressure of society, and the privatization of faith. They highlight the elements of the Christian message that resist integration, the irreconcilable opposition between faith and knowledge. But this confrontation takes place on the foundation of postmetaphysical thinking that shields the critique of modernity against reactionary anti-modernism (as demonstrated by the political stand of Barth and Bultmann against the Nazi regime).

On the other hand, existentialist philosophy also lays claim to the legacy of Kierkegaard. It follows him along the path to an ethics that attaches only a *formal* value to the historical mode of a self-critical, conscious conduct of life.[75] Karl Jaspers attempts to

---

[74] Georg Pfleiderer, "Karl Barth – Theologie des Wortes Gottes als Kritik der Religion," in Neuner and Wenz, *Theologen des 20. Jahrhunderts*, pp. 124–44, here p. 135.

[75] See Habermas, "Are There Postmetaphysical Answers to the Question: What is the Good Life?"

go further by rationally reconstructing the radical tension between transcendence and worldly existence from the secular standpoint of the "illumination of existence." He succeeds, however, only at the cost of assimilating the validity claim of philosophical assertions to the status of truths of faith. He generalizes Kant's concept of rational faith, which was tailored to the postulates of God and immortality, to philosophy as a whole and demarcates "philosophical faith" from scientific knowledge. This leads to a family resemblance between philosophical teachings and religious traditions as competing systems of belief. Philosophy can at best clarify the character of this conflict but cannot resolve it with arguments.[76]

(10) What can we learn from this rough sketch of the reception of Kant's philosophy of religion concerning its contemporary relevance? Today this question is posed from the perspective of a threat to the normative content of modernity as it arose in the West. Hegel characterized the achievements of modernity with the concepts "self-consciousness," "self-determination," and "self-realization." Self-consciousness is a function of the growth in reflexivity in the context of a perpetual revision of dissolved traditions, self-determination is the result of the predominance of egalitarian and individualistic universalism in law and morality, and self-realization the result of the pressure toward individuation and self-direction under conditions of a highly abstract ego-identity.[77] This self-understanding of modernity is also a result of secularization, and thus of the liberation from the constraints of politically powerful religions. But today this normative consciousness is threatened not just from outside by the reactionary longing for a fundamentalist countermodernity, but also from within the uncontrolled process of modernization itself. The division of labor between the integrative mechanisms of the market, bureaucracy, and social solidarity is out of kilter and has shifted in favor of economic imperatives that reward forms of social interaction

---

[76] Jaspers, *Philosophical Faith and Revelation*, trans. E. B. Ashton (New York: Harper & Row, 1967).

[77] Habermas, *The Philosophical Discourse of Modernity*, trans. Frederick G. Lawrence (Cambridge, Mass.: MIT Press, 1987), pp. 368ff.

oriented to individual success. In addition, the establishment of new technologies that deeply permeate substrates of the human person that used to be regarded as "natural" promotes a naturalistic self-understanding among experiencing subjects in their interactions with one another.[78]

This disruption of normative consciousness also manifests itself in the dwindling sensitivity to social pathologies, indeed, to social deprivation and suffering in general. A sober postmetaphysical philosophy cannot compensate for this lack, which was already felt by Kant. It can no longer draw on the kind of reasons that could elevate *a single* motivating worldview above all others, specifically, one which satisfies existential expectations, provides binding orientations for life as a whole, or even offers consolation. We have seen that, with his doctrine of the postulates, Kant wanted to rob religion of more substance than practical reason can in all seriousness endure.

What he meant with the mode of rational faith holds more for the reflective self-understanding of members of religious communities, and of cultural groups in general, shaped by strong, identity-forming traditions. This mode of faith resembles the propositional attitudes we adopt toward our own forms of life that we regard as authentic. We live in the certainty of our way of life when we are convinced by its values. But there are different, equally authentic ways of life, so in this respect certainty and truth-validity diverge in an interesting way. No matter how certain we are of such an existential self-understanding, this does not licence us in the least to confuse the underlying value judgments with universalizable moral convictions (or even theoretical statements). At any rate, we do not associate with value orientations that have existential significance for us (and members like us) the claim that they merit universal recognition.

Against Kant, we must first affirm that conceptions of the kingdom of God and of an "ethical community" are inherently plural. It was the Kant of the philosophy of religion rather than Hegel who first recognized that the rational morality that occurs in the singular and the institutionalization of human rights and

[78] Habermas, "The Debate on the Ethical Self-Understanding of the Species," in Habermas, *The Future of Human Nature*, pp. 16–100.

democracy in the constitution must be embedded in the thick
context of a form of life. However, they acquire driving force from
being embedded in the *diverse* contexts of worldviews and forms
of life involving *competing* final ends. Disagreement between them
is something to be rationally expected and must be articulated in
public discourses lest it foster mute hostility and breed violence.
Here, philosophy in the role of a translator can promote moral,
legal, and political harmony only if it fosters enlightenment concerning the legitimate diversity of the substantive life plans of
believers, members of different faiths, and unbelievers, but not if
it adopts the posture of a superior competitor. In this interpretive
role, it can even contribute to the revival of sensibilities, thoughts,
and motives that, although they spring from other resources,
would remain buried if they were not brought into the light of
public reason through philosophical conceptualization.

Kant's philosophy of religion set standards both for the self-
critical restraint of a reason that *draws boundaries* and for the
maieutic role of a public discursive *appropriation* of the particularistic semantic potentials contained in the languages of specific
communities. But it throws light on the constellation of faith and
knowledge in our contemporary, postsecular societies only in the
context of its history of reception. Each of the three historical
lines of reception mentioned – Hegelian Marxism, Culture Protestantism, and existential dialectics – highlights a different aspect
of this changed constellation. Let me make a brief remark on this
in conclusion.

(11) Hegel's genealogical gaze interprets the suggestive images
and thick narratives of the major world religions as the history
of a mind that awaits reflexive appropriation through the labor of
the concept. From this perspective, today philosophy also finds
in uncomprehended religious traditions and in misunderstood
communal practices insights, intuitions, expressive possibilities,
sensibilities, and modes of social interaction which, although
not inherently alien to public reason, are too enigmatic to be
spontaneously absorbed into the communicative circuits of society
as a whole. These contents have the potential to regenerate an
atrophied normative consciousness if they offer a basis for developing concepts that open up new perspectives. Thus, at one time
basic concepts such as "positivity," "alienation," and "reification" –

concepts that serve to deny their religious heritage in the prohibition on images and the fall from grace – transformed perceptions in general. They cast the triumphal march of capitalist modernization in a different light and revived sensibilities that had become blunted to social pathologies. The critical use of such concepts tore the veil of normality from established social relations.

After the breakdown in civilization of National Socialism, Benjamin's concept of "anamnestic solidarity" with past injustice, for example – a concept that manifestly tries to fill the gap left by the lost hope in a Last Judgment – recalled a form of collective liability beyond moral obligation.[79] The idea of approaching the kingdom of God, assimilated within the boundaries of mere reason, does not direct our gaze toward the future alone. This idea inspires a general awareness of collective responsibility for failures to offer help and failures to cooperate in averting imminent disaster or even simply to cooperate in improving shameful social conditions. To be sure, cooperation can meet this expectation only *in lucky moments*. But the weak responsibility for the collective fate of one's neighbors and of distant peoples is not lifted from our shoulders simply because our fallible powers are mostly inadequate or because it sometimes misleads obstinate or fanatical individuals who fail to recognize their own fallibility.

Kant, Hegel, and Marx goaded secular consciousness with the spur of the religious legacy. But only Schleiermacher and Kierkegaard demanded that philosophy should acknowledge religion as a counterpart of equal status. They freed Christianity from its alliance with Greek metaphysics and defended or criticized it on the Kantian level of postmetaphysical thinking vis-à-vis the learned and the indifferent among its critics.

Schleiermacher explains why religion is not merely a phenomenon of the past that must close itself off against the complexity of modernity. He shows how the Church, religious consciousness, and theology can stake out a position for themselves under conditions of social and cultural differentiation as contemporary, indeed

---

[79] Helmut Peukert, *Wissenschaftstheorie, Handlungstheorie, fundamentale Theologie* (Düsseldorf: Patmos, 1976), pp. 278ff. See also Habermas, "A Reply to my Critics," in John Thomson and David Held (eds), *Habermas – Critical Debates* (Cambridge, Mass.: MIT Press, 1982), pp. 245ff.

functionally specific, forms of spirit. Schleiermacher is the pace-maker for the consciousness of a postsecular society that accepts the continued existence of religion in an environment that is becoming progressively more secular. At the same time, he effects a modernization of religious consciousness from "within" that then links up with the normatively indispensable conditions of postconventional law, with the pluralism of worldviews, and with scientifically institutionalized factual knowledge. However, Schlei-ermacher meets a philosophy that wants to uncover the epistemic aspects of faith halfway to the extent that he brings about the reconciliation between religion and modernity with philosophical means.

Kierkegaard was the first to confront postmetaphysical thought with the irreducible heterogeneity of a religious faith that unre-servedly rejects the anthropocentricity of a form of philosophical thought that takes its point of departure from within the world. Philosophy first achieves a serious dialectical relation to the domain of religious experience through this challenge. The core of this experience resists the secularizing appropriation of philo-sophical analysis just as aesthetic experience resists rationalizing appropriation. Philosophy, after all, with its concepts of the beau-tiful, the ugly, and the sublime, can do little more than carefully circumscribe the wordless stimulation of the senses set in motion by the play of reflecting judgment. The source of sensuousness escapes the understanding. Something similar holds for a "tran-scendence" that penetrates the world from the outside. For, with this concept, philosophy circumscribes the archaic origins of the utopian energy for "promoting the highest good" over whose source a detranscendentalized reason no longer claims any power. It can provide a discursive reconstruction only of a transcendence from within.[80]

Philosophy can draw *rational* sustenance from the religious heritage only as long as the source of revelation that orthodoxy counterposes to philosophy remains a cognitively unacceptable imposition for the latter. The perspectives which are centered *either* in God *or* in human beings cannot be converted *into one another*. Once this boundary between faith and knowledge

---

[80] Habermas, *Religion and Rationality*, pp. 67–94.

becomes porous, and once religious motives force their way into philosophy *under false pretences*, reason loses its foothold and succumbs to irrational effusion [*Schwärmerei*]. Kant's self-critique of reason was not only supposed to clarify the relation between theology and practical reason. It was also supposed to differentiate reason itself, in its justified theoretical and practical uses, from excessive metaphysical claims to knowledge, on the one hand, and from supersensible religious truths of faith, on the other. These determinations of the limits of postmetaphysical (and post-Christian) thought can still provide standards in the search for orientation concerning the relation between faith and knowledge in the contemporary philosophical landscape.

(12) As a guide to a rough localization, I would like to distinguish (a) directions of thought which retreat behind the boundary that Kant draws to the metaphysical tradition from approaches which (b) respect the limits of postmetaphysical thinking or which (c) efface these markers again by "going beyond" a mode of thought that draws limits.

(a) The speculative need that Plato bequeathed to philosophy with the ascent to the Ideas and the liberation of mind from the fetters of matter has, of course, not come to rest. Thus the revival or dialectical appropriation – on the post-Kantian basis of self-consciousness – of forms of argumentation from the classical tradition serves, at least implicitly, to recover thoughts relevant for salvation. These motifs are often (e.g. in Leo Strauss) associated with currents of thought critical of modernity and corresponding political motives. However, the recovery of the tradition of Western metaphysics does not always focus on Greek origins but often also (as in Carl Schmitt) on medieval ontotheology. Then the point is not to heal the wounds inflicted by modernity through the contemplative reassurance of a cosmic order (being as a whole), thus along the "path to salvation" that connects the *bios theoretikos* with Oriental meditation practices. The concern is rather, as formerly in neo-Thomism or today in Islamic philosophy, with the metaphysical justification of the basic claims of monotheistic teachings. On certain readings, theological Hegelianism and analytic ontology can also be understood as continuations of classical apologetics with different means.

(b) Kant's differentiation between faith and knowledge presupposed the break with the totalizing epistemic claim of metaphysics. This turn toward postmetaphysical thinking devalued a certain ontological conceptual apparatus and a certain structure of explanation; it was supposed to raise philosophy to the level of modern science.[81] Of course, after this turn, philosophy adopted a variety of approaches to religion.

Modern apologetics, which remains centered on the Catholic philosophy of religion, differs from classical apologetics not only in the concepts it employs but also in the goal of its arguments. Granted, neither speaks, in the manner of theology, "in the name of," but only "with reference to," a tradition of faith *assumed to be true*, and both use contemporary philosophical approaches (which nowadays extend from Critical Theory to Wittgenstein) with the goal of rationally justifying the cognitive components of their preferred religious doctrines.[82] However, modern apologetics no longer shares with its classical counterpart the rejection of the spiritual foundations of secular society and culture. With an at once critical and apologetic intention, it brings about the internal rationalization of a religious heritage (alongside modern theology) with the aim of finding a satisfying dogmatic answer to the challenges posed by modern religious pluralism, the scientific monopoly on knowledge, and the constitutional state.

Scientism represents the opposite pole to this rational reconstruction of the contents of faith. For scientism, religious convictions are false, illusory, or meaningless *per se*. On this conception, legitimate knowledge must be able to find support at the "level" reached by the socially institutionalized empirical sciences at any given time. The validity of religious convictions, too, is measured exclusively by this yardstick; hence the religious language game, if only for grammatical reasons, must be rejected as cognitively

---

[81] Habermas, "Themes in Postmetaphysical Thinking," in Habermas, *Postmetaphysical Thinking*, trans. William Mark Hohengarten (Cambridge, Mass.: MIT Press, 1994), pp. 28–56.

[82] See, for example, Peukert, *Wissenschaftstheorie*; Matthias Lutz-Bachmann, "Materialismus und Materialismuskritik bei Max Horkheimer und Theodor W. Adorno," in Klaus J. Grün and Matthias Jung (eds), *Idee, Natur, Geschichte: Alfred Schmidt zum 60. Geburtstag* (Munich: Olms, 1991), pp. 143–59; Friedo Ricken, *Religionsphilosophie* (Stuttgart: Kohlhammer, 2003).

empty. The practical evaluation of religion – whether it must be regarded as dangerous and, if necessary, treated therapeutically or whether it must be resisted – depends solely on the empirical investigation of its causes, functions, and consequences. Scientism enters into a genuine relation of competition with religious doctrines, however, once it develops a naturalistic worldview and extends the scientifically objectivating standpoint into the life-world by applying it to acting and experiencing persons with the demand for the self-objectification of everyday knowledge.

Finally, I use the term "postmetaphysical," not only in a methodological sense that concerns procedures and conceptual means but also in a substantial sense, to describe agnostic positions that make a sharp distinction between belief and knowledge without assuming the validity of a particular religion (as does modern apologetics) or without denying the possible cognitive content of these traditions (as does scientism). Here I want to distinguish between *rationalist* approaches that (in the Hegelian tradition) *subsume* [*aufheben*] the substance of faith into the philosophical concept, from *dialogical* approaches that (following Karl Jaspers) adopt a critical attitude toward religious traditions while at the same time being open to *learning* from them.[83]

This classification is based on whether philosophy assumes or presumes to decide what is true or false in religion, or whether it leaves the internal questions of the validity of religion to disputes within rational apologetics and is solely concerned to salvage cognitive contents from religious traditions. All semantic contents count as "cognitive" in this sense which can be translated into a form of discourse decoupled from the ratcheting effect of truths of revelation. In this discourse, only "public" reasons count, hence reasons that have the power to convince also beyond the boundaries of a particular religious community. The methodological separation between the two universes of discourse is compatible with the openness of philosophy to possible cognitive contents of religion. This "appropriation" is free from any intention to interfere or to launch a "hostile takeover." As it happens, this at once tolerant and clear demarcation from religious dogmatics reflects the level of consciousness of secular citizens who are aware that they

[83] Jaspers, *Philosophical Faith and Revelation.*

live in postsecular society. This posture distinguishes the postmetaphysical self-understanding of the Kantian tradition from
the neopaganism that appeals – whether rightly or wrongly – to
Nietzsche.

(c) The attitude of philosophy toward religion not only
expresses the controversial self-understanding of philosophy, i.e.
what it thinks it can and cannot still accomplish. The interpretation of the relation between philosophy and religion also reveals
whether the attitude toward modernity is one of rejection or
one of critical affirmation. After all, the regenerative power
of the metaphysical heritage is supposed in this way to compensate for a felt *lack* in modernity. By contrast, postmetaphysical
thinking can draw back from the contents of a totalizing world-
construction out of nature and history because it *accepts* the
modern differentiations, even though with a critical intent; as
Kant's three "Critiques" demonstrate, it *associates* itself with the
already differentiated spheres of validity of science and technology, law and morality, art and criticism. Finally, the mostly
implicit connection between attitudes toward religion, on the one
hand, and modernity, on the other, becomes explicit among the
postmodern followers of Nietzsche.

Here the intention of a future-oriented revolutionary overcoming of a disastrous and *condemned* modernity is the salient theme.
However, this time the return to a "different beginning" leads back
behind Jaspers's "Axial Age." A self-obsessed modernity mindless
of tradition is supposed to represent the culmination of the history
of decline that dates from the beginnings of metaphysics *and*
religion with Socrates and Moses. This diagnosis of the age leads
to the leveling assessment of religion – like metaphysics itself,
it is treated as an expression of the forgetfulness of being. Only
the originary powers of a myth still to come can bring about the
longed-for turning away from the pretensions of the logos. Speaking from a place beyond the logos, however, this neopagan specu-
lation on "the flight or advent of the gods" must employ a rhetoric
that has turned its back on the power of rational argument and
replaced it with the incantatory self-glorification of the "great and
hidden individual."

Ironically, the only available vocabulary is the familiar eschatological one. Thus the late Heidegger speaks in terms of "terror,"
"venture," "leap," "resoluteness," "acquiescence," "remembrance,"

"thoughtfulness," "advent," "withdrawal," "devotion," "gift," "happening," and "turning." At the same time, he must cover the traces of the heritage of this language game. For he had long since dismissed the Christian message of redemption, whose semantics he nevertheless has to exploit, as the insignificant ontotheological interlude of an "obsolete theocracy."[84] Kant's limitation of reason to its practical use in his philosophy of religion today applies less to religious effusion than to an effusive philosophy that merely *borrows* the propitious connotations of the vocabulary of a religion of redemption to exempt itself from the rigor of discursive thought. Here, too, we have much to learn from Kant, for his philosophy of religion can be understood in general as a warning against "religious philosophy."

---

[84] Heidegger, *Contributions to Philosophy (From En-owning)*, trans. Parvis Emad and Kenneth Maly (Bloomington: Indiana University Press, 2006).

Part IV

Tolerance

9

Religious Tolerance as Pacemaker for Cultural Rights

(1) It was not until the sixteenth century, in the context of the Reformation, that the German language borrowed the word "Toleranz" from the Latin and French. In this context the concept immediately assumed the narrow meaning of toleration (or indulgence [*Duldsamkeit*]) of other religious confessions.[1] In the course of the sixteenth and seventeenth centuries, religious tolerance became a legal concept. Governments issued tolerance edicts that enjoined state officials and the population to be tolerant in their treatment of religious minorities, such as Lutherans, Huguenots, and Papists.[2] Legal acts of toleration by absolutist governments created the expectation that people (as a rule the majority of the population)[3] should behave tolerantly toward members of religious communities which until then had suffered oppression or persecution.

---

[1] See the *Allgemeine Handwörterbuch der philosophischen Wissenschaften nebst ihrer Literatur und Geschichte*, ed. Wilhelm Traugott Krug (2nd edn, 1832): "'Toleranz' (from the Latin *tolerare*, 'to tolerate' or 'put up with') is 'Duldsamkeit' [i.e. toleration or indulgence] . . . However, this word is mainly used in the narrower sense of religious tolerance, just as its opposite 'intolerance' is used in the sense of religious intolerance."
[2] In 1598, Henri IV of France issued the *Edict of Nantes*; see also the *Act Concerning Religion* passed by the government of Maryland in 1649, the *Toleration Act* issued by the king of England in 1689, and – as one of the last instances in this series of absolutist "authorizations" – the "Patent of Tolerance" issued by Joseph II in 1781.
[3] The case was different in Maryland, where a Catholic minority ruled over a Protestant majority.

English makes a more precise distinction than German between "tolerance" as a form of behavior and "toleration," the legal act through which a government grants more or less unrestricted permission to practice one's particular religion. In German, the predicate "tolerant" refers both to a legal order that guarantees toleration and to the political virtue of tolerant behavior. Montesquieu emphasizes the sequential link between toleration and tolerance: "When the legislator has believed it a duty to permit the exercise of many religions, it is necessary that he should enforce also a toleration among these religions themselves . . . It is necessary, then, that the laws require from the several religions, not only that they shall not embroil the state, but that they shall not raise disturbances among themselves."[4]

The concept retained not only its reference to religious addressees into the era of the French Revolution, but also the authoritarian connotation of *mere* toleration. That said, since Spinoza and Locke, the philosophical justifications offered for religious tolerance point away from the authoritarian act of *unilaterally* declared religious toleration toward a right to exercise one's religion freely based on the *mutual* recognition of everybody's religious freedom, which entails a right to protection against the imposition of alien religious practices. Rainer Forst contrasts the "permission conception" of authorities who grant religious freedoms to the "respect conception." The latter concurs with our understanding of religious freedom as a civil right that every person can claim as a human being, independent of her religious affiliation.[5]

Pierre Bayle came up with ever new examples designed to urge his intolerant opponents to adopt the perspective of other persons and to apply their own standards to their opponents as well:

If a mufti should take it into his head to send missionaries into Christendom, as the Pope does in India, and if these missionaries should be caught going into people's houses to carry out their mission to make converts, I do not see what right anyone has to punish them. If they were to answer the same thing that the Christian missionaries do in Japan, namely, that a zeal for making

[4] Montesquieu, *The Spirit of the Laws*, trans. Thomas Nugent (2 vols) (New York: Hafner Press, 1949), vol. 2, p. 52.
[5] See below, n. 11.

known the true religion to those who are in error and promoting the salvation of their neighbor whose blindness they lament moved them to share their insights, and if, without any regard to this answer or hearing about their reasons they had been hanged, would it not be ridiculous to complain when the Japanese do the same?[6]

Bayle – who is in this respect a forerunner of Kant – practices mutual perspective-taking. He insists on *universalizing* the "ideas" in terms of which we judge "the nature of human action."[7]

Reciprocal recognition of the rules of tolerant behavior also provides a basis for resolving the supposed paradox that famously prompted Goethe to reject tolerance as an insulting and patronizing form of benevolence. The ostensible paradox is that every act of toleration must circumscribe the range of behavior that everyone must accept, thereby setting limits to tolerance itself. There can be no inclusion without exclusion. And as long as this line is drawn in an authoritarian manner, i.e., unilaterally, toleration bears the stigma of arbitrary exclusion. Only the idea of equal freedoms for all and a definition of the domain of tolerance that all concerned find equally convincing can draw the sting of intolerance from tolerance. All those potentially affected by the future practice must take account of the perspectives of everyone else if they are to reach an agreement concerning the conditions under which they, as all meriting equal respect, wish to practice mutual tolerance.

The familiar conditions of a liberal social ethos among different religious groups satisfy this standard of reciprocity. They involve, first, the renunciation of the use of political power for missionary purposes and a freedom of association that, in addition, forbids religious authorities from exercising compulsion over the conscience of their members. Only if they find intersubjective recognition across confessional divides, can such norms provide justifications that *trump* the subjective grounds for rejecting alien religious convictions and practices. Even if Jellinek's suggestion

---

[6] Pierre Bayle, *Pierre Bayle's Philosophical Commentary: A Modern Translation and Critical Interpretation*, trans. Amie Godman Tannenbaum (New York: Peter Lang, 1987), pp. 145–6.
[7] Ibid.

that all human rights are rooted in religious freedom lacks any historical basis, there is certainly a *conceptual connection* between the universalistic justification for the basic right to religious freedom, on the one hand, and democracy and human rights as the normative foundation of the constitutional state, on the other.

For citizens can agree on where to draw the boundaries of a reciprocally demanded tolerance only if they submit their decisions to a form of deliberation that compels the parties involved, who are also those affected, to adopt each other's perspectives and to give equal consideration to the interests of all. But precisely this kind of deliberative will-formation is fostered by the democratic constitutional procedures. Religious tolerance can be guaranteed in a tolerant manner under the precise conditions under which the citizens of a democratic polity grant one another freedom of religion. The purported paradox dissolves with the right to the free exercise of one's own religion and the corresponding negative freedom to remain unmolested by other people's practice of their religions. From the perspective of a democratic lawmaker who makes the addressees of law into its authors, the legal act of mutual toleration fuses with the virtuous self-obligation to behave tolerantly.

However, the paradox that every limited conception of tolerance implies intolerance does not seem to be fully resolved by this reciprocal generalization of religious freedom into a basic right but instead seems to reemerge in a secular guise at the very core of the constitutional state. A democratic order that guarantees tolerance must take preventive measures against the enemies of the constitution. Since the "legal" transition from the Weimar Republic to the Nazi regime at the latest, we in Germany have been aware of the peculiar dialectic of the self-assertion of a "militant" democracy that is "prepared to defend itself."[8] Courts can pass judgment on the limits of religious freedom on a case-by-case basis by appealing to the law and the constitution. However, if the freedom-guaranteeing constitution itself is

---

[8] Karl Loewenstein, "Militant Democracy and Fundamental Rights, I," *American Political Science Review* 31 (1937): 417–32; see also his *Verfassungslehre*, 3rd edn (Tübingen: Mohr, 1975), pp. 348ff.

opposed by the enemies of freedom who make use of their political freedom to abolish the constitution that grants it, then the question concerning the limits of political freedom arises in a self-referential form: How tolerant can a democracy be toward the enemies of democracy?

If the democratic state does not wish to abdicate, then it must resort to intolerance toward enemies of the constitution, either by employing the mechanisms of political criminal law or by prohibiting particular political parties (Article 21.2 of the German Basic Law) and suspending basic rights (Article 18 and Article 9.2 of the same). The "enemy of the state," originally a concept with religious connotations, resurfaces in the guise of the enemy of the constitution, whether in the secularized form of the political ideologist who combats the liberal state or in the figure of the fundamentalist who violently attacks the modern way of life *as such*. But who is to define the enemy of the constitution if not the organs of the constitutional state itself? The constitutional state must protect itself against the hostility of its mortal enemies while simultaneously guarding against betraying its own principles, i.e. against the perennial danger of a self-incurred regression to an authoritarian practice of unilaterally defining the limits of tolerance. Those who are suspected of being "enemies of the state" may very well turn out to be radical defenders of democracy. Whereas religious tolerance can delegate the paradoxical task of limiting itself to democracy, the latter must deal with the paradox of constitutional tolerance within the legal medium that is proper to it.

The paradox is heightened when the constitution is protected in a paternalistic way. For a law reified into an "objective order of values" has, as Konrad Hesse recognized, "an inherent tendency to seek the security of the constitution and the state it constitutes in a well-oiled surveillance and counterintelligence system." We must not overlook the fact that "the substance of liberal democracy cannot be secured through restrictions on freedom."[9] A militant

---

[9] Konrad Hesse, *Grundzüge des Verfassungsrechts der Bundesrepublik Deutschland*, 17th edn (Heidelberg: Müller, 1990), marginal note 694; see Günther Frankenberg, *Die Verfassung der Republik* (Baden-Baden: Nomos, 1996), pp. 107ff.

democracy can circumvent the danger of paternalism by allowing the self-regulating democratic procedure to exercise its self-referential effects also in open-ended democratic debates over the correct interpretation of constitutional principles in particular contexts.

How a constitutional state deals with civil disobedience serves as a kind of litmus test in this respect. Of course, the constitution itself lays down how conflicts over the interpretation of the constitution are to be dealt with. When constitutional courts grant legal recognition to *"civil disobedience"* (which does not mean exempting it from punishment), the tolerant spirit of a liberal constitution also goes beyond the totality of existing institutions and practices in which its normative contents have found concrete embodiment. A democratic constitution that understands itself as the project of realizing equal civil rights tolerates the resistance of dissidents who continue to combat legitimate decisions even after all the legal channels have been exhausted – under the proviso, of course, that the "disobedient" citizens offer plausible reasons for their resistance by appealing to constitutional principles and employ nonviolent, i.e., symbolic means.[10] These two conditions define the limits of political tolerance in a constitutional democracy that defends itself against its enemies by nonpaternalistic means, limits that are also acceptable to its democratically minded opponents.

Recognizing civil disobedience is the democratic state's way of dealing with the paradox of tolerance that reappears at the level of constitutional law. It draws a line between a tolerant and a self-destructive treatment of ambivalent dissidents. It thereby ensures that dissidents, who could ultimately prove to be enemies of the constitution, nevertheless have an opportunity to contradict this appearance and prove themselves to be in fact the true constitutional patriots, that is, champions of a constitution understood in dynamic terms as an ongoing *project*. This self-reflexive

---

[10] On the problematic issue of civil disobedience, see "The New Obscurity: The Crisis of the Welfare State and the Exhaustion of Utopian Energies," in Habermas, *The New Conservatism: Cultural Criticism and the Historians' Debate*, ed. and trans. Shierry Weber Nicholsen (Cambridge, Mass.: MIT Press, 1989), pp. 48–70.

limitation of the limits of tolerance of the constitution can be understood, in turn, as an expression of the principle of the equal inclusion of all citizens whose universal recognition must be pre-supposed if tolerance of members of other confessions and of unconventional ideas is to be institutionalized in the right way.

Pluralism and the struggle for religious tolerance were not only driving forces behind the emergence of the democratic state, but remain important impulses for its consistent development up to the present day. Before addressing religious tolerance as the pacemaker for multiculturalism, correctly understood, and for the equal coexistence of different cultural forms of life within a democratic polity (3), I want to analyze the concept of tolerance a bit further and to explain the specific burden imposed on citizens by the expectation to behave tolerantly (2). For the purpose of conceptual analysis, it is useful to distinguish the two kinds of reasons involved, i.e. reasons to reject the convictions of others and reasons nevertheless to accept the common membership of people who disagree fundamentally within the same political community. From the latter reasons – political reasons for civic inclusion – the third kind of reasons I have already mentioned can be derived, namely, reasons for the limits of tolerance and the repression of intolerant behavior. These legal reasons then open the door to the justification of cultural rights.

(2) We have already mentioned in passing the three components of the modern concept of tolerance distinguished by Rainer Forst under the headings of *rejection* [*Ablehnung*], *acceptance* [*Akzeptanz*], and *repudiation* [*Zurückweisung*].[11] Tolerance rulings were the result of religious conflicts. The challenge posed by tolerance consists in the fact that, although the mutual *rejection* of convictions and practices is based on good subjective reasons, there is no reasonable hope of a cognitive resolution of the disagreement (a). Thus the persisting disagreement between believers, those

---

[11] Rainer Forst, "Toleranz, Gerechtigkeit und Vernunft," in Forst (ed.), *Toleranz* (Frankfurt am Main: Suhrkamp, 2000), pp. 144–61; Forst, "Grenzen der Toleranz," in Winfrid Brugger and Görg Haverkate (eds), *Grenzen als Thema der Rechts- und Sozialphilosophie* (Stuttgart: Steiner, 2002); see, furthermore, Forst, *Toleranz im Konflikt* (Frankfurt am Main: Suhrkamp, 2003).

of different faiths, and unbelievers must be uncoupled from the social level if they are to continue to interact peacefully as citizens of the same polity. However, this calls for joint *acceptance* of a foundation of impartial reasons that trump good reasons for rejection without neutralizing them (b). Finally, legally binding rulings call for a demarcation between what should be tolerated and what can no longer be tolerated. The impartiality of the mirror-image reasons for *acceptance and repudiation* is, as we have shown, ensured by an inclusive procedure of deliberative will-formation that requires the participants to respect one another and to adopt one another's perspectives. Then a corresponding imperative of neutrality addressed to the state also provides the normative foundation for generalizing religious rights into cultural rights (c).

(a) The general question of when a situation arises that calls for tolerant behavior and makes it possible is answered by spelling out the rejection components. The concept would be used in too loose a sense if "tolerance" were extended to include the patient and indulgent treatment of others or of strangers in general. Instead it means the legally noncoercible *political* virtue of citizens in their dealings with other citizens who adhere to a rejected conviction. We should respect the fellow-citizen in others even when we regard their beliefs or ideas as *false* and the corresponding way of life as *bad*. Tolerance protects a pluralistic society from being torn apart as a political community by conflicts over worldviews.

Thus only someone who has subjectively convincing reasons for rejecting the beliefs of people of other faiths can practice tolerance. Tolerance is not indifference; for indifference toward the convictions and practices of others, or even esteem for others and their otherness, robs tolerance of its proper object. The reasons for rejection that call for tolerance, however, must not be accepted on merely subjective grounds. They must be able to claim public legitimacy. Prejudices do not count. Tolerance can exist only when the parties involved can base their rejection on a *reasonable* ongoing absence of agreement. Not every rejection is reasonable in this sense. After all, we do not confront chauvinists or racists with calls for more tolerance, but with the demand that they should overcome their prejudices. Refraining from discrimination, and hence showing equal respect for everybody, is what is called for in the first instance toward those who *are* different, rather than the tolerance called for by those who *think* differently.

This points to an interesting conclusion: tolerance begins only once discrimination has been overcome. As in the case of religious freedom, we can call for tolerance only once the prejudices on the basis of which a minority was initially repressed have been overcome. Admittedly, the example of anti-Semitism demonstrates that the rejection of members of different faiths in fact remained connected with stubborn prejudices long after the legal emancipation of Jewish citizens. But, as in Lessing's play *Nathan the Wise*, the differences in religious beliefs that provide "good" reasons for rejecting the convictions and practices of others emerge for enlightened Christians, Muslims, and Jews only after all prejudices have been overcome. By contrast, once the corresponding prejudices against people of color, homosexuals, or women are overcome, no components of "otherness" remain to which a *justified* rejection that was generally recognized as legitimate could refer.

Aside from this qualification of the reasons for rejection founded on a *reasonable* ongoing disagreement, the rejected but tolerated views must themselves exhibit an internal relation to the practice. Thus salvation religions derive an immediate power to orient action from their significance for the personal salvation of the believer. But metaphysical worldviews and political ideologies also offer explanations of the world, of history, and of society in a "thick" normative language that has practical implications for the success or failure of one's life. Only conceptions with an ethical content of this kind can influence conduct and are potential targets of a demand for tolerance that places restrictions on behavior. We can adopt a critical, scrutinizing stance toward competing scientific theories, but not a tolerant one.[12]

In theoretical controversies, scientific specialization is sufficient to pre-empt the practical lifeworld conflicts that erupt in religious disputes because religious truths have immediate relevance for

---

[12] Jürgen Habermas, "Wann müssen wir tolerant sein? Über die Konkurrenz von Weltbildern, Werten und Theorien," *Jahrbuch des Berlin-Brandenburgischen Akademie der Wissenschaften* (Berlin, 2003): 167–78.

the personal conduct of one's life. Scientists are drawn into such conflicts only when the practice of research promises to have implications for the ethical self-understanding of persons beyond the domain of research (as in the case of research on embryos). As it happens, this shows that a naturalism based on a synthetic treatment of scientific information is itself a worldview and is situated on the same level as religious interpretations as far as the relevance of knowledge for ethical action goes.

On the other hand, only those conceptions call for tolerance that conflict for subjectively understandable reasons but where there is no reasonable prospect of reaching a rational agreement. Scientists assume that the problems they work on generally admit of convincing solutions, though ones that remain open to criticism. They are attempting to uncover truths that for us still lie in the future. Religious people, by contrast, see themselves as interpreters of a truth revealed in the past that does not admit of revision and can be defended against competing articles of faith with good reasons. In this respect, the conflict between the political views of parties competing for influence in accordance with democratic rules resembles a theoretical dispute among scientists more than a dogmatic dispute among theologians. The conflict of political opinions is also (methodically) regulated *mutatis mutandis* through democratic procedures in such a way that those involved conduct it with the goal of reaching rationally acceptable solutions. Granted, in political controversies the scope of the reasonably expectable non-agreement is broader than in scientific disputes. But the expectation that disagreement will endure is merely a function of the fact that political convictions are more deeply embedded in background convictions founded on worldviews.

We can speak of "political tolerance," therefore, only in a narrower sense – not in the everyday political affairs of a democracy but only in relation to conflicts between comprehensive political ideologies. As long as citizens engage in disputes over political problems that they believe can be solved, civil conduct is sufficient. Tolerance is not the same thing as the political virtue of civility. Granted, the definition offered by John Rawls of such a "duty of civility" comes very close to tolerance: "This duty . . . involves a willingness to listen to others and a fair-mindedness in deciding when accommodations to their views should reasonably be made."[13] Nevertheless, tolerance toward those who think differently should not be confused with the willingness to cooperate and to make compromises. Tolerance becomes necessary – over and above the patient pursuit of truth, openness, mutual trust, and a sense of justice – only when the parties with good reason neither seek agreement concerning controversial beliefs nor think agreement is possible.

(b) If we want to determine exactly what burden the demand for tolerance involves, we must offer an account of the acceptance of reasons that morally trump reasons for rejection. The burden in question is twofold: someone who is tolerant may, on the one hand, realize his own ethos only within the limits of what everyone is equally entitled to; on the other hand, he must also respect the ethos of others within these limits. It is not the rejected views and the competing validity claims that must be accepted. The individual's own truth claims and certainties remain undisturbed. The burden does not follow from the need to relativize one's own convictions but from the demand to restrict their practical efficacy. The imposition consists in the requirement that the mode of life prescribed by one's religion, or the ethos inscribed in one's worldview, may be practiced only under the condition of equal rights for everybody. This burden is of a cognitive nature insofar as the morality and law of a liberal polity must be reconciled with the religious convictions in which one's own ethos is embedded. What this means can be seen from the intellectual accommodations that have been demanded of religious consciousness in Europe since the Reformation at the latest.

Every religion is originally a "worldview" or, in Rawls's terminology, a "comprehensive doctrine," also in the sense that it claims the authority to structure a form of life *in its entirety*. Religion must renounce this claim to structure life in a comprehensive way that also includes the community once the life of religious groups becomes differentiated from that of the larger political community within pluralistic societies. The major religions must reappropriate the normative foundations of the liberal state *on their own premises* even if, as in the case of the Judeo-Christian legacy

---

[13] John Rawls, *Political Liberalism* (New York: Columbia University Press, 1993), p. 217.

in Europe, a genealogical connection exists between the two. Rawls chose the image of a module to represent how the morality of human rights is "embedded" within different religious comprehensive doctrines. The module fits into the various orthodox contexts of justification even though it is constructed exclusively on the basis of reasons that are neutral with respect to worldviews.[14] Viewed in functional terms, religious tolerance is supposed to absorb the social destructiveness of a persistent irreconcilable disagreement. But the required differentiation between the role of a member of the community and that of a citizen must be given a convincing justification from the perspective of the religion *itself* if conflicts of loyalty are not to continue to fester.

Religious membership harmonizes with membership of secular society only if the corresponding sets of norms and values not only differ from one another, but if the one can be derived consistently *from the other*, also from the internal perspective. If the differentiation between the two memberships is to go beyond a mere *modus vivendi*, the transformation must not be limited to a cognitively undemanding accommodation of the religious ethos to externally *imposed* laws of the secular society. It calls for a cognitive derivation of the social morality established by the democratic constitution *out of* the communal ethos. In many cases this necessitates the revision of attitudes and prescriptions that – as in the case of the dogmatic condemnation of homosexuality, for example – rest on a long-standing tradition of interpretation of sacred texts. In difficult cases, even the classification of a matter in need of regulation as a "moral" or an "ethical" question is controversial. Thus, in the case of abortion, for example, Catholics must allow the public courts to ascribe to them as part of their particular religious ethos a conception that, in their view, rests on moral judgments that claim universal validity.

It becomes even clearer from this complementary standpoint of respect for the ethos of others that the burdens of tolerance are not equal for believers and unbelievers. For the consciousness of the secularized citizen with light metaphysical baggage who can accept a morally "freestanding" or autonomous justification of

[14] Ibid., pp. 11ff.

democracy and human rights, the right – or the moral point of view – has priority over the substantive conceptions of the good. On this premise, the plurality of *ways of life*, each of which reflects a different worldview, does not generate any cognitive dissonance with one's own ethical convictions. For different ways of life merely incorporate different *value orientations*. And different sets of values are simply *other* values for one another; unlike different *truths*, they are not incompatible.

The reference to a first person, to the life history of an individual or the form of life of a collectivity, remains inscribed in ethical judgments. Thus what is good for one person in his own context may be bad for another person in a different context. If the evaluation of alien forms of life and life plans does not demand the same kind of *universal* agreement as do judgments concerning justice or factual assertions, we can show equal respect for each without needing to hold all forms of life in equal esteem. Thus secular consciousness has no difficulty in acknowledging that an alien ethos has the same authenticity and enjoys the same priority for others as our ethos does for us. Those who derive their ethical self-understanding from religious truths that claim universal validity, by contrast, cannot draw the same conclusion.

For the believer who travels with heavy metaphysical baggage, the good enjoys epistemic primacy over the right. The validity of the ethos on this assumption depends on the truth of the worldview in which it is embedded. The exclusive validity claims of the underlying worldviews are accordingly bound up with different ethical existential orientations and competing forms of life. As soon as one's conception of the good life is shaped by religious notions of salvation or metaphysical conceptions of the good, a divine perspective (or a "view from nowhere") opens up from which (or where) other ways of life appear not only different but *mistaken*. When an alien ethos is not merely evaluated in relative terms, but is judged in terms of truth and falsity, the demand to show every citizen equal respect regardless of his ethical self-understanding and his way of life represents an imposition. In contrast with competition between values, therefore, contradictions between ethical truths call for tolerance.

This asymmetry between the burdens borne by believers and by unbelievers is counterbalanced at most by the fact that religiously tone-deaf citizens confront an expectation of tolerance of a different kind. For the understanding of tolerance of pluralistic liberal societies not only demands that believers in their dealings with members of other faiths should recognize that they must *rationally* reckon with the fact of continuing disagreement. This same insight is also expected of unbelievers in their dealings with believers. But for secular consciousness this amounts to the requirement to determine the relation between faith and knowledge in a *self-critical* manner. For the expectation of an ongoing lack of agreement between rational factual knowledge and religious tradition deserves the predicate "reasonable" only when religious convictions are accorded an epistemic status that is not merely irrational from the perspective of secular knowledge.

But how can the advancing naturalization of the human mind be harmonized with this assertion of political theory? Today the issue of "faith and knowledge" that has exercised philosophy since the seventeenth century is again gaining explosive force in view of the advances in biogenetics and brain research. At any rate, the secular state can guarantee tolerance in an impartial way only if it ensures that the pluralism of worldviews in the political public sphere can develop unhindered, and without substantive prejudicial regulations, on the basis of mutual respect. There is a good reason for this. For political views on controversial questions that are expressed in religious language and from the perspective of a particular worldview can also open the eyes of citizens to aspects that were hitherto neglected. Hence they can influence the formation of majorities even when the matter itself is then decided upon under a description that is not shaped by worldviews.

(c) Having examined the reasons for rejection and reasons for acceptance, this brings us to the third conceptual component of tolerance. The *reasons for excluding intolerant conduct* reveal whether the state respects the imperative of neutrality and whether legislation and the administration of justice institutionalize tolerance in the right way. Thus Sikhs in Great Britain and the United States, for instance, have gained exemptions from generally binding safety regulations to permit them to wear turbans and carry ceremonial daggers (kirpans). In the relevant legal disputes in Germany, too, the key issue is where to draw the line between the practices and the laws of the Christian majority culture, on the one hand, and the claims of religious minorities, on the other. In the name of religious freedom, the latter demand equal treatment (such as the Jehovah's Witnesses who have fought in court for public recognition as a religious group) or exceptions from regulations (for example, for turbans or kosher food) or state services (for instance, instruction in schoolchildren's native languages in public schools). In these cases the courts must decide who must accept whose ethos and when. Must the Christian inhabitants of a village accept the call of the muezzin? Must native animal rights activists accept the ritual slaughter of calves? Must nonconfessional pupils or those of other confessions accept the headscarf of the Islamic teacher? Must the Turkish father accept coeducational physical education for his daughter?[15]

(3) Freedom of religion tests the neutrality of the state. The latter is often jeopardized by the predominance of a majority culture that abuses its historically acquired power of definition to lay down what shall count as the generally binding political culture in a pluralistic society according to its own standards.[16] This intact fusion can lead to a gradual infiltration of an essentially procedural constitution by cultural substance. For the essential moral content

[15] See the list offered by Dieter Grimm in the *Frankfurter Allgemeine Zeitung* (June 21, 2002), p. 49: "Can a Sikh riding a motorcycle be excused from obeying the general law to wear a helmet on grounds of his religious duty to wear a turban? Must a Jewish prisoner be offered kosher food? Does a Muslim employee have the right to briefly interrupt his work time in order to pray? Can an employee be fired because he did not appear for work on the high holy days of his religious community? Does an employee dismissed on these grounds forfeit his entitlement to unemployment benefits? Must Jewish businesspeople be permitted to open their businesses on Sundays because for religious reasons they are not allowed to work on Saturdays? Does a Muslim pupil have the right to be exempted from physical education classes because she is not allowed to show herself to other pupils wearing sports clothes? May Muslim schoolgirls wear headscarves in class? What about female teachers at a public school? Should the law be different for nuns than for Muslim teachers? . . . Must muezzins be allowed to broadcast their call to prayer by loudspeaker in German cities just as churches are allowed to ring their bells? Must foreigners be allowed to ritually slaughter animals although it contravenes the local animal protection regulations? . . . Must Mormons be permitted to practice polygamy here because it is permitted in their country of origin?"
[16] On the unity of the political culture in the multiplicity of subcultures, see Habermas, *The Inclusion of the Other: Studies in Political Theory*, trans. and ed. Ciaran Cronin and Pablo De Greiff (Cambridge: Polity, 1998), pp. 117ff.

of the constitutional principles is secured through procedures that owe their legitimizing power to the fact that they guarantee impartiality and the equal consideration of the interests of all. They forfeit this power when substantive ethical ideas infiltrate the interpretation and practice of the formal regulations. In this respect the imperative of neutrality can be violated as much by the secular side as by the religious side.

The *affaire foulard* is an example of the former, the response of the Bavarian state government to the crucifix verdict of the German Federal Constitutional Court an example of the latter. In the former case, the management of a French school forbade Muslim schoolgirls to wear their traditional headscarves; in the latter, the government of the German state opposed the judgment of the Federal Constitutional Court, which upheld the complaint brought by anthroposophical parents against the crucifix in their daughter's classroom. In the one case positive religious freedom, in the other negative religious freedom, came under scrutiny. The Catholic opponents of the crucifix verdict defend the religious symbol of the crucified Christ as an expression of "Western values," and hence as part of a culture that all citizens may be expected to share. This is a classic case of a political overgeneralization of a regionally dominant religious practice, as expressed in the Bavarian *Volksschulordnung* [i.e. Regulations for Elementary Schools] of 1983. By contrast, in France, Muslim schoolgirls are forbidden to wear headscarves on the secular grounds that religion must be treated as a private matter to be kept out of the public domain. Here we have a secularist interpretation of the constitution that must face the question of whether the republican tradition of interpretation dominant in France is not so "strong" that it inevitably violates the required neutrality of the state vis-à-vis the legitimate claim to self-representation and public recognition of a religious minority.

These legal disputes show why the spread of religious tolerance, which we have already identified as a pacemaker for the emergence of democracies, has also become a stimulus and model for the introduction of further cultural rights within constitutional states. The inclusion of religious minorities in the political community awakens and promotes the sensitivity to the claims of other groups that suffer discrimination. The recognition of religious pluralism can assume this model function because it throws an exemplary light on *the claim of minorities to civic inclusion*. To be sure, the debate over multiculturalism hinges less on slights to religious minorities than on flashpoints, such as regulations concerning national holidays and official language(s), the promotion of school instruction in the mother tongue for ethnic and national minorities, and quotas for women, blacks, and indigenous peoples in politics, in the workplace, or in higher education. From the perspective of equal inclusion of all citizens, however, religious discrimination takes its place in the long list of cultural and linguistic, ethnic and racial, sexual and physical discrimination.

Inclusion concerns one of two aspects of civic equality. Although discrimination against minorities is usually associated with social underprivilege, these two categories of unequal treatment should be kept separate. The one is a matter of distributive justice, the other of full membership.[17] From the perspective of distributive justice, the principle of equal treatment requires that all citizens should have equal opportunities to make *actual* use of formally equal rights and liberties in realizing their individual life plans. The political struggles and social movements that combat status inequalities rooted in class structures and seek to promote a redistribution of social life chances are fueled by experiences of injustice in the dimension of distributive justice. By contrast, a different kind of experience of injustice underlies the struggles over the *recognition of the integrity of a particular collective identity*, namely, the experience of disrespect, marginalization, or exclusion based on membership in a group stigmatized as "inferior" by the dominant majority culture.[18] In this dimension, overcoming religious discrimination is today becoming the pacemaker for cultural rights of a new kind.

Prohibitions on discrimination, whether based on religion, gender, sexual orientation, or race, are not directed in the first

[17] On this distinction, see Nancy Fraser, "From Redistribution to Recognition?," in Cynthia Willett (ed.), *Theorizing Multiculturalism* (Oxford: Blackwell, 1998), pp. 19–49.
[18] Such pathologies of the refusal of recognition are the primary focus of Axel Honneth, *Disrespect: The Normative Foundations of Critical Theory* (Cambridge: Polity, 1997).

place against unequal distributions of social life chances. In many
cases it is not even possible to provide compensation for the
impacts of inequalities in status, for homosexuals and women are
represented approximately equally among all social strata. Exclusion from particular domains of social life reveals what is denied
to those who suffer discrimination, i.e. full and unqualified social
membership. Structurally entrenched mechanisms of exclusion
are difficult to pin down. It is true that, under the banner of
formal equality, discrimination has retreated into more inconspicuous zones of informal interactions, and even into the domain
of body language; but even these more subtle forms of discrimination are still painful enough.[19]

Cultural rights serve, as does the freedom of religious exercise,
to guarantee all citizens equal access to the patterns of communication, traditions, and practices of a community that they deem
necessary to develop and maintain their personal identities. Cultural rights need not privilege ascriptive memberships in ethnic
groups but can refer just as well to social environments that are
chosen. Yet it is often the case that the means and opportunities
to reproduce one's language and form of life as desired are as
important for members of national, linguistic, or ethnic minorities
as the freedom of association, the transmission of religious teachings, and the exercise of their forms of worship are for religious
minorities. Hence, both in political theory and the administration
of justice, the struggle for the equal rights of religious communities furnishes arguments and inspiration for an extended concept
of "multicultural citizenship."[20]

Religious convictions and practices exercise a formative influence on the ethical conceptions of believers in all cultures. Linguistic and cultural traditions also have a similar relevance for the
formation and maintenance of the personal identity of speakers
or their dependants, which is invariably interwoven with collective identities. This insight suggests that we need to revise the

[19] See the phenomenology of racial discrimination in Charles W. Mills, *The
Racial Contract* (Ithaca, N.Y.: Cornell University Press, 1997), ch. 2, pp.
41–89.
[20] Will Kymlicka, *Multicultural Citizenship* (Oxford: Oxford University Press,
1995).

traditional concept of the "legal person." The individuation of natural persons occurs through socialization. Socialized individuals can form and stabilize their identities only within a network of relationships of reciprocal recognition. This has implications for the protection of the integrity of the legal person – and for an extension of the concept itself, which has hitherto been conceived in excessively abstract terms (and tailored to possessive individualism), in an intersubjectivist direction.

The rights constitutive for protecting an individual's integrity define her status as a legal person. These rights must also extend to guaranteeing access to the contexts of experience, communication, and recognition in which people can articulate their self-understanding and develop and maintain their identities. Accordingly, cultural rights that are fought for and implemented under the banner of the "politics of recognition" should not be understood as inherently collective rights. On the model of religious liberty, they are rather what is called in German law "subjective" rights designed to grant full inclusion.[21] They guarantee all citizens equal access to cultural environments, interpersonal relations, and traditions insofar as these are indispensable for forming and securing their personal identities.

Yet, cultural rights do not just mean "more difference" and "more independence." Groups that suffer discrimination do not enjoy equal cultural rights "free of charge." They cannot benefit from a morality of equal rights of inclusion without making this morality their own in turn. This is not especially difficult for the elderly, homosexuals, or handicapped people who suffer discrimination, for in these cases the group-forming characteristic that is decisive for the discrimination is not bound up with awkward constitutive traditions. By contrast, "strong" (secular) communities (such as national or ethnic minorities, immigrants or indigenous subcultures, the descendants of slave cultures, etc.) are shaped by shared traditions and have formed their own collective

---

[21] Charles Taylor, *Multiculturalism: Examining the Politics of Recognition*, ed. Amy Gutmann (Princeton, N.J.: Princeton University Press, 1994). See also, in the same volume, my critique of the communitarian conception of cultural rights as collective rights (pp. 107–48).

identities.[22] These traditions also open up "world-perspectives" that, like religious worldviews, can conflict with one another.[23] Hence mutual tolerance also demands that "strong" secular communities should establish cognitive links between their internal ethos and the morality of human rights that prevails in their social and political environments. Groups whose historical development is out of sync with the surrounding culture may find this even more difficult than religious communities that can draw on the highly developed conceptual resources of one of the major world religions.

The advance in reflexivity exacted from religious consciousness in pluralistic societies in turn provides a model for the mindset of secular groups in multicultural societies. For multiculturalism that understands itself in the right way is not a *one-way street* to the cultural self-assertion of groups with their own collective identities. The equal coexistence of different forms of life must not lead to segmentation. It calls for the integration of all citizens and the mutual recognition of their subcultural memberships within the framework of a shared political culture. The citizens as members of society may legitimately cultivate their distinctive cultures only under the condition that they all understand themselves, across subcultural divides, as citizens of one and the same political community. The same constitutional basic norms in terms of which cultural exemptions and authorizations are justified also define their limits.

---

[22] On the concept of such "encompassing groups," see Avishai Margalit and Joseph Raz, "National Self-Determination," in Will Kymlicka (ed.), *The Rights of Minority Cultures* (Oxford: Oxford University Press, 1995), pp. 79–92, here pp. 81ff.

[23] The more comprehensive cultural forms of life are, the stronger is their cognitive content, and the more they resemble ways of life structured by religious worldviews: "The inescapable problem is that cultures have propositional content. It is an inevitable aspect of any culture that it will include ideas to the effect that some beliefs are true and some are false, and that some things are right and others wrong." Brian Barry, *Culture and Equality* (Cambridge: Polity, 2001), p. 270.

10

Equal Treatment of Cultures and the Limits of Postmodern Liberalism

I

Classical liberalism, which traces its lineage in the first instance to Locke, uses the medium and concepts of modern law to tame political power and to promote the primary goal of liberal political thought, namely, the protection of the prepolitical freedom of individual members of society. The core of a liberal constitution is the guarantee of equal individual liberties for everyone. This corresponds to Kant's "Universal Principle of Right," according to which, "the freedom of choice of each can coexist with everyone's freedom according to a universal law." Even the "rule of the people" remains an instrument of the "rule of law." The political autonomy of citizens is not an end in itself but serves as a means to safeguard the equal private autonomy of members of society.

The appeal of liberalism resides in part in its elegant reconciliation of two powerful normative intuitions. On the one hand, the idea of equal individual liberties for all satisfies the *moral* standard of egalitarian universalism, which demands equal respect and consideration for everyone. At the same time, it satisfies the *ethical* standard of individualism, according to which each person must be granted the right to conduct her life according to her own preferences and convictions. The equality of all citizens is expressed in the generality of laws, whereas actionable rights, which are derived from laws in particular cases, accord each citizen a carefully circumscribed latitude in pursuing her own way of life. Hence, ethical individualism constitutes the essential meaning of the egalitarian universalism that modern law borrows from postconventional morality.

The differentiation between ethical life plans and questions of justice responds to the requirements of a postmetaphysical mode of thought. Since philosophy has renounced any ambition to compete with religious worldviews, it no longer presumes to offer ontotheological or cosmological justifications for universally binding models of a successful or not-misspent life. It claims universal validity only for moral claims concerning what is in the "equal interest of all," that is, what is equally good or tolerable for each person. This kind of moral theory refrains from committing itself to substantive conceptions of an exemplary way of life that are supposed to be authoritative *for everyone.* Having become "formal" in this respect, morality is exclusively associated with the idea of equal respect and consideration for each person. This idea of equality also crops up in the positive, compulsory, and individualistic form of modern law in the conceptions of "equal treatment" and "human dignity" (purged of all connotations of social rank).

This liberal idea of equality has been repeatedly subjected to criticism. The civic republicanism that had been pushed aside by liberalism first responded by objecting that the "freedom of the ancients" must not be sacrificed on the altar of the "freedom of the moderns." In fact, classic liberalism threatened to reduce the meaning of equal ethical liberties to a possessive-individualist reading of individual or "subjective" rights misinterpreted in instrumentalist terms. In so doing, it failed to do justice to an important normative intuition that also merits respect under modern social conditions, namely, the requirement of solidarity that unites not only relatives, friends, and neighbors in the private sphere, but also citizens as members of a political community beyond purely legal relations. Individual liberties tailored to the business transactions of private property owners and to the religious conscience and allegiance of private individuals constitute the core of a liberal legal system. This reading pointed to the narrow "egoistic" interpretation of ethical freedom that continued to echo in the polemic of the young Marx against the American and French declarations of rights. The objection is that individual freedom is not exhausted by the right to a utilitarian "pursuit of happiness" and hence cannot be reduced to the authorization to the private pursuit of temporal and spiritual goods.

To make good this deficit, the modern revival of civic republicanism brought into play a different, intersubjectively expanded conception of freedom associated with the role of the democratic citizen. Within this Rousseauean tradition, the equal communication and participation rights are not merely important for realizing subjective individual rights but rather make possible a joint civic practice understood as an end in itself. From a republican point of view, democratic self-legislation establishes a form of solidarity that – however abstract, because legally mediated – enables one citizen to take responsibility for the other (also with weapons in hand). The political ethos of the community is reproduced and revitalized in the democratic will-formation of a sovereign people. Equal rights in turn guarantee ethical freedom – but in this case not first and foremost the subjective freedom of the individual member of society but the freedom of a nation of citizens united in solidarity conceived in terms of sovereignty. This sovereignty branches internally into a communitarian understanding of the political freedom of the members of a national community and toward the outside into a collectivist understanding of the freedom of a nation that asserts its existence against other nations.

However, ethical republicanism accepts a limitation on egalitarian universalism as the price for this element of civic solidarity. Each citizen enjoys equal rights only within the limits of a particular ethos presumed to be shared by all members of the political community. The fusing of citizenship and national culture leads to a "monochrome" interpretation of civil rights that is insensitive to cultural differences. The political priority accorded an ethically tinged common good over the effective guarantee of equal ethical liberties inevitably leads to discrimination against different ways of life in pluralistic societies and to helplessness in the face of a "clash of civilizations" at the international level.

These problems can be solved in principle only from a universalistic egalitarian perspective that detaches the mobilization of civic solidarity from ethnic nationality and radicalizes it into a solidarity between "others." In binding itself to universalistic constitutional principles and to "human" rights, the sovereign will-formation of democratic citizens simply draws the unavoidable conclusion from the necessary presuppositions for a legitimate legal institutionalization of its own practice.[1] Historically evolved forms of solidarity are transformed, but not destroyed, by the interconnection between the republican idea of popular sovereignty and the idea of a rule of law spelled out in terms of basic rights. On this third reading, which reconciles liberalism with republicanism, the citizens understand their national political ethos as the intentional product of the democratic will-formation of a populace accustomed to political freedom. The internal relation between the private autonomy of individual members of society and the political autonomy of the citizenry as a whole is something that is *worked out* progressively over time and the historical experience accumulated in this process eventually finds expression in a form of national pride founded on the attainment of an intersubjectively shared consciousness of freedom.

Citizens can make appropriate use of their political rights only if they are able to judge and act independently because they enjoy equal protection of private autonomy in the conduct of their lives. On the other hand, members of society can enjoy equal unrestricted private autonomy only if they make an appropriate use of their political rights as citizens, that is, only if they do not use them exclusively to promote their self-interest but also with an orientation to the common good. The idea that the addressees of the law must be able to understand themselves at the same time as its authors, which Rousseau introduced and to which Kant gave a universalist twist, does not give a united democratic citizenry *carte blanche* to make any decisions it likes. It should enact only those laws that derive their legitimacy from the fact that they can be willed by all. The individual liberty to do as one pleases

---

[1] Jürgen Habermas, *Between Facts and Norms: Contributions to a Discourse Theory of Law and Democracy*, trans. William Rehg (Cambridge, Mass.: MIT Press, 1996); "On the Internal Relation between the Rule of Law and Democracy," in Habermas, *The Inclusion of the Other: Studies in Political Theory*, ed. and trans. Ciaran Cronin and Pablo De Greiff (Cambridge, Mass.: MIT Press, 1998), pp. 253–64; "Constitutional Democracy – A Paradoxical Union of Contradictory Principles?" *Political Theory* 29 (2001): 766–81, repr. in Habermas, *Time of Transitions*, ed. and trans. Ciaran Cronin and Max Pensky (Cambridge: Polity, 2006), pp. 113–28. For the following reflections, I am indebted to the participants in a seminar held at Northwestern University in fall 2002.

within the bounds of the law is the core of private, not civic, autonomy. On the contrary, based on this legally guaranteed freedom of choice, democratic citizens can be reasonably expected to exercise autonomy in the more demanding sense of a will-formation that satisfies requirements of rationality and solidarity – even though this cannot be legally required, but only *urged* upon them [*angesonnen*]. A legal obligation to show solidarity would be a contradiction in terms.

The democratic elaboration of the system of rights necessarily presupposed by a democracy operating within legal institutions rescues classical liberalism from the rigid abstraction of universal laws grounded in natural rights which are supposed to "rule" for the sake of equal individual liberties. On the other hand, the logic according to which the egalitarian universalism of the constitutional state makes possible citizens' ethical individualism remains intact. On the radical-democratic interpretation of political liberalism, however, this logic is no longer objectively imposed by the anonymous rule of law above the heads of the citizens, as it were; rather, this logic is internalized by the citizens themselves and is embodied in the democratic procedures of their political will-formation. The idea of equal liberties is no longer fossilized in natural law but takes on reflexive form in the process of self-legislation. It calls upon the participants in the democratic process to engage in reciprocal perspective-taking and joint generalization of interests with the goal of granting one another the rights called for under existing historical circumstances by the project of a voluntary and self-determining association of free and equal legal consociates.

The egalitarian project of making equal ethical liberties possible assumes the form of a process in the shape of a civic solidarity produced, renewed, and deepened through the democratic process. Under auspicious circumstances, this dynamic can initiate cumulative learning processes and lead to permanent reforms. A democracy with roots in civil society then acquires in the shape of the political public sphere a sounding board for the multiform protests of those who suffer inequality, underprivilege, or disrespect. This protest against social injustice and discrimination can serve as a spur for self-corrections that extend the universalistic content of the principle of civic equality progressively in the form of equal ethical liberties.

However, even this democratic reading of political liberalism does not silence criticism. Here I would like to distinguish three kinds of objections, namely, those which draw on social science, social theory, and the critique of reason, respectively. In the first place, chastening sociological reservations offer salutary corrections to the frank normativism (and concealed idealism) of a political theory that prioritizes conceptual analysis. However, if they are understood in a melioristic sense, then they do not necessarily solidify into the fundamental objection that normative theories are condemned to failure by social complexity. Purely normative considerations retain their relevance as long as we accept that complex societies can still shape themselves in a reflexive manner through law and politics.

Second, from Hegel through Marx to Foucault, the critique of the "impotence of the ought" has intensified within social theory. From this perspective, normative projects already meet with the glaring denial of an opposed reality because they are themselves an integral part of the overwhelming totality of a form of life that is denounced as "alienated" or "power-ridden." These more far-reaching critical diagnoses, however, attribute the criticized leveling and isolating power of the "abstract universal" to the facticity of social *structures*, and not to the violence exerted by the *concepts* of a normativity turned in upon itself. Thus, conformist standardization and individualization is supposed to be exerted by the oppressive mechanisms of the market and administrative power – i.e. by mechanisms of social integration that exercise a reifying power when they penetrate into the heart of the fragile, communicatively constituted lifeworld. This criticism is not yet directed at inherent conceptual contradictions in the norms themselves as long as the desiccation of the resources of social solidarity is seen as the result of pathological distortions of communicatively constituted private and public domains of the lifeworld caused by the invasion of exchange relations and bureaucratic regulations.[2]

In this respect, Adorno's work marks a transition to a third and deeper level of criticism which represents the exchange of equivalents and organizational power, the two systemic mechanisms of

---

[2] Habermas, "Conceptions of Modernity," *The Postnational Constellation*, ed. and trans. Max Pensky (Cambridge, Mass.: MIT Press, 2001), pp. 130–56.

social integration, in terms of a critique of reason. For Adorno they are expressions of an instrumental rationality that contradicts the noncoercive form of individuation characteristic of relations of solidarity. In limiting himself to a deconstruction of the basic concepts of critical theory, Derrida dissolves the link between the critique of reason and social theory that marks the tradition of Weberian rationalization theories going back to Lukács.[3] He is primarily concerned with the internal heterogeneity of a concept of law that is inextricably bound up with sovereign power.[4] However, Derrida's deconstruction of justice, like Adorno's critique, is still informed by an indeterminate messianic hope. At any rate, the fervent talk of the hesitantly anticipated "event"[5] supports the interpretation that Derrida "criticizes an existing, exclusionary and oppressive understanding of liberal equality from the perspective of a pending, expanding, and domination-free understanding of liberal equality."[6]

Derrida seems to be still inspired by the memory of the promise of radical democracy. It remains for him a source for the reticent hope in a *universal* solidarity that permeates all relations. Christoph Menke, by contrast, gives the project of the deconstruction of justice an anti-utopian twist. In the process, he develops an interesting and original postmodern reading of liberalism. It shares with the classical version the view that democratic procedures and the political participation of citizens do not play an essential role in determining the basic liberal idea of equal ethical freedoms. The critique of reason then takes the form of an attempt to demonstrate that the conception of equal liberties is self-contradictory. Equal treatment, no matter how reflective, fails to

[3] The "theory of communicative action" also upholds the connection in question. On the associated "reconstructive" approach, see Bernhard Peters, *Integration moderner Gesellschaften* (Frankfurt am Main: Suhrkamp, 1993), pp. 471ff.
[4] Jacques Derrida, "Force of Law: The 'Mystical Foundation of Authority,'" *Cardozo Law Review* 11 (1990): 919–1045, and *Politics of Friendship* (New York: Verso, 1997). On the constitutive relation between law and power, see Habermas, *Between Facts and Norms*, pp. 133–51.
[5] For example, in Derrida, "The University without Condition," *Without Alibi* (Stanford, Calif.: Stanford University Press, 2002).
[6] Christoph Menke, *Spiegelungen der Gleichheit* (Berlin: Akademie, 2000), p. ix.

do justice to the concerns of the individual because "the realization of equality can [always] conflict with the obligations implied by doing justice to the individual case."[7] Revolution, mercy, and irony are "three sovereign ways of dealing" with the irreducibly "paradoxical relation" between equal treatment and doing justice to the individual case.

The quietism involved in persisting in reflecting on the limits of freedom reveals the anti-utopian aspect of this conception. Although acts of equal treatment cannot achieve their declared purpose, this deconstructive insight should induce us to try even harder to achieve individual justice, conscious of the inevitability of failure.[8] On Menke's conception, by making philosophy aware of the hidden paradoxical nature of its own activity, deconstruction heightens awareness of finitude.[9] Conceptual analysis of this unconscious element is supposed to bring out the "performative contradiction . . . between acting and saying."[10] Of course, then we need to know how "philosophy" understands its own activity.

According to Menke, philosophy is concerned from the outset to grasp "what successful action involves," and it understands this transcendental knowledge, in turn, as an "insight into the good." In the process, it also wants to make a practical contribution toward promoting the good.[11] If philosophy did not understand itself in such metaphysical terms, deconstruction would lack the pathos that first lends it its significance on this reading. The demonstration that "the conditions of possibility" of a successful practice are simultaneously "the conditions of impossibility of its success" remains within the conceptual universe of metaphysical thought that seeks to grasp reality as a whole. For the true adversary of the critique of metaphysics is the postmetaphysical

[7] Ibid., p. 41.

[8] Ibid., p. 33.

[9] I am skeptical and set aside the question of whether Menke's interpretation of the method of so-called deconstruction applies to the practice or self-understanding of Jacques Derrida.

[10] See the editors' introduction in Andrea Kern and Christoph Menke (eds), *Philosophie der Dekonstruktion* (Frankfurt am Main: Suhrkamp, 2002), p. 9.

[11] Menke, "Können und Glauben," in Kern and Menke (eds), *Philosophie der Dekonstruktion*, pp. 243ff.

self-understanding of modernity that starts from the supposition of the autonomy of self-conscious subjects and responsible agents: "Deconstruction aims at the philosophical presupposition that the success of our praxis is something in our own power."[12] The goal of deconstruction on this reading is to awaken a disenchanted modernity from the assumption that its intellectual presuppositions are beyond question.

The theories of morality and justice that appeal to Kant's egalitarian universalism and his conception of autonomy represent a particular challenge for such a project. This forms the backdrop to the controversy with John Rawls[13] to which Christoph Menke has returned in an article in the *Deutsche Zeitschrift für Philosophie*.[14] His excellent analysis deserves attention not only for the clarity of its arguments but also for its subject matter. Menke develops his critique of the idea of equality through an examination of political liberalism, that is, a specific interpretation of the legally institutionalized equality of the citizens of a political community. He wants to uncover the harm inflicted by the violent abstraction of universal laws on the claims of the individuals concerned within the dimension of the relations between legal subjects. This concentration on law and politics is important because the argument for a "different" or "caring" justice points to a dimension *beyond* law. Morally binding mutual claims derived from the personal encounters and the communicative interconnections among individual life histories interwoven through relations of solidarity thereby advance to an exacting but inappropriate standard for criticizing law.

Of course, law owes its legitimacy in essence to its moral contents; however, constructed legal orders also complement the moral-practical orientations acquired through socialization with the goal of freeing citizens in unmanageably complex social contexts from the cognitive and motivational burdens of an exacting form of morality. This accounts for the formal differences between

---

[12] Ibid., p. 247.
[13] Menke, "Liberalismus im Konflikt," in *Spiegelungen der Gleichheit*, pp. 109–31.
[14] Menke, "Grenzen der Gleichheit," *Deutsche Zeitschrift für Philosophie* 50 (2002): 897–906.

morality and law that must be respected when speaking of "justice" in a moral in contrast to a legal sense. The fact that law must not contradict morality does not mean that it is situated on the same level as morality. The differences become especially apparent in the case of the claims based upon our positive duties toward our "fellows." Postmodern ethical ideas in particular turn "not unlike Adorno's unwritten theory of morality, . . . on the idea that it is only in dealing appropriately with the non-identical that the claim to human justice can be redeemed."[15]

In comparing these approaches, Axel Honneth has already drawn attention to the danger of overgeneralization. Lévinas's phenomenologically elaborated "unbounded concern for a singular, unique individual" is read off from face-to-face relations in existentially radicalized situations that shed light on the basic moral impulse and often ground positive duties of virtue, but are not typical for legal obligations. To be sure, the function of the administration of justice is also to apply laws in a way that does justice to the individual case in the light of its "particular circumstances." We must even expect the fair administration of justice to show an extraordinary hermeneutic sensitivity for circumstances whose relevance changes according to the individual biographical perspectives of those involved. Otherwise, it would not be able to discover the single "appropriate" norm or apply it in a sufficiently "flexible" manner.[16] Nevertheless, the individual claims of the *legal* persons are pre-formed, as it were, by the predicates of the legal norm; they are restricted in principle to what legal persons can expect from one another, that is, to an ultimately coercible conduct that falls under the formal determinations of the law. Legal norms regulate interpersonal relations among actors who recognize one another as members of a community that is abstract because it is first created by legal norms.[17]

I am interested in Menke's perceptive attempt to deconstruct the freedom-guaranteeing principle of civic equality as presented

[15] Axel Honneth, *Disrespect: The Normative Foundations of Critical Theory* (Cambridge: Polity, pp. 99–128, here p. 100.

[16] Klaus Günther, *The Sense of Appropriateness*, trans. John Farrell (Albany, N.Y.: SUNY Press, 1993), pp. 247ff.

[17] On the formal features of law, see Habermas, *Between Facts and Norms*, pp. 111ff.

in Rawls's political liberalism primarily because he restricts his examination to the liberal idea of equality in its classic form. He neglects the prior generalization of interests that should be performed by democratic legislation, that is, through joint deliberation on and agreed justification of the legal determination of equal individual liberties (II). Even on a reading that does justice to this aspect, the criticism is not dispelled if one thinks of the ambivalent consequences of group rights founded on multiculturalism. Such rights are supposed to strengthen the capacity of groups that suffer discrimination to assert themselves; but even assuming an exemplary democratic realization, they appear instead to produce a dialectical inversion of equality into repression (III). Finally, I will examine once again the conceptual coherence of the interconnection between freedom and equality in the equal treatment of cultures from a historical perspective, namely, in the light of the normative reasonableness of the costs that religious communities had to pay for their cognitive adaptation to the requirements of cultural and social modernization (IV).

II

Menke wants to show that, in the course of implementing the liberal program, the idea of equal ethical liberties for all becomes embroiled in a self-contradiction. Although he is not interested in the specific solution proposed by the later Rawls – i.e. the modular idea of an overlapping consensus[18] – the Rawlsian theory is just the right thing for the purpose of such a deconstruction. In view of the "fact of pluralism," it offers an explicitly "political" conception of justice that is neutral among worldviews and is equally acceptable to all citizens. A liberal constitution guarantees all citizens equal freedom to structure their lives according to their own "conceptions of the good." If it could be shown that the equal

---

[18] Rainer Forst, *Contexts of Justice*, trans. John Farrell (Berkeley: University of California Press, 2002), pp. 94–100; Jürgen Habermas, "'Reasonable' versus 'True,' or the Morality of Worldviews," in *The Inclusion of the Other*, pp. 75–101, here p. 100.

guarantee of ethical liberties were itself merely an expression of a particular, substantive view of the "correct" life, then citizens who did not share that liberal worldview would inevitably feel constrained in the spontaneous conduct of their lives. Let us assume for the sake of argument that the principle of equal ethical liberties is only valid within the context of a humanistic self-understanding, say within the context of belief in eighteenth-century French Enlightenment ideals. Then the pluralism of worldviews institutionalized in the liberal state would marginalize all religious doctrines in the long run.

Rawls must avoid such an *ethical* liberalism, which would *eo ipso* restrict the equal right of adherents of conflicting doctrines in the name of equal rights. Menke agrees with him in the formulation of the problem, though not in its solution. According to Menke, even the most reflective attempt to guarantee all citizens equal ethical liberties on the basis of a conception of justice that is neutral among worldviews will still fail for conceptual reasons. Admittedly, he does not want to discourage us from the continued attempt to *seek* justice on the basis of the equal treatment of all. But we should no longer presume that we can succeed in *establishing* justice *ourselves*.

In the tragic awareness of a supposedly irreconcilable conflict between justice for all and the individual good, the realization of political equality should remain "an object of hope and striving." Evidently, this is not intended in the trivial sense of an ineradicable difference between norm and reality but rather in the deeper metaphysical sense of the recognition of the "impossibility of any guarantee of successful completion." In Rawls's theory, too, the "pending state [*Im-Kommen-Sein*] of justice" can be demonstrated and hence the insight that "*the reign* of justice becomes independent of the subjective *implementation* of justice."[19] In Hegelian terms, the causality of fate retains the upper hand over abstract justice – only now, of course, no longer in the name of a surpassing objective or even absolute *reason*.

A conception of political justice cannot remain neutral in the sense that it lacks any normative content, even if the corresponding constitutional principles take the form of procedures for

---

[19] Menke, "Können und Glauben," *Philosophie der Dekonstruktion*, p. 250.

legitimately making and applying the law.[20] For the just political order Rawls claims (1) the "neutrality of aim" in relation to the ethical forms of life and worldviews common in civil society, but not (2) the "neutrality of effect or influence" that individual norms and measures have on different cultural groups.[21] Under both of these aspects, Menke believes that he can show that the conditions of possibility for an egalitarian-universalistic constitutional order turn out in an aporetic way to be conditions of the impossibility of its realization.

(1) The neutrality of the aim or goal of a conception of civic equality is measured by the complete and equal inclusion of all citizens. It must be possible to include all of the citizens in the political community without discrimination as to their ways of life or their understandings of themselves and the world. Of course, this aim demands both the *exclusion* of doctrines that are incompatible with the principle of civic equality (such as sexist, racist, or fundamentalist doctrines) and a *restriction* of the rights and duties of persons who are not yet (or are temporarily not) in the position to fulfill the roles of citizen or of competent legal persons (such as underage children or people who are of unsound mind). We shall return in Section III below to the specific problem of exclusion that arises with regard to fundamentalist worldviews and members of so-called illiberal groups.

Menke argues for the claim that neutrality of aim is unattainable, even with regard to groups and doctrines that accept liberal premises, as follows. In European and American constitutional history, we can identify with hindsight dramatic examples of exclusion of women, disadvantaged groups, nonwhites, and so on, that obviously violated the principle of equal treatment: "Each and every liberal conception of equality therefore stands not only in opposition to non-egalitarian ideas of justice and order, but represents the attempt to go beyond previous definitions of the idea of liberal equality and to overcome the

---

[20] See Rawls's critique of my procedural view in John Rawls, "Reply to Habermas," *Journal of Philosophy* 92 (1995): pp. 132–80, at pp. 170ff., and my reply, " 'Reasonable' versus 'True,' " pp. 98ff.

[21] Forst, *Contexts of Justice*, pp. 47f.

oppression still associated with them."[22] From the retrospective understanding of the *inconsistencies* of a painfully selective implementation of basic rights, however, Menke does not draw the obvious conclusion that progress is possible through a self-correcting learning process. Instead, he explains the at best partial success of past attempts to realize the idea of equal inclusion, which thereby contradicted the idea of equality, as a function of an *inconsistency* in the underlying idea of civic equality as such. The liberal idea of equal liberties can never be "specified" in a neutral way, because even future generations cannot know whether they do not err in turn in their attempts to correct the mistakes of the past.

Certainly later generations can at best "strive for" but cannot "guarantee" neutrality of aim. Practical reason is even more fallible than theoretical reason.[23] We must not rule out the possibility that our reforms *could* again turn out, from a future perspective, to be incomplete and in need of correction. But will they necessarily turn out to be false? After all, the fallibilist awareness in which we make an assertion does not mean that we somehow relativize or leave open the truth claim that we raise for the assertion. The understanding acquired from the retrospective view of a third person that *some* of our efforts to acquire knowledge consistently fail does not force us, from the participant perspective, to cease to credit ourselves with any knowledge *at all*.

However, this is the basis of Menke's objection. Since we do not find ourselves here and now in a fundamentally different epistemic position from earlier generations whose attempts to

---

[22] Christoph Menke, "Grenzen der Gleichheit," *Deutsche Zeitschrift für Philosophie 50* (2002): 901.

[23] Menke nonetheless rejects a fallibilist interpretation of his thesis without offering a plausible justification. The fact that the consequences of practical misjudgments are more serious, in general, than the consequences of theoretical misjudgments does not deprive moral judgments and legal decisions of the epistemic status of statements that can be right or wrong. See Habermas, "Rightness versus Truth: On the Sense of Normative Validity in Moral Judgments and Norms," in *Truth and Justification*, trans. Barbara Fultner (Cambridge, Mass.: MIT Press, 2003).

provide neutral definitions of the idea of equal treatment repeatedly failed, we cannot be sure "that our own proposals and definitions will not themselves appear in retrospect equally non-neutral and be criticized accordingly."[24] But even past generations were not mistaken in every respect. As the more than 200-year-old American constitutional tradition shows, later generations have corrected the errors of the founding fathers and predecessors, for instance, during Reconstruction, the New Deal, or the civil rights movement of the last century. Because the idea of civic equality points beyond its particular institutionalizations, it is possible to overcome exclusions which are recognized as unjustified under different historical conditions. Just as in theoretical areas, here too the relativization of old insights leads to the extension rather than the elimination of past achievements.

I fail to see how one can explain either the notorious blind spots of past interpretations of civic equality that are now obvious to us or the resulting practices of exclusion and discrimination in terms of *conceptual* "conditions of impossibility" supposedly implicit in the idea itself. The selective readings of norms that have the grammatical form of universal statements but at the semantic level are vulnerable to particularistic interpretations of their basic concepts, such as "person" or "human being," call for an *empirical* explanation. Of course, this must extend to the semantics of the background worldview that prejudices the interpretation of the norms of equality to the advantage of the dominant values.

Thomas McCarthy pursues this method in his analysis of the racial prejudices in Kant's anthropology: "Substantive worldviews – religions, cosmologies, metaphysics, natural histories, etc. – function like refractive media for *grammatically* universal norms . . . The meanings of key terms used in formulating universal norms have typically been inflected to mark distinctions of gender, race, ethnicity, class, status, or other forms of group membership and ascriptive identity, such that those who understand the language in question were sensible of the variations in the

---

[24] Menke, *Spiegelungen der Gleichheit*, p. 902. Note that Menke does not say at this point "could be criticized."

intended scopes of the norms."[25] Selective interpretations of universalistic principles are symptomatic of the incomplete differentiation between the "right" and the "good." But the lucky historical experience that we can *also* learn in this respect is not sufficient to establish the paradoxical nature of the *project* of guaranteeing equal ethical liberties to all as such.

(2) Rawls claims neutrality for his conception of justice as a whole, not for the differential effects of the individual norms that guarantee equality. Impartially justified norms by no means necessarily affect the ethical self-understanding and way of life of each and every addressee in the same way. Menke seems to regard this insight as a concession that already meets deconstruction halfway. But first let us examine the phenomena to which this proviso applies. The conceptual priority of the right over the good means that a norm that is in the equal interests of all may impose not only general restrictions on those affected but also unequal burdens on different groups of addressees. Such burdens may impede one group more than others in shaping its form of life and some individuals more than others in the pursuit of their individual goals. Liberal regulations on abortion place a greater burden on devout Catholics or on any supporter of a pro-life position based on a religious or other worldview than on secular citizens, who, even if they do not share the pro-choice position, can live more easily with the idea that the right to life of the embryo may be trumped by the right to self-determination of the mother under certain circumstances.

Again, Menke wants to restrict his analysis to the harm suffered by forms of life and worldviews that are not essentially anti-egalitarian. Therefore, he may not relate the non-neutrality of effects to identity groups that will "cease to exist in the well-ordered society of political liberalism." With that, Rawls has in mind "illiberal" groups whose continued existence depends,

---

[25] Thomas McCarthy, "Die politische Philosophie und das Problem der Rasse," in *Die Öffentlichkeit der Vernunft und die Vernunft der Öffentlichkeit*, ed. Lutz Wingert and Klaus Günther (Frankfurt am Main: Suhrkamp, 2001), pp. 627–54, at p. 633; trans. as "Political Philosophy and Racial Injustice: From Normative to Critical Theory," in *Pragmatism, Critique, Judgment*, ed. Seyla Benhabib and Nancy Fraser (Cambridge, Mass.: MIT Press, 2004), pp. 147–68.

for instance, on the fact that their membership "controls the machinery of the state and is able to practice effective intolerance."[26] An example would be the Shiite interpretation of the Qur'an by the Mullahs who currently govern Iran; but this could not be described as a "not in principle anti-egalitarian conception of the good." Rather, the question turns on whether an aporia inherent in the idea of equality itself can be developed out of the differential burdens that norms sometimes impose on their addressees, even when they are justified from the point of view of the equal consideration of the relevant interests of all.

Menke takes his orientation from the intuition that each specific determination of the idea of equal treatment is an abstract universal that inevitably does violence to the individual life of particular persons. Here we must avoid getting off on the wrong foot. Cognitively speaking, we always have the alternative between judging the facts of the case from the participant perspective of citizens who are involved in political opinion- and will-formation concerning collective goals and binding norms or from the first-person perspective of someone deliberating on his or her own way of life as a unique individual. The cognitive possibility of adopting either perspective does not imply, however, that they are equivalent for all normative purposes. The perspective of justice and that of evaluating one's own life are not equally valid in the sense that the morally required priority of impartiality can be leveled out and reversed in favor of the ethical priority of one's particular goals in life.

It is certainly open to those affected to subject the effects of intersubjectively justified norms on their lives to a personal evaluation from their subjective perspective. But this option – of which the participants must in any case make use *ex ante* during the process of justification – does not imply a balancing that gives ethical self-understanding the final say for normative purposes. In the process of reflecting and adopting the corresponding perspectives in examining issues of political justice, they do not both have equal weight.

---

[26] John Rawls, *Political Liberalism* (New York: Columbia University Press, 1992), pp. 196–7.

In the end, the symbiotic fusion of both perspectives is supposed to pave the way for the concept of a supposedly "higher" justice that guarantees the happy coincidence of the right with the individual good.[27] "Then the priority of liberal justice would not only be a priority for institutions – and for us as participants in institutions – but also a priority for us as individuals: not just a politically, but also an ethically valid priority."[28] The paradoxical nature of this surreptitiously introduced standard also explains why any "political justice" that is distributed in the currency of equal ethical liberties appears unworkable by this standard. For there are good reasons why political justice does not enjoy priority over other, more important individual values in the context of most life histories.

The mistake in this thought is not difficult to identify: the two opposing perspectives (of justice and the "good life") do not enter into a symbiosis, but remain for good normative reasons intertwined with each other in an asymmetrical way. Ethical self-understanding, undertaken from the first-person perspective, can succeed in the final analysis only under the proviso that the pursuit of individual aims does not violate moral consideration for others.[29] On the other hand, citizens in their role as democratic co-legislators are bound to procedures of *reciprocal* perspective-taking, so that the perspectives of the affected, who do not want their individual goals to be restricted in existentially unreasonable ways, also find their way into the perspective of justice.

Moreover, a norm can be appropriately applied only on the basis of such a democratic justification. That norm is "appropriate" for an individual case if it enables all relevant features of the conflict and of the participants in the conflict to be considered "exhaustively."[30] Whoever has only the *semantic* features of a

---

[27] Menke wants to place the idea of equality in a relation "with the obligations of individuality . . . which is not already determined from the beginning in favor of the priority of equality" (*Spiegelungen der Gleichheit*, p. 7).

[28] Ibid., p. 122.

[29] Martin Seel, *Versuch über die Form des Glücks* (Frankfurt am Main: Suhrkamp, 1999), pp. 191ff.

[30] Klaus Günther, "Ein normativer Begriff der Kohärenz," *Rechtstheorie* 20 (1989); "Warum es Anwendungsdiskurse gibt," *Jahrbuch für Recht und Ethik* 1 (1993).

universal norm in view, and then claims that it *cannot* do justice to the particularity of the case and to the context of the individual's life history, overlooks the *pragmatic* meaning of the "universality" of democratically justified norms. Norms of this kind are discovered and adopted in accordance with a procedure of discussion and decision that grounds the presumption of rational, and in this sense universal, acceptability. There can be no question of the constitutional state ignoring "the problem of the possible restriction of the individual good by political equality."[31] The non-neutral effects are the proper focus of the hypothetical scenarios fought out in the public arena and in the political debates of the democratic legislature *ex ante* and thus not only in the subsequent application discourses of the administration of justice.

Because the democratic procedure makes the legitimacy of decisions dependent on the discursive forms of an inclusive process of opinion- and will-formation, the norms that are supposed to guarantee equal rights can only come about in an awareness and assessment of the different burdens they impose. Menke describes the non-neutral effects of norms of equality as "unintended consequences" of "achieving equality."[32] That betrays a fixation on the observer standpoint of the theorist; he refuses to adopt the participant perspective of the citizens who also regard themselves as the authors of the law. Postmodern liberalism follows classical liberalism in excluding the democratic components, together with the lawmaker, from the guiding idea of equal liberties and ignores the dialectical connection between private and civic autonomy.

In this way, the process of "defining" equality takes place entirely in the mind of the philosopher observer. The space in which the participating citizens engage in communication does not feature in the analysis. But only there can the process of determining what calls for equal application as a universal norm be carried out as "self-determination" in the shape of democratic opinion- and will-formation. Those affected must participate in the process of differentiating the right from the good, both from the point of view

---

[31] Menke, "Grenzen der Gleichheit," p. 905.
[32] Ibid., p. 903.

of their own self-understanding and worldview and under the condition of reciprocal perspective-taking. Then the universal norms, which meet with general agreement after discursive consideration of the anticipated exclusions and restrictions, no longer confront them as an alien force that does violence to their individual lives (and, most importantly, not on account of their equality-guaranteeing generality).

A deconstruction of the idea of equality is not necessary in order to arrive at the result to which the democratic procedure is inherently geared. Political discourse focuses the participants' gaze on what is equally good for all, so it naturally still remains *connected* to the ethical judgments "that individuals reach in view of what is important and good in their lives."[33] As citizens, the participants can nevertheless accept a norm as just – for instance, a liberal abortion regulation whose effects they personally find harder to accept than other citizens – if this burden appears reasonable to them in comparison to the burden of the discrimination that is thereby eliminated. The norm must be legitimated by democratic means in an awareness and assessment of its non-neutral effects by all those who must live with the consequences. Hence, the asymmetric restrictions that are accepted on normative grounds are as much an expression of the principle of civic equality as the norm itself – and not a reflection of its "internal heterogeneity," as Menke claims.

Neither the actual failures in realizing the "neutrality of aim" (1) nor the "non-neutral effects" of formally equal rights (2) support the idea of a "limit to equality" inherent in the idea of civic equality as such. The "unavoidable suffering of individuals that every system of equality produces through its operations of exclusion and the effects of its restrictions"[34] cannot be established through conceptual analysis. Only the egalitarian universalism of equal rights that is sensitive to difference can satisfy the individualistic requirement that the fragile integrity of unique and irreplaceable individuals should be guaranteed equally.

---

[33] Ibid., p. 898.
[34] Ibid., p. 906.

III

Of course, this claim concerns only the conceptual relations on which deconstruction focuses, not the actual relations that are deformed by violence. Liberal "systems of equality" have, of course, hitherto covered up the flagrant injustices of social inequality. The impoverished districts of our cities and other desolate areas are populated by outcasts and "superfluous" persons for whom equal rights do not have "equal value." Under the pretense of equality, they suffer the misery of insecurity and unemployment, the humiliation of poverty and inadequate social provision, the isolation of a life on the margins of society, the wounding feeling of not being needed, the despair over the loss of (and denial of access to) all the means required to change their oppressive condition through their own initiative. However, these facts do not reflect a paradox in the normativity of the idea of equality itself. Rather, the contradiction between the normative claim that these conditions prompt and the morally obscene sight that they actually present gives rise to cognitive dissonances.

From the early socialists to present-day opponents of globalization, political protest has been spurred by facts that flout the normative claim to substantive equality of rights. This led to the promise of the welfare state that the guarantee of equal ethical liberties must also include the opportunity to make effective use of equal rights. Underprivileged citizens have a right to compensation when they lack the opportunities and resources to make use of their rights in accordance with their own preferences and values.

Of course, such contradictions between facticity and validity can become the political driving force for the self-transformation of society only as long as the cognitive dissonances are not robbed of their sting by being ontologized – through a form of deconstruction that projects the contradiction into normativity as such. However, we must examine whether the implementation of cultural rights for members of groups that suffer discrimination, as well as the introduction of social rights, follows a development in law governed by the principle of civic equality (1). The justification of cultural rights can explain a disturbing competition between group rights and individual rights (2) that gives rise to the paradoxical appearance of a dialectical inversion of equal rights into oppression (3).

(1) Recent court decisions in Western countries contain numerous examples of correctives to unreasonable asymmetrical effects of general laws: Sikhs are permitted to wear their turbans on motorcycles and to carry their ritual daggers in public; Muslim women and girls may wear their "headscarves" in the workplace and in school; Jewish butchers are permitted to slaughter livestock and poultry according to kosher methods; and so forth. Although these rulings seem to involve exceptions to general laws (concerning traffic safety, animal protection, and so on), interpreting them as exceptions to rules misleadingly suggests a dialectic in the idea of equality. In fact, these decisions are simply the logical consequences of the fact that Sikhs, Muslims, and Jews enjoy the same religious freedom as the Christian majority. They are not a matter of a mysterious "inversion of the universal into the particular," only trivial instances of basic rights taking priority over ordinary laws or public safety regulations. As in the decision handed down by the Federal Constitutional Court of Germany concerning the equal status of the Jehovah's Witnesses (who acquired the same privileges as the Churches in being recognized as an entity in public law), here it is also a matter of implementing the equal treatment of cultures through the normal process of applying the law to particular cases.

Both the regulations in the organizational section of the constitution (such as those conferring self-administration rights on regional authorities or special representation rights on cultural minorities) and multicultural policies designed to protect and promote groups that suffer discrimination (such as quotas in education, employment, and politics, subsidies for language programs and school curriculums, and regulations governing official languages, official holidays, and national symbols) constitute precautionary measures against the exclusion of groups with strong identities of their own. Such tendencies continue to operate below the threshold of formal recognition of equal treatment – as shown, among others, by the impressive study of Charles W. Mills.[35] More inconspicuous mechanisms of exclusion in the modes and communicative patterns of everyday interaction permeate the

---

[35] Charles W. Mills, *The Racial Contract* (Ithaca, N.Y.: Cornell University Press, 1997).

very semantics of body language. To be sure, the "politics of recognition" runs up against the structural limits of the legal medium,
which can, at best, bring about conformity in behavior but has
little impact on mentalities. But factual restrictions on the effects
of a steering medium such as law must not be confused with the
conceptual barriers of the allegedly self-contradictory idea of legal
equality.

We describe a political culture as "liberal" insofar as it is characterized by symmetrical relations of reciprocal recognition,
including those between the members of different identity groups.
These relations of recognition, extending across subcultural
divides, can only be promoted indirectly, but cannot be directly
produced, by means of politics and law. Cultural rights and policies of recognition can strengthen the capacity for self-assertion
among minorities that suffer discrimination and their visibility in
the public sphere; but the values of society as a whole cannot be
changed through the threat of sanctions. The aim of multiculturalism – the mutual recognition of all members as equals – calls
for a transformation of interpersonal relations via communicative
action and discourse that can ultimately be achieved only through
debates over identity politics within the democratic public arena.[36]
However, these processes also occur in a space constituted by
citizens' rights to political participation and communication.
Thus, the "self-reflection" oriented toward the "recognition of
difference" that Menke rightly calls for does not depend on an
entirely different politics – built on the ruins of deconstructed
equality – that would free itself from the chains of law and enter
the sphere of virtue.[37]

The discussion of "multiculturalism" calls for a more careful differentiation within the concept of civic equality. Discrimination

---

[36] Nancy Fraser, "Struggle over Needs," *Unruly Practices* (Minneapolis: University of Minnesota Press, 1989); Seyla Benhabib, *The Claims of Culture* (Princeton, N.J.: Princeton University Press, 2002), pp. 114–22.

[37] It is not clear to me what is meant by the thesis "that a politics of equality
must develop *in itself* the attitude or the virtue of doing justice to the suffering
and complaints of the individual," if this politics is supposed to be allowed "[to
go] to the extreme that equality limits itself in view of these limitations" (Menke,
"Grenzen der Gleichheit," p. 905).

or disrespect, nonpresence in the public arenas of society, or a collective lack of self-respect point to an incomplete and unequal inclusion of citizens who are denied full status as members of the political community. The principle of civic equality is violated in the dimension of membership, not in the dimension of social justice. The degree of inclusion concerns the horizontal relations among members of the political community, whereas the scope of the system of statuses concerns the vertical relations among citizens of a stratified society.

Social strata are conditioned by patterns of distribution of social wealth. Depending on their rank, citizens have at their disposal greater or lesser resources and a greater or lesser variety of opportunities for shaping their lives according to their own preferences and values. Among equal citizens, every system of statuses raises questions concerning the legitimacy of the permitted degree of inequality. Whatever counts as economic exploitation and social underprivilege (as measured by the socially accepted principles of distributive justice)[38] and whatever counts as deprivation (of the necessary means for an autonomous life), it violates the principle of civic equality in a different way from incomplete inclusion. The inequality lies in the dimension of distributive justice, not in the dimension of the inclusion of members.

Nancy Fraser recognizes the importance of making an analytic distinction between these two dimensions of civic inequality (even though they are almost always empirically intertwined) and has made a corresponding distinction between the politics of distribution and the politics of recognition.[39] This distinction makes clear why one misses the point of cultural rights by incorporating them into an extended model of the

---

[38] Herlinde Pauer-Studer, *Autonom leben* (Frankfurt am Main: Suhrkamp, 2000).

[39] Nancy Fraser, "From Redistribution to Recognition?" in Cynthia Willett, ed., *Theorizing Multiculturalism* (Oxford: Oxford University Press, 1998), pp. 19–49. Her subsequent revisions do not seem to me to represent improvements over the original formulation. See Fraser, "Rethinking Recognition," *New Left Review* 3 (May/June 2000): 107–20; also Nancy Fraser and Axel Honneth, *Redistribution or Recognition? A Political-Philosophical Exchange*, trans. Joel Golb and Christiane Wilke (London: Verso, 2003).

welfare state.[40] Unlike social rights, cultural rights must be justified in terms of their role in facilitating the equal inclusion of all citizens. Although this consideration demands an extension of the classic concept of the legal person, which was tailored to the dual role of economic citizen and member of a religious community, this revision seems at the same time to grant us ambivalent group rights that could conflict with individual rights under certain circumstances.

(2) The standard justification for cultural rights starts from the guarantee of equal ethical liberties for all.[41] These take the form of subjective rights that open up a well-defined range of options for decisions guided by preferences. The rights-bearer can enjoy this freedom of decision to lead an ethical life only if she has a sufficiently wide range of value orientations at her disposal that allow her to choose the ends of her actions and set goals. She only really enjoys equal ethical liberties if, in selecting her preferences, she can rely upon the orienting power of internalized cultural values. Therefore, the use value of equal ethical liberties depends upon guaranteed access to cultural resources from which the necessary values can be tapped (i.e. acquired, reproduced, and renewed).

This instrumental justification misses the real point of cultural rights. The concept of a person acting instrumentally who selects from fixed options according to culturally shaped preferences fails to clarify the intrinsic meaning of culture for an individual's way of life. Newborn children come into the world organically

---

[40] See Brian Barry, who reduces the claim to recognition of groups that suffer discrimination to a lack of "means and options" because he measures civic equality in terms of distributive justice, hence according to the necessary "opportunities and resources" for each citizen to enjoy equal opportunities to make actual use of equal rights. This assimilation of the lack of recognition to underprivilege that calls for material redress leads, for example, to the counterintuitive assimilation of religious convictions to preferences: "The position regarding preferences and beliefs is similar" (Barry, *Culture and Equality* [Cambridge, Mass.: Harvard University Press, 2002], p. 36). On this approach, the Sikhs would be permitted to wear turbans when riding motorbikes because otherwise their leeway in choosing a religious community would be unjustly restricted.

[41] Joseph Raz, "Multiculturalism: A Liberal Perspective," in *Ethics in the Public Domain* (Oxford: Oxford University Press, 1994).

immature and remain for a long period briefly dependent on the care of others. Only as social members of cultural communities can they develop into persons. Only by growing into an intersubjectively shared universe of meanings and practices through socialization can persons develop into irreplaceable individuals. This cultural constitution of the human mind explains the enduring dependence of the individual on interpersonal relations and communication, on networks of reciprocal recognition, and on traditions. It explains why individuals can develop, revise, and maintain their self-understanding, their identity, and their individual life plans only in thick contexts of this kind.

But if we relate the guarantee of equal ethical liberties to such an intersubjectively understood process for forming, reproducing, and developing personal identity, we must expand the concept of the legal person as the bearer of subjective rights accordingly.[42] Against this background, it makes sense to derive cultural rights directly from the principle of the inviolability of human dignity (Article 1 of the German Basic Law): the equal protection of the integrity of the person, to which all citizens have a claim, includes the guarantee of equal access to the patterns of communication, social relations, traditions, and relations of recognition that are required[43] or desired[44] for developing, reproducing, and renewing their personal identities.

This role for cultural rights explains how such rights can counteract the incomplete inclusion of the members of disrespected

---

[42] For an overview of the more recent discussion, see Stephan Kirste, "Dezentrierung, Überforderung, und dialektische Konstruktion der Rechtsperson," in *Verfassung – Philosophie – Kirche* (Berlin: Duncker & Humblot, 2001).

[43] Avishai Margalit and Moshe Halbertal, "Liberalism and the Right to Culture," *Social Research* 61 (1994): 491–510. Chaim Cans speaks of an "identity based argument" in *The Limits of Nationalism* (Cambridge: Cambridge University Press, 2003), pp. 43ff.

[44] This qualification is intended to pre-empt the restriction of cultural rights to access to *cultures of origin*. We must not reify cultural heritages – which are always hybrids resulting from the intermingling of different traditions – into closed totalities. Nor should we assume that people's identities remain dependent throughout their lives on a particular culture or even on rootedness in their culture of origin. See Jeremy Waldron, "Minority Cultures and the Cosmopolitan Alternative," *University of Michigan Journal for Law Reform* 25 (1992): 751–93.

religious, linguistic, ethnic, or racial minorities (as well as oppressed and marginalized women, children, elderly people, etc.). The aim of guaranteeing free access to the cultural background, social network, and communicative web of identity groups also accounts for the introduction of collective rights. Such rights strengthen the organizations responsible for the self-assertion of endangered cultures. Collective rights empower cultural groups to preserve and make available the resources on which their members draw in forming and stabilizing their personal identities.

Self-assertion rights grant the representatives of identity groups enhanced authority to organize and administer themselves. These rights are particularly interesting in the present context because they give rise to a type of conflict that is alien to systems of equality organized along individualistic lines. Typical conflicts of rights arise either between individual legal persons (one of whom violates the rights of the other) or between the individual citizen and the state (when the latter oversteps the legal boundaries of interference). The introduction of collective rights gives rise to conflicts of a different type, (a) when different identity groups dispute each other's rights or privileges, or (b) when, as is typically the case with multicultural claims, one group demands equal treatment with other groups, or (c) when, as in the complementary case, nonmembers see themselves as disadvantaged in relation to members of privileged groups (white people, for example, by quotas for nonwhites).

In the present context, a fourth case – (d) oppression within groups – is of primary interest. In these cases, elites use their expanded organizational rights and competences to stabilize the collective identity of the groups, even if it entails violating the individual rights of dissenting members of the group. When the communal life of religious groups is determined by a "law" that is guarded and interpreted literally by guardians of orthodoxy (as it is in Islamic countries and in Israel, for example), and when religious law supplements or even replaces civil law, especially within the sphere of the family, women and children in particular are exposed to repression by their own authorities.[45] Given the

---

[45] Ayelet Schachar, "On Citizenship and Multicultural Vulnerability," *Political Theory* 28 (2000): 64–89.

"special power relations" within the family, even the secular rights enjoyed by parents in Western countries can lead to similar conflicts (for example, when Turkish fathers keep their daughters out of coeducational physical education in public schools).

The point is not that rights are suspect *per se*. For example, the rights that a democratic constitution accords local authorities, provincial governments, or semi-public institutions are generally unproblematic because such transfers of authority can be justified on the basis of, and hence cannot conflict with, citizens' basic rights. But not all cultural groups whose position is strengthened by collective rights have an internal organization that satisfies liberal standards. Cultural groups are also not required to abide by liberal organizational principles (as are political parties). Thus, for example, the Catholic Church has the right to exclude women from the priesthood, even though the equality of men and women has constitutional standing and is implemented in other sectors of society. The Church explains this employment policy by appealing to an essential element of the doctrine to which its pastoral mission is devoted.[46] From the perspective of the liberal state, the principle of equality is not violated as long as members are not barred from expressing their dissent by leaving the group or by mobilizing counterforces within the organization itself. Yet, how should we view the religiously based racial discrimination of Bob Jones University, an American institution of fundamentalist Christians that, although it changed its restrictive admissions policy and accepted black students when it was threatened with losing its tax-exempt status, nevertheless prohibited interracial dating and marriage?[47] How do the two cases differ?

When the liberal state fulfills the conditions required to enable the reproduction of a cultural minority whose very existence would otherwise be threatened, and when it as a consequence accepts in return the violation of the basic rights of individual members, it seems that the dialectic of equality and oppression affirmed by Menke comes into play. Thus, the US Supreme Court in a notorious decision upheld the objection of an Amish community against

---

[46] See the discussion of the relevant legal cases in Barry, *Culture and Equality*, pp. 169ff.
[47] Ibid., pp. 165f.

the Department of Education of the state of Wisconsin and granted the plaintiff a collective exemption from the universal requirement of ten years of schooling. Amish parents were accordingly allowed to withdraw their children from the ninth and tenth grades because they would otherwise be familiarized with subjects judged to be incompatible with the survival of the worldview and way of life of the religious community. It seems that the right to protect the religious form of life and practice, which according to the principle of equality must be equally valid for the (otherwise law-abiding) Amish community as for other religious communities, can only be honored if the state accepts a violation of the civil rights of juveniles to the basic education that would enable them to make their way in complex societies.

Countless cases exhibit this classic pattern, which Brian Barry deals with in his study on "culture and equality." Barry draws on these examples in conducting a polemical debate with authors such as William Galston, Charles Taylor, and Iris Young. Assuming they exist, the paradoxical inversions of freedom into repression that are supposed to reveal a contradiction in the idea of civic equality as such would have to be demonstrated by the potential threat to individual basic liberties posed by collective rights guaranteeing the equal treatment of cultural groups.

(3) In order to dispel the air of paradox, Will Kymlicka has made a distinction between two types of group rights: legitimate rights through which an organization protects itself against external pressures from its social environment; and problematic rights through which it can impose its will internally on dissenting members of the group who threaten to destabilize the settled life of the community.[48] But this distinction ceases to be useful when the same collective rights simultaneously serve both functions, as in the Amish case. To be sure, empowering collective rights do not *necessarily* conflict with individual rights;[49] but the alleged paradox can only be resolved if it can be shown that group rights that are legitimate from the perspective of civic equality *cannot*

---

[48] Will Kymlicka, *Multicultural Citizenship* (Oxford: Oxford University Press, 1995), pp. 34–48.
[49] Ibid., p. 38.

conflict with the basic rights of individual group members. For, according to the liberal intuition, group rights are legitimate only if they can be understood as *derivative* rights – derived, that is, from the cultural rights of the individual group members.

The advocates of a "strong" multiculturalism dismiss this requirement and pursue a justification strategy that does not exclude collective rights that potentially restrict basic rights. They argue that if the equal right to ethical freedom obliges the state to guarantee equal access to cultural resources for any citizen who needs them to develop and maintain her personal identity, then the state must also see to it that such cultural resources are available – and remain available. The latter qualification marks the inconspicuous but decisive logical step from the availability of such resources in the present to *ensuring* their availability in the future. Only this step enables "strong" multiculturalism to justify a "politics of survival."

Thus Charles Taylor, for example, defends the thesis that the undisputed right of the French-speaking citizens of Quebec to continue their ancestral traditions implies the controversial obligation on the part of the provincial government to take whatever measures are required to ensure the *survival* of the French language:

> You could consider the French language, for instance, as a collective resource that individuals might want to make use of, and act for its preservation just as you do for clean air or green spaces. But this can't capture the full thrust of policies designed for cultural survival. It is not just a matter of having the French language available for those who might choose it . . . But it also involves making sure that there is a community of people in the future that will want to avail itself of the opportunity to use the French language. Policies aimed at survival actively seek to *create* members of the community, for instance, in their assuring that future generations continue to identify as French speakers.[50]

This argument justifies, among other things, the intrusion by the government of Quebec into the parental rights of its

---

[50] Charles Taylor, "The Politics of Recognition," *Philosophical Arguments* (Cambridge, Mass.: Harvard University Press, 1995), p. 246.

Francophone population. These citizens are obliged to send their children to French schools, even if they prefer to educate them in English-speaking institutions. The argument is based on the unspoken premise that cultural resources have a kind of priority over other rights of the individuals who enjoy them, or at least have an intrinsic value that justifies an independent claim to protection. This conception presupposes a metaphysically grounded ethics of the good, which I will not address further here.[51] The idea that rights can refer *directly* to cultural resources is not trivial. For then the claim to protection of these collective goods must be justifiable independently of citizens' interests in maintaining their personal identity.

Collective rights that strengthen a group, not in order to protect the cultural rights of its individual members, but to support the continued existence of the cultural background of the collectivity directly, even above the heads of its members, have the potential to promote internal repression: "Cultures are simply not the kind of entity to which rights can properly be ascribed. Communities defined by some shared cultural characteristic (for example, a language) may under some circumstances have valid claims, but the claims then arise from the legitimate interests of the members of the group."[52] Barry's objection, however, is based on a no less dogmatic inversion of his opponents' dogmatic assertion of the priority of cultural resources over their beneficiaries. What reasons support the claim that collective rights, which guarantee the availability of cultural resources, are justified solely by the individual member's cultural rights to access to such resources?

Barry's passing remark that cultures are "not the kind of entity" to function as rights-bearers offers a clue. Even if we do not already presuppose the individualistic character of modern legal orders on moral grounds,[53] the ontological constitution of

---

[51] On the theory of hyper-goods, see Charles Taylor, *Sources of the Self: The Making of the Modern Identity* (Cambridge, Mass.: Harvard University Press, 1989), pt. I; see also Jürgen Habermas, *Justification and Application: Remarks on Discourse Ethics*, trans. Ciaran Cronin (Cambridge, Mass.: MIT Press, 1993), pp. 69ff.

[52] Barry, *Culture and Equality*, p. 67.

[53] See my debate with Karl-Otto Apel in Jürgen Habermas, "On the Architectonics of Discursive Differentiation," above, ch. 3.

symbolic objects speaks against the idea that cultures qualify as
bearers of rights. A culture as such is not a suitable candidate for
the status of a legal subject because it cannot meet the conditions
for its reproduction from its own resources but depends upon
constructive appropriation by autonomous interpreters who say
"yes" or "no." Therefore, for empirical reasons the survival of
identity groups and the continued existence of their cultural background *cannot* be guaranteed by collective rights at all. A tradition
must be able to develop its cognitive potential in such a way that
the addressees are convinced that this tradition is really worth
pursuing; and the hermeneutic conditions for the continuation of
traditions can only be guaranteed by individual rights.

A culture can be conceived as an ensemble of enabling conditions for problem-solving activities. It furnishes those who grow
up in it not only with elementary linguistic, practical, and cognitive capacities, but also with grammatically prestructured worldviews and semantically accumulated stores of knowledge. However,
a culture cannot be maintained through conditioning or crass
indoctrination; neither can it be maintained solely through the
implicit habituation of the young to corresponding language games
and practices. Rather, traditions preserve their vitality by insinuat-
ing themselves into the ramified and interlinked channels of
individual life histories and, in the process, passing the critical
threshold of the autonomous endorsement of every single potential participant. The intrinsic value of a tradition can manifest
itself during adolescence at the earliest. Young people must be
convinced that they can lead a worthwhile and meaningful life
within the horizon of the assimilated tradition. The test of the
viability of a cultural tradition ultimately lies in the fact that challenges can be transformed into solvable problems for those who
grow up within the tradition.

Although this test also functions within closed societies, its
relevance increases with the number of alternatives that are
open to the individual. In pluralistic societies, cultural groups
can pass on their heritage from one generation to the next
only via the hermeneutic filter of the affirmations of individual
members who are in a position to say "no" to a range of genuine
alternatives. For this empirical reason, collective rights can
strengthen the cultural self-assertion of a group only if they
also accord the individual members the latitude to use them

realistically in deciding on reflection between critical appropria-tion, revision, or rejection.[54] Freedom of association certainly already safeguards the voluntary nature of group membership. But it is only the seal on a realistic right to exit. The guarantee of the internal latitude necessary to assimilate a tradition under conditions of dissent is decisive for the survival of cultural groups. A dogmatically protected culture will not be able to reproduce itself, especially not in a social environment replete with alternatives.

IV

The critique of "strong" multiculturalism boils down to the fact that the principle of civic equality confronts all cultural groups with the universal normative expectation that their members should not just become unconsciously accustomed to traditional convictions and practices, but should be taught to appropriate a tradition in a reflexive way. Of course, the more demanding the formulation of the exit conditions, the more they confirm the suspicion that "equal treatment of cultures" remains wedded to the anthropocentric and secularist ideas of the Enlightenment and humanism, and hence that its implementation must deny the "neutrality of aim" vis-à-vis other forms of life and worldviews. This brings us back to the issue of the fairness of the adaptive achievements that the liberal state demands from the traditional

---

[54] William Galston cites the following as "realistic" conditions for exit: "knowl-edge conditions – the awareness of alternatives to the life one is in fact living; capacity conditions – the ability to assess these alternatives if it comes to seem desirable to do so; psychological conditions – in particular, freedom from the kinds of brainwashing that give rise to heart-rending deprogramming efforts of parents on behalf of their children, and more broadly, forms of coercion other than the purely physical that may give rise to warranted state interferences on behalf of affected individuals; and finally, fitness conditions – the ability of exit-desiring individuals to participate effectively in at least some ways of life other than the ones they wish to leave." See Galston, "Two Concepts of Liberalism," *Ethics* 105 (1995): 516–34, here p. 533; for a feminist perspective, see Susan Moller Okin, "'Mistresses of their own Destiny': Group Rights, Gender, and Realistic Rights to Exit," *Ethics* 112 (2002): 205–30.

communities and doctrines whose origins long predate modern social conditions.

Let us begin with two distinctions. First, we must not confuse the normative demands of a liberal order with the functional imperatives of social modernization, which, among other things, also necessitate the secularization of state authority. Second, the structural adaptation of identity groups or religious communities to the requirements of modern life in general, and to the expectations of civic autonomy and demands for toleration of a liberal republic in particular, does not entail exposure to reflexive pressure that would inevitably undermine theocentric or cosmocentric doctrines and life-orientations in the long run.

Of course, there are tribal societies and forms of life and ritual practices that are not compatible with the political framework of an egalitarian and individualist legal order. This is shown by the commendable attempts of the United States, Canada, and Australia to rectify the historical injustice to indigenous peoples who were subjugated, forcibly integrated, and subjected to centuries of discrimination. These tribal groups use the concession of a broad autonomy to maintain or to restore specific forms of traditional authority and collective property, even though in individual cases these conflict with the egalitarian principle and individualistic character of "equal rights for all." According to the modern understanding of law, a "state within the state" should not exist. If an "illiberal" social group is nevertheless permitted to operate a legal system of its own within the liberal state, this leads to irresolvable contradictions.

When tribal communities, whose ancestors were forcibly integrated into the state of the conquerors are compensated with extensive self-administration rights on moral grounds, the obligations of individual *members of the tribe* may conflict with the rights they are entitled to as *citizens* of the larger political community. The self-administration rights possessed by Indian territories in the United States and Canada have such implications, especially for legal claims regarding property and family relations. Again, it is primarily women who are affected: "If a member of an Indian tribe feels her rights have been violated by her tribal council, she can seek redress in a tribal court, but she cannot (except under exceptional circumstances) seek redress from the Supreme

Court . . . These limits on the application of constitutional bills of rights create the possibility that individuals or subgroups within Indian communities could be oppressed in the name of group solidarity or cultural purity."[55]

In the special case of reparations for past injustices by the state, law and morality can become embroiled in contradictions, even if both are governed by the principle of equal respect for all. This is because law is a recursively closed medium that can respond in a reflexive manner only to *its own* past decisions, but is insensitive to episodes that predate the legal system.[56] Hence, this conflict is reflected *in* law but does not emerge *from* it. The way of life of illiberal groups constitutes an alien element within the liberal legal order. Therefore, the contradictory consequences that result from a morally justified legal toleration of alien structures remain external to egalitarian law itself. It is quite different with religious groups who adapt their doctrines and forms of life, notwithstanding their premodern origins, to the secularization of state and society in order to be able to assert themselves within the differentiated structures of modernity.

Judaism and Christianity, which not only shaped Western culture but also played an important role in the genealogy of the idea of equality, no longer have any fundamental difficulties with the egalitarian structure and the individualistic character of a liberal order. Like all world religions, however, at one time they raised exclusive claims to validity and authority that were by no means inherently compatible with the claims to legitimacy of a secular legal and political system. In the context of modern societies and secular power structures, religious consciousness has itself been induced to "modernize," if you will. The cognitive switch from the "transmission of tradition" to expectations to adopt a reflexive stance and realistic exit conditions is an example of this.

The question is whether such adaptation processes reflect the submission of the religious ethos to conditions of a *hypocritical*

---

[55] Kymlicka, *Multicultural Citizenship*, pp. 38f.
[56] Law and morality conflict in a different way in cases of claims for reparations for the descendants of the victims of the criminal policies of past governments for which their legal successors are made responsible.

neutrality that is merely a disguise for domination by a different conception of the good (namely, the secular ethos of equality). Is a religious community that renounces indoctrination and grants latitude for a self-conscious appropriation of religious truths merely falling in line with norms imposed by the state or is it acting on its own initiative? In Europe, long before the emergence of the neutral state, the Church had to brace itself against the anthropocentric ideas of humanism and the secular ideas of the new physics, not to mention the pressure to secular-ize exerted by the capitalist economy and a bureaucratized administration, while having to cope with the deep crisis of an internal schism. The neutralization of state power vis-à-vis worldviews was only the political response to the irreconcilable wars of religion. This not only served the state's interest in main-taining law and order but also responded to the need of the religious communities themselves to subject their traditional self-understandings to revision in an environment marked by a heightened critical consciousness.

The freedom of religion in the liberal state, generalized into a civil right, not only defused the political threat of the pluralistic polity being torn apart by conflicting worldviews but also pro-vided religious communities seeking a place within the differenti-ated structure of modernity with an institutional framework for solving their own problems. The political solution ensuring the equal coexistence of the feuding religious powers consisted in a conception of tolerance that took into consideration the absolute – hence, non-negotiable – character of the validity claims raised by religious convictions. For tolerance must not be confused with indifference.

An attitude of indifference toward alien beliefs and practices or esteem for the other in her otherness would render something like tolerance superfluous. Tolerance is expected of those who reject the convictions and practices of others for good subjective reasons, in the awareness that it is a matter of a cognitive, though in the long run irresolvable, disagreement. However, prejudices do not count as legitimate grounds for rejection; tolerance is only required and is only possible if those involved base their rejection on a *reasonable* persisting disagreement. We do not respond to racists or chauvinists with calls for more tolerance, but with the demand that they overcome their prejudice.[57] These specific requirements are clearly accommodating toward the dogmatic stance of religious communities. But what price must the latter pay for this? What is demanded of those who benefit from the tolerance of others?

With the basic right of free exercise of religion, the liberal state seeks to decouple from the social level a cognitively irreconcilable disagreement among believers, members of different confessions, and unbelievers so that it does not affect social interactions among the citizens of the political community. For the state, the point is to defuse the social destructiveness of a conflict of worldviews by largely neutralizing their impact on actions and interactions. For religious communities, by contrast, the fact that the state recognizes the legitimacy of the persisting disagreement is important. This guarantees them the leeway to adopt – from the internal perspective of their own doctrines whose substance remains unaffected – a cognitively intelligible stance toward the beliefs of other religious communities and toward the modes of thought and interaction in their secular environment. In this way, the functions that legally guaranteed tolerance fulfills for the one side complement those it fulfills for the other. It promotes the self-assertion of the religious communities in a progressively modernizing society as much as it does the political survival of the liberal state. But, once again, what price do the religious communities pay for this leeway for self-transformation? Are the conditions of possibility not at the same time unreasonable restrictions?

Every religion is originally a "*world*view" or "comprehensive doctrine" in the sense that it claims authority to structure a form of life *in its entirety*. A religion must relinquish this claim within a secularized society marked by a pluralism of worldviews. With the functional differentiation of social subsystems, the life of the religious community also becomes detached from its social surroundings. The role of "member of the community" becomes

---

[57] See Rainer Forst, "Toleration, Justice and Reason," in Catriona McKinnon and Dario Castiglione (eds), *The Culture of Toleration in Diverse Societies* (Manchester: Manchester University Press, 2003).

differentiated from the role of "member of society." And since the liberal state depends on a political integration of citizens that goes beyond a mere *modus vivendi*, this differentiation of memberships must not be confined to a cognitively undemanding conformity of the religious ethos to the *imposed* laws of the secular society. The formation of religious communities harmonizes with the secular process of socialization only when – also from the internal perspective – corresponding statements of norms and values are not only differentiated *from one another*, but when one statement follows consistently *from the other*. John Rawls chose the image of a module to describe this "embedding" of the egalitarian universalism of the legal order in the ethos of the various religious worldviews: the module of secular justice should fit into each orthodox context of justification even though it was constructed with the help of reasons that are neutral toward different worldviews.[58]

However, such a cognitive differentiation of the egalitarian social morality from the communal ethos is not just a normative expectation with which the state confronts the religious communities. Rather, it coheres with their own interest in asserting themselves within modern society and in gaining the opportunity to exercise independent influence on the society as a whole via the political public arena. By participating in national debates over moral and ethical questions, religious communities can foster a postsecular self-understanding of society as a whole in which the enduring vitality of religion in a progressively secularizing environment must be reckoned with.

Nevertheless, the question of whether the religious community must pay an unfair price for this from the perspective of civic equality is not yet answered. The imposition implied by the demand for tolerance has two aspects. Everyone is permitted to realize her own ethos only within the limits required by equal ethical liberties for all. Consequently, everyone must also respect the ethos of others within these limits. One is not required to accept the rejected views of others, since one's own truth claims and certainties remain untouched. The imposition results not from relativizing one's own convictions, but from restricting their

---

[58] Rawls, *Political Liberalism*, pp. 58ff.

practical effects; it is an implication of being allowed to realize one's own ethos only within limits and having to accept the practical consequences of the ethos of the other. But these burdens of tolerance do not fall equally on believers and unbelievers.

For the consciousness of the secularized citizen traveling with light metaphysical baggage who can accept a morally "free-standing" justification of democracy and human rights, the "right" can without difficulty be accorded priority over the "good." Under these conditions, the pluralism of *ways of life* in which each different worldview is reflected does not give rise to any cognitive dissonance with one's own ethical convictions. For from this perspective, different forms of life only embody different *value orientations*. And different values are not mutually exclusive like different *truths*. So secular consciousness has no difficulty in recognizing that an alien ethos has the same authenticity and the same priority for the other that one's own ethos has for oneself.

The situation is different for the believer who draws her ethical self-understanding from religious truths that claim universal validity. As soon as the idea of the correct life takes its orientation from religious paths to salvation or metaphysical conceptions of the good, a divine perspective (or a "view from nowhere") comes into play from which (or from where) other ways of life appear not just different but *mistaken*. When the alien ethos is not merely a question of relative value but of truth or falsity, the requirement to show each citizen equal respect regardless of her ethical self-understanding or her lifestyle becomes a heavier burden.

That the expectation of tolerance does not have a neutral effect on believers and unbelievers is not surprising but as yet does not reflect an injustice *per se*. For the burden is not one-sided. A price is also demanded from religiously tone-deaf citizens. The understanding of tolerance in liberal pluralistic societies requires not only believers to recognize that they must *reasonably* reckon with the persistence of disagreement in their dealings with adherents of other faiths. The same recognition is also required of unbelievers in dealing with believers. For the secular consciousness, this implies the nontrivial requirement to determine the relation between faith and knowledge *self-critically* from the perspective of secular knowledge [*Weltwissen*]. For the expectation that the disagreement between secular knowledge and religious tradition will persist merits the title "reasonable" only if religious convictions are accorded an epistemic status as not simply "irrational" from the perspective of secular knowledge.

The guarantee of equal ethical liberties calls for the secularization of state power, but it forbids the political overgeneralization of the secularized worldview. Insofar as they act in their role as citizens, secularized citizens may neither fundamentally deny that religious worldviews may be true nor reject the right of devout fellow-citizens to couch their contributions to public discussions in religious language. A liberal political culture can even expect its secularized citizens to participate in efforts to translate relevant contributions from the religious language into a publicly accessible language.[59] Even if these two expectations did not fully counterbalance the non-neutrality in the effects of the principle of tolerance, a residual imbalance does not place the justification of the principle itself in question. For in the light of the glaring injustice that is overcome by abolishing religious discrimination, it would be disproportionate of believers to reject the demand for tolerance because its burdens are not shared equally.

This observation paves the way for a dialectical understanding of cultural secularization. If we conceive of the modernization of public consciousness in Europe as a learning process that affects and changes religious and secular mentalities alike by forcing the tradition of the Enlightenment, as well as religious doctrines, to reflect on their respective limits, then the international tensions between major cultures and world religions also appear in a different light. The globalization of markets, the media, and other networks no longer leaves nations any realistic prospect of opting out of capitalist modernization. Neither can non-Western cultures evade the challenges of secularization and a pluralism of worldviews generated by an inadequately regulated process of modernization that they also actively pursue. They will only be able to assert their cultural distinctiveness against a capitalist world

---

[59] See Habermas, "Faith and Knowledge," in *The Future of Human Nature*, trans. Hella Beister and William Rehg (Cambridge: Polity, 2003).

culture shaped by the West by finding paths to "alternative modernities." But this means that they will be able to use their own cultural resources to resist the leveling violence *from the outside* only if the religious consciousness in these countries also opens itself up to modernization *from within*.[60] The challenge for these cultures is to find functional equivalents for the European innovation of the separation of church and state in responding to similar challenges. To the extent that they are successful, their constructive adaptation to imperatives of social modernization will not represent a submission to alien cultural norms any more than the change in mentality and detraditionalizing of religious communities in the West was merely a submission to liberal norms of equality.

[60] Charles Taylor, "Two Theories of Modernity," *Public Culture* 1 (1999): 153–74.

11

A Political Constitution for the Pluralist World Society?[1]

The prospects for the success of the project of a "cosmopolitan condition" are no worse today, following the invasion of Iraq in contravention of international law, than in 1945, following the catastrophe of World War II, or in 1989–90, following the collapse of the bipolar power constellation. This does not mean that the chances are good; but we should not lose a sense of proportion either. The Kantian project only found its way onto the political agenda with the League of Nations, in other words after more than two centuries; and the idea of a cosmopolitan order only acquired an institutional embodiment with the foundation of the United Nations. The UN has gained in political significance and has evolved into an important factor in global political conflicts since the early 1990s. Even the superpower found itself compelled to engage in a confrontation with the world organization when the latter refused to succumb to pressure to provide legitimacy for a unilateral intervention. The United Nations weathered the subsequent attempt to marginalize it so well that it was able to initiate the urgently needed reform of its core organization and subsidiary agencies.

The recommendations of a reform commission appointed by the Secretary General have been on the table since December 2004. As we shall see, the proposed reforms are the product of

[1] I am indebted to Armin von Bogdandy for his suggestions for corrections and his comments as an expert in international law.

an intelligent analysis of mistakes. This learning process is directing the political will unmistakably toward a continuation of the Kantian project. This project expresses not only the idea of an enduring state of peace. For Kant already extended the negative concept of the absence of war and violence into one of peace as an implication of legally granted freedoms. Today, the comprehensive concept of collective security also extends to the necessary resources to ensure conditions of life under which citizens in all parts of the world can actually enjoy formally granted liberties. We can still take our cue from Kant's idea of a cosmopolitan condition provided that we construe it in sufficiently abstract terms. I will first explain why I consider the Kantian alternative between a world republic and a league of nations to be incomplete (I) and how the Kantian project can be understood under contemporary conditions (II). Then I will explain why the viability of any form of democracy, including the democratic nation-state, depends on the success of this project (III) before addressing, in conclusion, two historical trends that work in favor of the project (IV and V).

I

Hobbes interpreted the relationship between law and security in functionalist terms: the state accords the citizens, as the subjects of law, the guarantee of protection in exchange for their unconditional obedience.[2] For Kant, by contrast, the pacifying function of law remains conceptually intertwined with the function of a legal condition that the citizens recognize as legitimate in promoting freedom. For the validity of law is based not only on the external threat of sanction by the state, but also on the internal reasons for the claim that it merits recognition by its addressees. Kant no longer operates with Hobbes's empiricist concept of law. However, with the idea of a transition from state-centered

---

[2] In the following I draw on my essay "Does the Constitutionalization of International Law Still Have a Chance?" in Jürgen Habermas, *The Divided West*, ed. and trans. Ciaran Cronin (Cambridge: Polity, 2006), pp. 115–93.

international law to cosmopolitan law, Kant also sets himself apart from Rousseau.

Kant breaks with the republican conception that popular sovereignty finds expression in the external sovereignty of the state – in other words, that the democratic self-determination of the people is internally linked to the collective self-assertion of a corresponding form of life, if necessary by military means. Kant recognizes that the democratic will has its roots in the ethos of a people. But that does not necessarily imply that the capacity of a democratic constitution to bind and rationalize political power must be restricted to a specific nation-state. For the universalistic thrust of the constitutional principles of a nation-state points beyond the limits of national traditions which are no doubt also reflected in the local features of a particular constitutional order.

These two operations – first, the linking of the idea of peace with a condition of legally guaranteed freedoms and, second, the separation between democratic self-determination in the domestic sphere and aggressive self-assertion toward other nations – clear the way for Kant to project the *"bürgerliche Verfassung"* (i.e. the type of constitution which had recently emerged from the American and French revolutions) from the national onto the global level. This marks the birth of the idea of a constitutionalization of international law. The extraordinary thing about this farsighted conceptual innovation was the implication that international law as a law of states would be transformed into cosmopolitan law as a law of individuals. For individuals would no longer enjoy the status of legal subjects merely as citizens of a nation-state, but also as members of a politically constituted world society.

However, Kant could construe the constitutionalization of international law exclusively as a transformation of international into intrastate relations. To the very end, he advocated the idea of a world republic, even though he proposed the "surrogate" of a league of nations [*Völkerbund*] as a first stage toward realizing such a commonwealth of nations [*Völkerstaat*]. This weak conception of a voluntary association of states that are willing to coexist peacefully while nevertheless retaining their sovereignty seemed to recommend itself as a transitional stage en route to a world republic. Many have wondered why he placed his hopes in such a conceptually flawed structure. From the vantage point of the legal and political networks of a pluralist, highly interdependent, yet functionally differentiated global society, it is easy to identify with the fortuitous hindsight of later generations the conceptual barriers that prevented Kant from overcoming this sterile alternative. Three reasons may have prevented him from conceiving the telos of the constitutionalization of international law, the "cosmopolitan condition," in sufficiently abstract terms to avoid assimilating it to the problematic model of a world republic and to prevent it from being dismissed as utopian.

The centralist French republic that served Kant as a model for a democratic constitutional state suggested that the sovereignty of the people is indivisible.[3] In a multilevel federalist system, however, the democratic will of the people already branches out at its very source into parallel channels of legitimation through elections to local, state, or federal parliaments. The model of the United States (and the debate conducted in the "Federalist Papers") provides early testimony concerning this concept of "divided sovereignty."[4] The image of a federalist world republic might have allayed Kant's fear that the normalizing pressure exerted by the "soulless despotism" of a global "state of nations" would rob particular nations of their cultural specificity and identity. This fear may explain his search for a "surrogate", though not yet why he felt compelled to conceptualize a cosmopolitan condition in the shape of an all-encompassing state in the first place.

The reason for this may have been another conceptual bottleneck, one which we have been able to overcome only recently as a result of the increasingly dense network of international organizations. Republicanism of the French variety explains the rationalizing effect of the subjection of political power to law in terms of a constitutive popular will that reconfigures political authority from the ground up. Rousseau's social contract implies that the state and the constitution are one because both arise *uno*

[3] Wolfgang Kersting, "Globale Rechtsordnung oder weltweite Verteilungsgerechtigkeit?" in Kersting, *Recht, Gerechtigkeit und demokratische Tugend* (Frankfurt am Main: Suhrkamp, 1997), pp. 243–315, here p. 269.
[4] On the theory of sovereignty in the constitutional state, see Martin Kriele, *Einführung in die Staatslehre* (Opladen: Kohlhammer, 1994), pp. 273ff.

actu, i.e. coevally, from the will of the people. Standing in this tradition, Kant neglected a different, competing constitutional tradition that rejects any such conceptual linkage of state and constitution. In the liberal tradition, the constitution does not have the function of constituting *authority* but only that of constraining *power*. The early modern assemblies of the estates already embodied the idea of a system of mutual checks and balances on the "ruling powers" (namely, on the aristocracy, the clergy, and the towns over against the monarch). Liberalism develops this idea further in the modern sense of the constitutional division of powers.

A political constitution primarily geared to setting limits to power founds a "rule of law" that can normatively shape existing power relations, regardless of their democratic origins, and direct the exercise of political power into legal channels. By rejecting the identity of the rulers with the ruled, a constitution of this type ensures the conceptual independence of three elements, namely, the constitution, the powers of the state, and citizenship.[5] Thus, here there is no fundamental conceptual obstacle to separating the elements that are so tightly intermeshed in the democratic state. In fact, the cooperation between different nations in multilateral networks or in transnational negotiation systems has in many cases produced the legal forms of a constitution of international organizations without state characteristics which dispense with the familiar forms of legitimation through the will of an organized citizenry. Such constitutions regulate the functional interplay among nation-states; even comprehensive global policy networks lack the "meta-competence" characteristic of states, namely, the power to define and extend their own competences.

Thus the liberal type of constitution that limits the power of the state without constituting it also provides a conceptual model for a constitutionalization of international law in the form of a politically constituted world society without a world government.

---

[5] See Günter Frankenberg, "Die Rückkehr des Vertrages: Überlegungen zur Verfassung der Europäischen Union," in Lutz Wingert and Klaus Günther (eds), *Die Öffentlichkeit der Vernunft und die Vernunft der Öffentlichkeit* (Frankfurt am Main: Suhrkamp, 2001), pp. 507–38.

With the transition from state-centered international law to a cosmopolitan legal order, nation-states will be restricted in their scope of action without being robbed of their status as subjects of a global legal order by the individual world citizens, who now acquire the additional status of subjects of cosmopolitan law. Rather, republican states can remain subjects of a world constitution without a world government alongside individual world citizens. That said, the fusion of the types of constitution that have hitherto emerged from competing legal traditions gives rise to the problem of how political decision-making above the national level can be fed back into national channels of legitimation.[6]

Before returning to this question, I would like to mention a third motive that may have prompted Kant to seek a surrogate for the extravagant idea of a world republic as a model for a cosmopolitan condition. The two constitutional revolutions of the eighteenth century led contemporaries, and later generations, to assume that political constitutions are the products of sudden acts of will performed at favorable historical junctures. The image of the events in Paris was marked by the spontaneous uprising of inspired masses grasping an opportune moment. The creation of a republican constitution appeared to be linked to a mythical act of foundation and a state of emergency. If the occurrence of a revolutionary moment in a particular place was improbable enough, the coincidence of such improbabilities in several places seemed inconceivable. I surmise that this intuition is what underlies Kant's curious assertion that the peoples of the earth "in accordance with their idea of international law" (i.e. their notion of sovereign self-determination) definitely "do not at all want" to merge into a state of nations.[7]

However, in the meantime we have become accustomed to the institutionalization of international law as a long-term process that is driven, not by revolutionary masses, but in the first

---

[6] Christoph Möllers analyzes this link using the European Union as an example in his introductory chapter on constitution and constitutionalization in Armin von Bogdandy (ed.), *Europäisches Verfassungsrecht* (Heidelberg: Springer, 2003), pp. 1–56.

[7] Immanuel Kant, "Toward Perpetual Peace," in Kant, *Practical Philosophy*, ed. and trans. Mary Gregor (Cambridge: Cambridge University Press, 1996), p. 328 (translation amended).

instance by nation-states and regional alliances of states. On the one hand, this process is deliberately pursued employing the classical mechanisms of international treaties and the founding of international organizations; on the other, it is also developing incrementally in response to the systemic stimuli that have been triggered and to unintended side-effects. This mixture of intentional action and quasi-natural spontaneity is exhibited by economic globalization (of trade, investment, and production) and (in response to the resulting need for coordination and regulation) by the expansion and reorganization of the institutional core of the global economic regime. The latter was initially the result of straightforward political decision-making and only subsequently, in response to the resulting need for coordination and regulation, gave rise to an inexorably expanding global economic regime.

The temporal pattern of such a long-term process, in which political intervention is combined with systemic growth, suggests that we should speak here of stages or even degrees of constitutionalization.[8] The prime example is European unification, which keeps advancing in spite of the fact that its normative parameters have not yet provided an answer to the question of *finalité* – i.e. whether the European Union will evolve into a federal state of nations with pronounced internal differentiations, or whether it will continue to expand at the level of integration of a supranational organization without taking on the qualities of a state. The "path-dependence" of a mode of decision-making that gradually restricts the scope of future alternatives, even against the will of participants, through the cumulative effects of past decisions plays an important role in this context.

Hitherto, I have discussed three aspects from which the Kantian idea of transforming state-centered international law into cosmopolitan law can be freed from its misleading instantiation in the form of a world republic. I first drew attention to the federalist notion of divided sovereignty and the general concept of a multilevel system. Then I introduced the distinction between two types of constitution that focus on constituting political

---

[8] This is emphasized by Thomas Cottier and Maya Hertig, "The Prospects of 21st Century Constitutionalism," MS, 2004 (Institute of European Economic Law, University of Berne).

authority and on constraining power, respectively, which could
be linked in a new way in the political constitution of a world
society without a world government. And, finally, I pointed to
the process of gradual advances in the constitutionalization of
international law that are initiated and supported by governments rather than by citizens, before they exercise wide-scale
effects thanks to the gradual internalization of anticipatory legal
constructions.

With an eye to the present-day structures, we can outline a
conceptual alternative to the cosmopolitan republic (and its
contemporary variants) on this basis.[9] This calls for three further
adjustments within the conceptual apparatus of political theory:
(a) the concept of national sovereignty must be adapted to
the new forms of governance beyond the nation-state; (b) we
must revise the conceptual linkage between the state's monopoly on force and compulsory law in favor of the idea that
supranational law is backed up by the sanctioning powers
that remain the preserve of nation-states; and (c) we must identify the mechanism that explains how nations can change their
self-understanding.

(a) According to the tradition of liberal nationalism, the core
norms of international law, i.e. the principle of state sovereignty
and the prohibition on intervention in domestic affairs, follow
from the principle of popular sovereignty. The competence of the
state to assert itself toward the outside is the reflection of the
democratic self-determination of the citizens within the state.[10]
The state must have the right and the ability to uphold the identity and the form of life supported by the democratic community
and to protect itself against other nations, if necessary with military force. Internal self-determination requires protection against

---

[9] On "cosmopolitan democracy," see Daniele Archibugi and David Held (eds),
Cosmopolitan Democracy (Cambridge: Polity, 1995); David Held, *Democracy and
the Global Order* (Cambridge: Polity, 1995); on a federal world republic, see
Otfried Höffe, *Demokratie im Zeitalter der Globalisierung* (Munich: Beck,
1999).
[10] Michael Walzer still defends this view in *Just and Unjust Wars* (New York:
Basic Books, 1977) and *Arguing about War* (New Haven, Conn.: Yale University
Press, 2005). See also the essays on "Twenty Years of Michael Walzer's *Just and
Unjust Wars*," *Ethics and International Affairs* 11 (1997): 3–104.

the threat of foreign domination. However, this conception encounters difficulties in a highly interdependent global society. If even a superpower can no longer guarantee the security and welfare of its own population without the help of other states, then "sovereignty" is losing its classical meaning.[11]

Whereas internal state sovereignty is no longer restricted to simply maintaining law and order but also includes the effective protection of the civil rights of citizens, "external sovereignty" today calls for the ability to cooperate with partners as much as the capacity to defend oneself against external enemies. Fulfilling the social contract also presupposes that the sovereign state is willing and able to participate equally in collective efforts to address problems that arise at the global and regional levels and can only be solved within the framework of international or supranational organizations.[12] This presupposes both the renunciation of the right to go to war and the recognition of the duty of the international community to protect the population of a criminal or failing state against its own government or what is left of it.

(b) Interestingly enough, the international community can transfer this right to impose sanctions and to intervene to a world organization without at the same time equipping the latter with a global monopoly on force. Contrary to the conventional understanding of compulsory state law, a gap is opening up between supranational legislative authority and national agencies that can draw on legitimate means of force to implement that law. The individual states retain their monopoly on force, although as members of the United Nations they formally cede the right to decide on when military force should be used to the Security Council (except in the case of justified self-defense). In line with

---

[11] Erhard Denninger advocates rejecting the concept of sovereignty altogether; see "Vom Ende der nationalstaatlichen Souveränität in Europa," in Denninger, *Recht in globaler Unordnung* (Berlin: Berlin Wissenschafts-Verlag, 2005), pp. 379–94.

[12] See the corresponding definition of "new sovereignty" in Abram Chayes and Antonia Handler Chayes, *The New Sovereignty: Compliance with International Regulatory Agreements* (Cambridge, Mass.: Harvard University Press, 1995).

the pattern of behavior that has evolved within collective security systems, the effectiveness of a Security Council resolution to intervene in the affairs of a nation-state is ensured by a sufficient number of powerful members making their forces available for executing consensually agreed-upon missions. The European Union is a convincing example of how higher-order legal norms can have binding force, even though they are only backed in this circular way by formally subordinate member states. The means of force available to impose the sanctions called for by laws decided in Brussels and Luxembourg remain in the hands of the individual states, which then "implement" this law without resistance.

(c) This example also illustrates the hypothesis concerning the empirical effectiveness of norms[13] without which it would be difficult to render the Kantian project of promoting a cosmopolitan condition empirically plausible. The constitutional norms and legal constructs introduced by political elites in supranational arenas exercise anticipatory effects in the sense of a *self-fulfilling prophecy*. This kind of lawmaking anticipates the change in consciousness that it provokes among the addressees only in the course of its gradual implementation. The accompanying political discourses provide the medium in which the spirit of legal regulations, whose letter is initially recognized only in a declamatory manner, can be gradually internalized. This holds for the states and their citizens alike. How national contracting parties understand their role can shift in the course of such a constructive, self-referential, and circular learning process. As collective actors used to making autonomous decisions become accustomed to forms of cooperation that are initially agreed upon in a sovereign manner, their self-understanding is transformed into the consciousness of members of international organizations with rights and duties. In this way, even sovereign states can learn to subordinate national interests to the obligations they have assumed as members of the international community or as players in transnational networks.

---

[13] On the importance of the social constructivist concept of learning for the theory of international relations, see Bernhard Zangl and Michael Zürn, *Frieden und Krieg* (Frankfurt am Main: Suhrkamp, 2003), pp. 118–48.

II

In the light of these preliminary clarifications, I would now like to flesh out the idea of a cosmopolitan condition in a form that remains in touch with existing realities while at the same time pointing beyond them. On my understanding, the constitutional-ized world society, which I have outlined elsewhere,[14] is a multi-level system that can make possible a global domestic politics that has hitherto been lacking, especially in the fields of global eco-nomic and environmental policies, even without a world govern-ment. Whereas the state-centered system of international law recognized only one type of player – the nation-states – and two playing fields – domestic and foreign policy or internal affairs and international relations – the new structure of a constituted cos-mopolitan society is characterized by *three arenas* and *three kinds of collective actors*.

The *supranational arena* is dominated by a single actor. The international community assumes institutional form in a *world organization* that has the ability to act in carefully circumscribed policy fields without itself taking on the character of a state. The United Nations lacks the authority to define or expand its own powers at will. Its authority extends to the effective, and above all non-selective, fulfillment of two functions, namely, securing peace and human rights on a global scale, and is restricted to these two fundamental, but clearly circumscribed, functions. Hence, the pending reform of the United Nations must focus not only on strengthening core institutions but also on detaching them from the extensive web of special UN organizations, in particular those networked with independent international organizations.[15]

Of course, opinion- and will-formation within the world orga-nization should be connected back to the circuits of communica-tion within national parliaments and should be subject to more effective monitoring by NGOs and other representatives of

---

[14] See Habermas, *The Divided West*, pp. 115ff. and 176ff.
[15] For an overview of the UN family, see David Held, *Global Covenant* (Cambridge: Polity, 2004), pp. 82f.

a mobilized world public. Yet even an appropriately reformed world organization would remain composed of nation-states in the first instance and not of world citizens. In this respect, it resembles more a league of nations [*Völkerbund*] than Kant's idea of a universal state of nations [*Völkerstaat*]. For there cannot be a world parliament, however modest, without a world republic. The collective actors would not disappear *without a trace* into the new order, which they must first establish with the only instrument available to them, namely, a treaty under international law. The world organization must be permanently buttressed by power centers organized at the state level if it is to constitute the main pillar of a legal pacifism backed up by power.[16] Alongside individuals, states remain subjects of an international law transformed into a cosmopolitan human rights regime that is capable of protecting individual citizens, if necessary even against their own governments.

As members of the international community, nation-states must retain a privileged status also with a view to the far-reaching agenda that the United Nations has recently announced under the imposing title "Millennium Development Goals." The legal guarantees spelled out in the UN's human rights compacts are no longer limited to basic liberal and political rights but include the "empowering" material conditions that would first enable the world's most vulnerable populations to make use of the rights accorded them *in abstracto*.[17] The worldwide political efforts demanded by such an agenda overtax the capacities and political will of the international community. At present

---

[16] On the "indispensability of the nation-state," see Edgar Grande, "Vom Nationalstaat zum transnationalen Politikregime," in Ulrich Beck and Christian Lau (eds), *Entgrenzung und Entscheidung* (Frankfurt am Main: Suhrkamp, 2004), pp. 384–401.

[17] On "material equality of rights" [*Rechtsinhaltsgleichheit*], see Habermas, *Between Facts and Norms*, trans. William Rehg (Cambridge: Polity, 1998), pp. 484ff.; on the relation of the younger generation of basic rights to the classical core, see ibid., pp. 156f. In this connection, the conception of "social democracy" in the theoretical tradition in constitutional law which can be traced back to Hermann Haller has also gained acceptance in international law. See Thomas Meyer and Lew Hinchman, *The Theory of Social Democracy* (Cambridge: Polity, 2007).

we can observe this in the arena of increasingly numerous and interconnected *transnational* networks and organizations designed to cope with the growing demand for coordination of a world society that is becoming more complex.[18] However, regulation in the form of the "coordination" of governmental and nongovernmental actors is only sufficient to address a particular category of cross-border problems.

The largely institutionalized procedures of information exchange, consultation, control, and agreement are sufficient for handling "technical" issues in a broader sense (such as the standardization of measures, the regulation of telecommunications, disaster prevention, containing epidemics, or combating organized crime). Since the devil is always in the details, these problems also call for a balancing of conflicting interests. However, they differ from genuinely "political" issues that impinge on entrenched interests which are deeply rooted in the structures of national societies, such as, for example, questions of global energy and of environmental, financial, and economic policy, all of which involve issues of equitable distribution. These problems of a future world domestic policy call for regulation and positive integration, for which at present both the institutional framework and actors are lacking. The existing political networks are functionally differentiated, multilateral, and at times even inclusive international organizations in which government representatives generally bear the responsibility and have the final word, irrespective of who else is granted admission. At any rate, they do not provide a forum for legislative competences and corresponding processes of political will-formation. Even if such a framework were to be established, collective actors capable of implementing such decisions would still be lacking. What I have in mind are *regional or continental regimes* equipped with a sufficiently representative mandate to negotiate for whole continents and to wield the necessary powers of implementation for large territories.

Politics cannot intentionally meet the spontaneous need for regulation of a systemically integrated, quasi-natural global

---

[18] Anne-Marie Slaughter offers an impressive list of the international organizations in *A New World Order* (Princeton, N.J., and Oxford: Princeton University Press, 2004), pp. xv–xviii.

economy and society until such time as the intermediate arena is populated by a manageable number of global players. The latter must be strong enough to form shifting coalitions, to produce a flexible system of checks and balances, and to negotiate and implement binding compromises – above all on issues concerning the structure and boundary conditions of the global ecological and economic systems. In this way, international relations as we know them would continue to exist in the transnational arena in a modified form – modified for the simple reason that under an effective UN security regime even the most powerful global players would be denied recourse to war as a legitimate means of resolving conflicts. The problem that, with the exception of the United States, there are at present no viable actors at the intermediate or transnational level directs our attention to the *third level*, namely, the lower level of the nation-states.

This level began to emerge on a global scale only during the process of decolonization. An inclusive international community of nation-states arose only in the latter half of the twentieth century, during which time the number of UN member states increased from fifty-one to 192. Thus these nation-states are a comparatively recent political formation. Although, as the "original" actors, they remain the most powerful actors with the greatest scope for action, the nation-states are now coming under pressure. The growing interdependencies of the global economy and the cross-border risks of a world society are overtaxing their territorial range of operation and their chains of legitimation. Globalized networks in all dimensions have long since made nonsense of the normative assumption in democratic theory of a congruence between those responsible for political decision-making and those affected by political decisions.[19]

Thus on all continents individual nation-states find themselves compelled to establish regional alliances, or at any rate closer forms of cooperation (APEC, ASEAN, NAFTA, AU, ECOWAS, OAS, etc.). However, these regional alliances represent weak beginnings. The nation-states need to enter into closer

---

[19] David Held and Anthony McGrew (eds), *The Global Transformations Reader* (Cambridge: Polity, 2003).

alliances than forms of intergovernmental cooperation if they are to assume the role of collective pillars of a global domestic politics at the transnational level. Only in this way can they acquire the scope for action of global players and confer the necessary democratic legitimacy on the outcomes of transnational political accords. To date, only the first-generation nation-states have made an attempt to create stronger political entities of this type. In Europe, the motivation to found a political union was provided by the self-destructive excesses of radical nationalism.

Today, the European Union has at least reached the stage that it can plausibly claim to be a global player. Its political muscle is comparable to that of "natural" continental regimes such as China or Russia. The latter powers emerged comparatively late from the social and political structures of the ancient empires following a transitional phase of state socialism. The European Union, by contrast, could provide a model for other regions because it harmonizes the interests of formerly independent nation-states at a higher level of integration, thereby creating a collective actor on a new scale. However, European unification can serve as a model for constructing regional political alliances only if it achieves a level of political integration that enables the EU to pursue democratically legitimized common policies both at home and abroad.

Thus far I have not mentioned the cultural pluralism that could pose problems for a constitutionalized world society at all three levels. The current worldwide political instrumentalization of the major religions also increases tensions at the international level. Within a cosmopolitan order, this perceived clash of civilizations would above all impede the transnational negotiation systems. However, the fact that the nation-states would have to learn to change both their behavior and their self-image within the multilevel system outlined would make it easier to cope with such conflicts.

One of the required learning processes involves internalizing the norms of the world organization and acquiring the ability to pursue one's own interests by prudently merging into transnational networks. Even without formally relinquishing their monopoly on force, the sovereign states must come to see themselves in a constitutionalized world society as peaceful members of the international community and at the same time as capable players in international organizations. The other learning process relates to overcoming a stubborn mindset that is historically closely interconnected with the formation of the nation-state. Nationalism provided the basis for what is by any standards a highly abstract form of civic solidarity. This national consciousness must now be raised to an even higher level of abstraction in the process of integrating nation-states into continental regimes. A mobilization of the masses through religious, ethnic, or nationalist agitation will gradually become less likely the more the expectations of tolerance inherent in a liberal civic ethos permeate political culture also at the national level.

Here, at the latest, we must face the objection of the "impotence of a mere ought." I do not want to discuss the normative superiority of the Kantian project over other visions of a new world order here.[20] However, projects remain without consequences, no matter how normatively well grounded, if reality does not meet them halfway. This was Hegel's objection to Kant. Instead of merely juxtaposing the rational idea with an irrational world, he wanted to elevate the actual course of history into the realization of the idea. However, Hegel and later Marx compromised themselves badly with this attempt to ground rational ideas in the philosophy of history. Before I discuss two historical trends that may work in favor of the revised Kantian project, I would like to draw attention to the possible benefits and risks of the success or failure of this project. The issue is whether we must finally bid farewell to the very idea of constitutional democracy or whether the normative core of the vanishing world of democratic nation-states can be recovered within the postnational constellation.

III

Modern conceptions of the constitution refer explicitly to the relationship between citizens and the state. But in addition they

---

[20] Habermas, *The Divided West*, pp. 183–93.

also implicitly prefigure a comprehensive legal order encompassing the state and civil society (in the Hegelian and Marxist senses)[21]
– in other words, the totality comprised of administrative state,
capitalist economy, and civil society. The economy comes into
play for the simple reason that the modern, tax-based state
depends on market transactions regulated by civil law. In social
contract theories, civil society is thematized as the network of
relations among the citizens – whether, following the liberal tradition, as the relations between private utility maximizers or, following the republican tradition, as relations of solidarity between
citizens.

To be sure, the legal construction of a community of free
and equal citizens is the focus of any constitution. The topics
of "security", "law," and "freedom" place the emphasis on the
self-assertion of the political community toward the outside
world, on the one hand, and on the rights that free and equal
persons accord each other as members of a voluntary and
self-administering association, on the other. The constitution
lays down how organized force within the state is transformed
into legitimate power. However, this problem of "law and
freedom" cannot be solved without implicitly defining the roles
that the economy, as the basic functional system, and civil
society, as the arena in which public opinion and political will
are formed, are supposed to play in relation to the administrative
power of the state.

With the expansion of the catalogue of tasks to be performed
by the state beyond the classical functions of maintaining law and
order, this implicit, comprehensive character of the constitutional
order becomes especially apparent.[22] Social injustice must
be overcome in a capitalist society, collective dangers must be
averted in a risk society, and the equal rights of members of

---

[21] These two elements were not initially differentiated from each other in the
classical concept of civil or bourgeois society [*bürgerliche Gesellschaft*]; see
Habermas, "Further Reflections on the Public Sphere," in Craig Calhoun (ed.),
Habermas and the Public Sphere (Cambridge, Mass.: MIT Press, 1992), pp.
421–61.
[22] The nineteenth-century liberal constitutions were comprehensive legal orders
in this sense long before the policy fields had extended beyond the classical tasks
of maintaining law and order.

different religions, cultures, and ethnicities must be guaranteed in a pluralist society. In the class differences produced by capitalism, in the risks produced by science and technology, and in the tensions intrinsic to cultural pluralism, the state encounters problems that do not immediately respond to the instruments of politics and law, i.e. the means of coercion available to the state. But the state cannot simply shirk its general political responsibility either, because it depends on the systemic integration promoted by private functional systems – in the first instance, on the economy – and on the social integration fostered by civil society. The state, in its role as provider of welfare, must cope with the internal logic of functional systems and the cultural dynamics of civil society.[23] The corporatist mode of negotiation is an indicator of this new style of state as a moderator which nevertheless continues to take its orientation from the constitution or from an interpretation of the constitution suitably adapted to the times.

The triple reference of the constitution to the state, the economy, and civil society can be explained in sociological terms by the fact that all modern societies are integrated through exactly three media, "power," "money," and "communication" (or "mutual understanding"). In functionally differentiated societies, social relations come about either through "organization," the "market," or consensus-formation (i.e. communicative actions, values, and norms). Corresponding types of social interaction assume concrete form in the bureaucratic state, the capitalist economy, and civil society (as a separate sphere differentiated from both). The political constitution is geared to shaping each of these systems by means of the medium of law and to harmonizing them so that

---

[23] See the special issue of the *European Review*, vol. 13, Supplement 1 (May 2005), edited by Stephan Leibfried and Michael Zürn, on the transformation of the state and the heterogeneous list of state functions in the editors' introduction, "A New Perspective on the State," p. 2: "The state regulates the labor market, steers the economy, fights crime and provides some form of education; it regulates traffic, provides a framework for democracy, owns businesses, enters wars and makes peace treaties, creates a reliable legal structure, supports social welfare, builds streets, provides water, imposes military service, maintains the pension system, collects taxes and deploys some forty per cent of the gross national product, represents national interests and generally regulates daily life down to the smallest details."

they can fulfill their functions as measured by a presumed "common good." The constitutional design is supposed to prevent system-specific pathologies in virtue of the structuring effects of the legal system as a whole, thereby contributing to maximizing the common good.

In this way, the state is supposed to employ political power to implement law and guarantee freedom without resorting to repressive, patronizing, or normalizing force. The economy is supposed to promote productivity and affluence without violating the standards of distributive justice (by ensuring that as many people as possible are better off and nobody suffers disadvantage); and civil society is supposed to foster solidarity among independent citizens without resorting to collectivist integration or fragmentation or provoking ideological polarization. The postulated "commonweal" is jeopardized not only by "failures of the state" (legal uncertainty and repression) but likewise by "failures of the market" and by a lack of solidarity and mutual recognition among citizens. The indeterminate character of the essentially contested common good[24] results especially from the difficulty in striking a balance between these interdependent variables.

Even if the state discharges its proper tasks of maintaining security and freedom, it cannot preserve the necessary level of legitimacy in the long run unless a functioning economy fulfills the preconditions for an acceptable pattern of distribution of social rewards and unless an active civil society fosters a sufficient orientation to the common good among citizens.[25] The converse also holds. For this reason, the constitution burdens the democratic state with the paradoxical responsibility of satisfying the economic and cultural preconditions for maintaining the society as a whole. Although the state can try to meet these demanding requirements and bring them under political control with the instruments at its disposal, such as legal regulations and political pressures, it cannot provide legal guarantees of success. Unemployment and social segmentation cannot be eliminated by

[24] Claus Offe, "Wessen Wohl ist das Gemeinwohl?" in Wingert and Günther (eds), *Die Öffentlichkeit der Vernunft*, pp. 459–88.
[25] Hasso Hofmann, "Verfassungsrechtliche Annäherung an den Begriff des Gemeinwohls," in Herfried Münkler and Karsten Fischer (eds), *Gemeinwohl und Gemeinsinn im Recht* (Berlin: Akademie Verlag, 2002), pp. 25–42.

prohibitions or administrative decrees any more than can a dete-
rioration in social solidarity.

This asymmetry between the image of society inscribed in the
constitution and the limited scope of the political tools available
to the state was not harmful as long as the economy coincided
with the nation-state and civic solidarity among a comparatively
homogeneous population was sustained by a corresponding
national consciousness. As long as the system of free trade with
fixed exchange rates established with the 1945 Bretton Woods
agreements existed, the opening of national borders to free trade
did not deny nation-states a certain degree of control over economies that remained embedded in their territories. Under such
conditions, governments retained a considerable scope for political regulation and intervention, one which moreover was perceived as sufficient. They could in any case be relied upon to
master publicly relevant social processes by political means.

This presupposition that problems are "politically manageable"
is the key to the constitutional construction of a society that has
the ability to exert a formative influence upon itself through state
agencies in accordance with the will of its citizens. Indeed, the
democratic substance of a constitution that makes the citizens the
authors of the laws to which they are at the same time subject as
addressees stands or falls with this presupposition. The political
autonomy of citizens acquires concrete content only to the extent
that a society is capable of influencing itself by political means.
This is the crucial point for the present discussion. However, the
expansion of the domains of political responsibility and the new
forms of corporatism have placed the channels of legitimation of
the nation-state under intolerable strain.[26] And with the switchover to a neoliberal economic regime these channels have definitively reached breaking point.

We are currently witnessing an ever more extensive privatization of public services that were hitherto provided by the nation-
state for good reasons. The connection of these services to the

---

[26] Dieter Grimm, *Die Zukunft der Verfassung* (Frankfurt am Main: Suhrkamp,
1991), pp. 372–96; Grimm, "Bedingungen demokratischer Rechtsetzung," in
Wingert and Günther (eds), *Die Öffentlichkeit der Vernunft*, pp. 489–506, here
pp. 500ff.

dictates of the constitution is being loosened by their transfer to private firms. This becomes all the more risky the further privatization advances into the core areas of sovereignty, such as public security, the military, the penal system, or the energy supply. Since the globalization of the economy has developed a dynamic of its own, however, ever more processes that are vital for maintaining the rule of law, freedom, distributive justice, and equal rights are escaping political supervision and control. At any rate, the asymmetry between the responsibilities accorded the democratic state and its actual scope of action is becoming increasingly pronounced.[27]

With the deregulation of markets and the globalization of flows of traffic and information in many further dimensions, a need for regulation arises that is being absorbed and processed by transnational networks and organizations. Their decisions, even when national officials collaborate in making them, make deep inroads into the public life of nation-states without being connected with processes of legitimation at the national level. Michael Zürn has described the impact of this development as follows:

> The democratic decision-making processes within nation-states are thus losing their anchorage. They are superseded by organizations and actors who indeed are mostly accountable to their national governments one way or another, but at the same time are quite remote and inaccessible for the nationally enclosed addressees of the regulations in question. Given the extent of the intrusion of these new international institutions into the affairs of national societies, the notion of "delegated, and therefore controlled authority" in the principal and agent sense no longer holds.[28]

If this description is accurate, then the postnational constellation confronts us with an uncomfortable alternative: either we must abandon the demanding idea of the constitution as a self-administering association of free and equal citizens and resign

---

[27] David Held, Andrew McGrew, David Goldblatt, and Jonathan Perraton, *Global Transformations* (Cambridge: Polity, 1999).

[28] Michael Zürn, "Global Governance and Legitimacy Problems, Government and Opposition," *International Journal of Comparative Politics* 39 (2004): 260–87, here 273f.

ourselves to a sociologically disillusioned interpretation of constitutional democracies that have been reduced to empty façades; or
we must detach the fading idea of a democratic constitution from
its roots in the nation-state and revive it in the postnational guise
of a constitutionalized world society. Needless to say, a philosophical thought experiment describing how the normative substance of the idea can be *conceptually* preserved in a cosmopolitan
society without a world government does not go far enough. The
idea must also find *empirical* support in the real world.

The nation-states have long since become entangled in the
interdependencies of a complex world society. The latter's subsystems effortlessly permeate national borders – with accelerated
information and communication flows, worldwide movements of
capital, networks of trade and production, technology transfers,
mass tourism, labor migration, scientific communication, etc. This
global society is also integrated through the same media of power,
money, and consensus as the nation-states. Why should a constitution, which successfully drew upon these sources of integration
at the national level by shaping them through politics and law, be
doomed to failure at the supranational and transnational levels?
There are no necessary socio-ontological reasons why solidarity
between citizens and the regulatory capacity of the constitution
should stop at national borders. As mentioned, however, it is not
enough to show through a philosophical thought experiment how
the normative content of the idea of the constitution of a nation-
state can be *conceptually* translated into that of the cosmopolitan
order of a constitutionalized world society.

In a multilevel global system, the classical function of the state
as the guarantor of security, law, and freedom would be transferred
to a *supranational* world organization specialized in securing peace
and implementing human rights worldwide. However, it would
not shoulder the immense burden of a global domestic policy
designed to overcome the extreme disparities in wealth within the
stratified world society, reverse ecological imbalances, and avert
collective threats, on the one hand, while endeavoring to promote
an intercultural discourse on, and recognition of, the equal rights
of the major world civilizations, on the other. These problems
differ in kind from violations of international peace and human
rights. They call for a different kind of treatment within the context
of *transnational* negotiation systems. They cannot be solved directly

by bringing power and law to bear against unwilling or incapable nation-states. They impinge upon the intrinsic logic of functional systems that extend across national borders and the intrinsic meaning of cultures and world religions. Politics must engage with these issues in a spirit of hermeneutic open-mindedness through the prudent balancing of interests and intelligent regulation.

In searching for actual trends that meet the idea of a cosmopolitan constitution halfway, the distinction between the supranational and the transnational levels points, on the one hand, to the pending reform of the United Nations (IV) and, on the other, to the dynamics triggered by an ever clearer awareness of the lack of legitimacy of current forms of global governance (V).

IV

In his reflections on the gap between the is and the ought, John Rawls distinguished between "ideal" and "real" theory. This methodological distinction did not go far enough in detranscendentalizing the Kantian distinction between the world of noumena and the world of phenomena. Ideas find their way into social reality through the unavoidable *idealizing presuppositions of everyday practices* and in this way inconspicuously acquire the status of stubborn social facts. For example, citizens participate in elections because they assume from their perspective as participants that their vote counts, irrespective of what political scientists report from an observer perspective concerning the effects of electoral geography and voting procedures. Likewise, litigants do not stop going to court with the expectation that the judge will treat their case impartially and reach the correct decision, irrespective of what law professors or judges have to say about the indeterminate character of law. However, ideas produce effects only through the idealizing presuppositions of established or institutionalized practices. Only when the practices have acquired a foothold in legal institutions, for example, must the fictions or presuppositions on which participants operate be taken seriously as facts.

The United Nations is such an institution. Over the decades, normatively loaded practices and procedures have emerged within the framework of this institution of international law. I would like to examine how realistic the Kantian project is by tracing a reform of this world organization already in progress. With this we leave the terrain of a theory constructed primarily with normative arguments and shift to the constructive interpretation of a domain of enacted law [*positiven Rechts*] undergoing rapid development. The validity of international law has in the meantime become assimilated to the mode of validity of national law, in the process shedding its status as *soft law*. At the transnational level, "we are dealing with a novel combination of national and supranational law, of private contracts and public law"; at the supranational level "we are in addition witnessing the emergence of a global constitutional law."[29] The controversy between the dualistic conception of the relation between national and international law, on the one hand, and the monistic doctrine of the fusion of national and international law in the global legal system, on the other, has thereby been rendered moot.[30]

At any rate, many experts construe the accelerated development of international law as a process of "constitutionalization" promoted by the international community with the goal of strengthening the legal position of the individual legal subject, who is gradually acquiring the status of a subject of international law and a cosmopolitan citizen.[31] The High-Level Panel put in

[29] Anne Peters, "Wie funktioniert das Völkerrecht?" *Basler Juristische Mitteilungen* (February, 2004): 24.

[30] Hans Kelsen, "Sovereignty," in Stanley Paulson and Bonnie Litschewski Paulson (eds), *Normativity and Norms* (Oxford: Clarendon Press, 1998), pp. 525–36.

[31] Christian Tomuschat, "International Law: Ensuring the Survival of Mankind on the Eve of a New Century: General Course on Public International Law," *Recueil des cours* 281 (1999), (The Hague, 2001): 163f.: "Today, the international legal order cannot be understood any more as being based exclusively on State sovereignty . . . Protection is afforded by the international community to certain basic values even without or against the will of individual States. All of these values are derived from the notion that States are no more than instruments whose inherent function is to serve the interests of their citizens as legally expressed in human rights . . . Over the last decades, a crawling process has taken place through which human rights have steadily increased their weight, gaining momentum in comparison with State sovereignty as a somewhat formal principle." On this, see also Armin von Bogdandy, "Constitutionalism in International Law: Comment on a Proposal from Germany," *Harvard International Law Journal* 47 (2006): 223–42.

place by Kofi Annan[32] also starts quite naturally from the premise that the overdue reform of the world organization must pursue the line already laid down by the UN Charter with four far-reaching innovations:

(a) (in common with Kant) the Charter explicitly links the objective of securing international peace to the global implementation of human rights;

(b) the Charter backs up the prohibition on violence with the threat of sanctions, including interventions to enforce peace (and hence creates the prospect of a penalization of war as a mechanism for solving interstate conflicts);

(c) the Charter relativizes the sovereignty of the individual member states to the goal of international peace and collective security; and

(d) by admitting all nations into an inclusive world organization, the Charter creates a key condition for the precedence and universal validity of international and UN law.

(a) In contrast to the League of Nations, the UN Charter links the objective of world peace (in Article 1.1 and Article 2.4) with the "respect for human rights and for fundamental freedoms for all without distinction as to race, sex, language, or religion" (Article 1.3). This obligation to promote the worldwide validity of constitutional principles hitherto guaranteed only within nation-states has increasingly shaped the agenda of the Security Council and has led in recent decades to a progressively broader interpretation of what constitutes a breach of peace, an act of aggression, and a threat to international security. The High-Level Panel infers from this development that it is necessary to extend the "new security consensus" to include the indivisible triad of protection against basic dangers, promotion of individual liberties and rights of participation, and emancipation from unworthy and undignified

---

[32] On December 1, 2004, the High-Level Panel on Threats, Challenges and Change presented its report, *A More Secure World: Our Shared Responsibility* (New York: United Nations Department of Public Information, 2004; hereinafter "TCC"). Kofi Annan incorporated its substance into his report to the General Assembly on the reform of the UN on March 21, 2005: "In Larger Freedom: Toward Development, Security and Freedom for All."

living conditions. It extends the sources of danger beyond classical interstate conflicts to include not only civil war and internal conflicts, international terrorism, the possession of weapons of mass destruction, and transnational organized crime; with an eye to the developing countries, it expands this catalogue of sources of danger to cover the mass deprivation of the population through poverty and disease, social marginalization, and environmental degradation.

Preserving international security is in the process conceptually fused with the postulate of the fulfillment of the covenants on civil and political and on economic, social, and cultural rights (ratified by the General Assembly in 1966). The High-Level Panel expressly advocates a demilitarization of the concept of security when it points out, for example, that the influenza pandemic of 1919 killed an estimated 100 million people within a year,[33] far more than the bloody military conflicts during the whole of World War I. It states at the very outset of its report that "any event or process that leads to large-scale death or lessening of life chances and undermines States as the basic unit of the international system is a threat to international security" (TCC, p. 2).

(b) The core of the UN Charter comprises the general prohibition on the use of force in connection with the authorization of the Security Council to impose the appropriate sanctions in the case of violations. With the exception of coercive measures imposed by the UN itself, the general prohibition on the use of force is only qualified by a narrowly defined right of self-defense in the case of a clearly identifiable and immediate threat of attack. The High-Level Panel reaffirms the Security Council's prerogative to object to unilateral actions of major powers that arrogate a right of preventive first strikes.[34] At the same time, it insists on the Security Council's right to intervene militarily: "Collectively authorized use of force may not be the rule today, but it is no longer an exception" (TCC, p. 32). It emphasizes this also with

---

[33] The number of 100 million cited (in TCC, p. 14) is disputed by some historians; but that in no way mitigates the scope of the pandemic.

[34] TCC, p. 62: "There is little evident international acceptance of the idea of security best preserved by a balance of power, or by any single – even benignly motivated – superpower."

regard to the now established practice of intervention in domestic conflicts: "We endorse the emerging norm that there is a collective international responsibility to protect, exercisable by the Security Council authorizing military intervention as a last resort, in the event of genocide and other large-scale killing, ethnic cleansing or serious violations of international humanitarian law which sovereign Governments have proved powerless or unwilling to prevent" (TCC, p. 66).

Based on a thorough analysis of past errors and shortcomings, the Panel proceeds to criticize the implausible selectivity of perception and the shamefully unequal treatment of relevantly similar cases (TCC, pp. 34, 65–6).[35] The report makes proposals

- for a more exact specification of possible sanctions and their monitoring;
- for a more appropriate differentiation between peacekeeping and peace-enforcing missions;
- for the correct weighting of the constructive tasks of post-conflict peace-building, which the UN must not shirk from taking on following a military intervention; and, most importantly,
- for strict conditions governing the legitimate use of force (seriousness of threat, proper purpose, last resort, proportional means, balance of consequences).

However, the High-Level Panel does not address the pressing question concerning what consequences follow for humanitarian international law from the transformation of military force into a global police force. When armed forces carry out a mission authorized by the Security Council, the focus is no longer on limiting military violence and the so-called collateral damage of warfare

---

[35] TCC, p. 19: "Too often, the United Nations and its Member States have discriminated in responding to threats to international security. Contrast the swiftness with which the United Nations responded to the attacks on 11 September 2001 with its actions when confronted with a far more deadly event: from April to mid-July 1994, Rwanda experienced the equivalent of three 11 September attacks every day for 100 days, all in a country whose population was one thirty-sixth of that of the United States."

within civilized bounds. Once war has been overcome, the key issue becomes that of obligating a global *police force* to act on behalf of the basic rights of cosmopolitan citizens who need protection against their own criminal governments or other violent gangs operating within states.

(c) If we read the UN Charter literally, then there is a contradiction between Article 2.7, which appears to affirm the classical prohibition on intervention in the internal affairs of any sovereign state, and Chapter VII, which accords the Security Council the right of intervention. In practice, this inconsistency has often paralyzed the work of the Security Council, especially in cases of humanitarian disasters that have unfolded behind the shield of the sovereignty of a criminal or complicit regime.[36] However, the international community violates its legal obligation to protect human rights worldwide if it simply sits back and watches mass murders and mass rapes, ethnic cleansing and expulsions, or a policy of deliberately exposing people to starvation and disease, without intervening (TCC, pp. 65–6). The High-Level Panel recalls that the United Nations was not intended to be a utopian project. Rather, the establishment of the Security Council was intended to equip the principles with adequate political power and to subordinate international relations to compulsory legal regulations (TCC, p. 13).

Given the fact that the monopoly on the means of legitimate violence continues to be dispersed among so many states, this can only work if the Security Council acquires enough authority to borrow the relevant means of sanction required to enforce higher-level UN law from cooperating members in *all* cases. The proposals on reforming the Security Council as regards its composition, its voting procedures, and the provision of resources thus serve to

---

[36] TCC, p. 65: "The Charter of the United Nations is not as clear as it could be when it comes to saving lives within countries in situations of mass atrocity. It 'reaffirms faith in fundamental human rights' but does not do much to protect them, and Article 2.7 prohibits intervention 'in matters which are essentially within the jurisdiction of any State.' There has been, as a result, a longstanding argument in the international community between those who insist on a 'right to intervene' in man-made catastrophes and those who argue that the Security Council . . . is prohibited from authorizing any coercive action against sovereign States for whatever happens within their borders."

strengthen the willingness of powerful members to cooperate and to engage a superpower that understandably has the greatest difficulty in changing its self-image from that of an autonomous player to that of one player among others.

If necessary, UN law must be implemented against opposed or ineffectual states by means of the combined capacities of the other member states, each of which still retains its monopoly on force. This is not an altogether unrealistic premise, as the example of the European Union shows; but it is certainly not yet satisfied at the supranational level of the world organization. In this context, the High-Level Panel recommends that the Security Council should cooperate more closely with regional alliances. For neighboring armed forces bear a special responsibility when it comes to carrying out UN missions in their regions.

Assuming that member states provide the UN with the means it requires to implement higher-level law, an elegant solution to the dogmatic question of how we should understand the "sovereign equality" of states suggests itself: "In signing the Charter of the United Nations, States not only benefit from the privileges of sovereignty but also accept its responsibilities. Whatever perceptions may have prevailed when the Westphalian system first gave rise to the notion of State sovereignty, today it clearly carries with it the obligation of a State to protect the welfare of its own peoples and meet its obligations to the wider international community" (TCC, p. 17). The nation-state continues to be equipped with strong competences, but it now operates as the fallible agent of the international community. The sovereign state remains responsible for guaranteeing the human rights enshrined in constitutional basic principles within national borders; the constitutional state fulfills this function on behalf of its democratically united citizenry. However, in their role as subjects of international law – as cosmopolitan citizens – these citizens have also issued the world organization a kind of indemnity that authorizes the Security Council to act on their behalf as a stand-in in cases of emergency when the primary agent, their own government, is no longer able or willing to protect their rights.

(d) Whereas the League of Nations was supposed to consist of an avant-garde of liberal nations, the United Nations, which now comprises 192 members, was designed from the outset to include all the world's nations. Alongside nations with liberal constitutions, it also includes various authoritarian, sometimes despotic or even criminal regimes, whose practices fly in the face of the wording of the UN Charter that they formally recognize and UN resolutions that they nominally support. Full inclusion thereby meets a necessary condition for the universal validity of cosmopolitan law while at the same time undermining its binding character. This consciously accepted tension between facts and norms becomes most drastic in the case of human rights violations by the major powers that enjoy veto rights and can block any Security Council resolutions directed against them. For similar reasons, the credibility of other institutions and procedures has been damaged by the use of double standards. This applies in particular to the practice of the Commission on Human Rights, which the High-Level Panel suggests should be reformed from the ground up: "Standard-setting to reinforce human rights cannot be performed by States that lack a demonstrated commitment to their promotion and protection" (TCC, p. 89).[37]

The gap between norm and reality also works the other way round and exerts pressure to conform on authoritarian member states. The changed international perception and public stigmatization of states that violate the established standards on security and human rights have led to a materialization of the rules governing the international recognition of states. The principle of effectivity, according to which a state is recognized as sovereign if it maintains law and order within its own borders, has been largely superseded by the principle of legitimacy.[38] The regular reports submitted by global monitoring agencies such as Human Rights Watch or Amnesty International have played a major part in stripping such "outlaw states" (John Rawls) of their legitimacy.

The desired recognition of the International Criminal Court is especially important in this context. The practice of a court that

---

[37] On Kofi Annan's institutional proposal for a new Council for Human Rights, see Annan, "In Larger Freedom," pp. 181–3.

[38] Jochen A. Frowein, "Konstitutionalisierung des Völkerrechts," in *Völkerrecht und internationales Recht in einem sich globalisierenden internationalen System: Bericht der Deutschen Gesellschaft für Völkerrecht*, vol. 39 (Heidelberg, 2000), pp. 427–47, here pp. 429ff.

specifies what constitute violations of international law and would in future monitor the relevant Security Council resolutions would not only strengthen the binding character of supranational law vis-à-vis the sovereign claims of nations of dubious repute and in general foster the autonomy of UN institutions vis-à-vis the nation-states' monopoly over the means of legitimate violence. Such a court would also lend an authoritative voice to a diffuse global public sphere that is stirred by mass political crimes and unjust regimes.

V

This brings us to the question of the need and capacity for legitimation of political decisions in international organizations. Such organizations are founded on multilateral treaties between sovereign states. If such organizations are burdened with the tasks of "governance beyond the nation-state," the growing need for legitimacy soon outstrips the type and scope of legitimacy that international treaties can ideally enjoy in virtue of the democratic character of the signatory states. Such a discrepancy seems to exist even in the case of the world organization, which is expected to monitor international security and worldwide compliance with human rights standards.

The High-Level Panel recommends including NGOs in the consultation process for the General Assembly (TCC, p. 109), which would at least enhance the visibility of the UN and its decisions in the global public arena. Direct connections to the national parliaments in the member states might also be helpful in this regard.[39] The convention that stipulates that "foreign affairs" are the privileged domain of the executive branch becomes obsolete in any case as state sovereignty shifts from unilateral policymaking to institutionalized multilateralism. Let us not fool ourselves, however; these reforms, desirable though they may be, are not extensive enough to establish a connection between the supranational and the national levels in such a way that an

---

[39] Andreas Brummel, *Internationale Demokratie entwickeln* (Stuttgart: Horizonte, 2005).

uninterrupted chain of legitimation would run from the nation-states to the world organization. A gap remains.

On the other hand, we must ask whether the need for legitimacy that would arise from the future interaction of a reformed Security Council with a universally recognized ICC would require this gap to be bridged in the first place. On closer inspection, it transpires that what legitimacy requires is different at the supranational and the transnational levels. Insofar as the development of international law follows the intrinsic logic of an explication and extension of human rights and international politics increasingly conforms to this trend, the issues that the world organization faces tend to be more of a legal than a political kind. This would be even more emphatically true in a perfectly constitutionalized world society. Two reasons suggest that embedding a reformed world organization in a (for the present still under-institutionalized) global public sphere would be sufficient to confer the requisite legitimacy on decisions taken by its two central, but nonmajoritarian institutions.

Let us assume for the sake of argument that the Security Council were to deal with litigable issues of securing peace and protecting human rights in accordance with fair procedures, hence in an impartial and nonselective manner. And let us assume further that the ICC had dogmatically analyzed and defined the major crimes within its jurisdiction (presently characterized as threats to international security, acts of aggression, breaches of the peace, and crimes against humanity). Thus reformed, the world organization could count on a worldwide background consensus in a threefold sense. The agreement would be geared, first, to the political goal of a substantively expanded conception of security, second, to the legal basis of the human rights pacts and conventions of international law passed by the General Assembly and already ratified by many states (i.e. the core domain of *jus cogens*), and, third, to the procedural principles in terms of which a reformed world organization would tackle its problems. This practice can expect to gain due recognition if, as we assume, it abides by just those principles and procedures that reflect the result of long-term democratic learning processes. Confidence in the normative force of existing judicial procedures can tap into the reserve of legitimacy made available by the exemplary histories of proven democracies for the collective memory of mankind, as it were.

Of course, these assumed agreements within the background global public sphere do not yet explain why we may accord the latter a critical function. In this regard, Kant was already quite optimistic, because "a violation of justice on *one* place of the earth is felt in *all.*"[40] Decisions taken at the supranational level concerning war and peace and justice and injustice do indeed attract the attention and critical responses of a global public – just think of the interventions in Vietnam, Kosovo, and Iraq, and the cases of Pinochet, Milošević, and Saddam. The dispersed society of world citizens becomes mobilized on an *ad hoc* basis through spontaneous responses to events and decisions of such import. Shared moral indignation extends across the gulfs separating different cultures, forms of life, and religions as a response to egregious human rights violations and manifest acts of aggression. Such shared reactions, including those spawned by sympathy for the victims of humanitarian and natural disasters, gradually produce traces of cosmopolitan solidarity.

The negative duties of a universalistic morality of justice – the duty not to commit crimes against humanity or to launch wars of aggression – have roots in all cultures and luckily correspond to the yardsticks used by the institutions of the world organization to justify their decisions. This is too narrow a basis, however, for regulations negotiated at the transnational level that go beyond the classical tasks of promoting security, law, and freedom. Such regulations impinge upon issues of redistribution familiar from the national arena where the corresponding policies call for the kind of legitimation that can only be provided, albeit poorly, through proper democratic channels. But once we bid farewell to the dream of a world republic, this channel is blocked at the transnational level. Thus a deficit in legitimation arises that is increasingly recognized as a problem.[41]

---

[40] Kant, "Toward Perpetual Peace," p. 330.

[41] Mattias Kumm, "The Legitimacy of International Law: A Constitutionalist Framework of Analysis," *European Journal of International Law* 15 (2004): 907–31. However, this proposal focuses exclusively on legitimizing legal principles and neglects the institutional level. The counterfactual example of a climate control regulation to limit emissions of carbon dioxide enacted by the Security Council (ibid., pp. 922ff.) shows that Kumm does not take account of the genuinely political character of issues relating to distribution and the need for legitimation they engender.

In conclusion, I would like to mention three responses to the legitimation problem produced by the more interesting among the new forms of governance beyond the nation-state. Over and above offering a correct description of the problem, the United Nations does not do much more than issue helpless appeals (a). For neoliberal and legal pluralist apologists of the status quo, the whole problem dwindles in importance because legal pluralism and the conception of a world society under private law deflate the supposedly misleading claims for legitimation. But the appeal to the legitimizing force of nonmajoritarian institutions does not go far enough (b). Even if we assume that the economic theory underlying the neoliberal neutralization of the problem of legitimacy is correct, the policy switch from political regulation to economic self-regulation poses a disturbing question: Can we take responsibility for promoting the worldwide political self-limitation of the leeway for possible political interventions? (c)

(a) The expansion of the concept of international security makes it unthinkable for the United Nations to restrict itself to the central tasks of peacekeeping and human rights policy. The Economic and Social Council (ESC) was originally intended to ensure the linkage between these policies and the onerous tasks of global development. But the UN quickly ran up against its limits in these areas. An international economic regime was established under the hegemony of the United States outside of the UN framework. This experience is reflected in the following sober statement: "decision-making on international economic matters, particularly in the areas of finance and trade, has long left the United Nations and no amount of institutional reform will bring it back" (TCC, p. 86). The institutional design of the United Nations offers a simple explanation for this. Assuming the sovereign equality of all members, the UN is geared more to normatively regulated consensus-formation than to political struggles over conflicts of interests, and hence it is not suited to the constructive tasks of a global domestic politics.

On the other hand, the Global Economic Multilaterals (GEMs) – first and foremost, the World Trade Organization (WTO), the World Bank (WB), and the International Monetary Fund (IMF) – are nowhere near tackling the collection of tasks emerging for the first time under the banner of the "new security consensus." This is the context of the High-Level Panel's observation concerning the "sectoral fragmentation" in the way international organizations function and cooperate. The self-referentially closed circuit of communication between ministries of finance and international monetary institutions, between ministries for international development and international development programs, and between ministries of the environment and international environmental agencies hinders even an appropriate perception of the problems:

> International institutions and States have not organized themselves to address the problems of development in a coherent, integrated way, and instead continue to treat poverty, infectious disease and environmental degradation as stand-alone threats . . . To tackle the problems of sustainable development, countries must negotiate across different sectors and issues, including foreign aid, technology, trade, financial stability and development policy. Such packages are difficult to negotiate and require high-level attention and leadership from those countries that have the largest economic impacts. (TCC, p. 26)

The call for an institution in which not only technocrats and ministerial delegates with specialized expert knowledge but also responsible representatives of governments with global authority or councils of ministers meet to address the problems in context-sensitive ways, and resolve them within a broader perspective, can be understood as an implicit answer to the legal pluralist defense of a "disaggregated world order." However, the informal meetings of heads of state in the style of the G-8, or the formation of *ad hoc* coalitions such as the G-20 and G-77, can hardly be regarded as convincing starting points for constructing an enduring global domestic politics. With the exception of the United States and China (and perhaps also of Russia), today's nation-states are ill-suited for the role of global players. They would have to achieve the aggregate scale of continental or subcontinental regimes, without thereby incurring substantial democratic deficits.

(b) The counterproposal to this vision of a global domestic politics has the advantage of reinforcing the existing structure of global policy networks. From the viewpoint of legal pluralism, the functional requirements of a differentiated world society are

giving rise to transnational networks that intensify communication between the expanding functional systems that were
hitherto national in scope. The networked flows of information
foster the spontaneous production of legal norms and promote
coordination and benchmarking, the stimulation and regulation
of competition, and the balancing and mutual prompting
of learning processes.[42] Beyond the nation-state, vertical,
power-based dependencies are receding behind horizontal interactions and functional interconnections. Anne-Marie Slaughter
links this analysis with the thesis of the disaggregation of state
sovereignty.[43]

From this perspective, the functionally specified exchange relations acquire structural precedence over territorially bound power
relations to the extent that the transnational networks achieve a
certain degree of independence, and thus act back upon the
national governments from which they originated. The centrifugal
forces of transnational networks drain the sovereignty from the
member states and disaggregate their centralized hierarchies. State
sovereignty disintegrates into the sum of the various functionally
autonomous subsidiary authorities. The state loses the competence to define its own competencies and to operate on the
domestic and international stages as an actor with a single voice.
This image of the disaggregation of state sovereignty also illuminates the increasing uncoupling of regulatory decisions that intervene in nation-states from above or outside from popular
sovereignty as organized within the nation-state. Although the
competences and decisions transferred to the GEMs remain formally within the responsibility of the governments concerned, the
agreements reached in those remote organizations are *de facto* no
longer exposed to public criticism, deliberation, and political reaction by affected citizens in their respective national arenas.[44] On
the other hand, no substitute for this growing deficit of legitimacy

---

[42] For a position that emphasizes the role of private actors, see Gunther Teubner,
"Globale Zivilverfassungen: Alternativen zur staatszentrierten Verfassungstheo-
rie," *Zeitschrift für ausländisches öffentliches Recht und Völkerrecht* 63 (2003):
1–28.
[43] Slaughter, *A New World Order*, pp. 12ff.
[44] Michael Zürn, "Global Governance and Legitimacy Problems," pp. 273f.: see
text to n. 28 above.

at the national level is emerging beyond the nation-state either.[45]

Anne-Marie Slaughter responds to the issue of the legitimation deficit at the transnational level with a proposal that exposes and illuminates the problem without solving it: "The members of government networks [must] . . . first . . . be accountable to their domestic constituents for their transgovernmental activities to the same extent that they are accountable for their domestic activities. Second, as participants in structures of global governance, they must have a basic operating code that takes account of the rights and interests of all peoples."[46] But to whom are the delegates of the executive branch accountable when they negotiate binding multilateral regulations that their domestic electorate would not accept? And who decides what is in the interest of all of the peoples affected as long as negotiating power in transnational settings is as unequal as the military power and economic weight of the participating countries in the real world?[47]

Another line of defense is more promising, namely, the neoliberal strategy of playing down supposedly *excessive* demands for legitimacy. The legitimizing power of democratically elected governments who send their officials as delegates to international organizations is held to be quite sufficient for international agreements, even if there is no public discussion of the relevant issue in the countries in question. On this reading, the unequal distribution of voting power and influence within the GEMs is not a serious problem, because democratic representation is simply the wrong model. What is lacking in terms of accountability can be offset (over and above increased transparency of negotiations, better information for those affected, and if necessary the involvement of NGOs) especially by the self-legitimizing force of the

[45] Patrizia Nanz and Jens Steffek, "Global Governance, Participation and the Public Sphere," *Government and Opposition* 39 (2004): 314–35.

[46] Anna-Marie Slaughter, "Disaggregated Sovereignty: Toward the Public Accountability of Global Government Networks," *Government and Opposition* 39 (2004): 163.

[47] Christian Joerges and Christine Godt, "Free Trade: The Erosion of National and the Birth of Transnational Governance," *European Review* 13, Supplement 1 (May 2005): 93–117.

rationality of experts. Here the professionalism of nonmajoritarian institutions serves as a model: "Contemporary democracies have assigned a large and growing role to nonmajoritarian institutions, such as the judiciary . . . and central banks . . . The accountability of international institutions, particularly global ones, may compare favorably to these domestic analogues."[48]

However, these supposedly extenuating analogies are in fact misleading. The independence of central banks is explained by the (as it happens, controversial) assumption that the stabilization of a currency calls for complex arguments and decisions that should be left to experts. The decisions taken by the GEMs, by contrast, are politically controversial because they have major impacts on the interests of national societies and on occasion even on the structure of entire national economies. For this reason, the WTO now features a Dispute Settlement Body and an Appellate Body designed to ensure that the interests of third parties also receive due consideration. For example, they adjudicate conflicts between economic interests, on the one side, and standards for health or environmental protection and the protection of consumer or employee rights, on the other. However, this nonmajoritarian institution in the shape of an arbitrating body, whose "reports" have the function of binding "judgments," throws the lack of accountability of the WTO into sharp relief.[49]

Within the framework of the constitutional state, the legitimacy of judicial decisions relies essentially on the fact that courts apply the law laid down by a democratic legislature and that court decisions can be corrected via the political process. In the WTO there is no legislative authority that could lay down or *amend* norms in the domain of international business law. Because cumbersome multilateral negotiations cannot serve as a substitute for such an authority, the autonomous arbitration body develops new

---

[48] Miles Kahler, "Defining Accountability Up: The Global Economic Multilaterals," *Government and Opposition* 39 (2004): 133.

[49] The following argument is based on von Bogdandy, "Verfassungsrechtliche Dimensionen der Welthandelsorganisation," *Kritische Justiz* 34 (2001): 264–81; also 34 (2001): 425–41; and his "Law and Politics in the WTO – Strategies to Cope with a Deficient Relationship," in *Max Planck Yearbook of United Nations Law*, vol. 5 (The Hague: Kluwer, 2001), pp. 609–74.

law with its detailed reports, and thereby also implicitly performs legislative functions. Devoid of any discernible legitimation, such informal regulations could impact on national legal systems and (as in the famous dispute between the United States and the EU over artificial hormones) impose painful adjustments.[50]

(c) The argument that governmental policy networks should be relieved of exaggerated demands for legitimation would work only on the assumption that the GEMs function as integral parts of a liberal global economic regime order that *is assumed to be legitimate* to implement the worldwide deregulation of markets against government interventions. There is an elective affinity between the neoliberal program of creating a global "civil law society"[51] and the organizational structure of the existing GEMs composed of managers and controlled by governments. The envisaged division of labor between the integration of the world society through liberalized markets, on one side, and the shifting of the costs of any remaining social and ecological obligations to the nation-states, on the other, would render any form of global governance superfluous. From this perspective, the vision of a global domestic policy is a dangerous pipedream.

But what is the real danger? The worldwide export of the project of a neoliberal world order that President Bush again impressively expounded in November 2003 on the occasion of the twentieth anniversary of the foundation of the National Endowment for Democracy[52] does not enjoy worldwide democratic support. The so-called Washington consensus rests rather on a fallible and highly controversial theory, in particular, a combination of the economic dogmas of the Chicago School and a liberal version of modernization theory. The problem is not that these theories could turn out to be wrong like any other. Far more disquieting is an implication of a long-term neoliberal restructuring of the global economy. The political goal of switching from political forms of regulation to market mechanisms tends to per-

---

[50] See the Göttingen inaugural lecture by Peter-Tobias Stoll, "Globalisierung und Legitimation" (MS, 2003).

[51] Ernst-Joachim Mestmäker, "Der Kampf ums Recht in der offenen Gesellschaft," *Rechtstheorie* 20 (1989): 273–88.

[52] "President Bush Discusses Freedom in Iraq and Middle East" (www. whitehouse.gov/news/releases/2003/11/print/20031106-2.html).

petuate such a politics, since a change in policy becomes more difficult to the extent that the scope for political intervention is curtailed. The deliberate political self-limitation of the room for political maneuver in favor of systemic self-regulation would rob future generations of the very means they would require for a future course correction. Even if every nation "consciously and democratically decides to be more of a 'competition state' than a 'welfare state,'" such a democratic decision would inevitably destroy its own foundations if it led to a form of social organization that made it impossible to overturn that very decision by democratic means.[53]

This assessment of the consequences recommends itself not just in the foreseeable event of the failure of neoliberal forecasts. Even if the theoretical assumptions should prove to be accurate *grosso modo*, the old slogan concerning the "cultural contradictions of capitalism" could take on new meaning.[54] Competing social models of capitalism coexist even within the domain of Western culture, which is the cradle of capitalist modernization and remains the source of its dynamism. Not all Western nations are prepared to accept the social and cultural costs at home and abroad of the unrectified global disparities in wealth that the neoliberals would foist upon them for the sake of a more rapid increase in affluence for the time being.[55] The interest in maintaining a certain political scope for action is all the greater in *other* cultures which are willing to adjust and transform their own ways of life with access to the global market and acceptance of the dynamics of social modernization, but are not prepared to *abandon* these ways of life and allow them to be replaced by imported patterns. The many cultural faces of the pluralist global society, or *multiple modernities*,[56]

[53] Von Bogdandy, "Verfassungsrechtliche Dimensionen der Welthandelsorganisation," p. 429.
[54] Daniel Bell, *The Cultural Contradictions of Capitalism* (New York: Basic Books, 1976).
[55] David Held, *Global Covenant: The Social Democratic Alternative to the Washington Consensus* (Cambridge: Polity, 2004), develops a social democratic alternative to the prevailing Washington Consensus.
[56] Charles Taylor, "Two Theories of Modernity," *Public Culture* 11 (1999): 153–74.

do not fit well with a completely deregulated and politically neutralized world market society. For this would rob the non-Western cultures that are shaped by other world religions of their freedom to assimilate the achievements of modernity with their own resources.

Index

nuclear weapons, 22
Nuremberg trials, 18

outsiders, 16–17

Peirce, Charles Sanders, 14, 25, 32,
  33, 43, 44, 73, 140
Perelman, Chaim, 44
philosophy
  ancient Greece, 110, 142, 209,
    241
  claims, 272
  function, 278–9
  philosophers as citizens, 145
  philosophers' biographies, 12
  religious input, 108–10, 142–3,
    209
Piaget, Jean, 48
Pinochet, Augusto, 344
Plato, 12, 15, 243
Platonism, 7, 20, 42, 96, 218
platonism, meaning, 55, 57, 66, 67
Plessner, Helmut, 188n7
pluralism
  cultural pluralism and world
    order, 326
  liberalism, 281–90
  modernity and, 87
  multiculturalism and equality,
    291–303
  politics of recognition, 269, 293,
    294
  religious tolerance and
    multiculturalism, 265–70
  secularism and, 119, 310–11
  tolerance, 258
  ways of life, 263, 273, 309
Poland, 116
polarization, 6
politics of recognition, 269, 293,
  294
postmetaphysical thinking, 79–81,
  97, 101, 110, 119, 140–3,
  210, 237, 239, 241–6, 278–9
postmodernism, 107–8, 277–9
pragmatism, 25, 27, 36, 73
prejudices, 258, 259, 306–7

privatizations, 332, 350
Protestantism, 229, 234, 235, 240
psychologism, 29, 55
Putnam, Hilary, 44, 205

Quakers, 134
quasi-naturalness, 195–6, 198
Quebec, 300–1
Quine, Willard van Orman, 66

racism, 258, 306–7
rationalism, Europe, 116
Ratzinger, Cardinal Joseph,
  101n1
Rawls, John, 101, 112, 119–26,
  131, 134n43, 145–7, 260–2,
  279, 281–6, 308, 334, 341
reason
  Adorno, 182–208
  deconstructionism, 24–6
  democratic polities, 132
  detranscendentalization, 7,
    29–52, 77–8, 165, 187
  faith and, 6, 137
  Kant, 24, 26–31, 34–5, 40, 53,
    140, 142, 210–11, 214, 227,
    231, 243, 247
  natural reason, 120
  public use, 119–47
  pure reason, 24, 26–7, 29
  secularism and, 108–9
  tolerance and, 258–9, 306–7
Reformation, 136, 140, 261
regionalism, 324–6
religion
  beneficial influences, 124
  conflicts, 114, 115
  faith and knowledge, 209–47,
    264
  freedom, *see* religious freedom
  fundamentalism, *see*
    fundamentalism
  Hegel, 228, 229–32, 238, 239,
    240–1
  Kant, 211–47
  Kierkegaard, 229, 232, 235–8,
    237, 241, 242